WHERE
GHOSTS
WALKED

WHERE GHOSTS WALKED

Munich's Road to the Third Reich

DAVID CLAY LARGE

W. W. NORTON & COMPANY ■ NEW YORK ■ LONDON

For information about permission to reproduce selections from this book, write to
Permissions, W. W. Norton & Company, Inc., 500 Fifth Avenue, New York, NY 10110.

The text of this book is composed in Granjon with the display set in
Granjon and Bembo.
Composition by JoAnn Schambier
Manufacturing by Quebecor Printing, Fairfield Inc.
Book design by BTD

LIBRARY OF CONGRESS CATALOGING-IN-PUBLICATION DATA
Large, David Clay.
    Where ghosts walked : Munich's road to the Third Reich / by David Clay Large.
        p. cm.
    Includes bibliographical references and index.
    ISBN 0-393-03836-X
    1. Munich (Germany)—Social conditions. 2. National socialism—Germany—Mu-
nich. 3. Conservatism—Germany—Munich. 4. Munich (Germany)—Intellectual life.
I. Title.
DD901.M83L36   1997
943'.364—DC21   97-4263
                                                                  CIP

W. W. Norton & Company, Inc., 500 Fifth Avenue, New York, N.Y. 10110
http://www.wwnorton.com

W. W. Norton & Company Ltd., 10 Coptic Street, London WC1A 1PU

1   2   3   4   5   6   7   8   9   0

To Henry and Wilma

ACKNOWLEDGMENTS

ANY FOOL CAN make history, but it requires time and money to write it. I wish to thank Montana State University for giving me numerous leaves of absence to work on this project (and for not telling me too often that I wouldn't be missed). For financial support, I wish to acknowledge the National Endowment for the Humanities, the German Academic Exchange Service, and the Research Creativity Committee of Montana State University.

The staffs of the following archives and libraries were helpful in providing me with the source materials for this book: Bundesarchiv, Koblenz; Bundesarchiv-Militärarchiv, Freiburg; Bayerisches Hauptstaatsarchiv, Munich; Bayerische Staatsbibliothek, Munich; British Library, London; Doe Library, University of California, Berkeley; Green Library, Stanford University; Hoover Institution, Stanford; Institut für Zeitgeschichte, Munich; Library of Congress, Washington, D.C.; Public Record Office, London; Renne Library, Montana State University; Staatsarchiv, Munich; Stadtarchiv, Munich; Stadtbibliothek, Munich; Sterling Library, Yale University; Widener Library, Harvard University; Wiener Library, London.

Affiliation as a Visiting Scholar with the University of California, Berkeley during the years 1994–1995 and 1996–1997 greatly facilitated my work; I am grateful to Professor Gerald D. Feldman for arranging this hospitality.

Professor Gordon Craig of Stanford University kindly allowed me access to his unpublished diary covering his time in Munich in 1935.

Steven Forman, my editor at W. W. Norton, deftly guided the project through its various stages.

Finally, I wish to thank my wife, Margaret, for her patience and support during the long gestation of this book.

CONTENTS

INTRODUCTION
"Athens on the Isar"

ON 25 MAY 1913 Adolf Hitler, then twenty-four years old, moved from his native Austria to Munich, capital of the kingdom of Bavaria. "The city was as familiar to me as if I had lived for years within its walls," he later claimed. For the next thirty-two years Hitler's life was closely intertwined with the history of this handsome town on the Isar River.

The future Führer was among the throng in Munich's Odeonsplatz welcoming the outbreak of war in August 1914; he rushed off to a local recruiting station to enlist in the Bavarian Army. Upon Germany's defeat in World War I he returned to Munich and witnessed the emergence of a short-lived Bavarian soviet regime. Working as a Munich-based army intelligence operative, he investigated, in 1919, a recently formed political group called the German Workers' Party, which he joined and quickly transformed into the National Socialist German Workers' Party, or Nazis.

After building the Nazi movement into a credible force on the local scene, Hitler sought to use Munich as a springboard to national power in his ill-fated Beer Hall Putsch of November 1923. Following the putsch's failure and his own brief incarceration, Hitler retained Munich as party headquarters—against much internal opposition—when he reconstituted the Nazi movement and began a new assault on power, culminating in his appointment to the German chancellorship in January 1933.

Upon consolidating his dictatorship in Berlin, Hitler named Munich Capital of the Movement and Capital of German Art. Although he governed the Reich from Berlin, he kept his official residence in the Bavarian city and returned there often, for he felt much more at home on the banks of the Isar than on the banks of the Spree. As Führer he saw to it that in Munich the Nazi ideology found expression in monumental new buildings, art exhibitions, and political street theater.

The new world war that Hitler instigated in 1939 brought devastation to Munich as it did to other great cities of the Reich. Yet some of the most prominent Nazi buildings there survived the Allied bombing; they became a lasting, if little acknowledged, legacy to the man who made his favorite city the spiritual center of the German evil between 1933 and 1945.

IT IS ONE of the more piquant ironies of modern European history that the birthplace of Nazism, "capital" of the Nazi movement, and chief cultural shrine of the Third Reich had gained in the decades before Hitler's arrival a reputation around the world as the most tolerant, democratic, and fun-loving city in Germany. If Prussian Berlin stood for militaristic authoritarianism and pushy assertiveness, Munich meant baroque buildings, fine art museums, and easygoing *Gemütlichkeit*. The atmosphere was so egalitarian and congenial, people said, that one could almost forget one was in Germany.

The image of democratic amiability, it seems, had much to do with Munich's most famous product, its beer. "Beer is a great constitutional, political, and social leveler," wrote the American consul in 1874. "One sees at the Oktoberfest [Munich's famous beer festival] great and small crowded together on the rough benches." Max Halbe, a playwright who had fled bustling but "Mammon-ruled" Berlin for Munich in 1895, insisted that in

Brobdingnagian beer halls like the Hofbräuhaus there was "no distinction between rich and poor, elegant and simple, even between ministers of state and coach drivers." "Few other places are so democratic," agreed the American traveler Robert Schauffler in an article entitled "Munich—A City of Good Nature" (1909): "In the great beer halls where Munich spends many of its leisure moments, one man is exactly as good as another. There you will find a mayor and an army captain rubbing shoulders with a sweep and a peddler, and all talking and laughing together with no sense of constraint."

But such effusions, while no doubt true enough on the surface, disguised or overlooked another aspect of Munich's beer hall scene: frequent brawls and riots, in which heavy earthenware steins, emptied of their liquid bliss, became dangerous weapons. These stein wars were often ignited by ideological disagreements, since the massive beer halls were ideal forums for pitchmen of all political stripes. Colliding aesthetic judgments could also lead to blows. Alfred Pringsheim, a passionate Wagnerian (and future father-in-law of Thomas Mann) smashed his stein over the head of a fellow drinker who had dared insult the Master. For this act he proudly bore the title *Schoppenhauer,* "beer glass swinger," a pun on the name of the famous German philosopher.

Whatever the sociopolitical implications of Munich's beer culture, the city's claim to fame rested on more than its fabled brew. It was also, as a Bavarian character in Katherine Mansfields' story "Germans at Meat" (1911) brags, the repository of "all the Art and Soul life in Germany." Hitler might proclaim Munich Capital of German Art during the Third Reich, but the city had been celebrated as a great art center long before he took power, indeed well before he appeared on the local scene. A proper understanding of Munich's political and cultural role in the first half of the twentieth century must therefore begin with a brief account of the city's emergence as a mecca of the muses in the previous century, when it became known far and wide as Athens on the Isar.

Munich's rise to cultural prominence began with the reign of Bavaria's second king, Ludwig I (1825–1848), who declared (stealing a line previously applied to Cologne): "No one shall know Germany who does not know Munich." Having spent much of his time as crown prince in Greece and Italy, Ludwig was determined to turn his humble *Residenzstadt* into a radiant enclave of imposing buildings, grand boulevards, and rich collections of art. Among this ambitious king's most important contributions were the Königsplatz, a broad square framed with neoclassical structures; the Alte Pinakothek, which displayed the ruling Wittelsbach family's splendid collection of Old Masters (later Ludwig added the Neue

Pinakothek, for contemporary art); the Feldherrnhalle, a neo-Renaissance loggia dedicated to Bavaria's greatest generals; and the Ludwigstrasse, a grand corso lined with Italianate public buildings, including the Bavarian State Library and the Ludwigs-Maximilians-Universität, which the king had transferred to Munich from Landshut in 1827.

Modern Munich's greatest patron might have done even more for his capital had he not abdicated his throne during the revolutions of 1848. One of his reasons for renouncing power involved a feud with the citizens of Munich over what he regarded as another cultural asset for the city, his recently acquired mistress, the "Spanish dancer" Lola Montez. Née Maria Dolores Eliza Rosanna Gilbert, Lola was in reality of Anglo-Irish descent. Court lore had it that she gained the king's favor by baring her breasts to him at their first meeting, proving that these wonders were "nature's work alone." (Lola's most recent biographer discounts this story, no doubt justifiably, but it is worth noting that Ludwig later wrote a poem entitled "On Lola's Bosom.") Not only did Lola flop as a dancer in the court theater, but she infuriated the locals by her life of luxury at the king's expense, her brutality toward tradesmen, her interference in royal politics, and her assumption of the title Countess of Landsfeld. She became so hated that Ludwig had to send her away for fear she might be lynched by the populace.

Ludwig's son and successor, Maximilian II (1848–1864), was not as generous a benefactor as his father, but he added in important ways to Munich's luster. On the architectural front he presided over the construction of another new boulevard, the Maximilianstrasse, which proved rather livelier than the Ludwigstrasse because it provided much-needed space for private housing, art studios, shops, and hotels. King Max also commissioned the Glaspalast (Glass Palace), a 837.2-foot-long iron and glass structure modeled on Sir Joseph Paxton's Crystal Palace in London. Like that building, the Glaspalast was designed to house industrial exhibits, but it soon found more consistent use as an exhibition hall for painting, sculpture, and graphic arts. Another modern structure commissioned by Max was the glass and iron Central Train Station, which became a focal point in Bavaria's railway development. Above the banks of the Isar he built the hulking Maximilianeum, an innovative educational institute where Bavaria's brightest students could study at state expense for careers in the civil service.

Max enriched the culture of his capital also by importing talented scientists, scholars, and writers from other parts of Bavaria and Germany. Among his most prominent acquisitions were the great chemist Justus von Liebig, the historian Heinrich von Sybel, the poet Emanuel Geibel, and the poet-dramatist Paul Heyse. Geibel and Heyse became fixtures in the Munich Poets' Circle, known for its richly textured works that combined purity of form with otherworldliness of content. The circle dominated Munich's literary life long after its royal patron died in 1864. Heyse in particular enjoyed great success; he built a palatial villa in the Luisenstrasse and became the first German to win a Nobel Prize for Literature in 1910.

Although Max's imports gained influence across Germany, some of them inspired resentment in Munich as "outsiders" who led privileged lives as favorites of the king. Mockingly dubbed *Nordlichter* (northern lights) by a local journalist, they were widely seen as too pushy and arrogant in their relations with the townsfolk, whom they sometimes disparaged as barely civilized bumpkins. Nonetheless, they lighted the way south for many more northern luminaries in subsequent decades.

Bavaria's best-known ruler, King Ludwig II (1864–1886), began his reign with the ambition of turning his capital into Europe's premier venue for neoromantic music and communal theater. To that end he invited the composer Richard Wagner, whose innovative music dramas were inspiring both admiration and revulsion across Europe, to make Munich his new creative home. Fully sharing Wagner's dream of revolutionizing opera, Ludwig promised to build him a splendid new theater in the Bavarian capital where he could mount his great work in progress, the *Ring of the Nibelungen.* As he excitedly told Wagner, "In my mind's eye I see our longed-for building rising before me in all its majesty. . . . I hear the first mysterious chords and watch the curtain rise. . . . I see gods and heroes standing before me, see the dreadful curse of the Ring slowly fulfilled."

But as so often in his melancholy life, the young king had allowed fantasy to crowd out reality. His ministers balked at committing state funds for the project, while the people of Munich insisted that contrary to the king's and Wagner's assertions, they did not need Wagnerian theater to achieve spiritual and political enlightenment. Moreover, the citizenry was up in arms over Wagner's luxurious lifestyle, which was subsidized by Ludwig. "What [Wagner] demands in everyday life and comfort," protested the *Allgemeine Zeitung,* "seems to be of so exquisitely sybaritic a nature that not even an oriental *grand seigneur* would object to lodging permanently with him . . . and eating at his table." Münchners were also appalled by the composer's openly conducted love affair with Cosima von Bülow, the wife of the pianist and conductor Hans von Bülow, whom Wagner had summoned from Berlin to help transform the musical culture of Munich. To complete his transgressions, Wagner interfered in royal politics and looked down his Saxon nose at the locals. "The Münchner," huffed an indignant society lady, "is benevolent and respectful toward friendly talents, but will by no means put up with being condescended to or humiliated by arrogant foreigners." Thus, like Lola Montez, Wagner became so hated that his royal benefactor was forced to send him away in 1865. The composer ultimately built his cherished Festival Theater not in Munich but in Bayreuth, near Nuremberg.

Ludwig II did not abdicate his throne over this loss, but he never forgave Munich for making him part with his "Dear One." For the rest of his reign he avoided his capital as much as possible, spending the bulk of his time in the nearby Alps, where he began building, at enormous expense, his spectacular rural retreats: Neuschwanstein, Linderhof, and Herrenchiemsee. His apparent inability to curb his mania for mountain castles, combined with his increasingly bizarre behavior—he conversed with imaginary guests during dinner, spoke of wanting to fly across the sky in a chariot pulled by peacocks, and made his valet wear a bag over his head in his presence—prompted his ministers to have him declared congenitally insane and unable to carry out his royal duties. However, in June 1886, before he could be safely locked away in a gilded cage, he drowned mysteriously in Lake Starnberg south of Munich along with the psychiatrist who had (without ever interviewing him) signed the certificate of insanity. From that moment on a romantic cult flourished around the memory of Ludwig II, above all in Munich, the city he had rejected.

Although Ludwig II personally did not do as much as his father and grandfather for Munich's enrichment, his capital continued to act as a cultural magnet, especially in the plastic arts. In 1885 the Bavarian capital had more painters and sculptors than Berlin and Vienna combined. In addition to being thick on the ground, the artists exerted considerable social influence. A visiting painter from England was astonished to note that Munich's artists enjoyed a level of prestige "equal to that of a general in the army." Some of them, like the "painter princes" Wilhelm von Kaulbach, Franz von Lenbach, and Franz von Stuck, became so wealthy that they could build grand villas.

Munich's painters sold much of their work at large annual exhibitions, which were truly cosmopolitan affairs. The First International Exhibition, held in 1869 in the Glaspalast, featured paintings by Courbet, Corot, and Manet, as well as hundreds of German works. These events were sponsored by the Münchener Künstlergenossenschaft (Munich Artists' Society), which encouraged relationships between artists and "friends of the arts." It organized dinners, processions, and (at Carnival time) costume balls and bacchanalian parties. The constant round of artists' revels was instrumental in furthering Munich's reputation as Germany's answer to Paris. As one contemporary observed, "a single successful fête organized by the artists, an effective parade, did more to popularize Munich art than half a dozen auspicious exhibitions."

While it was known primarily for its painters and art schools, Munich in Ludwig II's era continued to attract writers and musicians, many of whom did their most productive work there. Hermann Levi, a gifted conductor from Giessen, used his tenure as Kapellmeister in Munich (1872–1896) to make the court orchestra there one of the finest musical ensembles in Europe. Levi's Jewishness, however, caused him to be attacked in the local press as an "alien" who had no business conducting "German music." The Norwegian dramatist Henrik Ibsen, who moved to Munich in 1875, had an easier time of it in the Isar city, where he lived until 1891, surrounded by friends and admirers. He too sometimes ran afoul of local conservatives—one critic accused him of purveying "soulless materialism"—but he was impressed enough by the cultural ambiance of the Bavarian capital to dub it "a genius among cities."

HOW WAS IT, then, that this genial place, this center of beery good cheer and magnet of the muses, came to play the crucial role it did in the development of National Socialism? This question has puzzled students of the German scene for years. Summing up the quandary in a pioneering essay in 1957, the Bavarian scholar Georg Franz asked: "Why precisely Munich? Why, of all places, should this 'Athens on the Isar' have been regarded as the cradle and nursery of that cataclysmic force?" Franz's query is a small but significant piece of that much larger puzzle: How was it that the land of *Dichter und Denker* (poets and thinkers) became the country of *Mörder und Henker* (murderers and hangmen)?

To the extent that commentators have dealt with the Munich dimension of the German catastrophe, they have tended to focus on the immediate background of the Nazi Party's Foundation, the revolution of 1918–1919. Munich, alone among major German cities, experienced an escalation of revolutionary chaos that culminated in back-to-back soviet regimes, the last of which amounted to a grimly brutal attempt to emulate the Bolshevik model in Russia. The Munich soviet experiment quickly collapsed, but the trauma of those days seared the consciousness of the city's middle classes to such a degree that they were highly receptive to the anti-Marxist message of the Nazis. As Franz puts it, "The fundamentally anti-revolutionary mood of the Bavarian population may be regarded as the basis for the antirevolutionary movement of which the Nazi party was a part. In the story of the revolution, therefore—the story of the bolshevik soviet republic in Munich and its rejection—lies the key to the place of Munich in the history of the Nazi party."

One of the operating principles of this book is that Munich's fateful political role between 1919 and 1945 is best understood by starting the story in a rather different setting—in the so-called golden age of Munich that encompassed the three or four decades before World War I. During most of this period Bavaria basked under the benevolent tutelage of Prince Regent Luitpold (1886–1912), who ruled on behalf of Ludwig II's younger brother, Otto. (Otto could not take power himself because he was considerably more demented than Ludwig; he was hidden away from public view at the Fürstenried Palace until his death in 1916.) Our study begins in the Prince Regency period because, as I shall argue in detail in the first chapter, fin de siècle Munich's much-celebrated culture had a deeply problematical side in terms of the ideological legacy it left behind. It was a culture that generated not only outstanding works of the modernist spirit—one thinks, for example, of the paintings of the *Blaue Reiter* school and the pioneering designs of the *Jugendstil* movement—but also an internal critique of cosmopolitan modernity and political liberalism that could easily be embraced by the Nazis and their *völkisch* allies. Indeed, a Nazi commentator in Munich had this protofascist cultural heritage in mind when he proposed in 1935 that the Bavarian capital had always remained "healthy in its essence" and that there were extensive ties connecting the Hitler movement to the historical life of the city.

Important lines of continuity can also be detected in the realm of socioeconomic and political developments. Under Prince Regent Luitpold, who was loved for his common touch and lack of stuffiness, Munich was often praised as a "classless" and "harmonious" city. Yet in reality the Prince Regency era was a time of escalating social discord and rising political tension. The "good old days" of Luitpold's rule coincided with an upsurge of population growth, ethnic diversification, and industrial expansion—in short, with Munich's emergence as a modern metropolis. Boisterous *Gemütlichkeit* was as evident as ever in the beer halls, but increasingly it had an aggressive edge to it, as if one could repress unwanted change with a hearty song and a thump of the stein. Munich's difficult passage to metropolitan modernity, like its troubled transition to cultural prominence, helped set the stage for the political and ideological battles of the twentieth century.

Munich had been growing steadily through the first two thirds of the nineteenth century, its numbers climbing from approximately 34,000 in 1800 to 230,000 in 1880. In the next three decades the population more than doubled, reaching 596,000 in 1910. Most of the newcomers came from other parts of Germany or from eastern Europe. By the turn of the century almost half the city's inhabitants were not native-born.

With rapid population growth came the usual urban ills. Many of the newcomers crowded into seedy, congested districts like Giesing and the Au. Local boosters liked to tout these quarters as "picturesque," but the residents generally saw things differently. "We had a room and a kitchen," recalled a working-class girl from the Au. "My sister slept on the floor in the kitchen; I slept between my parents in the other room. That was completely normal for workers. It was unheard of for children to have their own beds, or for workers to have living rooms or bathrooms in their houses." Humorist Karl Valentin's nine-member family lived in one room, which had "one good feature—running water—which ran day and night down the walls." As the tide of immigrants rose, new working-class districts sprang up outside the old city center. The housing there consisted of drab stack-a-prole *Mietskasernen* (rental barracks), which, like their better-known counterparts in Berlin, featured long, dingy corridors and cavernous inner courtyards where light scarcely penetrated.

Neither the old hovels nor the new flats came cheaply. "Munich is an expensive city," observed the American consul in 1893, "especially as far as rents are concerned. I speak from personal experience in Paris, London, Rome . . . and other cities in Germany." The poor were particularly hard hit by the frequent rent increases, which forced them to move repeatedly in search of affordable quarters.

The high cost of living also bred a plague of begging. In 1886 the city's largest newspaper, the national liberal *Münchener Neueste Nachrichten,* complained that hordes of beggars were congregating around the beer halls and popular tourist sites. These predators, admonished the paper, should not be confused with the "genuinely helpless people to whom Münchners' hearts are always open." Rather, they were "work-shy thieves" whose presence was a threat to the city's orderly image. The police responded to the begging plague with periodic roundups of "doubtful characters."

Another by-product of the expanding metropolis was prostitution, which increased dramatically with the influx of rural migrants and the escalating cost of living. Prostitution was legal in Munich so long as the women registered with the police, submitted to periodic medical exams, and stayed away from the fancy tourist areas. Needless to say, these restrictions ensured that the majority of Munich whores never bothered to register. In 1907 there were 107 registered prostitutes, but a poll among the prostitutes put the number at more than 2,000, a figure accepted by the vice police. Whatever the actual tally, whores certainly seemed omnipresent. A pamphlet entitled *The Secrets of Munich* (1910) complained: "Neuhauser-strasse, Kaufingerstrasse, and Marienplatz are particularly infested. Every six paces, it seems, one encounters a prostitute. If they do not whisper 'Come along' or a similar phrase, they give you a challenging look or even grab you by the sleeve." Another report insisted that whores and their pimps were so numerous around the Isartorplatz that "no decent woman can walk there."

More dangerous than female prostitution, from the standpoint of vigilant moralists, was a proliferation of homosexuality and a growing sex trade in young boys. *Das Bayerische Vaterland,* an archconservative paper, claimed that a "flood of homosexuality" was inundating Germany, citing the Eulenburg affair in Berlin as a case in point. (Count Philipp zu Eulenburg, a prominent diplomat and close friend of Kaiser Wilhelm II's, was exposed as a homosexual by the muckraking journalist Maximilian Harden in 1908.) The homosexual flood had reached Munich, complained the paper, because local liberals were treating this phenomenon as a "mental illness" rather than as a willful perversion, thereby giving it "scientific respectability." A similar message was conveyed by a Munich cabaret song: "Years ago no one knew the homosexual curse / Love was normal then, not perverse / But now not just Eulenburg loves this way / Our city teems with creatures of his sway / Warm friendship blooms rank on rank / Aside the pretty Isar bank."

Local homosexuals did not confine their attentions to fellow adults, noted alarmed conservatives, but exploited the services of *Strichjungen,* young male prostitutes. The Munich police brought a number of cases of male prostitution before the courts in the first decade of the twentieth century, but they insisted that these were just the tip of the iceberg since this "antisocial vice" was practiced "in the greatest secrecy."

Munich's economy was also in a state of flux during the Prince Regency period. Although small producers and purveyors to the court—traditionally the backbone of the local economy—continued to play an important role, the city began to develop a significant manufacturing base with a substantially larger labor force. Between 1882 and 1895 the number of licensed firms operating in the city increased by 68.1 percent, and from 1895 to 1907 grew another 21.9 percent. Artisanal shops increasingly took on the quality of small factories, doubling in average size between 1882 and 1907, when one third of the plants were classed as *Grossbetriebe* (large enterprises employing more than fifty workers).

These changes greatly increased tensions in the labor market. In the mid-1880s Munich surpassed Nuremberg as Bavaria's major center of labor unrest. Complaining of job competition from foreigners willing to work for lower wages, factory workers and artisans repeatedly went on strike, prompting the employers to band together in protective associations and to rely even more heavily on recent immigrants. After the turn of the century the strike movement abated, but not because the workers had made significant progress. In 1912 a Munich police report stated that the "welcome" decline in strikes was due "solely to the employers' ability to match the workers in solidarity."

Munich's emergence as a metropolis also brought significant changes on the political front. The city's political scene had been dominated since mid-century by its business and professional elites, which tended to take a relatively liberal stance on issues of religion and economics. That is, they favored minimal clerical influence in daily life and opposed state or guild control of business and trade. Small in number, the wealthy elites used franchise restrictions to maintain their hold on power. But in the last decades of the century new forces emerged to challenge liberal dominance. While varying in composition and orientation, the new parties shared a populist commitment to democratizing the political order. Yet democratization could also bring, as it did in Vienna and Budapest, a tip toward religious sectarianism, nativism, hypernationalism, and anti-Semitism.

The first group to challenge the liberal parties in Munich was the Patriots Party, which had been established in 1868 by militant Catholics to fight for religious prerogatives and states' rights following the Bavarian-Austrian defeat by Protestant Prussia in 1866. Capitalizing on widespread fears of a "Prussianization" of the emerging German nation, the Patriots (renamed the Bavarian Center Party in 1887) won a slight majority in the Bavarian Landtag (diet) in 1869. When, two years later, Germany became unified under Prussian domination, the Patriots used their strength in the Landtag to combat German Chancellor Otto von Bismarck's anticlerical program, known as the Kulturkampf (cultural struggle). They also fought against liberal cultural policies pursued by the government of Prince Regent Luitpold. While continuing franchise restrictions at the municipal level kept them from penetrating the Munich City Council, their influence in the Bavarian legislature exerted—as we shall see—a dramatic impact on the cultural politics of "Isar Athens" in the early twentieth century.

In 1887 Social Democracy, the party of Germany's industrial working classes, came to Munich in the form of the Munich Social Democratic Workers' Association. Despite a flurry of new anti-Socialist laws introduced at the national level, the fledgling party grew quickly. As early as 1878 Socialists won 14 percent of the vote in Munich's two Reichstag (national parliament) districts. (Voting for the Reichstag was by universal manhood suffrage.) This success was due in large part to the party's leader,

Georg von Vollmar, a folksy figure who eschewed Marxian dogmatism for pragmatic reformism. Vollmar himself won one of Munich's Reichstag seats in 1884. Six years later, in 1890, the Social Democratic Party (SPD) captured both of Munich's Reichstag seats. At the Bavarian Landtag level they won one mandate from Munich in 1893, four in 1899, and (after a reduction in franchise restrictions) eight in 1907.

Another new political force was virulent anti-Semitism. Like many western and central European cities, Munich experienced an upsurge of anti-Semitism in the last decades of the nineteenth century. In part this stemmed from a sudden growth in the size of the Jewish population. As late as 1875 only 3,451 Jews lived in Munich. By 1900, however, the figure had reached 8,739. Though still tiny by the standards of Berlin or Vienna, this was the largest concentration in southern Germany. Some of the growth came from within Bavaria and other parts of Germany, but many of the new migrants were *Ostjuden* (Eastern Jews) from Galicia, Poland, and Russia. They congregated in specific districts, such as Bavariaring and the Gärtnerplatz. With their distinctive dress, habits, and speech, the *Ostjuden* hardly went unnoticed. As early as 1895 a local chronicler wrote: "Like the Chinese to California came the Jews to Munich: diligent, frugal, numerous, and thoroughly hated."

Munich's more established Jewish community, while not readily distinguishable from the rest of the population in speech or dress, was also "noticeable" because of its tendency to cluster in certain professions or businesses. The University of Munich was said to function as a "secularized Talmud high school" for the many Jews who obtained degrees there. Like their counterparts in Berlin, Vienna, Budapest, and Prague, many Munich Jews parlayed their professional skills into illustrious careers. The Eichtal, Hirsch, and Auhäuser families were prominent in banking, the Bernheimers and Wallachs were distinguished in the art trade, and Hermann Tietz dominated the new department store business. Alfred Pringsheim, who had converted to Protestantism, was one of Munich's leading art patrons.

Such prominent and successful figures liked to think that they were well assimilated into the local social establishment, a perception that was undoubtedly enhanced by Bavaria's promulgation of legal equality for Jews in 1869. But legal equality did little to change the fact that even the most assimilated Jews were often seen as not fully German. Nor did efforts at assimilation shield Jews from charges that they were responsible for many of the social ills associated with rapid urbanization and industrialization. Indeed, their successes made them all the more despised by those who were falling by the wayside in the new economic environment. Thus the retailer Hermann Tietz, who built Munich's first department store, was accused of driving his salesgirls to prostitution by paying them less than a living wage. Jewish financiers were said to be behind the speculation in urban real estate that was driving up rents and building costs.

Hostility toward Jews was vented in a variety of ways, from innuendo-filled newspaper articles to occasional physical attacks by "patriotic" louts. One satirical weekly, the *Grobian,* made anti-Semitism its chief theme. The conservative *Staatsbürgerzeitung* complained of "a terrifying increase in the Jewish element" that was threatening to "destroy the healthy kernel of the Munich middle class." Popular folk singers who worked the raucous beer halls around the Platzl (little square), and whose songs both reflected and shaped public opinion (much like today's talk show hosts), conjured up horror visions of a city being overrun by strange, foul-smelling creatures from the East. A couple of examples will suffice: "One sees these animals by the score / Hirsch and Low and many more / From Russia and Galicia they roam / Settle here and call it home." Or: "Take a stroll down the Thal / Look at the people, one and all / Some natives from Regensburg you'll surely spy / But the hordes from Jerusalem will stick in your eye." Munich's most popular folk singer, Weiss Ferdl (Little White Horse), identified Jews with the obnoxious by-products of technological modernization. "Cohen and Sarah go motoring for a blast / Up front it stinks of garlic, and out back of gas."

Malicious toward unassimilated *Ostjuden,* Ferdl and his colleagues were no easier on Jews who sought to blend in with Gentile society by converting to Christianity or by changing their names. On the contrary, they targeted these Jews for special abuse. "A Schutz remains a Schutz, come rain or shine / And a Jew stays a Jew, though he converts a hundred times." Or: "Kohn changes his name to help escape the shame / But 'Julius Schmid' he cannot chew / Ask his name and he'll blurt out 'Schmulius Jew.' " Munich's populist folk singers were expressing in their beery idiom what influential scientists around Europe were retailing in learned lectures: the doctrine that biology was destiny.

Such sentiments soon became the stuff of organized politics. In December 1891 a group calling itself the Deutsch-Sozialer Verein (DSV) registered with the police as Munich's first anti-Semitic party. Composed primarily of craftshop owners, small retailers, and low-level officials, it besieged the state government with petitions detailing the grievances of Bavaria's "little men." Viktor Welcker, the group's chief propagandist, cried: "In the interest of national self-preservation, we cannot allow that our people are sucked dry by the international Jewish stock-exchange pump. Nor can we tolerate that our peasants and middle classes, the backbone of our monarchical system, are proletarianized and driven into the arms of Social Democracy by a cartel of usurious Jewish cattle dealers, heartless clearance-sale jobbers, and aggressive pushcart peddlers—all backed up by liberal laws on trade and commercial mobility."

A newspaper allied to the DSV, the *Deutsche Volksblatt,* urged the Bavarian government not just to rescind laws liberalizing trade but to prohibit outright such "Jewish" commercial enterprises as department stores, chain stores, cut-rate bazaars, rental agencies, and street peddling. It also urged curbs on the recently instituted stock exchange, an alleged bastion of "unproductive Jewish capital." New limited liability companies should be subjected to a special tax, and the proceeds used for the relief of small producers and retailers who did not "enjoy the protection of international high finance." The paper also urged the government to overturn the emancipation law of 1869, to exclude Jews from public office, and to reduce Jewish participation in the medical and legal professions. "The future belongs to those nations that are most successful in freeing themselves from the curse of the Jews."

In addition to being a hotbed of anti-Semitism, fin de siècle Munich figured prominently in a corollary movement: Pan-Germanism. Alhough, once again, Munich was hardly alone in pushing this cause, Pan-Germanism was particularly militant there owing to the competing presence of Bavarian Catholic particularism and the city's geographical location on the southeastern periphery of the Reich. Munich's hypernationalists, many of whom were Protestants, were anxious to prove that they were just as "German" as the folks in the heartland. Here they had much in common with their counterparts in Vienna, who saw themselves as an island of Germanic purity in a sea of ultramontane Catholicism, Judaism, and rising Slavic nationalism.

Munich's branch of the Pan-German League, established in the mid-1890s, was one of the largest in the Reich. Serving as hosts for the league's annual meeting in 1898, leaders of the Munich chapter advertised their city as the "kernel" of Pan-German thinking. In his greeting to the delegates, a representative of the municipal government urged that Munich play a key role in the league's expansion into Austria and Bohemia. This would be a "natural mission" for the Bavarian capital, said the speaker, because Munich had originally "colonized" this region for German culture.

One of the founders of the Munich branch of the Pan-German League was a local publisher of medical and scientific books named Julius Friedrich Lehmann. Later to be awarded the Nazi Party's first Golden Medal of Honor, Lehmann used his publishing business to distribute extreme racist and nationalist literature. Convinced that the Berlin government was not doing enough to expand German influence outside the Reich, he created a "war fund" to "strengthen Germandom on our language borders and abroad, to support German settlers, students, libraries, and economic enterprises, and [to help establish] colonies throughout the world."

Lehmann was quick to add, however, that the struggle for Germandom abroad could not prosper if the *Volk* at home fell victim to corrupting influences. Although he and his colleagues often railed against the Germans' subservience to foreign cultural values, especially those of France, they believed that the greatest danger came from those "internal aliens" the Jews. "[W]e are not conducting a pogrom," wrote Lehmann in 1903, "but we seek, as much as possible, to exclude [Jewish] influence from our political and cultural life."

Convinced that mainstream Christianity, with its Judaic foundations, was no effective antidote to Jewish "corruption," Lehmann called for a "Germanic Christianity" that would incorporate the myths and legends handed down from pagan ancestors. While the publisher found both Protestants and Catholics remiss in their attitude toward German national values, he singled out the latter for especial abuse, accusing "Rome" of deliberately favoring Slavs over Germans in the Habsburg monarchy. At home he saw an insidious conspiracy between political Catholicism and Judaism to thwart the growth of German culture and identity. He hoped that Germany might give birth to a "new Luther" who would "bring on a struggle which will shake our foundations [and] compel the entire nation—indeed the whole world—to take a stand on the great questions of our time." Lehmann could hardly have known, at the turn of the century, that his "Luther" would appear so soon or that he would do so in his own hometown.

WHEN ADOLF HITLER arrived in Munich in 1913, he settled on the edge of Schwabing, the city's artistic and intellectual quarter. He did so because he considered himself an artist and wanted to be close to the center of action. By this time, the eve of World War I, Schwabing's creative bloom was beginning to fade, but in the last decades of the nineteenth century the district had harbored one of the most exuberant avant-garde scenes in the world. If Munich as a whole had established itself as Germany's Athens, then Schwabing was Germany's bohemia. Yet it was a very troubled bohemia, not a refuge from but a hothouse of the pressures and antagonisms afflicting the new German Reich.

Walls where ghosts still risk to walk,
Soil as yet untouched by bane,
Oh town of folk and youth!
Of home we dare not speak,
Until we see Our Lady's spires reign.

—*Stephan George, "Munich"*

WHERE
GHOSTS
WALKED

1

Germany's Bohemia

"**SCHWABING WAS A** spiritual island in the great world, in Germany, mostly in Munich itself," observed Wassily Kandinsky, the Russian painter, who lived in the district from 1897 to 1908. Erich Mühsam, an anarchist who was to play a major role in the Munich revolution of 1918, wrote: "I think of the free spiritual wind that blew through Schwabing and made the district synonymous with culture." Such phrases well capture the popular image of Munich's famed artists' quarter at the turn of the century. The Bavarian capital, it was said, had produced in these vibrant streets lying just north of the Old City a

German Montmartre or Chelsea, a freethinking, free-living antidote to the stuffy authoritarianism of the Wilhelmian Reich. The notion of Schwabing as a bohemian paradise became so well established that fifty years later, after a lot of very dirty water had flowed under Munich's bridges, the physicist Werner Heisenberg, a native Münchner, could speak of "live-and-let-live Schwabing," whose "spirit of tolerance" had set the tone for the entire town.

Like many clichés, this one was not without some validity: Schwabing was undoubtedly a "beautiful place to live," as Viktor Mann, Thomas Mann's younger brother, insisted in his memoirs. Yet such elegiac imagery obscured the complex realities of the quarter in the decades just before World War I. As Kandinsky noted, Schwabing was an "island" not only in the great world but also in Greater Munich. Many of the city's established residents had little use for the hordes of non-Bavarian artists, intellectuals, and students who frequented the quarter. Native Münchners labeled the expatriates *Schlawiner*—a derogatory term for Eastern Europeans—and generally looked askance on their unorthodox lifestyles.

Like the *Nordlichter* of Max II's day, the *Schlawiner* were in turn often contemptuous of the natives. The writer Theodor Lessing, an ex-Berliner, appreciated the locals' "sensual sloppiness" but found them "bearlike in their dim brains and fat hips." Lujo Brentano, an academic import, considered the Münchners so "decisively hostile to high culture that they [were] destined to go under, like the Sioux in North America." Even Thomas Mann, who had a genuine affection for his adopted town (he had moved there from Lübeck in 1894), could complain that Munich was "the *unliterary* city par excellence. Banal women and healthy men—God knows what a lot of contempt I load into the word 'healthy'!" Mann's first novel, *Buddenbrooks* (1901), caricatured the typical Münchner via a character named Alois Permaneder, a hops dealer interested only in marrying into money and drinking his three liters of beer a day.

True Schwabinger preferred cafés to beer halls. Among the district's many *Künstlercafés,* the most famous was the Stefanie, whose patrons sat around declaiming poetry and solving the problems of the world amid a perpetual cloud of cigarette smoke. Talk was cheap, and a good thing too, for most of the talkers were broke; the headwaiter carried a battered little book in which he marked down debts that rarely got paid. "He who entered this place to become a regular patron crossed the rubicon of his life," recalled the writer Richard Seewald. "Here he could lay the basis for later fame or totally come a cropper. Here he could find himself by wandering through a jungle of philosophies or become hopelessly lost and go to seed in some back alley." Not without reason was the Stefanie known as Café Grössenwahn (Café Grand Illusion).

Aflame with their grand illusions, the Schwabingers waged protracted battles over intellectual turf. The streets were alive with sectarian rancor, personal feuds, and ideological discord. As one veteran of the scene recalled, "[We were] enemy nomadic tribes occupying the same never-never land of self-importance. When our warpaths converged, we crossed cutting glances like sword blades." It was here, in the first years of the new century, that a Russian émigré named Nikolai Ulyanov took the pseudonym Lenin and launched a revolutionary magazine called *Istra* (Spark). In 1904 Lev Trotsky spent a few months in the Schwabing apartment of a local Socialist publisher. And of course it was here that Germany's own future world burner, Adolf Hitler, was to find a congenial home.

Looking back on Prince Regency Schwabing after World War II, the philosopher Ludwig Klages argued: "Here, and here alone, the die was cast, and the thirty years' war of 1914–1945 was only the working out of fate." Klages's assertion undoubtedly overshot the mark, for Munich-Schwabing was hardly the only intellectual foundry in which the weapons of the coming ideological struggle were forged. Another observer of the Munich scene, the cultural historian Moritz Julius Bonn, was closer to the mark when he observed that "A good many spiritual threads connect [Hitler] with the bohemian crowd that by and by came to be known by the name of Schwabing."

The Modern Life Society

Munich-Schwabing's avant-garde culture may be said to have been launched on 18 December 1890, when a group calling itself the Gesellschaft für modernes Leben (Modern Life Society) registered with the Munich police. According to its statutes, this "nonpolitical literary-artistic association" would cultivate "the modern creative spirit" through lectures, stage productions, art exhibitions, and a periodical. The society welcomed "all people . . . who wish to engage actively in the fight for the modern spirit." The group's declared enemies were the cultural traditionalists around Paul Heyse's Munich Poets' Circle, which, though established under Maximilian II, still commanded considerable influence. Another foe was the clerically supported Center Party, which tended to equate artistic modernism with political and religious subversion.

Publication of the society's goals generated so much interest that when it held its first public lecture evening, on 29 January 1891, the hall was sold out. A police observer reported that there were "many Social Democrats present, as well as many young businessmen and Jews; also many elegantly dressed women whose toilettes suffered in the crush."

The meeting was opened by the group's principal founder, Michael Georg Conrad, a journalist from Franconia (northern Bavaria) who had made a name for himself in Munich through his advocacy of literary naturalism and his biting attacks on the conservative Catholic establishment. On this occasion he was surprisingly mild, as were the comments of two other charter members, the litterateurs Otto Julius Bierbaum and Julius Schaumberger. Conservatives who had come to be scandalized must have been disappointed.

They found ample cause for indignation, however, in the performance of the evening's last speaker, a young journalist and playwright named Hanns von Gumppenberg. The son of an impoverished Bavarian nobleman who worked in Munich's post office, Gumppenberg believed that one of literature's main functions was to slaughter sacred cows. Thus he used his hour on the stage at the Modern Life Society to deliver a withering parody of the "forever yesterdays" of the Munich Poets' Circle. "Mocking, angry, and threatening cries flew at me from the excited crowd," he recalled in his memoirs. "[In] the wake of my performance, the evening ended full of discord and a general escalation of passions."

In the following days Bavaria's conservative newspapers ran alarming stories about the Modern Life Society. "How happy the Social Democrats will be," wrote the Catholic *Bayerischer Kurier,* "over these pioneers who prepare the way for them." The *Münchener Fremdenblatt* labeled the Modern Lifers "Socialists in tailcoats" who were more dangerous than the proletarians because they sought to "carry out among the upper ten thousand the work that the Social Democrats are performing among the 'socially dispossessed.' "

Believing that the society's critics were misrepresenting its constructive posture, Conrad published the lectures of the inaugural meeting. But instead of calming passions, this (in the self-important words of Gumppenberg) "split Munich into two rival camps." A Catholic critic wrote verses attacking the society, while Schaumberger weighed in with another parody of the Munich Poets' Circle. Gumppenberg, disguised as a beggar woman "to confuse our opponents," handed out copies of the parody on the Maximilianstrasse. Although not seeing through his disguise, an angry mob set upon him and forced him to take refuge in the ladies' room of the Parsifal restaurant.

While Gumppenberg saved his skin for the moment, he soon ran afoul of the conservatives once again, this time more seriously. Shortly after the Modern Life Society's inaugural lecture, a new play of his called *Messias* (The Messiah) appeared in Munich's bookstores. The play depicted Christ as a purely human apostle of peace and social progress who had duped his followers by faking miracles.

Predictably, Bavaria's Catholic press pounced on the playwright, condemning his work not only as blatantly atheistic but also as politically subversive. "The church is his first target, the state his second," cried the *Fremdenblatt*. Munich's clerical authorities demanded that the government take legal action against the author. Gumppenberg's father, hoping to protect his job, hurriedly bought up the entire stock of *Messias*. The young artist, meanwhile, responded with a new lecture entitled "The Atheistic Treatment of Religious Subjects." Here he argued that "it is not I, but my opponents, who are atheists."

This tack failed to impress the Catholic press, which insisted that Gumppenberg had ridiculed Christ as a "laughable fool" and "disgusting figure." As the church hoped, this induced the police to bring formal charges of blasphemy against the playwright, which in the event of conviction could have led to a jail term. The charges were dropped, however, when Gumppenberg was able to prove that he had not actually said that Christ was loathsome and ridiculous, only that the Catholic *image* of him suggested absurdity.

It had been a close call, and the Catholic establishment was now more determined than ever to put the playwright behind bars. Gumppenberg played into their hands with another provocative foray. At the Modern Life Society's third lecture evening he read a number of poems by the radical Berlin naturalist Karl Henckell. One of them, entitled "Monarchs Who Have No Time," took some unmistakable jabs at the new kaiser, Wilhelm II, whose restless traveling allegedly left him no time to concentrate on problems at home. Gumppenberg got an inkling of the stir he was causing when two officers stalked out of the room.

Immediately after the meeting the Catholic *Fremdenblatt* demanded that Gumppenberg be charged with lèse majesté. The Bavarian cabinet was sensitive to this accusation, for in the wake of its treatment of King Ludwig II in 1886 it was anxious to show its loyalty to monarchical institutions. The government also hoped that by tossing the disgruntled Catholics the occasional errant artist they might stave off the Center Party's push for control of the cabinet.

Brought to trial for lèse majesté, Gumppenberg argued that he had not intended to undermine the monarchy. The judges conceded this point but insisted that he must have known that his recitation would be "provocative" in the given context. They handed down a sentence of two months' incarceration. "The ultramontane court wanted to make an example of me," declared the playwright.

While controversy swirled around Gumppenberg, Conrad sought to defend the Modern Life Society against charges of irreligiosity by announcing that it stood "on the ground of the Gospels, not on the ground of atheism." Conrad's declaration did not sit well with younger members of the society, who interpreted it as a craven retreat before the forces of reaction. Bierbaum and Schaumberger declared that they were "fully committed to the consequences of the modern ideal in this domain [religion]."

Conrad's backpedaling did not pacify the Catholics. On 7 February 1892 the *Fremdenblatt* charged that anyone who listened to Conrad and his friends would know that they glorified divorce, encouraged suicide, promoted the doctrine of "natural sensuality," and waged war against "positive religion." The paper also revived the charge that the naturalists were agents of political subversion. The Modern Life Society, it insisted, "walks arm in arm with the Socialists."

This last charge was not entirely groundless, for some of the younger members of the society had indeed lectured before working-class audiences, and workers had been well represented at the group's meetings. Believing that it might advance social progress, the Socialist *Münchener Post* had applauded the formation of the society. The paper had also backed some of the group's cultural causes, including its appeal for an independent "people's theater" that could mount uncut versions of socially critical plays.

The Catholics' claim that the Modern Life Society was an artistic front for the SPD enraged Conrad, who feared that the charge might lead to legal suppression. But his indignation also stemmed from his conviction that the accusation was unfounded. If the society made contact with workers, Conrad said, it was to wean them from the SPD, whose revolutionary agenda it rejected in favor of a reconciliation between the masses and the monarchy. As if to show that avant-garde artists could be respectable monarchists, Conrad represented the society at a party honoring the prince regent's seventieth birthday; he even toasted the ruler in the name of Munich's progressives. In the society's new journal, *Moderne Blätter* (Modern Leaves), he threw the Socialists into the same pot with the ultramontane Catholics, insisting that both worked for "the destruction of the national spirit."

Conrad claimed to be speaking for the Modern Life Society, but he was actually speaking for himself. His stance prompted a new revolt from other members of the society that angered him so much he resigned his chairmanship in December 1891. As he explained to the police, he could no longer tolerate "the radical undercurrents of the thoroughgoing modernists."

With Conrad's resignation, the Modern Life Society quickly lost whatever coherence it had ever possessed. Gumppenberg, Schaumberg, and Bierbaum remained members but spent most of their time working on projects unconnected with the society. A police report in 1892 observed that the group's meetings lacked the verve of earlier gatherings. With its members pursuing different aesthetic visions and with no strong leader to impose unity, the society voluntarily dissolved in February 1893.

The Modern Life Society's brief history revealed certain tendencies in Munich's fledgling avant-garde that persisted over the next quarter century. Every bit as self-righteous as their opponents, the Modern Lifers believed they were on a mission to purify German culture of outmoded forms. Although they sometimes denied harboring any political intentions, they understood that art was a weapon and used it as such. While taking obvious delight in attacking clerical traditions, they were ambivalent when it came to prevailing secular authority. Some toyed with socialism, though none did much to promote the SPD's cause. Gumppenberg might make fun of Kaiser Wilhelm II, but he and his colleagues considered themselves staunch German nationalists—indeed the purest patriots in Bavaria. They respected the Bavarian ruling house, for the Wittelsbachs had been crucial sponsors of cultural progress. Their problem, however, was that the new regency was finding it ever harder to defend "blasphemous" artists against an increasingly assertive clerical establishment. By insisting that the Modern Life Society's attacks on religion were also attacks on the state, the church was making it very difficult for the secular authorities to turn a blind eye. At the same time, the confrontations with the authorities exacerbated internal divsisions within the group. Enamored with visions of the artist as lonely hero, the Modern Lifers could not work together to maintain a common front.

Oskar Panizza: Bavaria's Bruno

The Modern Life Society's collapse by no means calmed the conflict between Munich's avant-garde and clerical establishment since some of the modernists stepped up their anticlerical crusade in the wake of the society's demise. A society veteran named Oskar Panizza (1853–1921) emerged in the last years of the century as Munich's most notorious Catholic baiter.

Panizza, like Conrad, hailed from Franconia, where he had learned to hate Catholics from his Protestant mother. She wanted him to be a clergyman, but he decided to become a psychiatrist, a prophetic choice of pro-

fessions inasmuch as he was to end his days in an insane asylum. In the late 1880s he found employment as an army doctor but devoted most of his time to writing plays and poetry. His work came to the attention of Conrad, who invited him to join the Modern Life Society in May 1891.

By this time Panizza had gained a well-deserved reputation for eccentricity. A partial cripple with a bent back and large head, he was called "a limping Mephistopheles with a monk's face." He was accompanied everywhere by a little terrier, Puzzi, whose observations on life he recorded in his "Diary of a Dog." Appropriately his first presentation at the Modern Life Society was called "Genius and Madness."

Conrad soon had reason to regret his sponsorship of Panizza, for a contribution by the doctor led the police to confiscate a society anthology in September 1891. The offending piece, entitled "The Crime in Tavistock Square," was a mock detective story featuring garden plants practicing nightly masturbation. When word reached Panizza's military superiors that their unit physician had written a story about *Pflanzen-Onanie,* they ordered him to give up his literary avocation. He refused, and they cashiered him.

Panizza now embarked full-time on the mission he knew to be his true calling, that of skewering the self-appointed guardians of traditional morality. At the seventh meeting of the Modern Life Society, on 2 December 1891, he called attention to a recent "morality conference" of pietist pastors that had condemned modern realistic art in the name of "the eternal rules of morality." The pietists obviously did not realize, observed Panizza, that the record of German literature from Roswitha, a nymphomaniac nun of the tenth century, to Heinrich Heine was "one long chain of sensuality."

In other works Panizza defended prostitution as a "natural human drive"; praised Martin Luther for having slept around before his marriage; interpreted the *Grimm's Fairy Tales* as explorations in incest and zoophilia; appraised Wagner's *Parsifal* as "spiritual fodder for pederasts"; and, in a play entitled *The Council of Love,* depicted the Holy Family as a circle of drugged debauchés who conspire with Lucifer to infect humanity with syphilis.

The Council of Love was so patently offensive that the Munich prosecutor's office ordered the confiscation of all copies that could be found in local stores. In January 1895 the state began legal proceedings against Panizza for "crimes against religion, committed through the press." The dramatist now saw himself as a Bavarian Bruno, ready to don "the bloody halo." "It is time," he said, "for the public to learn that atheism too is not without its heroes and martyrs."

And martyr he became. The court sentenced him to a year's imprisonment, more than the prosecutor had asked for. Yet one of the jurors declared that Panizza should be happy with his sentence; had he been tried in a Lower Bavarian village, the juror said, "that dog would not have gotten out alive."

This was the harshest sentence yet levied for blasphemy in modern Germany, and Panizza's colleagues in the Modern Life Society were shocked at its implications for artistic expression. They insisted, as Conrad put it, that "the only forum" to which artists were responsible was the aesthetic criticism of their peers. Theodor Lessing protested that "Questions of literature do not belong before bourgeois courts."

For all his strident iconoclasm, Panizza was in certain ways more in tune with community standards than he was given credit for. There was another side to his work that in retrospect seems at least as important as his attacks on traditional values. In his defense of prostitution as "natural," for example, Panizza insisted that he was upholding the female's "inveterate tendency toward sluttishness" and seduction. This was a view of female nature that many conservative males, horrified by the dawning movement for women's rights, could readily accept. The main difference between Panizza's perspective and more conventional fin de siècle takes on "female perversity" is that he did not advance the usual Madonna/whore dichotomy; he left out the Madonna part. Panizza also espoused an unabashed anti-Semitism. Like most racialist commentators of his day, he considered Jews artistically inferior to Gentiles, albeit "superior in craft." Although (or perhaps because) he was himself no fine specimen of Nordic manhood, he made much of the Jews' alleged ugliness. In a nasty little story called "Der operierte Jud" (The Surgically Altered Jew), he wrote of a wealthy Jew who underwent several nose operations to rid himself of his Semitic features, only to be betrayed by his circumcised penis on his wedding night. Panizza also announced that while some Jews lusted after nubile Nordic women, most preferred young boys, a proclivity they shared with Catholic priests. Both Catholicism and Judaism, he declared, were marked by "something weak, formless, soft, timid, cowardly, and evasive." If the Germans hoped to become dominant, he insisted, they must overcome the influence of sexually inverted priests and Jews.

After his release from jail in 1896 Panizza decided to move to Switzerland. As he left Munich, he railed against its "perennial rejection of genius and creativity." The Münchners' only passion, he cried, was for beer and roast beef; woe be to anyone who tried to make them "chew on ideas!" If the town was called Athens on the Isar, he added, that was only because it had "harbored a few insane princes who had raised themselves above the prevailing butcher's mentality and built museums rather than slaughterhouses."

Panizza did not last long in Switzerland; a messy affair with a prostitute led to his deportation to France in 1898. Increasingly losing his mental grip, he blamed his deportation on Wilhelm II. From his new refuge in Paris he published a collection of verses called *Parisjana,* which heaped scatalogical abuse on the kaiser. The German authorities retaliated by confiscating Panizza's trust fund, which forced him to return to Munich to stand trial for lèse majesté. He evaded going to court by running naked through the streets. Declared insane in 1904, he was sent to an asylum outside Bayreuth, where he died in 1921.

Simplicissimus: *The Red Dog of Satire*

While Panizza was languishing in jail in 1896, a new and more lasting mouthpiece of literary satire made its appearance on the Munich scene: the magazine *Simplicissimus.* Taking its title from a seventeenth-century novel by Hans Jakob von Grimmelshausen, the new magazine lampooned Wilhelmian Germany's puritanical social mores, elevated cultural pretensions, and boastful political posturing. Strongly anti-Prussian, it also mocked backwardness at home. The Catholic clergy came in for much abuse, as did beer-swilling Munich burghers. In fact, a *Simpl* cartoon of 1897 showing a fat Münchner sitting drunkenly in a tavern inspired Thomas Mann's caricature of Herr Permaneder in *Buddenbrooks.*

Simpl's trademark was a red bulldog that had broken its chain. The fierce-looking totem was appropriate, for as Peter Gay has argued, aggression is one of the preeminent motives behind humor, especially satirical humor. *Simpl* was pugnacious in a double sense: It attacked Wilhelmian foibles while embracing some of that society's most aggressive ideals. Indeed, its role can best be appreciated when we recall that it emerged against a backdrop of German agitation for a place in the sun.

The man who unleashed Munich's red dog of satire was a twenty-seven-year-old publisher named Albert Langen. He borrowed the idea from the French satirical weekly *Gil Blas Illustré.* In Munich-Schwabing, where he had moved from Paris in 1895, Langen assembled a brilliant staff of young writers and graphic artists. His chief assistant was Ludwig Thoma, a Bavarian who savored earthy jokes that buried their targets in verbal offal. The magazine's best graphic artist was Thomas Theodor Heine, a Jew from Leipzig who drew urbane cartoons caricaturing the philistine taste and caste pride of imperial Germany's plutocrats, civil servants, and army officers. But perhaps *Simpl*'s sharpest pen was wielded by Benjamin Franklin ("Frank") Wedekind, a dramatist whose struggles against his superficially liberal father led him to detest hypocrisy in all authority figures.

Simpl was so bold that even its advertisements were on the cutting edge. In addition to fashionable new gadgets like motorcars and "Brownie Kodaks," the journal pushed contracaptive devices and "male strength pills." A regular advertiser was Dr. Franz Müller's sanatorium, which treated addiction to alcohol, morphine, opium, and cocaine.

From its inception until World War I *Simpl*'s favorite target was Kaiser Wilhelm II and the personality cult surrounding him. "Am I really the king or just suffering from megalomania?" asks a "fairy-tale prince" in one cartoon. "Perhaps both," responds the court jester. In another cartoon a bourgeois citizen asks the mayor why he keeps a shoe on display. The mayor responds: "That's a precious relic. Our Most Noble All-Highest spit on that shoe on the occasion of His Sublime Majesty's recent visit to our city." Even more graphically, a cartoon entitled "The Cigarette Butt or True Popularity" has citizens fighting to retrieve a cigarette end that the prince has thrown into a pile of horse droppings. One citizen exults: "It fell upon some manure. People stepped on it, horses pissed on it, but . . . I ran to where it lay and gladly licked it clean."

Simpl's most celebrated attack on the kaiser was a send-up of his voyage to Palestine in 1898. Alongside a cartoon by Heine showing the ghosts of Godfrey of Bouillon and Friedrich Barbarossa snickering about "pointless" crusades, there appears a poem by "Hieronymus Jobs" (Wedekind) containing the lines:

> Though men are lazy, not too fond of action,
> They have the greatest need to be admired,
> To show off, to be Number One Attraction,
> Like you who strut so gorgeously attired,
> In sailor suit or ermine robes arrayed,
> Or in rococo suit of stiff brocade,
> As sportsman, huntsman, always on display,
> Oh photogenic Prince! Accept this lay.

The kaiser insisted upon prosecution of the journal. The case was handled by the Saxon government, since *Simpl* was printed in Leipzig. Charges of lèse majesté were leveled against Langen, Heine, and Wedekind. Langen escaped to Paris, where he remained for five years until he was pardoned. Heine was arrested, tried, and sentenced to six months in jail. Wedekind fled to Switzerland but soon returned to stand trial in order to avoid permanent exile. Also convicted, he was given seven months' imprisonment.

The arrests did not succeed in muzzling the red dog. New writers and editors, including Thomas Mann, were hired to fill the vacancies. The controversy, moreover, was a boon to sales. "The fury of the Saxon authorities," wrote acting publisher Korfiz Holm, "had the result that our circulation rose within four or five weeks from fifteen thousand to, I think, eighty-five thousand. We were happy about this, although even then we barely broke even financially."

In their efforts to suppress *Simplicissimus,* conservatives sometimes claimed that the magazine held no principles dear. This was far from the case, especially in the political realm. In fact, *Simpl*'s attacks on the political establishment stemmed not from a contempt for authority per se but from an urge to defend state power against abuse by those who wielded it. Certainly this was evident in the lampooning of the kaiser. At bottom *Simpl*'s complaint was that Wilhelm II was all bluster and no substance: He spoke loudly and carried a little stick. His strutting theatricality was reducing the art of government to a vaudeville show. Recalling *Simpl*'s deep frustration with the kaiser's antics, Ludwig Thoma later wrote: "None of us was so clairvoyant as to see the consequences of these musical-comedy politics, but we knew that they were ridiculous, and behind our mockery lay a lively discontent. And it was natural that we as artists should be repelled by the whole show."

Repelled also, he might have added, by the fact that Germany's middle classes seemed all too delighted by this flashy production. When *Simpl* made fun of German professors and businessmen who scrambled after titles and court receptions, it was exposing the failure of the intellectual and commercial elites to impose some discipline or focus on the mercurial kaiser. To the disgruntled artists, this failure confirmed the German bourgeoisie's political immaturity.

Simpl's treatment of Germany's military leadership reflected similar concerns over misdirected or inadequately realized power. The magazine was full of cartoons savaging the officer corps' caste pride, dim-wittedness, addiction to spit and polish, and brutalization of enlisted personnel. There were jokes about the fashionable officer who could issue no IOUs because he could not sign his name, about the elegant young aristocrat who did not worry about being unable to lead a platoon because he would soon be commanding a brigade. A cartoon entitled "Barracks Discipline" had a pair of officers standing over a dead recruit. "It's a good thing he didn't resist the punishment," says one; "otherwise he would have gotten two years in the stockade."

The motivation behind these attacks was arguably not knee-jerk antimilitarism but a desire for a more efficient and potent army. Like many German national liberals, *Simpl*'s contributors believed that the military could realize its potential only if it rooted out remnants of feudalism in favor of promotion by merit, along with improved technical training and civilized treatment of personnel. Significantly, the magazine never joined Socialist crusades to reduce the army's budget.

Simpl joined no such crusades because in many ways it was just as bellicose as imperialist lobby groups like the Pan-German League. When the German government backed down in a 1903 confrontation with America over Berlin's attempt to penetrate the Caribbean, *Simplicissimus* barked in rage. A Heine cartoon skewered Germany's ambassador to Washington for meekly accepting the Monroe Doctrine. Taken to court for insulting the government, Heine argued that his cartoon was meant as a protest against Berlin's lamentable tendency to be misled by "its love of peace into self-abasement before a foreign power."

Simpl's depiction of the foreign powers with which Germany was competing in the decades before World War I also revealed pronounced nationalist tendencies. France was not too badly savaged because it was a favorite haven for persecuted German artists, but Britain emerged as a shallow, meanspirited, hypocritical land whose people spoke incessantly about democracy while imposing a brutal colonial yoke on half of the world. *Simpl*'s contributors, like many Germans (including the kaiser), were particularly outraged by Britain's suppression of the Boers in South Africa. Echoing Wilhelm II's famous Kruger Telegram, *Simplicissimus* cheered the Boers on, instructing them to "shoot the English in the mouth, where they are the most dangerous." Another cartoon showed King Edward VII and a colonial officer stamping on the inmates of a concentration camp in South Africa. "The blood from these devils is befouling my crown," complains Edward. These slurs caught the attention of British visitors to Munich, whose complaints prompted the Bavarian authorities, watchful protectors of the tourist industry, to confiscate *Simpl*'s Boer War issue. Thoma, however, was very happy to have given offense. "I hate the English," he wrote, "and if I could shoot one of them, I'd be delighted."

The magazine was even more rabid about the Russians, casting them as barbarous, superstitious, and reactionary. In the wake of the abortive revolution of 1905, Nicholas II was pilloried as "The Blind Czar," strolling club in hand across a landscape littered with severed heads and broken bodies. Because Nicholas was related to the Prussian Hohenzollerns, *Simpl* could conflate Russian and Prussian "autocracy" as a double evil. A cartoon entitled "At Russia's Service" (1904) showed Prussian monkeys picking lice from the fur of a Russian bear: " 'Tis the Prussians' greatest love / To delouse the Russian bear / Filth and dirt they're not above / They perform this service with nary a care."

Simpl's hatred of Russia derived in part from a broader contempt for all Slavs, so it is not surprising that the magazine heaped abuse on other Eastern European peoples, including the Poles and the Serbs. Like most of the German intelligentsia, *Simpl*'s contributors saw the Balkans as a benighted region where the people were too primitive to do anything but flay one another in incessant tribal wars. The Serbs always fought to the death, proposed one cartoon, because they could never find a flag white enough to signal surrender. Yet the magazine presciently sensed danger in the perennial Balkan quarrels. A cartoon entitled "The Politics of Insect Bites" (1908) noted that "when there's an itch down in the Balkans, all Europe has to scratch."

If in its coverage of international affairs *Simplicissimus* often showed itself more in tune with traditional ways of thinking than might seem appropriate for a magazine claiming "advanced" status, such was true also of its stance on many domestic issues of the day. In Germany's ongoing class confrontation, *Simpl* liked to champion the cause of the workers, but its advocacy was heavily tinged with paternalism. Its depiction of working-class people hardly deviated from Victorian-era stereotypes of inarticulate wretches in need of guidance from their intellectual betters. A Heine cartoon called "An Impertinent Person," for example, shows a cadaverous woman and her malnourished child bowing before a pair of overstuffed burghers, whose dog is devouring a plate of bones. "If Herr Dog cannot eat it all?" pleads the woman. *Simplicissimus* also trafficked in stereotypes of the Jews. There were Jews on its staff, and it sometimes attacked instances of racial prejudice, but its cartoons implied that Jews could never become fully assimilated. They appear as overfed types crassly exploiting their wealth to assault the upper reaches of Gentile society. A cartoon by Bruno Paul, called "The Aristocratic World View," shows a dwarfish Jewish bride being given by her father in marriage to a chinless aristocrat. It reads: "Honor, love, and hunger make the world go around; for honor, we have the duel; for love, the corps de ballet; and for hunger, thank God, marriage for money." Down-at-the-heel Junkers and social-climbing Jews, the cartoon suggests, deserved each other.

If the humor purveyed in *Simplicissimus* reflected the pugnacious instincts of the magazine's producers and consumers, it also betrayed other emotions characteristic of aggressive humor: inner insecurity and self-doubt. The bitter derision of Germany's foreign rivals stemmed partly from fears regarding the Reich's ability to find its place in the sun, while the caricatures of Jews and workers suggested disorientation in a time of rapid socioeconomic change. And perhaps the kaiser came in for such ferocious abuse because in the end he was not all that different from his critics at *Simpl*: more bark than bite.

The Eleven Executioners: Bourgeois Society on the Chopping Block

Both aggression and insecurity were amply evident in Munich's theatrical equivalent to *Simplicissimus,* the satirical cabaret Die Elf Scharfrichter (The Eleven Executioners). Like the angry red dog, the Eleven Executioners became a prominent fixture on the Schwabing scene, though the famous cabaret lasted only from 1901 through 1903. During its brief moment of glory it wielded the sword of satire with lusty abandon, yet it also showed just how double-edged that sword could be.

Cabaret, of course, was not a Munich invention. Paris's legendary Chat Noir (1881–1897) was the prototype of this genre, and it spawned a host of imitators across Europe, from Barcelona's El Quatre Cats and Berlin's Überbrettl to Moscow's Bat. The Eleven Executioners had direct Parisian affinities, for one of its founders, Marc Henry, was an expatriate Frenchman who had worked in the cabaret scene there. Convinced that Schwabing would provide fertile soil for Parisian-style cabaret, Henry brought together about a dozen Munich writers and artists to discuss the venture. According to him, they envisaged "a sort of artistic-literary republic with a clearly defined program." Their cabaret would boast the latest technical innovations, including an auditorium of original design, but "everything in miniature," so the audience's experience would be "intimate and exclusive." By registering as a private club and allowing admission only to members, the enterprise could avoid paying Munich's theater tax and evade censorship regulations applicable to public theaters.

Once the cabaret opened in April 1901, however, it proved anything but low-profile. Located in the back room of a tavern in the heart of Schwabing, it boasted appointments that were calculatedly outrageous. The black walls were adorned with illustrations from *Simplicissimus* and pornographic Japanese woodcuts. The defining motif was an executioner's block complete with the cloven head of a bewigged philistine. The cabaret's printed program magazines were also studies in provocation.

One cover depicted a policeman drawing his sword over a woman baring her leg; another showed a nude lady hurling her red gloves in the face of the viewer; yet another featured a naked girl admiring herself in a hand mirror while a group of old crones look on disapprovingly. As for the cabaret's name, one of the founders explained that it "was intended to suggest that judgment was sharp and execution summary in the battle against reaction and obscurantism."

The performers did their best to live up to their name. The eleven Executioners, decked out in bloodred robes and hangman's masks, marched onto the stage singing a song addressed to the protectors of the traditional Catholic order:

> A shadow-dance a puppet's joke!
> You happy, polished people—
> In Heav'n on high the same old bloke
> Guides puppets from his steeple.
> For good or ill he guides their moves,
> Each doll an anthem sings,
> But then, just when it least behooves,
> We cut the puppets' strings.

After the opening song came an appearance by the resident femme fatale, Marya Delvard, an extremely thin woman with flaming red hair, black-rimmed eyes, and luminescent skin. Dressed in a long black gown and bathed in violet light, she looked as though she had just crawled out of a coffin. Hardly moving or changing her pitch, she moaned songs about dawning sexuality, suicide, and murder. "She was frightfully pale," recalled the writer Hans Carossa. "One thought involuntarily of sin, vampirically parasitical cruelty, and death. . . . She sang everything with a languid monotony which she only occasionally interrupted with a wild outcry of greedy passion."

After Fräulein Delvard had warmed up the audience, the Executioners got down to serious business: political and religious satire. Their first program included a puppet play called *The Fine Family,* the family in question being the European Great Powers. Like *Simplicissimus,* the play condemned both the British for their suppression of the Boers and the German government for not pursuing a more aggressive colonial policy. Thus, as one commentator has pointed out, the "same people who desired greater domestic liberties also demanded a stronger German stance in Asia and Africa." This posture was typical of the national liberals of the Wilhelmian era, who believed that greater openness and intellectual freedom at home would make Germany a stronger contender abroad.

True to their anticlerical liberal ethos, the Executioners also hacked away at the Catholic Church. Among their early presentations was a play by Otto Falckenberg that claimed to illuminate the lascivious mental world of Lucrezia Borgia's father confessor. Reminiscent of Panizza's *Council of Love,* this work could not help but appall the authorities. A police officer informed Bavaria's archconservative minister of the interior, Max von Feilitzsch, that the play constituted an "insult to the institutions of the church" since the priest performed "his sensual gesticulations in a most immoral manner."

On Feilitzsch's orders, the Eleven Executioners lost its status as a private club in 1901; henceforth it would have to submit all its material to prior censorship. The cabaret was also reclassified as a vaudeville "devoid of the higher interest of art and science," which meant that it could be closed down by the police at any time.

With the authorities' ax hanging over their heads, the Executioners became more careful in their selection of targets and less violent in their theatrical techniques. One of their most popular skits in 1902 made fun of Munich's building commission for stipulating that a new public toilet must blend in with the city's historical architecture. Rather more daring were Frank Wedekind's explorations of adolescent eroticism; though not explicitly political, they challenged a moral order that considered sexual freedom the first step to anarchy. The Executioners also swung their swords against the contemporary art scene. Hanns von Gumppenberg mocked the pious Ibsenites and the cult of mysticism surrounding the symbolist poet Maurice Maeterlinck. Gumppenberg and his colleagues even poked fun at one another in parodies of modernist cabaret.

Although the Executioners' self-parody showed that the group found nothing too sacred to mock, it also suggested a growing frustration with the work at hand. The satirists were honest enough to see that their "literary republic" was not having much of an effect on the society around them. Their bourgeois audiences were titillated but hardly galvanized to action. Their skits had no resonance with workers, who were rarely in attendance. For all their aggressive talk and trappings, the artists had not wounded, let alone "executed," the reigning powers of the day.

Indeed, political gains by conservatives in 1903 helped put the Eleven Executioners itself on the block. In an effort to appease the Catholic-dominated Landtag, Prince Regent Luitpold dismissed his relatively liberal prime minister, Krafft von Crailsheim, in favor of the much more conservative Clemens von Podewils. Now the cabinet acceded to the Center Party's demands for even tighter controls over Die Elf Scharfrichter and other modernist theater groups. In November 1903 the government ordered the suppression of four major pieces planned by the cabaret. When he criticized the censorship, Henry, as a French citizen, was threatened with deportation. Under such conditions, the group concluded that it could not go on. Already unsure about the resonance of its message, it closed up shop in 1903.

The Eleven Executioners' demise—partly imposed and partly self-inflicted—illustrated the growing fragility of Munich-Schwabing's modernist culture at the beginning of the twentieth century. In retrospect the cabaret's collapse may be seen as an early exit from a battlefield that was soon almost entirely vacated by its once-so-doughty defenders.

The "Queen of Schwabing"

Simplicisimmus and Die Elf Scharfrichter were prominent bastions of Munich's modernist culture, but they were also commercial businesses with payrolls and deadlines to meet. As such they could not fully exemplify the bohemian ethos that seemed so central to the Schwabing mystique. That role could be performed only by an individual, someone prepared to lead a life of daily rebellion against the conventions and restrictions of bourgeois society. In the end no one person could embody all aspects of this place and time, but the figure that perhaps came closest was Countess Franziska zu Reventlow, known widely in her day as the Queen of Schwabing. Her tumultuous life in the Bavarian capital, which she richly documented in diaries and autobiographical novels, illustrated the possibilities, as well as the limitations, of free-spirited rebellion in bohemian Munich. And her world view, a curious amalgam of the advanced and the reactionary, reflected the deep ambiguity of turn-of-the-century Schwabing's ideological legacy.

Like most of the artists and intellectuals who had enriched the cultural life of Munich since the era of Ludwig I, Franziska ("Fanny") zu Reventlow hailed from northern Germany. Her father owned a large estate and two of her brothers were members of the Reichstag. From an early age Fanny showed signs of rebellion. Instead of learning needlework she read "advanced" novels. "People are horrified," she wrote to a friend, "when young women want to develop their own character. They aren't allowed to be anything but pieces of furniture or household pets, hemmed in by thousands of ridiculous prejudices."

In 1886, hoping to crush Fanny's budding rebelliousness, her mother sent the fifteen-year-old to a strict Lutheran school for young noblewomen. Fanny caused so much trouble, however, that she was expelled. Shortly thereafter her family moved to Lübeck, Thomas Mann's native town. (She shared this connection not only with Mann but also with *Simplicissimus*'s Korfiz Holm and the anarchist Erich Mühsam. "Why did they all have to come from Lübeck?" groaned that city's conservative mayor.) In Lübeck Fanny joined the Ibsen Club, where young people discussed the latest plays by the Norwegian dramatist, as well as works by other modernists like Émile Zola and Ferdinand Lassalle. Nietzsche too was a potent influence, as he was for the entire German avant-garde. Fanny declared that *Zarathustra* was the "sacred source" from which she quenched her intellectual thirst.

Meanwhile, she was satisfying her physical needs through a liaison with a fellow Ibsenite, which prompted her mother to lock her up in a convent. Fanny refused to be kept down, and on her twenty-first birthday she escaped to Hamburg, the nearest big city. But Hamburg proved too staid for her tastes; in 1894, determined to become a painter, she decamped for Munich.

Twenty-two years old when she arrived in Munich, Fanny was a strikingly handsome woman, with blue eyes, dark blond hair, and a voluptuous figure. One of her admirers called her the Venus from Schleswig-Holstein. But she was a sloppy Venus, already cultivating the bohemian look. She did not bother to launder her dresses or to use makeup. "She took too little interest in her toilette to be elegant," commented one of her new friends.

Shortly after settling in Schwabing and beginning painting lessons at the Royal Academy, Fanny received word that her father was dying. She rushed home, only to learn that she was being disinherited for soiling the family name. In despair she sought out a former lover in Hamburg and agreed to marry him. This was unwise, for Fanny was simply not cut out to be a Hamburg hausfrau. Within a year she had left her bewildered husband and was back in Schwabing, furiously partying with her bohemian friends. "My life was young, ripe, and hot, and sin was so sweet and beautiful," she wrote in her diary. "[Sin] pulled me down into its glowing whirl, and I became its priestess."

Now dependent largely on her own resources, Fanny tried to make a living from her painting. This would have been difficult even if she had possessed unusual talents, as she did not. In the year of her arrival Munich was overflowing with artists. There were some 1,180 "registered" painters and sculptors, about 13 percent of all those living in the Reich. Their output overwhelmed the local market because there were too few patrons willing to invest in contemporary art. The American market, long a profitable dumping ground for Munich's artists, had fallen off sharply when Washington imposed a 30 percent tariff on art imports in the mid-1880s. To survive in such tight circumstances, many artists resorted to fringe employment, like retouching photographs, making kitsch for tourists, forging Old Masters, and studio modeling.

Countess zu Reventlow was as hard up as any of her peers. Her paintings did not sell, and her savings quickly dried up. Reducing her meals to one a day, she soon fell dangerously ill and was unable to paint. "Art is the only way I can hold myself together," she wrote. "but a sick person cannot work." Lying feverish in her flat, she threw glasses at the walls to remind her landlord to bring her crusts of bread and water. Frequently she used laudanum to combat the pain from a bleeding ulcer.

In January 1897, not long after her marriage had been officially terminated, Fanny learned that she was pregnant. Pregnancy brought on further bouts of illness, but she was ecstatic about her impending motherhood. Nietzsche's *Zarathustra* states: "Everything about women is a puzzle, and everything about women has a resolution—pregnancy." Apparently remembering this adage, Fanny wrote in her diary: "It now seems to me that the puzzle of my identity has resolved itself . . . that I can see with new eyes, understand everything, feel everything, and be everything to those who stand close to me."

Fanny's baby, a son named Rolf, was born in September 1897. She did not identify the father, perhaps could not, for since coming to Schwabing, she had slept with dozens of men. In any event she was determined not to bind herself to a man for the sake of economic convenience, and she did not want to share Rolf with a live-in father. "I want him exclusively for myself," she wrote. While having an illegitimate child was nothing unusual, Fanny's determination to remain unattached as a "free mother" helped turn her into a liberationist icon, a "pagan Madonna."

Fanny said that Rolf was her "salvation," but he was also a heavy responsibility. She immediately began looking for the kind of work that would put food on the table without depriving her of time to paint and rear her child. For a while she peddled insurance, but she was happy every time someone slammed a door in her face. She tried to open a milk shop but gave up after three days when she found herself knee-deep in unsold product. A total failure in commerce, she returned to art or to a kind of art. She found that she had a talent for forging medieval religious drawings and sketching likenesses of Ludwig II on beer steins. "L'art pour l'art gives pleasure but it doesn't pay the bills," she noted pragmatically. She also sold a few jokes to *Simplicissimus*. Her largest literary paychecks came from translating French novels for Albert Langen's press.

Her own novels, lightly fictionalized accounts of her upbringing and colorful existence in Schwabing, earned almost nothing. In writing, as in painting, her address was decidedly Grub Street.

Desperate, Fanny began selling her body. Schwabing's many bars and cafés provided a steady source of customers. "Spooned up a French writer who wants to study life," reads a diary entry for 15 July 1898. On another occasion she engaged in a ménage à trois with three students, who gave her 150 marks to advance her "acting career." "One can't become a star on 150 marks," she noted, "but the boys are dears, so energetic."

No doubt Fanny could have earned more money in this trade had she turned herself into a full-time prostitute, but this would have interfered with her parenting and painting. "I don't have time to make [streetwalking] a serious profession," she wrote in 1898. "Anyway, what comes of it? My Frenchman is already gone, and the 300 marks [he paid] are gone as well, like ice in the sun. I can never make a real go at this." Yet ten years later she was still at it. On Carnival Tuesday, 1909, she noted: "Evening [Café] Luitpold. Yesterday's gallants are not so approachable. . . . A bad night at the Tip-Top Bar." And a little later: "Another bad night with the Tip-Top people. They picked me up at 11:00, drove me to Pullach. The next morning they took me to the train station and disappeared."

Despite her material difficulties, Fanny continued to reject men who wanted to "keep" her. "One can be my lover only for a moment," she wrote. "I have no interest in constancy, need only sensuality. If someone wants to possess me, I retreat." Or: "I love one man but desire six more, one after another. It's precisely the variety that excites me, the new 'strange man.' "

In fact, it often seemed that men were little more than sex objects for Fanny. She remembered them not by their faces but by their penises—sometimes a "cudgel," sometimes a "pencil." In an erotic memoir entitled "Amouresken," she referred collectively to her men as Paul. "Paul is always an amusing thing, basically trivial and without consequence. Fortunately he shows up again and again, in varying shapes and sizes." Fanny's own libidinal needs were so strong that she did not resent sexual aggression in men, regarding it as a "point of honor" never to repulse a fellow's advances. "To be desired by a man is never an insult," she declared, "even when the desire is fleeting and without deeper feeling."

Such views, Fanny well knew, were more typically articulated by men. But why, she asked, should not women also celebrate their sexuality and adopt the credo of "free love"? Frenchwomen, she believed, were more advanced in this regard than their German sisters. Now it was time for the latter to shake off their "cold Nordic dutifulness and guilt complexes."

She saw herself as a role model, boasting that her liberating influence was working "like yeast on many daughters from good houses."

Yet Fanny's tough talk about sex and freedom should not be taken at face value. She was miserably lonely much of the time, frustrated by her inability to settle down to a more "normal" existence. "I pined for solitude but could not stand being alone," says the heroine of her autobiographical novel, *Ellen Olestjerne.* Her life, it seemed, was a bitter struggle between material necessity and the imperatives of the free spirit. Eventually the hardship became so great that Fanny began searching, albeit reluctantly, for a companion who might provide support for her and her son. The search was difficult because, as Fanny admitted, "A woman with a past is about as acceptable in society as a man who has served time in jail."

For all her preaching about female sexuality and independence, moreover, Fanny was not a prophet of women's emancipation in the conventional sense. She had nothing but contempt for her sisters who, in Germany and elsewhere, were campaigning for female suffrage. Organized politics of any sort she found boring and useless. In this regard she was the quintessential "unpolitical German," though her hostility toward political engagement was rooted not in high-minded idealism but in the cult of sensuality. She also had no interest in expanding women's economic horizons. Why fight for the right to be a banker or broker when the frock-coated males who pursued these occupations were so dreary? she asked. No woman worth her ovaries, thought Fanny, would ever want to be a stockjobber. "Women were not created for work, the heavy business of the world," she wrote, "but for lightness, joy, and beauty." The feminists who were stridently campaigning for socioeconomic rights were mean-spirited "viragoes" whose unhappy example was causing too many women "to lose their allure and producing an ever more boring and sexless world." Instead of angry assaults on the male sphere, she said, the world needed a "women's movement that works to free females as sexual creatures, that teaches them to demand free control over their own bodies."

Such views were advanced enough to scandalize Munich's conservatives, and Fanny's writings were roundly condemned. Yet her perspective was readily exploitable by enemies of the political and economic advancement of women. No wonder she was sometimes quoted by those who believed that women "by nature" had no business in business, not to mention in the political arena. Her brother Ernst, a nationalist politician and future supporter of Hitler, had at least one thing in common with his errant sister: the conviction that a woman's proper place was in bed.

Fanny's views on motherhood were equally problematic. While her championship of single motherhood typed her as a rebel, her insistence that women found their true calling in pregnancy and child rearing put her in league with cultural conservatives who were leading a backlash against the "New Woman." Late-nineteenth-century *völkisch* writers, like the Nazis a generation later, preached the virtues of broodmares that were all womb and no brain. As one of them wrote, "The way of the *Volk* is the way of the woman, anonymous, without person, producing unconsciously, at work quietly like Nature."

Fanny was celebrated in Schwabing for her rebelliousness, but her rebellion in the end was incomplete. Like many of her colleagues, she combined bold attacks on official culture with affirmations of some highly traditional views. More important, her very assaults on bourgeois values contained ideological ingredients that were as easily exploitable by the Right as by the Left. It is not surprising, therefore, that at the height of her Schwabing career she became close to (but also amusingly critical of) a coterie of self-absorbed intellectuals whose views were authoritarian and protofascist.

"Criminals of the Dream"

The group in question was known as the Cosmic Circle. It included Ludwig Klages, a graphologist and self-taught philosopher; Alfred Schuler, an amateur archaeologist; Karl Wolfskehl, a Jewish professor of German literature; and Stefan George, a noted symbolist poet who later became the center of a larger aesthetic cult.

Like Fanny, who was introduced to the group by Klages, the *Kosmiker* hoped to revivify the arid, overly cerebral modern world through a "renaissance of paganism." Though they disagreed on some of the finer points of their revolutionary project, they all shared a repugnance for industrial modernity, liberal rationalism, parliamentary democracy, and orthodox Christianity. They harbored a common inclination toward mysticism and the occult, agreeing that the only route to higher consciousness lay along "obscure and secret paths." Those who knew these paths might consider themselves *Enormen* (giants), whereas all others were *Belanglosen* (inconsequentials). Summing up the group's self-perception, Fanny wrote that it constituted "an intellectual movement, a direction, a protest, a cult, and above all an effort to retrieve new religious possibilities out of ancient rituals."

Ludwig Klages moved to Munich from Hanover in 1893. He came to the Bavarian capital to study chemistry but quickly tired of his studies and drifted into the bohemian scene. Tall, blond, and handsome—an admirer called him a "Nordic pine"—Klages became a fixture at the Café Luitpold, a favorite bohemian "muse temple." He was very excited to be in Schwabing, which he called, perhaps more presciently than he knew, the "world-suburb in which the fate of the next generation will be decided."

Not long after arriving in Schwabing, Klages stumbled upon a book that he said made him a "new man." It was *Mutterrecht* (Matriarchy), written in 1861 by the Swiss historian Johann Jakob Bachofen. From this work Klages learned that matriarchal orders had preceded patriarchal societies and were culturally superior to them. Matriarchy enshrined the life and power of the soul and spirit, whereas patriarchy brought the triumph of shallow, desiccated rationalism. "The oldest wisdom of humanity was the possession and privilege of women," concluded Klages, citing as proof the Pythian oracle, sibyls, Valkyries, and swan maidens.

Dilating on these themes in his most famous work, *Der Geist als Widersacher der Seele* (The Mind as Opponent of the Soul), Klages argued that the patriarchal mind, operating through abstraction and logic, created artificial concepts that distorted raw experience. The soul, on the other hand, was linked directly to the potent mysteries of the blood through the intercession of women. Drawing on Bachofen's observation that the lives of women were bound up in the ebb and flow of blood—menstruation, deflowering, childbearing—Klages argued that only men in touch with their inner women were capable of true creativity.

Much of this sounded like Klages's better-known English contemporary D. H. Lawrence, who also spent time in Schwabing and became a follower of Bachofen's. But unlike Lawrence, Klages gave the *Mutterrecht* doctrine a racist twist. Artistic creativity, he argued, had strong racial foundations, for the ur-Nordic peoples had been governed by their feminine "blood souls," whereas their racial antagonists, the Jews, had repressed the feminine power of blood in favor of patriarchal rationalism. As archrationalists the Jews could never create anything themselves, could only feed on the energy and accomplishments of others. "The Jew is the vampire of mankind," he wrote, "*collecting* the fragments of the broken urn of paganism."

For Klages, the victory of life-denying reason was painfully evident in the sad relationship between modern urban man and nature. Contemporary urban peoples, he argued, had lost touch with the natural environment. "Walled into their cities, their vision blocked by smokestacks and their hearing dulled by street noise," modern men no longer knew what nature was. In their sensual myopia and technological arrogance they were willing to turn their physical environment into a wasteland of polluted rivers, clear-cut forests, and befouled air. "An unprecedented orgy of destruction has been carried out in the name of 'progress and civilization,' " he wrote.

This too sounded like Lawrence (and few of us today would question its accuracy), but Klages's "environmentalism," like his "feminism," was thoroughly caught up in irrationalist mysticism and racist dogma. For him the spirit of the pagan Nordics, who had sanctified their forests and rivers, might be recaptured by modern Germans if only they had the wisdom to listen to their blood. By contrast, the Jews, rootless urbanites par excellence, were incapable of taking anything but a predatory view of nature. Should their perspective continue to hold sway, said Klages, the earth was doomed.

Klages's personal relationships were also mired in metaphysics. He fell violently in love with Fanny zu Reventlow, who to him embodied "Nordic paganism in unadulterated purity." The fact that she was a mother added greatly to her allure. He himself hoped to father a child with her, believing that the mere sight of their pure blond offspring might generate a "pagan revival through which the whole world would be rejuvenated." He even toyed with the idea of going off with her to some unpolluted corner of the globe to found a Nordic pagan colony. (Klages may have been inspired by the example of Nietzsche's sister Elisabeth and her militantly anti-Semitic husband, Bernhard Förster, who with a select group of followers traveled in 1886 to the remote jungles of Paraguay to establish an Aryan colony called Nueva Germania. Internecine squabbles and the harsh realities of life in the jungle soon wrecked the enterprise, but a few distant descendants of the original settlers are still there.)

Unlike Nueva Germania, Klages's pagan outpost never got beyond the planning stage. Fanny, moreover, became increasingly restless as her friend pushed to make her his permanent soul mate and disciple. It also did not help that he apparently talked a better sexual game than he played. Fanny told an acquaintance that Klages wanted to "overpower me intellectually and achieve through his personality what he cannot achieve as a man." After their break she wrote in her diary: "My God, what is Klages, exactly? At bottom just another man with illusions of grandeur and a captivating mind that pulled us all in." For his part, Klages concluded that Fanny was not his pagan goddess after all, for she had included Jews among her bed partners.

At the time Fanny met Klages he was already close to Alfred Schuler, who shared many of his views. Schuler cut a very different figure from Klages. Short, corpulent, and prematurely bald, he had a huge head and bulging, bloodshot eyes. Like a pagan monk, he darted through the streets of Schwabing in a black cloak with a cowl. Originally from Mainz, he now lived with his widowed mother in a roomy apartment on the Luisenstrasse. "Mama" gave him a generous allowance, which he supplemented by passing a collection plate at his poetry readings. His work left him plenty of time to ponder philosophical questions and to fantasize about young soldiers and sailors, boxers and wrestlers in overalls and heavily muscled lads in lederhosen. Apparently he had no actual lovers and slept only with his cat. Fanny zu Reventlow found him strange, declaring that his life played itself out in long-forgotten patterns. Klages, on the other hand, attested to the brilliance of Schuler's ideas, which he conveyed in a "heavy voice that seemed to emanate from a vault."

Among the few works that Schuler left to posterity are some lectures he delivered on ancient Rome. In these he argued that republican Rome had been a sterile, life-denying society where men ruled tyrannically over women, the city's true creative spirits. Schuler prized instead late imperial Rome, whose ripe sexual decadence should be emulated by the modern world.

Schuler, like Klages, advanced the "cosmic concept" of *Blutleuchte* (blood glow), which postulated that blood was central to human creativity because it was the repository of lingering energy from the ancient matriarchal past. Only those races who possessed a viable *Blutleuchte* could hope to tap into this ancient wellspring of cultural potency. Other peoples, burdened with inferior bloodlines, had to employ the underhanded wiles of Logos to get ahead. Among these peoples, Schuler included the Prussians, whose blood he said was too polluted with Slavic infusions to allow true Nordic status. The Prussians had achieved power through soulless science and industrialization—a curse for Germany. But the most devious practitioners of logic chopping, Schuler contended, were the Jews. They undermined all belief with their corrosive reason. Because of their weak blood, moreover, they needed to feed on the superior substance of their mother pagan antagonists the Nordics. In one of his poems he wrote: "Up to the heart of Life crawled the Weasel Jew. He eats away the hot, beating, foaming, dreaming Mother Heart." Branding the Jews as Moloch, devourer of children, Schuler admonished neopagans to "kill the father before he can eat your child; unleash against him the ancient coil, the thousand-spoked wheel of fire."

The "coil" to which Schuler referred was the swastika, an old and almost omnipresent symbol variously suggesting the wheel of the sun, the coupling of God-father with Earth-mother, or two human figures locked in coitus. The swastika was an appropriate emblem for Schuler because as the psychoanalyst Wilhelm Reich observes in his *Mass Psychology of Fascism,* this image awakened a stimulus in the psyche "that proves to be that much more powerful the more dissatisfied, the more burning with [unspent] sexual desire, a person is." Schuler could fall into semiorgiastic transports simply by seeing a swastika design on an ashtray. "Swastika! Swastika!" he would stammer, his eyes bulging.

Yet there was an ugly method in the madness here, for Schuler's swastika was not just a primeval sexual emblem but the visual representation of racial and religious counterrevolution, the fire wheel that would burn away everything (and everyone) impeding "cosmic renewal." "We throw fire into the night, a copper fury, so that everything bleeds and boils from the city to the village to the charcoal-burner's hut," he wrote. The hooked cross of racial renewal would sweep away the "limp cross of Christianity," which was just a "castrated swastika" on which pious postpagans, both Christians and Jews, would "come to a sticky end like flies on flypaper."

Given his apocalyptic neopaganism, Schuler not surprisingly advertised himself as a Nietzschean. The Nietzsche he loved was the great destroyer and prophet of new beginnings, the lonely sage who believed that new sources of vitality could reveal themselves only after the collapse of existing value structures. In 1896, besotted with Nietzsche, Schuler hatched a scheme to rescue the philosopher's mind, which had been darkened by insanity for six years. He planned to do this by subjecting the thinker to the Dionysian powers of ancient corybantic dance as interpreted by a band of virile young men wearing nothing but copper bracelets. Alas, Nietzsche's sister, back from the jungles of Paraguay, vetoed this plan.

Although Schuler had no luck with Nietzsche, he became guru to some of Munich's most prominent rightists, including the publisher Hugo Bruckmann and his socialite wife, Elsa, who ran a *völkisch* salon after the First World War. Schuler (who died in 1923) was often present at the Bruckmanns' evenings, holding forth on the cosmic meaning of the swastika and the need for pagan revival.

Karl Wolfskehl would not have been welcome at the Bruckmanns', for he was Jewish. Scion of a prominent Darmstadt banking family, Wolfskehl moved to Munich to assume a professorship in German literature at the university. An irrepressible bon vivant, he collected wine, women, books, and paintings. Among his many female conquests was the perennially available Fanny, who called him "a manly beautiful Assyrian Prince," a reference to his great height, wild black hair, and jutting beard. For a while Fanny wrote him glowing love letters every day. "Carlo, it strikes me that you and I have experienced the Primeval Awakening together, the earliest spring, which is so soft and magical, but also humid and ripe like a glowing summer day full of yearning." Carlo responded in kind, sometimes averaging three letters a day.

As much as Fanny, Wolfskehl was considered the soul of Schwabing. The designer Emil Preetorius recalled that he was "the very center and glory of everything" that made Schwabing an artistic mecca. Aside from his ebullient personality, one of the reasons for his prominence was his secure bourgeois position. Unlike most of his bohemian friends, he could afford to maintain a well-stocked apartment where young artists could comfortably celebrate their freedom from materialism. "From early morning until late at night," wrote Preetorius, "Wolfskehl's apartment was the favorite meeting place to find color and stimulation. It was a curious environment, filled to overflowing with art as well as odds and ends, objects of every provenance, valuable or worthless, serious or scurrilous, yet united by a secret significance they had for their owner. And to this confusing jumble was added an inexhaustible selection of the most beautiful and rarest books of all epochs." Through these rooms, recalled another acquaintance, Wolfskehl paced like a caged animal, "his great head with its hawk beak thrown back, his half-blind eyes, lit from within, flitting over people and objects, while he held forth at great length about the most amazing things."

Like his fellow *Kosmiker,* Wolfskehl espoused the glories of a lost pagan matriarchy. He spoke of a "sunken world in which many of the conditions governing modern life were not yet present. Not man, but woman, governed here; not calculating mind, but the expanding soul, filled with myth and symbolic power." Among the ancient rites that fascinated him were the orgiastic festivals of Dionysus and the Grecian *Totentanz* (dance of death). He was also obsessed with runes, the ancient alphabet supposedly invented by Wotan to help unlock the secrets of the universe. Wolfskehl insisted that the runes conveyed magical powers to those who could penetrate their mysteries.

Wolfskehl was by all accounts a commanding personality, but he felt like an unworthy suppliant in the presence of the fourth member of the Cosmic Circle, the poet Stefan George. "I am your slave and I will be your Peter," Wolfskehl exclaimed in a poem to George. It was from George's example, he said, that the "world received its meaning"; through him "one knew why one existed and to what end." In payment for such adoration, George consented to live rent-free in Wolfskehl's apartment.

George's route to Germany's bohemia was circuitous. He grew up in Rüdesheim on the Rhine, where his father ran a wine business. Stefan was meant to take over the firm but instead decided to become a poet. Convinced that his own country lacked an authentic poetic spirit, he wandered through Europe in search of enlightenment. Via London, Amsterdam, Montreux, and Turin, he found his way to Paris, where he fell in with the symbolist poets around Stéphane Mallarmé. Like them, he thought that poetry should be a secret code open only to the elect. Accordingly he wrote verse that few could decipher but that nonetheless was highly seductive and ultimately very influential, at least among a self-appointed elite. His looks too suggested a man anxious to set himself apart from the vulgar crowd. He kept himself immaculately groomed in black velvet frock coats with silver clasps. According to André Gide, who met him in Paris, he had a blue-white complexion, beautiful bone structure, and "a convalescent's hands, very slender, bloodless, very expressive."

The longer George stayed in Paris, the more he became convinced that he could employ the poetic medium not just to explore hidden corners of the psyche but also to elevate the cultural tone of his nation. He came to see the poet's role as that of cultural messiah, as prophet of a new national awakening. And where better to launch such an awakening than in Munich-Schwabing, where Germany's most daring and innovative artists were congregating as if in a huge church?

Arriving in Munich in 1895, George quickly became part of the cultural ambiance. Although he detested the Bavarian city's cult of beer (a "vulgar drink"), he found Munich "a thousand times better" than Berlin, which he disparaged as "an amalgam of minor civil servants, Jews, and whores." Schwabing he found to be even more exciting than his cherished Montmartre. "Here were powers," he intoned, "united in the knowledge that things could not go on as they were, that mankind was ruining itself, and that no social utopia would help, but only Miracle, Action, Life!"

Falling in with Klages and his friends and soon attracting a larger circle of his own. George began hosting literary-philosophical evenings at his room at Wolfskehl's or in some other acolyte's apartment. He would send out beautifully lettered invitations delivered by a liveried messenger. Invitees were expected to bring flowers and wine. Women, with the exception of Fanny and few others, were not welcome, for George did not share his fellow *Kosmiker's* faith in the special powers of the female sex. On the contrary, he considered women inferior to men in all matters of the spirit. "In council [woman] is evil and nefarious," he preached.

The young men who made up George's circle were subjected to a tyrannical order. They had to respect the Master's edict that all nouns be set in lowercase. They were required to recite his works by memory in a ghostlike chant. They had to open their apartments to him at a moment's notice should he desire to honor them with an extended visit. In preparation for his stay, rooms had to be cleared of newspapers (they smacked of grubby politics) and of most books, for one of his edicts was that fifty books were enough for any decent human being. (He made a special exception here for Wolfskehl, who could not give up his bibliomania.) Finally—and this was distinctly odd for a German—he would tolerate no music, believing, like the Italian humanist Settembrini in Thomas Mann's *The Magic Mountain,* that music's subjectivity corroded the mind.

The atmosphere prevailing during the Master's literary evenings was suffused with religiosity and ecstatic megalomania. The best description of these affairs, and one of the more prescient analyses of their broader implications, was provided by Thomas Mann in a little story called "At the Prophet's" (1904). While not a member of the George set, Mann knew whereof he spoke, for he had once attended one of its evenings in the company of his future mother-in-law, Hedwig Pringsheim. His story begins with a brilliantly ironic evocation of the physical and emotional context in which George and company operated:

> Strange regions there are, strange minds, strange realms of the spirit, lofty and spare. At the edge of large cities, where streetlamps are scarce and policemen walk by twos, are houses where you mount till you can mount no further, up and up into attics under the roof, where pale young geniuses, criminals of the dream, sit with folded arms and brood; up into cheap studios with symbolic decorations, where solitary and rebellious artists, inwardly consumed, hungry and proud, wrestle in a fog of cigarette smoke with devastatingly ultimate ideals. Here is the end: ice, chastity, null. Here is valid no compromise, no concession, no half-way, no consideration of values. Here the air is so rarified that the mirages of life no longer exist. Here reign defiance and iron consistency, the ego supreme amid despair; here freedom, madness, and death hold sway.

The climax of the evening comes when a "short-necked and ill-favored young man" (modeled on the George disciple Ludwig Derleth) delivers a series of semireligious "proclamations":

> The "Proclamations" consisted of sermons, parables, theses, laws, prophecies, and exhortations resembling orders of the day, following each other in a mingled style of psalter and revelation with an endless succession of technical phrases, military and strategic as well as philosophical and critical. A fevered and frightfully irritable ego here expanded itself, a self-isolated megalomaniac flooded the world with a hurricane of violent and threatening words. *Christus imperator maximus* was his name; he enrolled troops ready to die for the subjection of the globe; he sent out embassies, gave inexorable ultimata, exacted poverty and chastity, and with a sort of morbid enjoyment reiterated his roaring demand for unconditional obedience. Buddha, Alexander, Napoleon and Jesus—their names were mentioned as his humble forerunners, not worthy to unloose the laces of their spiritual lord. . . .

As Mann perceived at the time, these cosmic evenings revealed an intriguing mixture of uncompromising absolutism, hunger for grand solutions, hero worship, and eagerness for self-sacrifice in the name of purification and redemption. A half century later, looking back on his moment "among the prophets," Mann was to locate the spiritual origins of the German catastrophe in just this kind of all-consuming megalomania.

There was an air of self-dramatization and extravagant egotism even in the costume parties that the *Kosmiker* frequently organized in Schwabing. Here the best source is Fanny zu Reventlow, who was a regular participant. According to her accounts, George came dressed as Caesar or Dante; Wolfskehl as Homer, Dionysus, or Ulysses; and Schuler as Nero, Caligula, or a Roman earth mother. On one occasion George demanded that a young acolyte (Roderich Huch) take off all his clothes in the manner of a Greek Olympian. Huch demurred, stammering that the Master would not find his body pleasing enough. George was furious at such insubordination. At another party Wolfskehl, dressed as Dionysus, danced around swinging a long staff, which a girl broke by trying to climb. "At this moment," recounts Fanny, "[Wolfskehl] lost his pagan cool." Once when Schuler was dressed as Magna Mater, "Mama" also came to the party. Schuler refused to talk to her on the ground that it would not look right for the earth mother to be seen conversing with his real mother.

Although not ill disposed toward George and his young men, Fanny obviously enjoyed making fun of their pretensions. In a little newspaper she edited called the *Schwabinger Beobachter,* she referred to George as Weihenstephan, a pun on a famous local brewery; Klages she called Dr. Langschädel (Dr. Long Skull), while the Schwabing milieu they inhabited became Wahnmoching, the field of delusion. She ran naughty little jokes mocking the *Kosmiker*'s self-infatuation: "How do I become an 'enormous one'?" a young disciple asks Weihenstephan. "Rub up against my masterpiece," he replies. In a novel about the *Kosmiker* called *Herrn Dames Aufzeichnungen,* Fanny took up the delicate issue of anti-Semitism, albeit lightly, as if it were just another foible. A Jewish disciple laments that most of the *Kosmiker* "prize blond people much more than dark ones." They have "no respect for my race," he says; they "appreciate only long skulls." Another character observes that in Wahnmoching "the Aryans represent the constructive, cosmic principle, whereas the Semites embody the destructive, negative-molochistic forces."

Whereas Fanny tended to emphasize the ludicrous side of the *Kosmiker*'s antics, most middle-class Münchners saw George and his circle as evil and dangerous. "Much nonsense was spread about George," recalled Theodor Lessing. "The harmless symposia of his order were decried as fanatical orgies." George himself, Lessing added, took a certain pleasure in this hysteria. When there was talk of "satanic masses with violet lights," he would say, "Don't forget the dish of smoking blood that stood before me!"

Such self-mockery was untypical of the Master, however. Certainly there was little humor or irony in his most characteristic work, a magazine devoted to the dissemination of his aesthetic principles entitled *Blätter für die Kunst* (Leaves of Art). This journal contained esoteric poems and essays punctuated according to George's private rules. The cover was emblazoned with a swastika. The publishing house under whose auspices the *Blätter* appeared, Bondi, also adopted the swastika as its trademark. Ironically Bondi was a Jewish firm. "Those who know the kind of books we publish," explained a Bondi brochure, "know that they have nothing to do with politics."

George's own attitude toward Jews was somewhat ambivalent. He was very close to Wolfskehl, and his wider circle included other prominent Jews. Yet he acknowledged in his Jewish disciples only financial and organizational skills. "Jews make the best politicians," he once said; "they are gifted in the distribution and conversion of values. Of course they cannot experience things as elementally as we do." Under the malignant influence of Klages and Schuler, George produced some ugly racist drivel. One of his poems, for example, speaks of the "blood-shame" resulting from miscegenation; it argues that races that do not retain their purity are bound to lose their vitality.

George's continuing personal ties to Jews, however, alienated Klages and Schuler. "What binds you to Juda?" Klages asked. He and Schuler especially resented the Master's loyalty to Wolfskehl, who had responded to the growth of anti-Semitism by founding Munich's chapter of the International Zionist Federation in 1897. Schuler suspected that Wolfskehl and his Jewish associates were cultivating a Semitic *Blutleuchte* of their own to ensure world domination. In January 1904 he dispatched a black-bordered "declaration of war" to Wolfskehl. Fearing for his life, Wolfskehl bought a pistol and began practicing with it. In the course of his instruction he shot himself in the leg.

Meanwhile, Schuler turned against his friend Klages. "Klages comes from Hanover," he observed, "and the Phoenicians penetrated as far as Hanover. Therefore Klages is a Jew." Nonplussed by this logic, Klages questioned (it was about time) Schuler's sanity. Amid a storm of acrimony the Cosmic Circle blew apart in mid-1904.

The Decline of Kunststadt München

In 1902 Thomas Mann wrote a short story about his adopted hometown called "Gladius Dei." Many read it as a paean to the city's beauty and cultural verve. The much-quoted opening lines certainly sound laudatory enough:

> Munich was radiant. Above the gay squares and white columned temples, the classicistic monuments and the baroque churches, the leaping fountains, the palaces and parks of the Residence there stretched a sky of luminous blue silk. . . . Young people, the kind that can whistle the Nothung motif, who fill the pit of the Schauspielhaus every evening, wandered in and out of the University and Library with literary magazines in their coat pockets. A court carriage stood before the Academy, the home of the plastic arts, which spreads its white wings between the Türkenstrasse and the Siegestor. And colorful groups of models, picturesque old men, women and children in Albanian costume, stood or lounged at the top of the balustrade.
>
> Indolent, unhurried sauntering was the mode in all the long streets of the northern quarter. There life is lived for pleasanter ends than the driving greed of gain.

As Mann's story progesses, however, the mood darkens. A youth who has emphatically not given himself over to sensual pleasure enters the scene. Dressed in a black cloak and hood, haggard and ugly, the young man joins a crowd assembled outside an art shop next to the Feldherrnhalle. The crowd is admiring a reproduction of a painting newly purchased by the Neue Pinakothek, a "modern" Madonna who smiles provocatively while her child plays with her bare breast. Appalled by this blasphemy, the cloaked young man (Hieronymus) enters the shop and demands that the offending picture be removed from the window at once. Ascertaining that the youth has no official status, the shop owner ignores him. Hieronymus then launches into a tirade about the true purpose of art. "Art is no conscienceless illusion, lending itself to reinforce the allurements of the fleshly. Art is the holy torch which turns its light upon all the frightful depths, all the shameful and woeful abysses of life; art is the godly fire laid to the world that, being redeemed by pity, it may flame up and dissolve altogether with its shames and torments." This outburst results in the youth's being told to leave the shop or be thrown out. Defiant, Hieronymus now demands that the owner, Herr Bluthenzweig, burn everything in his shop, "for it is a filthiness in God's sight." Claiming that he stands for the freedom of art, Bluthenzweig duly orders his burly warehouseman to throw Hieronymus into the street. In front of the

Feldherrnhalle, the young man calls for a great bonfire of the vanities to consume this sinful Babylon of a city.

Although Hieronymus was meant to be a ludicrous figure, he had some heavy allegorical weight behind him, for he was modeled on Savonarola, the Jesuit monk who imposed an ascetic Christian republic on decadent quattrocento Florence. Although Mann was hardly proposing a similar fate for twentieth-century Munich, he could certainly see that much was rotten and fraudulent under the gleaming surface of the city's cultural life. This beautiful place was really just a stage on which most of the props were borrowed. The artwork at the center of the controversy was a reproduction, like everything else in the shop. Herr Bluthenzweig claimed to defend artistic freedom, but his real motives were commercial. Ridiculous though Hieronymus seemed, he represented a broadly based antipathy toward an art whose primary purpose was to shock. Mann seemed to be suggesting that if Munich's modernists were not careful, they might indeed bring forth a modern Savanorola, eager to light a purging fire.

In preparation for his story Mann had read a pair of articles that appeared in 1901 in a Berlin newspaper under the title "Münchens Niedergang als Kunststadt" (Munich's Decline as an Art City). The author, Hans Rosenhagen, argued that Munich was a shadow of its former innovative self, a place where "imitation," reactionary historicism, sleazy commercialism, and scandalmongering were the dominant concerns. Berlin, the critic predicted, would soon supplant Munich as Germany's true capital of the avant-garde.

Rosenhagen implied that Munich's decline as a center of progressive culture was partly the fault of the artists themselves. There was much truth to this. The city's celebrated artistic Secession of 1893, which involved a revolt by modernist painters and sculptors against the domination of the Old Guard, quickly became derivative and hidebound in its own right. Secessionist artists began working to shut out new talents that might have offered effective competition. The avant-garde painter Wilhelm Trübner left for Berlin in 1896 with a bitter blast at Isar Athens: "A city like Munich, where only rubbish gets recognized, should be avoided at all costs if one does not want to do oneself serious harm." Similar frustrations were voiced by the brilliant experimentalist Lovis Corinth, who upon departing for Berlin told a friend: "I really can't stand Munich any longer." Complaining of the Secession's lack of support for innovative craftsmanship, the *Jugendstil* pioneer Hermann Obrist fumed that in Munich one could expect "no action, just reaction"; hence he also left for greener pastures. Wassily Kandinsky, who saw all nine of the paintings he submitted to the Secession in 1906 rejected, remained in the

Munich area (in the village of Murnau) but was thoroughly sated with the pseudoprogressive art scene in the Bavarian capital. After visiting the Secession Exhibition of 1907, he told his friend Gabriele Munter that he found nothing new or interesting, just the "same bunglers. . . . In a half hour I was completely done with the exhibition and gallery and didn't even get tired."

Munich's avant-garde art community was also undermined by a steady growth of censorship sponsored by the Catholic Center Party and moral vigilante groups like the Munich Men's Association for Combating Public Immorality. Pressure from these groups resulted in the removal (for "indecency") of Max Slevogt's *Danaë* from the Secession Exhibition of 1903. On the theatrical front, in addition to dulling the swords of the *Scharfrichter,* the censors banished the innovative cabaret artist Josef Vallé and the radical promoter Karl Schuler. Sometimes the vigilantes had the cooperation of artists anxious to placate the authorities. Thus in 1913 Munich's Censorship Advisory Board, made up of twenty-three writers who advised the police commissioner, turned thumbs down on an uncut performance of Wedekind's *Lulu* plays. The atmosphere became so oppressive that *Simplicissimus* ran a cartoon showing two searchlights mounted on the twin towers of the Frauenkirche, Munich's Gothic cathedral.

But censorship per se was not the only arrow in the cultural conservatives' quiver. An even more effective weapon was financial starvation through restrictions on state funding of the arts. Largely because of the Center Party's growing influence in the Bavarian Landtag, no funds were added to the state's art-purchasing budget between 1890 and 1913, despite great increases in the number of artists working in the city. In 1904 the critic Theodor Goering lamented: "There is much suffering for the artist here! The capacity, the capability, is there, but one does not find enough support." This was especially true for avant-garde artists, whose experimental paintings were anathema to the Center. In 1910 a local paper called for the arrest of the Munich-based Blue Rider painters, Franz Marc, Paul Klee, Wassily Kandinsky, and August Macke. They were not arrested, but by 1914, when the outbreak of World War I suspended official art purchases, Munich's great state museums had not purchased a single work by the now-famous group.

The harsh realities of Munich's art market fostered an atmosphere of nationalism and xenophobia, of bunkering down against the outside world. As early as 1897 the leader of Munich's Secession. Fritz von Uhde, lambasted a Berlin art journal for suggesting that Berlin's Max Liebermann was a more important artist than he. Uhde attributed the judgment to "Semitic tendencies" characteristic of a *Berliner Judenblatt*

(Berlin Jewish rag). Increasingly, Munich artists grumbled about the number of foreigners working in the city. Two former members of the Secession, Karl Vinnen and Paul Schultze-Naumburg, insisted that Munich be identified exclusively with a "healthy" and "rooted" art of the German soil. In 1911 they sponsored a Protest of German Artists aimed against French cultural influences in the fatherland. Of the 118 artists who signed the protest, 57 lived in Munich or other parts of southern Bavaria. The document concluded with a call for parochial patriotism: "A great, powerfully upward striving culture and people like ours cannot forever tolerate spiritual usurpation by an alien force. And since this dominion is being imposed on us by a large, well-financed international organization, a serious warning is in order: let us not continue on this path; let us recognize that we are in danger of losing nothing less than our own individuality and our tradition of solid achievement."

A year before the publication of this document, Fanny zu Reventlow moved to Ascona, Switzerland, a budding art colony that became a kind of neo-Schwabing, a magnet for abstract painters, free verse poets, modern dancers, anarchist philosophers, vegetarians, Theosophists, faith healers, and long-haired sun worshipers. She died there in November 1918, just as the First World War—and the German Empire she had grown to hate—came to an end. Her flight from Schwabing to Ascona can be seen as the ultimate symbol of Munich's decline as a center of bohemian culture and avant-garde art in the first decade of the twentieth century.

"A Brother"

The proposition that Munich was in decline as a *Kunststadt* would have meant nothing to Adolf Hitler, who, as mentioned above, had chosen to settle in Munich in 1913. For the young Austrian, Munich was the place to be in Germany if one wanted to become an artist.

Before moving to Munich, Hitler had been trying to launch an artistic career in Vienna and had compiled a portfolio of renderings of major buildings in that city. But he had failed twice to gain admission to the Art Academy. He was advised to study architecture instead, but he could not do so because he lacked the necessary high school diploma. Drawing on his small inheritance, Hitler had lived an idler's life, getting up at noon, sitting in cafés, visiting museums, going to the opera, and gazing at the buildings along the Ringstrasse. As the years went by, he had become increasingly withdrawn and isolated, giving up a shared apartment for anonymous flophouses. He had managed to sell a number of his watercolors and oils but had made no impression on the local art world. Blaming polyglot Vienna for these failures, he had concluded that he would have better luck in Munich, where he imagined that a talent like his would be more appreciated.

Hitler's search for a place to live in Munich took him to the western edge of Schwabing, where he found a furnished room above Popp's tailor shop. The address was Schleissheimerstrasse 34, a few blocks from where Lenin had once lived. He signed in as "Adolf Hitler, architectural painter from Vienna." According to his landlady, Frau Popp, Hitler began working right away, turning out several paintings a week and hawking them in the streets. He insisted that his goal was to earn enough money through his painting to finance studies in architectural drawing. But he made no effort to undertake formal studies; as in Vienna, his painting served simply as a way to earn his keep. His specialty, again as in Vienna, was famous buildings: the Hofbräuhaus, Frauenkirche, Feldherrnhalle, Alter Hof, Theatinerkirche, and so forth. His renderings of these structures were pleasing enough to people who liked to know exactly what it was they were looking at. He was able to sell a few of his works in the local beer halls and shops. Like most Munich artists, however, he had trouble when winter came and there were fewer tourists. Contemporaries who dealt with him described him as a somewhat pathetic creature, thin and shabbily dressed, awkward in his desperation to make a sale.

Nonetheless, Hitler was content to be in Munich, which appealed to him on a number of levels. Much of what he later wrote in his autobiography, *Mein Kampf,* is inaccurate, but the following testimonial about his move to Munich rings true:

> [A] heartfelt love seized me for this city . . . almost from the first hour of my sojourn there. A *German* city! What a difference from Vienna! I grew sick to my stomach when I even thought back on this babylon of races. In addition, the dialect, much closer to me, which particularly in my contacts with Lower Bavarians, reminded me of my former childhood. There were a thousand and more things which were or became inwardly dear and precious to me. But most of all I was attracted by this wonderful marriage of primordial power and fine artistic mood, this single line from the Hofbräuhaus to the Odeon, from the October Festival to the Pinakothek, etc. If today I am more attached to this city than to any other spot of earth in this world, it is partly due to the fact that it is and remains inseparably bound up with the development at my own life; if even then I achieved the happiness of a truly inward contentment, it can be attributed only to the magic which the miraculous residence of the Wittelsbachs exerts on every man who is blessed, not only with a calculating mind but with a feeling soul.

Of all the Wittelsbachs, Ludwig I appealed to Hitler the most; this king was, Hitler believed, a great visionary who had made Munich into a place that one had to have seen "to know German art." Alas, not much of value had been added since Ludwig, Hitler concluded. "[T]ake from present-day Munich everything that was created under Ludwig I, and you will note with horror how poor the addition of significant artistic creations has been since that time." Hitler was also convinced that Ludwig's buildings had made Munich a center of German national unity. "By pushing Munich from the level of an insignificant provincial capital into the format of a great German art metropolis, [Ludwig] created a spiritual center which even today is strong enough to bind the essentially different Franks to this state."

Hitler's celebration of Ludwig I as a German cultural hero was part of his effort in the twenties to reinterpret his move to Munich in terms of political ideology as well as artistic ambition. He claimed to have left Vienna as "a confirmed anti-Semite, a deadly foe of the whole Marxist world outlook, and a pan-German." He went to Munich, he said, to find "a wider field for political activity."

Had politics indeed been Hitler's prime concern, he would have been better advised to go to Berlin, where the political action was. In truth, however, he was not motivated by a desire for political engagement, and he greatly exaggerated the coherence of the ideology he brought from Vienna to Bavaria. He undoubtedly considered himself "German" and despised the multiethnic Habsburg Empire, but he was not unusually anti-Semitic and had no developed views on Marxism. (All that came later.) Once settled in Munich, he made no effort to contact that city's bustling community of anti-Semites or Pan-Germans. He claimed later to have read extensively on Marxism, but in reality he read little more than the daily press. He certainly did not go around preaching the dangers of Social Democracy.

In fact, he seems to have done rather little preaching at this point, save for the occasional anti-Habsburg harangue in a beer hall. As in Vienna, his human contacts were meager and shallow. When not painting or trying to sell his paintings in the streets, he sat by himself in a café or in the Bavarian State Library reading newspapers. His literalist paintings suggested no affinity for the local avant-garde, and indeed, he loathed all experimentalism in art. While he frequented the cafés where Schwabing's artists held court, he made no effort to join any of their circles or to attend their gatherings.

Yet if Hitler made no mark on prewar Schwabing, he was firmly in his element in Germany's bohemia. After all, he fancied himself a rebel against bourgeois conventions and habits. He was attracted to a milieu where ordinary work was disparaged and daydreaming considered an honorable profession. Like the other habitués of Café Grössenwahn, he imagined himself destined for great things, though (as yet) he did not know what they might be. Strolling around Munich, he could be comforted by the fact that, for all its eccentricity, this city was indeed a very *German* place, much more so than Vienna. As a provincial nativist (which is what Hitler always remained), he could feel at home in a town that was often fearful of its own urbanism and that longed for "healthy" rusticity. While not yet an active participant in Munich-Schwabing's political discourse, he was already partial to the style of thought that prevailed there: the disdain for measured analysis and the delight in absolutist proclamations. But above all, young Hitler could identify with this city's artistic self-image, its conviction that preeminence in the arts endowed it with a purer and more refined perspective on the problems of the world.

Thus Thomas Mann was insightful when, twenty-five years after he and Hitler first shared the streets of Schwabing (though apparently never meeting), he wrote a piece about the Führer called "A Brother":

Ah, the artist! I spoke of moral self-flagellation. For must I not, however much it hurts, regard the man as an artist-phenomenon? Mortifyingly enough, it is all there: the difficulty, the laziness, the pathetic formlessness in youth, the round peg in the square hole, the "what ever *do* you want?" The lazy, vegetating existence in the depths of a moral and mental bohemia; the fundamental arrogance which thinks itself too good for any sensible and honorable activity, on the ground of its vague intuition that it is reserved for something else—as yet quite indefinite, but something which, if it could be named, would be greeted with roars of laughter.

On 18 January 1914 Hitler's bohemian idyll was interrupted when a Munich police officer served him with a summons to present himself to the Austrian military authorities in Linz on 20 January. This summons could not have been a total surprise to the young man, for he had left Austria without performing his required military service or obtaining an official deferment. In fact avoiding the Austrian draft was one of the main reasons for his sudden flight to Germany. The Munich policeman took him under arrest to the Austrian Consulate, where he lachrymosely pleaded that the stress of supporting himself as an orphaned artist had caused him to overlook his duty. Taking pity on him, the consul allowed him to postpone his draft appearance by two weeks and to report to Salzburg rather than to Linz. On 5 February he underwent a physical examination in Salzburg and was found unable to bear arms. Apparently his bohemian existence had paid off, for he had the dilapidated constitution of a coffeehouse warrior. Released from the clutches of the hated Habsburgs, Adolf Hitler was free to return to Schwabing and his hand-to-mouth existence as part-time painter and full-time dreamer.

2
The Great Swindle

ON 20 JUNE 1914 the First Heavy Cavalry of the Bavarian Army celebrated its one-hundredth anniversary with parades and parties in Munich. Officers and men filled the city's beer halls, toasting glorious battles of times past. Yet the political anxieties of the present—above all, the rising tensions between the Great Powers—imposed a certain seriousness on the festivities. For the fist time the soldiers wore their new field gray tunics rather than their traditional colorful dress uniforms. The change in dress was appropriate: One week later Austria's Archduke Franz Ferdinand was assassinated in Sarajevo by a Serbian nationalist. A month after that Europe was at war.

"It was the so-called First World War that put an end forever to the idyll of aesthetic innocence and dionysiac easygoingness in the Isar City," says the narrator in *Doktor Faustus* (1947), Thomas Mann's penetrating novel about the German condition in the first half of the twentieth century. Mann's perception notwithstanding. Munich had lost—or at least had begun to lose—its aesthetic innocence well before the Great War began. Nonetheless, the war unquestionably had a tremendous impact on the city, catapulting it into paroxysms of patriotic fervor and then magnifying internal divisions to the degree that the entire sociopolitical fabric ripped apart at the seams.

There was nothing unusual in this experience. What happened in Munich happened in other German cities, and indeed across much of Europe, under the pressure of the first "total war" of modern times. In fact, the Bavarian capital was in many ways a microcosm of the European home front. Yet the scene in Munich between 1914 and 1918 did not simply reflect developments on the broader stage; it also initiated trends that were to transform Germany and Europe in the coming generation. Wartime Munich, like prewar Schwabing, was a breeding ground for the new world.

On the Eve of War

Prince Regent Luitpold, the ruler of Bavaria since 1886, died at age ninety-one on 12 December 1912. For the last year of his life he had been so inactive that Münchners joked he was already dead but could not be informed because the news might overexcite him. Munich's affection for the regent was evident in the huge throngs that turned out to watch his funeral procession wind its way to the Theatinerkirche, where he was buried in the Wittelsbach crypt. After the war many Münchners looked back on Luitpold's death as the end of Old Bavaria.

Luitpold was succeeded in the regency by his oldest son, Ludwig. Already sixty-seven when he took up his duties, Ludwig was a study in unpretentious sobriety. Bald, fat, and bearded, he squinted at the world through old-fashioned glasses, wore trousers that fanned out like accordion bellows, walked with a stoop, and always carried a badly rolled umbrella. He looked more like a slightly down-at-the-heels businessman than a ruler.

Yet for all his lack of grandeur, he was discontent to be a mere regent and managed to have himself crowned King Ludwig III in November 1913. His coronation was legally problematical because Otto, Ludwig II's mad brother, was still alive. Ludwig could become king only through a constitutional amendment allowing the transfer of royal power outside the direct line of succession. For this he needed the blessing of the Center, the conservative Catholic party that was now the largest in the state. In exchange for its support, he promised to rule according to strict Catholic principles.

Among his first acts as king Ludwig sold the Neue Pinakothek (the art museum founded by Ludwig I and owned by the royal house) to the state of Bavaria. This move, which shocked many Münchners, was an indication of how little the new sovereign cared for the cultural life of his capital. Indeed, he was to play the role of Maecenas only occasionally and with great reluctance. He generally stayed away from Munich's theaters and concert halls, preferring to go bowling. He showed up for the unveiling of a Richard Wagner monument at the Prince Regency Theater in May 1913 only because the ceremony was an important step in Munich's ongoing crusade to claim the composer for its own. He also attended Munich's 1913 premiere of *Parsifal* (before then the work had been reserved for Wagner's Festival Theater at Bayreuth), but he swore that wild horses could not drag him to hear Wagner again. On the other hand, he was passionately interested in technology and launched a project to build Germany's largest museum of science and industry on an island in the Isar River. Unfortunately construction had to be suspended because of the war, and Ludwig was no longer around when the museum finally opened in 1925.

In addition to industrial technology, Ludwig had a passion for scientific agriculture, which had been his field of study at the university. He set up a model dairy farm at his estate at Leutstetten, where he always felt most at home. What grandiose castles and Wagnerian operas had been for Ludwig II, contented cows and fragrant dung heaps were for Ludwig III.

Munich duly marked Ludwig's coronation with a royal procession and proclamations of loyalty from the Rathaus, but there was much disgruntlement over the event among the city's liberals and Socialists, who rightly saw it as confirmation of their ruler's dependence on the Catholics. Some Münchners were also troubled by the fact that as king Ludwig would be entitled to a higher personal budget than he had had as regent and would therefore cost the taxpayers more. As a local tabloid, *Die Ratschkathel,* complained, "We now have a . . . king and must hope that we also have better economic times so we can pay for him. Unfortunately, it doesn't look as if this will be the case, and therefore everyone is afraid of the new taxes that the royal accession will bring."

Like Ludwig II, who had ascended the Bavarian throne on the eve of the wars of German unification, Ludwig III assumed royal power at a time of heightened international tension. The powerful new German Empire challenged the old balance of power laid down in 1815. Germany's bellicose policies under Kaiser Wilhelm II prompted the creation of the Triple Entente (Great Britain, France, and Russia), which in turn inflamed German desires to break out of its "encirclement." Russia and Austria meanwhile were at loggerheads in the Balkans, where the precipitous collapse of Turkish power was creating new opportunities for the Habsburgs and their Serbian antagonists, who enjoyed the protection of St. Petersburg.

Munich, which had a large population of Slavic refugees and students from Russia and Serbia, was fully caught up in the tensions of the hour. The Munich police received anonymous tips that the "Serbian Academic Reading Group" was a den of dangerous Pan-Slav radicals. Nationalist papers like the *Münchener Neueste Nachrichten* warned that war might be imminent. On 21 March 1914 Rosa Luxemburg, the Polish-born Socialist, told a huge crowd of workers at the Kindl beer hall that the SPD would obstruct any effort to plunge Europe into war. "If a man of blood and iron like Bismarck could not overcome us, how can the pipsqueaks now running the country manage it?" she asked. The crowd passed a resolution condemning the preparations for war.

Before leaving power in 1890, Bismarck had predicted that the next big war would start over "some damn fool thing in the Balkans." He was right, as usual. In the immediate aftermath of the assassination of Franz Ferdinand, the Great Powers began frantically putting their armies on a war footing even as they made last-ditch efforts at a diplomatic resolution of the Bosnian crisis. In early August they gave up and turned matters over to the generals.

The Spirit of August

The outbreak of hostilities in August 1914 brought rejoicing in all the great cities of Europe. Everywhere people imagined that they were about to witness a bracing and heroic spectacle. Patriotic citizens welcomed the sudden sense of national unity and common purpose. Leaders of political parties, unions, and interest groups solemnly swore to suspend internal conflicts for the duration of the struggle.

The city of Munich was as high on war fever as any place in Europe. This should not surprise us. In the decades since the unification of Germany by "blood and iron," military enthusiasm had become as much a part of the city's atmosphere as its famed *Gemütlichkeit*. Pride in Bavaria's military traditions was evident in the huge Army Museum, which went up in the Hofgarten between 1900 and 1905. Local regiments played a prominent role in the public life of the town, from the annual Corpus Christi parade to the Oktoberfest. Citizens took delight in daily changings of the guard by the magnificent *Leiber* (King's Own Regiment), all of whom stood a dizzying five feet nine inches or taller. Many Münchners hoped that the war would give Bavaria an opportunity to display its dedication to the national cause. At the same time, some also hoped that the conflict would strengthen Bavaria's hand within the Reich and allow it to stand equal with its old rival, Prussia. "The high enthusiasm in the streets of our town proves that the people are still true to their king, are good Bavarians and good Germans," observed the Munich writer Lena Christ in August 1914. "They are glad to fight for king and fatherland."

In Munich official notice that the long peace was about to end came on the night of 31 July 1914. Thirty drummers marched through the city sounding the alarm for mobilization. During the next few days, following Germany's declaration of war against Russia and France, people streamed into the streets singing the "Wacht am Rhein" and dropping cigars or cigarettes into blue and white boxes labeled "For the Front." Recruiting stations were jammed with young men anxious to trade their civilian garb for military tunics. Large crowds assembled before the Austro-Hungarian Consulate to cheer Germany's primary ally, whose insistence upon punishing Serbia for Franz Ferdinand's murder had done much to turn this issue into a major war. Another crowd gathered in front of the Residenz, where King Ludwig III soberly warned of the great test ahead, concluding with the admonition "Now go home and do your duty." Munich's governing mayor, Wilhelm von Borscht, spoke rapturously of a "storm of national enthusiasm that blows away everything that separates [German from German], yielding a single people of brothers." Swept up in the storm, a group of students demolished the Café Fahrig on the Karlsplatz because the house band got tired of playing the national anthem over and over again.

Munich's artists and intellectuals also leaped eagerly on the patriotic bandwagon. Many of them had become restless under the long peace, convinced that it was producing a shallow materialist ethos, internal divisions, and their own alienation from the rest of the nation. The conservative writer Ludwig Thoma allowed that he was "vastly relieved" when he learned of Germany's decision to fight. "Gone was the pressure, gone was the uncertainty," he exulted. Looking back on this heady moment, Thomas Mann asked how the "soldier in the artist could not but praise God for the collapse of a peace-time world of which he had become sick, thoroughly sick. War! It meant a cleansing, a liberation . . . and an extraordinary sense of hope. . . ."

Not just conservatives like Thoma and Thomas Mann took this line. The anarchist playwright Frank Wedekind, who before the war had written of the "glowing feeling of solidarity among the cultural nations against military rule," now spoke of the "loyal brotherhood of arms" between Socialism and the High Command. The young Munich writer Oskar Maria Graf was astonished by the overnight patriotism of his leftist friends. "Where had they all gone, those who had taught me that an anarchist must never serve the state, that he must especially reject all military or war service?" he asked. They had "run in droves to the nearest recruiting station to volunteer!" The leaders of the Bavarian SPD welcomed the chance to prove that Socialists were not, as Kaiser Wilhelm II had once claimed, "rascals without a fatherland," but loyal Germans ready to carry their share of the burden. The fact that czarist Russia had mobilized against Germany made shouldering this burden all the easier. As the *Münchener Post* editorialized on 1 August, "When it comes to the duty to protect our country from bloody czarism, we will not allow ourselves to be considered second-class citizens." Thus Bavaria's Socialist delegates to the Reichstag voted with the majority of their SPD colleagues in favor of war credits—to the consternation of more radical leftists like Rosa Luxemburg.

No one in Munich was more swept away by the spirit of the moment than that recent transplant from Vienna Adolf Hitler. Despite having dodged the Austrian draft, Hitler was convinced that war was "healthy." He was among the huge crowd that assembled in the Odeonsplatz on 1 August as Germany declared war on Russia.

The future Führer is easily recognizable in a now famous photograph of the scene; he gazes rapturously up at the Feldherrnhalle, his mouth half open, his hair uncut and wild. Later, in *Mein Kampf,* he described his emotions on that day: "To me those hours seemed like a release from the painful feelings of my youth. Even today I am not ashamed to say that, overpowered by stormy enthusiasm, I fell down on my knees and thanked heaven from my overflowing heart." On 3 August, after having submitted a petition to King Ludwig to allow him to enlist as a foreigner in the Bavarian Army, Hitler stood outside the Residenz waiting for the king to speak. When Ludwig appeared, Hitler whispered to himself: "If only the king has already read my application and approved it." In fact, the very next day Hitler received his approval to enlist. "My joy knew no bounds," he recalled later. "Within a few days I was wearing the tunic that I would not take off until almost six years later."

The uninhibited joy experienced by Hitler and so many others was hardly the only emotion generated by the opening of hostilities. Fear was another. Rumors swept through Munich that enemy agents had infected the water supply with typhus. Dynamite was said to have been found under several bridges. Because spies were reportedly everywhere, natives were instructed not to talk to strangers and to keep a sharp eye out for signs of treachery.

In such an atmosphere long-standing suspicions of foreigners quickly turned into open hostility. Newspapers urged the populace to take "self-defense measures" against resident Serbs and Russians. Anyone who looked out of place was in danger of being attacked in the streets. Walking on the Kaufingerstrasse, the conductor Bruno Walter, who had just arrived from Vienna, was accosted by a wild-eyed man who pointed at him, yelling, "A Serbian! A Serbian!" Walter replied that he was not from Serbia, but that his accuser must certainly come from Eglfing (site of an insane asylum). His knowledgeable riposte saved him from further acrimony. A pair of young women who were overheard speaking French did not get away so easily; they were attacked by a mob and savagely beaten. Ernst Toller, a student from Posen (and later a prominent revolutionary), was set upon simply for wearing a French-looking hat. He too might have been bloodied had he not found a policeman who quieted the mob by holding up Toller's German passport. Shortly after Britain declared war on 4 August, a mob destroyed the English Pharmacy in Munich on the assumption that "it must be penetrated by the English spirit." Some citizens urged the city council to change the name of Munich's great park, the Englischer Garten, to Deutscher Garten. The municipality demurred—a rare act of sanity in this environment of patriotic breast-beating and intense xenophobia.

Culture versus Civilization

One of the first cultural casualties of the war was Schwabing—or, more accurately, what was left of that quarter's beleaguered bohemian spirit. A number of local artists expressed their patriotism by rushing off to the front. Among them were the Blue Rider painters August Macke and Franz Marc and the prominent writer Richard Dehmel. Many of the artist-warriors, including Macke and Marc, never returned from the trenches. Schwabinger who stayed behind felt increasingly isolated. In summer 1915 Frank Wedekind gloomily predicted to his anarchist friend Erich Mühsam that there would henceforth be an unbridgeable gap between artists who had served at the front and those who had not. "[The veterans] will sit around and talk about their heroic deeds, and when people like us want to give their opinions on questions of art or religion, they'll shout us down: 'You weren't there, how can you expect to have a say?' "

Many conservative Münchners, meanwhile, were pleased that the war was cleansing their city of its remaining bohemian trash. As early as November 1914 a contributor to the nationalist *Allgemeine Rundschau* gleefully celebrated the dispersal of the "Schwabing crowd," that pack of self-proclaimed cosmopolitans who had always been so anxious "to complain to the world about Bavarian backwardness." He hoped that the "literary and artistic bohemianism signified by the word Schwabing" was gone forever. "German discipline is the demand of the hour," he proclaimed.

Simplicissimus certainly agreed with this last sentiment. For a moment after the war's outbreak, *Simpl*'s editors wondered whether a magazine noted for its gibes against illiterate lieutenants should not simply shut down. T. T. Heine, however, argued convincingly that it was "wrong to think that *Simpl*'s time was over." Indeed, the magazine could prosper if it "adjusted to the facts" and came down solidly for the war. After all, he continued, "at a moment like this the Fatherland needs a magazine . . . with international prestige to back the military leadership at home and abroad." The other editors quickly fell into line. "They all felt like good patriots and were pleased to find a way to secure their existences," noted Hermann Sinsheimer, a member of the board.

During the next four years *Simpl* emerged as one of the more strident jingoist voices in the Reich. When Germany's war machine slammed through Belgium, the red dog yelped for joy. A cartoon depicting German soldiers planting the flag of victory over the Belgian fortress of Lüttich (Liège) featured some bathetic doggerel from Ludwig Thoma: "We listened full of care / Then came a signal through the air / Rang over mighty mountains and valleys fair / The Germans! The Germans have taken Lüttich." With the failure of the Marne offensive and the onset of trench warfare, *Simpl* began devoting most of its space to the war effort. A cartoon of 1915 showed happy troopers entraining for the front, eagerly receiving flowers and coffee from buxom Fräuleins. The Prussian generals whom the magazine had once disparaged as caste-bound dolts were now held up as heroes of the hour. *Simpl* was especially enthusiastic about Hindenburg and Ludendorff, who were winning significant victories on the Eastern Front. Germany's enemies, on the other hand, were mercilessly lampooned as conniving, greedy, rapacious, barbarous, and hypocritical. One cartoon depicted Germany as St. George the Dragon Slayer, running his spear through cowering bears and reptiles. Thoma's caption reads: "Were the world filled with monsters, bent on making us their feed / We wouldn't be very frightened / For we know we will succeed."

By deciding to throw its creative energies behind the war effort, *Simpl* became part of a broader cultural war that was to accompany the battlefield carnage over the next four years. Munich, as the self-proclaimed capital of German culture, played a central role in this enterprise.

The tone of the wartime cultural crusade was signaled early on by an appeal from the rectors of the Bavarian universities to the academic youth: "Students! The muses are silent. The issue is battle, the battle for German *Kultur*. . . . The enthusiasm of the wars of liberation [against Napoleon] flares, and the holy war begins!" A little later several professors from Munich joined their colleagues at other German universities in issuing an Appeal to the World of Culture. They were disgusted with the Western powers for claiming to defend European cultural values while fighting alongside "Asiatic" Russians and black colonial troops. "The claim to be defending European civilization can be raised least convincingly by those who ally with Russians and Serbs, and who engage in the revolting spectacle of siccing Mongols and Blacks on a white nation."

To help protect German culture on the home front, Munich's cultural institutions tried to shut out foreign influences. The Court Opera curtailed its French and Italian repertories. The Royal Theater dropped plays by Racine, Molière, and Shaw. The city's music halls, whose "tinseled ladies" had earlier "passed out their coquettish adventures and alcove secrets in couplet form," now gave themselves over to patriotic reviews. A performer at the Circus-Varieté discarded his prewar stage name of Hopkins and reverted to Hoppke. "His performance," exclaimed the *Münchener Zeitung* piously, "has not become worse for his broadcasting his German name."

The push to purge Munich's cultural life of "un-German" influences was accompanied by attacks against resident Jewish artists. The experience of Bruno Walter is a case in point. Since his arrival in 1913, when he participated in that year's Wagner centennial, Walter had been disparaged by Munich critics as an "alien" figure who had no business tampering with German music, least of all with that of the Master. Such criticism accelerated during the war, as Walter continued to conduct Wagner operas and works like *Palestrina,* by the hypernationalist composer Hans Pfitzner. In 1916 Walter complained of a "measureless agitation against me in which the entire Munich press is unanimous." He was tempted to move to Boston, which had invited him to become resident conductor. But he stayed on in Munich, and a few local supporters rallied to his defense. The philologist August Mayer attacked Walter's critics as a pack of beer hall louts given to slamming down their opinions like steins on a *Stammtisch* (table reserved for regular guests). The offended critics promptly took Mayer to court and won a libel judgment against him. In 1934 the Nazi paper *Völkischer Beobachter* looked back on this judgment as "the first victory in Germany over the great power of Judaism . . . the dawn signaling the eventual triumph of the Hitler movement."

Meanwhile, most of Munich's newspapers jettisoned any social or political perspectives that could have been seen as critical of the ruling establishment or High Command. The periodical *Zeit im Bild* (Time in Pictures), which before the war had been serializing Heinrich Mann's *Der Untertan* (*Man of Straw*), a brilliant satire of kaiser worship, abruptly halted the project on 1 August. The editor explained to Mann:

> At this moment a great public organ cannot criticize German conditions in the form of satire. Only very few readers would, in such anxious times, either notice or accept the distinction between art and life: they would hold the contents of *Der Untertan* as matters of fact. In this light certain parts of the novel might easily give offense among the general public in the present critical situation. But apart from this we might face the most severe censorship problems were we to publish anything of the least political intent, particularly regarding the person of the Kaiser.

Despite such efforts at self-censorship, Munich's opinion makers, like those across the rest of Germany, became subject to increased governmental regulation as the war dragged on. A year after *Zeit im Bild* suspended *Der Untertan,* the Bavarian Ministry of War banned the periodical *Das Forum* for displaying "unpatriotic aestheticism and Europeanism." At the same time, local authorities warned theater and cabaret managers not to mount any skits or plays that might offend "religion, morality, public decency, political institutions, or public order."

Demands for political and moral purity, however, sometimes collided with Munich's desire to retain a reputation for artistic exuberance and lighthearted gaiety. Over vehement protests from conservatives, Frank Wedekind's *Frühlings Erwachen* (*Spring Awakening*), a daring play about adolescent sexuality, was allowed to run from 1915 to 1917. After an initial display of self-sacrificial Spartanism, moreover, the city began to loosen up somewhat. In 1915 *Der Zwiebelfisch,* a nationalist paper, reported disgustedly that some citizens were carousing in expensive bars and restaurants as if there were no war going on. Another commentator was revolted by the sight of scantily clad music hall chanteuses proclaiming their "lewd desire to hop in bed with furloughed soldiers."

One prominent Munich artist who showed no signs of cultural back-sliding was Thomas Mann. As we have seen, Mann greeted the war enthusiastically, though he feared it might "ruin" him financially. Despite his bellicosity, Mann was not inclined to join the rush to the trenches—earlier he had evaded completing his military obligation by finagling a discharge for flat feet (an experience he later worked into his comic novel *Felix Krull*)—but he was determined to compensate for his physical absence from the front through intellectual militance. In late August 1914 he put aside work on his novel *The Magic Mountain* to produce an essay entitled "Thoughts in Wartime," which he called "a war service with the weapon of thought." The heart of the piece was a polemical embroidering of Nietzsche's famous distinction between "culture" and "civilization." The former, which Mann identified with Germany, implied tribal unity, spiritual profundity, soulful irrationalism, youthful vitality, deep yearning for absolute values, and innocent uncontaminated strength. "Civilization," associated with Germany's Western enemies, especially France, connoted arid rationalism, secularism, pseudoenlightenment, shallow literary gamesmanship, spiritual softness, overbreeding, parliamentary fetishism, crass materialism, fake humanism, and the unhealthy atrophy of instinct. Mann argued that Germany's efforts to protect its *Kultur* from the onslaught of civilization demanded a heroic struggle that would be salutary for the national soul.

Mann's "Thoughts in Wartime," which appeared in the *Neue Rundschau* in November 1914, was merely the first salvo in an ideological barrage he maintained for almost the entire war. In December 1914 he expanded on the themes of his first war essay with a sixty-page harangue called "Frederick and the Great Coalition." By celebrating Frederick's "historically necessary" invasion of Saxony, Mann sought to justify Germany's overrunning of neutral Belgium at the outset of the present war. Frederick's unquenchable spirit during the darkest days of the Seven Years War, said Mann, lived on in the embattled Germany of 1914. "Germany today is Frederick the Great. It is his battle that we have to wage again and to win."

In May 1915, after Germany had used poison gas on the Western Front and bombed London, Mann wrote a shrilly defensive letter to a Swedish newspaper in response to an editorial about the bloody collapse of European unity. Europe *was* united, said Mann: united against Germany. Since the beginning of the war Germans had had to put up with a chorus of hypocritical cant about German "barbarism." It had gotten to the point where black colonial troops, "animals with lips as thick as cushions" and "gray paws" for hands, were demanding that German soldiers be executed as "war criminals." Explaining his country's need to continue fighting, Mann proposed that in the current struggle Germany recognized "the herald of her *Third* Reich," an emerging "synthesis of *might* and *mind*. . . ."

While Mann sometimes aimed his wartime writings at Germany's foreign critics and enemies, he also had in mind a target closer to home: his older brother, Heinrich. After a flirtation with conservative nationalism, Heinrich had become a champion of the Western democratic ideals openly despised by his younger brother. When Thomas's "Thoughts in Wartime" appeared, Heinrich was horrified. His friend Wilhelm Herzog recalled that Heinrich read these lines "with revulsion and indignation." He found it hard to believe that an otherwise "well-tempered spirit" could stray so far from the path of decency.

Heinrich's own literary response to the political and cultural issues raised by the war came chiefly in the form of an essay on Émile Zola that he published in November 1915. Here Heinrich celebrated Zola as a humanist intellectual who, in his defense of the alleged "spy" Alfred Dreyfus, had dared put abstract principles of justice over claims of national interest. Heinrich saw his own intellectual odyssey as a variation on Zola's, both having come to realize that, as Heinrich put it, "literature and politics have the same subjects, the same goals, and must mutually condition each other." This last comment was meant for brother Thomas, who, like most conservative Germans of the idealist school, had argued that politics must be avoided by all true artists (as if his own impassioned defense of the authoritarian state did not constitute a form of politics).

The arrow did not fail to hit its mark. Aside from the business about artists' needing to be politically engaged, Thomas was sure Heinrich had him in mind when he wrote:

"[Artists] who appear assertive and self-possessed in their early twenties are the most likely to dry up later on." The younger Mann condemned this remark as an example of "truly French spitefulness," a "glittering piece of sham" redolent of "slander and deception."

Thomas's fury with Heinrich was partly responsible for his decision, in 1916, to unlimber his "weapon of thought" once again on behalf of Germany and its sacred cause. Even this prolific writer, who sometimes joked about his tendency to run off at the pen, could not have guessed that this new effort would balloon to 650 pages, take two years to complete, and appear only when the cause it defended was already lost.

The work in question, *Die Betrachtungen eines Unpolitischen* (*Reflections of a Nonpolitical Man*), was a personal reckoning with brother

Heinrich, a defense of Thomas's own literary ideals, an apologia for Germany's military endeavor, and a tortured exploration of German identity in the early twentieth century. At its core, once again, was an impassioned argument for saving German *Kultur* from the predations of Western *Zivilisation*.

In the prefaces Thomas described the *Reflections* as the work of an artist "whose existence was shaken to its foundations, whose self-respect was brought into question and who was so upset he could produce nothing else." Yet as an inveterate pumper of irony, Mann was also aware that there was something odd about this entire project. Here was a literary man defending a nation he called "unliterary" and by so doing perhaps assisting the conquest of Germany by "civilization."

Like Schopenhauer and Nietzsche, Mann thought that music, not literature, was Germany's true art. He considered it more deeply spiritual, an unmediated expression of the soul's inner voice. Though music was mathematical in construction, its power to transport was, he thought, essentially irrational and religious. Only later would Thomas Mann conclude that music's "demonic" capacity to subvert the world of Logos made it an ambivalent and dangerous art, especially in the hands of Germans.

Whatever the author thought about his *Reflections,* posterity must judge it a problematical work. For all its agonized nuances, it was full of bombast regarding Germany's right to assert itself against an uncomprehending and jealous world. It was an unabashed reassertion of Hegel's "might makes right"—at least when the might in question was employed in the name of high cultural principles. As Mann's son, Klaus, later wrote, "[Thomas] confounded the reckless arrogance of the Prussian imperialists with the splendors of Dürer, Bach, and Schopenhauer. The deadly ecstasies of Tristan and Isolde became an argument in favor of the Teutonic expansion and unrestricted submarine warfare."

While Thomas's wartime convictions deepened his alienation from his brother and set him sharply apart from what remained of Munich's Left-literary culture, these views strengthened his broader spiritual identification with the town he had come to call home. Munich, he now believed, was Germany writ small, the quintessence of the beleaguered German spirit. In his martial mood he even loved the bovine anti-intellectualism of its shopkeepers and butchers, the visceral xenophobia of its superficially urbanized peasants. Having once despaired over the city's lack of literary sophistication, he now believed that this confirmed the deep Germanness of the place. Certainly he meant it as a compliment when he wrote, in the *Reflections,* "Munich is completely unliterary; literature there has no basis."

While Thomas Mann was agonizing over the fate of German culture in the modern world, another adoptive Münchner, Oswald Spengler, was beginning to forge his magnum opus, *Der Untergang des Abendlandes* (*The Decline of the West*), a book that Mann initially claimed was "thoroughly related" to his own ideas, though he later turned sharply against it.

Spengler had moved to Munich from Hamburg in 1911. He chose Munich because he had fallen in love with the city during a year's study there in 1901. Ten years later he found Munich changed for the worse, full of "sterile" *Jugendstil* buildings and nonsensical Expressionist paintings. Nonetheless, he settled in for good and allowed the town to work its seductive influence on him. Soon this staid North German was strolling through Schwabing carrying a knapsack full of books from the State Library. Like many of the artists and intellectuals who had flocked there over the years, Spengler had no regular job, living hand to mouth from a small inheritance. Staying well outside Munich's cultural and academic mainstream, he managed to find a few kindred spirits in the Schwabing cafés he frequented. In the end, wrote one of his biographers, his life in Munich amounted to a strange mixture of lingering northern discipline and newfound bohemian rebellion.

Spengler's writings, above all, his monumental *Decline,* also displayed a restless impatience with conventional intellectual boundaries. He had originally planned to write a philosophical novel about a young painter living in Munich, which he saw as a rich and cultured city bypassed by the modern zeitgeist. "Munich is the old-fashioned city par excellence in Germany" he wrote. "It is a place that lives off the artistic romanticism of its past and is therefore no longer able to produce. The spirit of Munich is now being thoroughly displaced by the spirit of Prussia-Berlin. From now on . . . Germany means Berlin."

Munich's historical fate, however, soon merged in Spengler's mind with broader patterns of cultural ebb and flow. The city's decline seemed symbolic of a disintegration of European civilization that was following the pitiless laws of historical evolution. Europe's tense political climate in the prewar era also helped define his thinking. He became convinced that a world war was about to begin that would serve as "the inevitable man-ifestation of the [contemporary] historical crisis," and his task must now be "to comprehend [this crisis] from an examination of the preceding cen-turies—not years."

Spengler spent almost a decade putting together his huge *Decline of the West,* but the crucial work was done during the First World War, which cast its grim shadow over the whole enterprise. Like Thomas Mann's *Reflections,* Spengler's book elaborated on distinctions between culture and civilization, albeit with a Darwinian twist. For him, "culture" denoted the phase in a society's development when it was young, virile, and instinctively creative; "civilization" came when the society turned to material comfort and theoretical refinements of earlier untutored creations. He did not attach a specific time frame to each phase, but he insisted that the transition from culture to civilization was as inevitable as the changes of the seasons or the biological stages in an individual's life.

Spengler believed that in his own age, the dawning twentieth century, Western civilization was taking a fateful turn toward great bloody conflicts in which charismatic Caesars would fight each other for mastery of the world. In the process humanity would sink into a uniform mass, most people living in enormous "barracks cities" like London, New York, and Berlin. Like the inhabitants of imperial Rome in its dotage, these masses would do the bidding of any leader who provided bread and circuses.

Spengler's *Decline* was not only gloomy but very long and badly organized. Its length and turgidity may have helped make it popular in Germany, where, as one commentator has noted, "long, wretchedly organized books had been the tradition" and where profundity was (and often still is) thought to be incompatible with brevity and lucidity. But the *Decline*'s main appeal was undoubtedly its very gloominess. Because the first of its two volumes appeared in 1918, at the end of the great slaughter, it harmonized perfectly with the dominant mood. Never before, noted the critic Ernst Cassirer, had a philosophical book gained such quick and universal popularity, finding an audience among ordinary readers as well as professional philosophers and historians. Cassirer thought that this was attributable more to the book's apocalyptic title than to its actual content. "The title . . . was like an electrical spark that ignited the reader's imagination. [When the book appeared], many of us recognized that there was something foul in the firmament of our highly praised Western civilization. Spengler's book brought this generalized discontent sharply to the surface."

"Dotschland, Dotschland über Alles"

Although various self-appointed guardians of German culture continued to demand unqualified enthusiasm for the war even as it degenerated into a stalemated contest over a few miles of mud, signs of disarray were beginning to show across the Reich as early as 1915. The cause was not only the mounting casualties at the front but increasing suffering at home. While the disillusionment was almost universal, it was particularly intense in

Bavaria, whose citizens came to feel that they were suffering more than other Germans and especially more than the Prussians. Munich was the center of this discontent, the place where Germany's wartime *Burgfrieden* (civil truce) broke down earliest and most dramatically.

At the outset of World War I Munich had ceased to be the glorified village imagined by many postwar nostalgia-mongers, but the long conflict greatly accelerated the process of social and economic change. For the first time Munich developed a sizable arms industry, as the Essen-based Krupp firm established an artillery factory in the suburb of Freimann, and local firms like the Bayerische Flugzeugwerke (Bavarian Aircraft Works) and Bayerische Motorenwerke (BMW) converted to war production. Munich's rapidly expanding industrial infrastructure required a larger work force than the town could provide, so thousands of workers were imported from other parts of Germany, especially from Saxony and the Ruhr. Meanwhile, to replace men called to the front, women took over industrial jobs in increasing numbers: Among the 9,402 women employed in Munich's war industries in 1917, only 19.5 percent had previously worked in a factory. For traditionalists among the native population, these changes were highly unwelcome; they portended an end to the comfortable old city they had known—or thought they had known.

While the war created employment for munitions and industrial workers, it also took jobs away from the city's artists, actors, and writers. Those who did not enlist in the army or arrange a war-related sinecure found that the home market for their services had significantly atrophied. Many citizens believed that in a time of national emergency it was improper to spend money on "frivolities" like the theater, novels, or paintings. Even King Ludwig III got into this spirit by banning the 1914 Okoberfest because of the "present political situation."

Munich's culture market became so depressed that after a few weeks of war several literary magazines and publishing houses shut down or curtailed operations. In October 1914 the Munich branch of the League for the Protection of German Writers lodged an appeal with the Bavarian Ministry of Culture on behalf of journalists and writers who had lost their jobs. "The war," said the letter, "has almost fully taken the possibility for existence from a large part of our colleagues who did not go along into the field or who were not able to dedicate their services to the fatherland in another way." The league urged the ministry to find suitable new positions for the artists, but few such jobs opened up, and Munich therefore harbored a growing community of unemployed intellectuals and writers who tried their best to turn their own misfortune into a crisis of state.

The situation in the theater was even worse. At the outbreak of war local officials closed all the theaters to demonstrate the city's no-nonsense commitment to the struggle. This caused an outcry, and after a few weeks the theaters were allowed to reopen, though not all of them did so. While some could not function for lack of actors or patrons, by 1916–1917 the main problem was an acute shortage of coal, which forced closures or curtailments of performance schedules in the winter months. As early as 1915 Munich's chapter of the Brotherhood of German Stage Artists complained that some two thirds of its members were unemployed, a figure that increased in the wake of the 1916–1917 closings. By the last two years of the war many of Munich's actors and actresses were reduced to performing impromptu street theater for people standing in breadlines.

But artists and actors were hardly the only ones to suffer economically from the impact of war. The conflict was especially hard on white-collar employees and small businessmen. Lacking the powerful unions deployed by manual workers, the white-collar workers were unable to obtain the wage increases necessary to keep up with the high wartime inflation. A Bavarian labor leader reported that white-collar workers were contemplating behaving like blue-collar workers and going out on strike. "The great need of the white-collar workers is demonstrated by the fact that the thought of striking is discussed in an ever more lively way in their ranks," he wrote. "This is the result of the failure of all their efforts to improve their condition. Until now the organizations have not approved of this idea; they are proud of the fact that they have chosen a path different from that of the [manual] workers."

The owners of small shops and companies, meanwhile, were in no position to compete for the huge military contracts awarded by the central government in Berlin, nor could they fight effectively for scarce raw materials or manpower. While these pressures exacted their toll on smaller businesses throughout the Reich, their impact was strongest in Bavaria, since the economy there, despite the new war industries, remained dominated by smaller firms. The Reich government's tendency to favor the megafactories of the North at the expense of Bavaria's nascent industry was the subject of a bitter protest to Berlin lodged by Crown Prince Rupprecht of Bavaria in 1917:

> Bavaria will find it much more difficult to recuperate from the consequences of the war than North Germany because her industry is less developed. But her further development is also being made more difficult during the war because, on the pretext that she is not sufficiently capable of producing, she receives relatively fewer contracts from the central agencies. Heavy industry is now supreme in Germany. . . . Using the needs of war in the most ruthless

fashion, the Berlin business people have managed, by the creation of all the central agencies set up in Berlin, to bring the entire internal economic life of Germany under their control and power, and the consequence will be that, after the war, the middle class, which already finds itself in dire distress, will disappear and a trustification worse than America's will set in. For Bavaria, where the middle class is rather numerous, this will be catastrophic. The members of this class, who were previously very monarchically minded, are now in part more antimonarchical than the Social Democrats because they blame the government for their misfortune.

Rupprecht's protests, and others like it, had little impact on the central government. A growing number of smaller Munich factories were forced to close for want of contracts, materials, coal, or labor. Their owners focused their bitterness largely on Berlin, though the "antimonarchical" sentiment noted by Rupprecht applied increasingly also to the Wittelsbachs, who were seen to be impotent when it came to protecting local interests.

As if bankruptcies and unemployment were not enough, the war also dramatically exacerbated Munich's housing shortage. The large wartime immigration made the demand for private dwellings greater than ever, while a lack of raw materials caused by priorities for the military forced Munich's builders to suspend most construction of new housing. Fewer than three hundred new dwellings were built during the entire war. The sight of families scouring the city for a place to live became so common-place that a local folk singer wrote a ditty about a wretched housewife slogging across town without ever finding an apartment for her family. Of course, the housewife's grief was the landlord's boon: The "devils" could charge forty marks for "two rooms in the building out back."

Agonizing as the housing crunch undoubtedly was, food shortages constituted the single greatest grievance during the First World War. The civilian food crisis, in Munich and elsewhere, came about largely because of the British blockade, inadequate resources for agricultural production, and massive demands by the military. In an effort to ensure that everyone received enough to eat, the Munich authorities began rationing foods in May 1915 and constantly added items to the list. (Food distribution and production were coordinated by a large bureaucracy in Berlin, the War Food Office.)

Despite such efforts, scarcities were such that long lines formed outside every bakery and butcher shop, and almost everyone complained about not getting enough to eat. In May 1916 Oswald Spengler wrote to a friend in the countryside:

I have a request—namely, that you send me some food as quickly as possible. . . . White bread and flour have not been available here since 1 February and probably will not be attainable until the next harvest. . . . Fresh vegetables and meat preserves are also no longer to be found. I'm living on 1/5 [kilo] Limburger and 1/4 [kilo] bad sausage a week. Recently in the Pschorr Brewery Restaurant the only "meat" dish they had was a piece of cod. . . . Yesterday I stood in line for one and a half hours to buy 200 grams of ham; this required one and a half weeks of ration coupons, so I can't eat in any restaurants. On Wednesday I stood in line for three quarters of an hour to get a little pack of saccharin, only the second one I've had since New Year's. These are truly matters for philosophical contemplation.

From his vantage point as the child of a much more prosperous writer, young Klaus Mann remembered the war chiefly in terms of inadequate food. "To us children, as well as the average citizen, war primarily meant not enough to eat. With the food situation constantly and rapidly deteriorating, it became a general obsession to discuss all aspects and implications of this one paramount problem: how, where, at what price and risk one could obtain the necessary victuals." On one occasion Klaus and his sister, Erika, discovered a tiny store in a distant suburb where they might buy some eggs for their mother. They stood in line in the bitter cold for six hours to make their purchase. But in trying to carry the eggs home in his numb hands, Klaus dropped them on the sidewalk. "It was bitter beyond description to watch the beautiful yolks, a mucilaginous rivulet, oozing away between the paving stones. It now seems to me that our tears froze even while running along our cheeks and adorned our bewildered faces like biting little jewels. Everything was glacial and forbidding and infinitely sad." Klaus recalled that even his august father became obsessed with food, and he speculated that Thomas's gloomy *Reflections* might, among other things, have been the product of "the inadequate food and the chilly temperature in his studio during the winter months." (If this was true for Thomas Mann's wartime opus, it might also hold for Spengler's *Decline of the West*; if ever a book bore the mark of having been written on an empty stomach, it was this one.)

With the shortage of foodstuffs, Münchners, like other Germans, were obliged to consume ersatz (substitute) products in lieu of genuine butter, coffee, sugar, eggs, milk, and so forth. Ersatz milk was a watery mixture that neither looked nor tasted like milk, ersatz eggs had a yellowish color but otherwise bore no resemblance to the original, and the substitute coffee simply did not bear drinking. More seriously, this was also true of beer, which was heavily watered down. Fake pastry was another abomination. Constance Hallgarten, a leader in the local women's movement, ordered a birthday cake from her baker in the hope that he might have secret supplies of real flour and eggs. "He sent something that looked like a cake," she recalled. "But one could hardly cut the thing and it tasted like pasteboard encased in gelatin—vile!" Summing up the universal contempt for ersatz products, Ernst Toller observed in his memoirs: "Eminent scientists proved that clay had the same food value as flour, that saccharin-sweetened jam was healthier than butter, that dried potato tops were better for the nerves than tobacco and tasted just as good. But the pronouncements of scientists were of little avail to the stomach, which reacted to this nonsense in its own way: People collapsed, fell sick, grew desperate."

Despised as the ersatz innovations were, however, the prime symbol for wartime deprivation was not a ghastly food substitute but a true product of nature, the lowly *Dotsche* (turnip), which began to replace the potato as the main staple during the infamous "turnip winter" of 1916–1917. With bitter humor Germans altered the opening lines of their national anthem to read "Dotschland, Dotschland über Alles."

Münchners responded to the multitude of laws governing the distribution of foodstuffs by violating them at every opportunity. Those who could bought food on the black market and hoarded it at home like pack rats (an offense called hamstering); others raided nearby farms for produce. Indeed, the food crisis brought out a streak of daring criminality in a people not otherwise known for their open flouting of the law. Recalled Klaus Mann: "The hoarding of illegal food was not only a necessity but a sport; more than that, a mania. Some people deployed the most uncanny skill in tracing devious sources of milk, lard or honey. With unflagging ingenuity they explored the countryside in search of chickens, rabbits, and potatoes. The funny papers and the criminal records were full of stories concerning the reckless wiles employed by the egg-ham-and-butter hunters."

City folks might regard their evasion of the food laws as a sport, but the authorities did not. Hundreds of Münchners were prosecuted for such offenses during the war. Even less amused were the farmers whose crops were regularly raided by hungry urbanites. The peasants responded by establishing armed patrols that beat and often killed would-be poachers.

As elsewhere in the Reich, some Münchners fared much better than others when it came to the challenges of wartime existence. Those with money and connections could bribe officials for extra ration cards, trade in the black market, and eat in restaurants that still had access to coveted items like *Weisswurst* (white veal sausage). Meanwhile, ever increasing prices for essentials meant that the poorest elements of the population were not just stealing from farmers but hunting urban "game" as well. As a popular folk song had it, "Squirrels, weasels, martens / We did kill, and a dog and a cat / Fox and mole and jay and crow / Safe weren't even mice and rats." But perhaps there was a shortage of these delicacies too, for by the middle of the war the children of poorer families were showing signs of severe malnutrition.

Monitoring these iniquities, the Munich police understood how dangerous they might become. "The easily avoidable, but long tolerated, injustice in food distribution," said a police report in March 1917, "is a far more dangerous enemy to public order than the shortage of food per se." The military command in Munich agreed. Because of "gross disparities in living standards," it said, "growing frustration and bitterness" were spreading through the lower classes.

On 18 June 1916 Munich witnessed the first of a series wartime food protests. Indignant over cuts in the bread ration, hundreds of people, mostly women and children, demonstrated in the front of the Town Hall. The mob was eventually dispersed by mounted police. According to Erich Mühsam, who witnessed the clash, people cursed the authorities as "Prussian lackeys" and shouted that "Even the French wouldn't treat us like this." Mühsam was convinced that the rioting would lead to full-fledged revolution.

With time, many people began to hold King Ludwig III personally responsible for the food shortages. Milk-starved Münchners accused him of shipping milk from his model dairy to northern Germany in order to make large profits. To help him appreciate their anger, some malcontents tied an empty milk can to his carriage. Others blamed him for the watered beer, on the ground that he allowed the export of Bavarian hops to the North. In summer 1917 rumor had it that the Münchners were so angry at the king that he had fled to Saxony. The story was false, but an ominous harbinger.

The popular perception of Ludwig as a toady to Berlin was part of a much larger animosity toward the central government, especially toward the Prussians, who dominated it. Hatred of Prussia, of course, was an old story in Munich and Bavaria, but it reached new levels of virulence in the later phases of the war. Locals often spoke more bitterly of the *Saupreussen* (pig Prussians) than of the enemy.

As the costs of war mounted and hopes of quick victory receded, Münchners began blaming the central government for dragging them into a war they claimed never to have wanted. They also accused the High Command of conducting operations in a way that South German troops took more than their share of the casualties. More precisely, Bavarians claimed that Prussian generals habitually threw Bavarian soldiers into the most dangerous engagements, treating them as cannon fodder.

Regarding developments on the home front, Bavarians complained that Prussia was using the war to gut states' rights in favor of a "dictatorship" from Berlin. Nowhere was this more evident, they said, than in the centralized military procurement policies directed from the Reich capital. On the one hand, these policies starved South German industry by favoring northern firms; on the other hand, they "ruined" Bavarian peasants by commandeering food products at artificially low prices.

Perhaps inevitably, beer became a centerpiece in the dispute with Berlin. Bavaria's brewers fumed that Berlin was providing plenty of raw materials to Prussian schnaps makers, while cutting hops quotas for beer production in the South. Berlin did this, said the brewers, knowing full well that in Bavaria beer "was not just a necessary food supplement for hard-working laborers, but, along with bread, the chief nutriment for poor people in the countryside." Ernst Toller put the complaint a little more bluntly: "Just because the Prussian swine didn't mind bad beer, the Bavarians also had to swallow dishwater."

In their bitterness over "Prussian hegemony," a delegation of Bavarian noblemen and prominent citizens of Munich petitioned Ludwig III in November 1917 to seize control over the war effort. But Ludwig's government chose to remain loyal to Berlin and to continue to enforce its edicts. Of course, Bavaria and Munich also continued to pour men into the meat grinder on the Western Front, which became even more grimly efficient with the arrival of fresh American troops in mid-1918. By summer 1918 Munich alone had lost 13,725 soldiers.

The war also demanded ever greater material sacrifices from the home front. On orders from Berlin, in 1917 the Bavarian government began requisitioning items that might be of military use; these included metal pots and pans, kitchen refuse, old paper, and organ pipes. In the same year the Imperial War Ministry seized and melted down 35 percent of Munich's church bells for ammunition. Aside from food shortages and bad beer, no wartime measure caused more consternation in Munich than this transformation of bells into shells.

Münchners also fretted over what the war was doing to the city's schoolchildren. School hours had been drastically cut because most male teachers had been drafted, and many school buildings had been turned into military hospitals or barracks. The local school commission worried that the cuts in schooling, along with disruptions of family life occasioned by the war, were rapidly producing a new generation of "wild" and "raw" youngsters. "The strong hand of the educator is gone," lamented a school commission report. "The father has been drafted, the mother works outside the home, and schooling has been sharply curtailed." A prominent Munich pedagogue warned that the more severely afflicted children "might have to live with the damage [suffered during the war] throughout their entire lives." As adults, he feared, they would either instinctively reject all authority and discipline or, conversely, surrender themselves blindly to anyone who promised to bring order and direction into their chaotic lives.

Pacifism and Polarization

In response to the manifold horrors of war, some Münchners, along with like-minded citizens across the Reich, began to cry that enough was enough. In February 1916 the first pacifist flyers and posters started showing up in Munich's streets; they declared that the war was a huge "swindle." According to the Bavarian War Ministry, most of the antiwar agitation was aimed at women. Whether or not this was true, it made good sense, for women had been carrying much of the war's burden at home. Among the earliest antiwar protesters in Munich were well-educated women like Anita Augsburg, Constance Hallgarten, and Lida Heymann. Starting in 1916, through rallies and printed broadsides, these ladies encouraged their sisters to stop doing all the things that helped keep the war machine oiled and running. They should stop filling men's places in the ammunition factories, stop sewing uniforms, and stop volunteering in military hospitals. The authorities did not take kindly to such agitation, and the Bavarian government ordered the expulsion of Heymann, who was not a Bavarian citizen. (She evaded the order by hiding on Augsburg's estate south of Munich.)

No one was more appalled by this pacifist and defeatist sentiment than Private First Class Adolf Hitler, who returned to Munich briefly in the depth of the "turnip winter" to continue convalescing from a leg wound he had suffered on the Somme in October 1916. Before joining a replacement battalion in Munich on 2 December, Hitler had spent time in a military hospital near Berlin, where he encountered (in his words) "spineless cowards" who had deliberately injured themselves in order to get away from the front. In Berlin itself, which Hitler now visited for the first time, he found pacifist agitators spreading their poisonous views in the streets. Thoroughly disgusted, he went down to Munich expecting to experience a more uplifting and patriotic atmosphere. To his horror, however, he discovered a monstrous nest of slackers and Jews. He recalled it in *Mein Kampf*:

When I was discharged from the hospital as cured and transferred to the replacement battalion [in Munich], I thought I could no longer recognize the city. Anger, discontent, cursing, wherever you went! In the replacement battalion itself the mood was beneath all criticism . . . to be a slacker passed almost as a sign of higher wisdom, while loyal steadfastness was considered a symptom of inner weakness and narrow-mindedness. The offices [in the city] were filled with Jews. Nearly every clerk was a Jew and nearly every Jew was a clerk. I was amazed at this plethora of warriors of the chosen people and could not help but compare them with their rare representatives at the front.

To Hitler's further horror, most Münchners did not seem to know who their true enemy was; they thought it was Prussia, not the Jews! Hitler had nothing but contempt for this anti-Prussian phobia, for though an adoptive Münchner himself, he regarded Bavarian (or any other) particularism as a betrayal of the national cause. Again, to quote *Mein Kampf*:

At this time [winter 1916–1917] I saw with horror a catastrophe approaching which, unless averted in time, would inevitably lead to collapse.

While the Jew robbed the whole nation and pressed it beneath his domination, an agitation was carried on against the "Prussians." At home, as at the front, nothing was done against this poisonous propaganda. No one seemed to suspect that the collapse of Prussia would not by a long shot bring with it a resurgence of Bavaria; no, that on the contrary any fall of the one would inevitably carry the other along with it into the abyss.

While Hitler expedited his return to the front in early 1917, grateful to be back in the only place he felt at home, agitation for an end to the war picked up steam across the Reich. In July 1917 the Reichstag passed a Peace Resolution calling for a negotiated settlement and a repudiation of annexationist war aims. This initiative found strong backing in Munich because the city was close the Southern Front, where Germany's Austrian allies were experiencing growing difficulty against the Italians. However, neither the parliament's belated effort to contain the war nor all the spontaneous pacifist protests had much effect on the German High Command. It seemed increasingly apparent that only a more radical and better organized antiwar campaign could bring an end to the slaughter.

On 16 May 1917 Munich hosted a meeting of the Independent Social Democratic Party (USPD), which had been formed the month before by embittered leftists (among them Rosa Luxemburg) to push for an early end to the war. The Bavarian capital became a major USPD bastion in large measure because of the man who took control of the movement in the Isar city, Kurt Eisner.

Eisner was without doubt the most unlikely figure ever to gain power and prestige in Bavaria. He was not only a Jew but a Jew who hailed from Berlin. Physically there was nothing earthy or robust about him; it was impossible even to imagine him in lederhosen. He had a spindly, bent frame; a large head sprouting wild white hair; a silver gray beard that hung like a dead animal over his dirty frock coat; a prominent hooked nose that was a caricaturist's dream; pale, unhealthy-looking skin; and dark, runny eyes enlarged by a pair of pince-nez glasses. Looking as he did, Eisner could find a certain niche in the small world of Schwabing's bohemia, where he became a fixture after moving to Munich from Nuremberg in 1911 and taking up a position as drama editor for the Socialist paper *Die Münchener Post*. Yet even here he was something of an odd (and sometimes unwelcome) duck. Otto Zarek, a student at Munich University during the war, wondered who among the denizens of the Café Stefanie might mobilize the growing discontent: "Perhaps, Herr Kurt Eisner, a dirty little man from Berlin who had succeeded in becoming dramatic critic on the Social Democratic newspaper."

Like almost all German Socialists, Eisner had backed the war when it broke out in 1914. "Now Tsarism has attacked Germany," he wrote in in the first days of August, "now we have no choice, now there is no looking back." But within a year, earlier than most of his colleagues, he did start looking back, becoming convinced that it was German militarism that was primarily responsible for the continued slaughter.

In December 1916 he delivered his first antiwar speech to a small group of USPD members. He must have had a way with words and, despite his odd looks, a certain magnetism, for he was soon attracting larger crowds to his speeches. His message was that the war would end only when the system that sponsored it was drastically changed. At first he was not very specific about how this might be done or what the new system should look like. Coffeehouse intellectual par excellence, he dealt in glowing abstractions and grandiloquent phrases. "Friends!" he cried. "The people of today are stunted and crippled because of the system of yesterday. But deep in every heart slumbers the yearning for a new world, for a new humanity."

Nebulous though this was, it had genuine appeal at a time when misery and deprivation set men dreaming of a new epoch for mankind. The poet Rainer Maria Rilke, who was on hand for some of Eisner's speeches, spoke for many such dreamers when he gushed: "I confess that I was able to feel a certain quick and happy confidence in the [revolutionary] overturn . . . for I had urgently wished that we turn an entirely new page in history, one onto which the sins of the past would not be carried over." Trying to explain Eisner's growing popularity from a different perspective, the liberal politician Ernst Müller-Meiningen observed: "There was nothing so stupid that it would not have found thousands of willing believers in Munich." No doubt this was true, but in the end it was a truth that would redound more to the advantage of the Right than of the Left.

In early 1918 Eisner began to get more specific with respect to the means by which the war and existing political system might be brought to a quick end. Taking a cue from Russia, where massive political strikes had recently helped bring down the czar, he started calling for crippling walkouts across the Reich. But he also—and this was the most astounding yet shrewdest part of this ex-Berliner's appeal—effectively exploited the Bavarians' wild antipathy toward Prussia. A police report quoted him telling a large audience at the Colosseum Beer Hall on 27 January 1918: "Here in Bavaria we have always been much more generous and open than [the people] up there in Prussia. The people here are also much more freedom-loving, not bound by Prussian hyperdiscipline. I myself, a Prussian, came for this very reason to the South. My ambition is not to encourage a separation between North and South, only to get rid of the Prussian militaristic system that has dominated Germany." The next day, urging an audience of metalworkers to go out on strike, Eisner spoke eloquently about the evils of industrial war, citing in particular a "cruel ammunition invented by a Berlin professor" that was being used on the Italian front. He was warmly applauded for his words, while an SPD speaker who called for patience and moderation was shouted down.

In late January workers in many plants in Berlin walked out in a demonstrative strike. Inspired by their example, employees at Munich's Krupp arms factory laid down their tools on 31 January. Other workers followed suit, and by the late afternoon of that wintry day some nine thousand men and women were parading down the streets of Munich, shouting revolutionary slogans.

The demonstration inspired a series of quick countermoves by the local authorities. That very evening Munich police arrested Eisner and packed him off to Stadelheim Prison. Shortly thereafter they picked up young Ernst Toller and other members of the USPD. At the same time, supported by the more conservative SPD, the Bavarian government employed a combination of force and vague promises of reform to bring the strikes to an end. For the next eight months, as Eisner and his radical colleagues sat in jail, the revolutionary forces in Munich remained quiescent.

While Munich's Left lapsed into temporary lassitude, the nationalist Right escalated its push for victory at the front and suppression of dissent at home. Like its counterparts elsewhere in the Reich, Munich's chapter of the Pan-German League sponsored rallies demanding "total war"—the unrestricted use of submarines, air power, and poison gas. Prodded by the rightist publisher Julius Lehmann, the Pan-Germans also insisted that Germany take over vast new territories in the East. Lehmann cried that it was "a matter of life and death for Germany to win the new land she needs to become strong and agriculturally and industrially independent from foreign influence." The problem, he realized, was that Germany's projected Lebensraum was already inhabited by other peoples, mainly Slavs who might "corrupt" the Germans who moved in after the conquest. Therefore, prior to Germanic settlement, Lehmann insisted that the region be "depopulated" by resettling the present inhabitants elsewhere.

Another urgent necessity, said the publisher, was a thorough ethnic purging of the Reich itself. Lamentably the imperial government in Berlin had allowed alien and racially inferior elements to undermine the purity of the *Volk*. It had forgotten the fundamental Darwinian rule that "Men of excellence must defend themselves—with all possible authority and power, and, if need be, by vile means—against the vile." One reason for this fateful lapse, Lehmann proposed, was that the leaders in Berlin had fallen under the influence of the international Jewish conspiracy, which was doing its best to bring Germany down. In his darkest moments Lehmann also suspected that the imperial elite had itself become Judaized through failure to keep its blood pure. He therefore declared that his publishing house would devote itself to the dissemination of the lessons of racial hygiene, which he said had been "fundamentally deepened and transformed" by the war. He also saw to it that Munich's Pan-German League established a special committee to study ways to deal with the "Jewish problem."

Wartime Munich also became a bastion of the Fatherland Party (established in Berlin on 2 September 1917), a militantly pro-annexationist group presided over by Admiral Alfred von Tirpitz. The purpose of this organization was to ensure that nationalist and militarist elements would have a stronger voice in the Reichstag at a time when that body, along with the imperial cabinet under Chancellor Theobald von Bethmann-Hollweg, was showing signs of irresolution. In August 1917 the Fatherland Party sponsored a mammoth rally in one of Munich's largest beer halls. *Simpliccisimus*'s Ludwig Thoma, a leader in the local branch, proposed that the recent Reichstag Peace Resolution be treated as a "day of national mourning."

Another significant development in Munich during the later phases of the war was the founding, on 17 August 1918, of the Thule Gesellschaft (Thule Society). Although it claimed to be nothing more than a "study circle" absorbed with early Germanic history and culture, Thule was in reality a semisecret sect promoting German power abroad and racial purity at home. The central figure behind it was a convicted forger calling himself Freiherr von Sebottendorff (but known to the police as Adam Glauer). According to Sebottendorff, who later wrote a history of the society entitled *Bevor Hitler kam* (Before Hitler Came), "Thule" referred to an ancient land in the Far North where the original Nordics had resided. Like Atlantis, Thule had vanished long ago, but its secrets could be recovered through magical rituals that allowed present-day Nordics to commune with their departed ancestors. Thule's secrets, once revealed and put to use, would enable twentieth-century Germans to create a new master race. To promote its cause, Thule launched a newspaper called *Der Münchener Beobachter.* The paper disguised itself as a "sports sheet" to deter Jewish readership; everyone knew, said Sebottendorff, that Jews read only business papers.

Regarding itself as an exclusive sect, Thule was careful to keep its membership small and pure. Potential members had to prove that their ancestry was exclusively German going back at least three generations. Aspirants also had to possess facial and body features conforming to the society's image of what the ancient Thulites had looked like. A certain fastidiousness was expected in the realm of sexual morals. "Always remember that you are a German! Keep your blood pure!" admonished the leadership. To symbolize its racial purity, Thule selected as its logo a dagger encircled in oak leaves crowned by a rounded swastika emanating shafts of light, like a pagan halo.

Swastika daggers figured prominently in the interior decorations at Thule's headquarters, a suite of rooms in Munich's most expensive hotel, the Vier Jahreszeiten. The group could afford such opulent quarters because its 250-person membership included some very wealthy and well-placed figures. There were industrialists, brewers, judges, lawyers, doctors, high police officials, university professors, and courtiers. Significantly, a number of Thule figures went on to play important roles in the Nazi movement. Among them were Dr. Rudolf Buttmann, head of the Nazis' Bavarian Landtag delegation; Dr. Ernst Pöhner, police-president of Munich until 1921 and an early Hitler backer; Karl Fiehler, mayor of Munich after 1933; Rudolf Hess, Hitler's deputy; Alfred Rosenberg, chief ideologist and head of the Nazis' foreign political office; Hans Frank, Bavarian minister of justice from 1933 to 1939 and wartime governor-general of Poland; and Dietrich Eckart, an early Nazi publicist and close Hitler confidant. With such a lineup there was some justice to Sebottendorff's boast that Thule set the stage in Munich "before Hitler came."

Another stage setter was a "guest member" of the Thule Society named Anton Drexler. As a toolmaker in Munich's railway yards, Drexler was too plebeian to socialize with the likes of Buttmann and Pöhner. Yet he became a prominent figure in the city's radical nationalist milieu in the last year of the war. On 9 January 1918, as talk of a possible general strike spread in Munich, Drexler wrote an article in the rightist *München-Augsburg Abendzeitung* seeking to rally local workers around the flag. He argued that an annexationist victory would greatly benefit the German workingman. "Hold Fast!" he urged. To promote this ideal, Drexler founded the Free Labor Committee for a Good Peace in March 1918. In addition to pursuing territorial annexations, the group promised to combat those "secret powers"—international Jewry, Freemasonry, Marxism, and Big Capital—that were conspiring to keep the "little people" of Germany in bondage. Drexler's organization never had more than about forty members and never exercised much influence on Munich's workers. Nevertheless, like the more august Thule Society, it did its part to pave the road to the Third Reich. The Free Labor Committee served as the nucleus for Drexler's postwar German Workers' Party, which Adolf Hitler transformed into the Nazis.

Defeat

Little did Drexler realize that just as he was admonishing his countrymen to stand fast on the home front, the battlefront was inexorably caving in. In the spring of 1918, ignoring the Reich's lack of manpower reserves and its inability to match its enemies' productive capacities, General Erich Ludendorff launched a massive offensive. It not only failed to achieve the desired breakthrough but also overstretched Germany's lines and dramatically reduced the supply of manpower necessary to hold the exposed positions.

In late summer the Allies counterattacked. In addition to their superior numbers, they made effective use of tanks, a weapon the Germans had failed to appreciate. (Upon seeing the first German-made tanks in February 1918, Field Marshal Hindenburg had sneered: "I do not think that tanks are of any use, but as they have been made, they may as well be tried.") British tank assaults in August and September produced panic in the German lines and provided officers with a welcome excuse to give up positions without much struggle. "The tanks had arrived," they reported; "there was nothing more to be done."

Ludendorff and Hindenburg railed at their subordinates for these losses, never admitting any blame on their part. For the time being they were also careful to hide the extent of the reversals from the kaiser, who in any event preferred to live in a world of illusion. In early September the High Command posted placards in the larger cities, including Munich, proclaiming: "We have won the war in the East, and we shall win it in the West." Ludendorff justified the deception as politically necessary. "If I had told the statesmen the truth," he said, "they would have completely lost their heads."

Actually it was Ludendorff who was losing his head. With every "strategic redeployment" he became more unstable, falling prey to insomnia, outbursts of vicious temper, and crying fits, none of which was helped by his home remedy of heavy drinking. Alarmed by his deteriorating condition, a physician at the German headquarters in Spa put him on a strict regimen of rest, walks, deep-breathing exercises, medicinal waters, and light reading. The general was also instructed to sing German folk songs upon awakening and to contemplate the beauty of the roses in the villa garden.

Ludendorff preferred to contemplate miraculous developments that might yet save Germany from defeat. Recalling how Catherine the Great's death had spared Frederick the Great in 1763, he proposed that the Spanish flu epidemic that was beginning to sweep the front would save Germany by wiping out enemy troops. Such fantasies suggested, at the very least, that the regimen of folk song singing and rose contemplation might have been insufficient.

On 28 September, as Germany's armies reeled from a new flurry of enemy blows, and Berlin's ally Bulgaria announced that it was withdrawing from the war, Ludendorff cracked. This supreme martinet, who had ordered soldiers jailed for uttering the word *defeat,* now called on Hindenburg to demand that Germany sue for an armistice. To delay, he said, would be to risk the complete destruction of the German Army and in all likelihood to provoke a revolution.

Supported by Hindenburg, who had also become pessimistic, Ludendorff took these grim tidings to the kaiser. Wilhelm was shocked to learn how desperate the situation had become, but he accepted the necessity for an armistice, hoping that a speedy peace might allow him to stay on the throne. Yet—and this is the crucial point—neither the kaiser nor his generals wanted to take on the onus of arranging an armistice after having spent four years telling the German people that a glorious victory was imminent. They all agreed that this unhappy task should be entrusted to civilian politicians, who would act in the name of the Reichstag, which would be given more authority. Moderate democratization, the generals hoped, might also take some wind out of the sails of the radicals calling for a German republic.

Accordingly, on 1 October 1918 the kaiser asked his cousin Prince Max of Baden to become Germany's chancellor and preside over a series of constitutional changes designed to bring effective parliamentary government. The reforms, which made the cabinet responsible to the legislature and subordinated the military command to the civilian government, were drawn up and passed through parliament in record time. Max also appealed to President Wilson to broker an armistice based on his Fourteen Points.

But the shock of impending defeat, coming after years of deprivation and promises of victory, overwhelmed these efforts. A few days of reforms, people said, could not make up for "years of lies."

The sense of having been "swindled" was as strong in Bavaria as anywhere in the Reich. Indeed, it was undoubtedly stronger there, for as we have seen, Bavarians had long felt that they were being victimized by the central government. As announcements of Max's armistice appeal were posted in Munich, sporadic rioting broke out and beer hall orators cursed Berlin more bitterly than ever. "In October of 1918," a prominent Munich liberal declared, "we finally considered ourselves, *everyone without distinction of party,* deceived and duped."

Thomas Mann captured the despair prevailing among the city's cultural conservatives when he insisted that one could trust neither the new regime in Berlin nor Germany's Allied conquerors. He wrote in his diary on 4 October:

> Prince Max von Baden appointed chancellor. Establishment of the new, democratic government in which the Social Democrats predominate. Formal peace offer and armistice terms from the "New Germany" are impending. Belief in "power" is being solemnly abjured—though Germany's enemies are steeped in that belief. The self-abnegation, remorse, and penitence are boundless. We now say that the enemy is in the right, admit that Germany needed to be reformed. Lethargic, tormented, half sick.

Mann was especially sickened by the fact that Germany's fate was now in the hands of President Wilson, whom he considered a naive do-gooder of the worst sort. Perhaps it would be best, he mused, if Wilson and the other victors *did* impose a harsh peace; at least then Germany might reject the democracy that was being forced down its throat. As he wrote on 5 October, "It is certainly a bit painful that everything now hangs on the wisdom of a Quaker [*sic*] whether Germany obtains a peace that does *not* inject into her bloodstream undying outrage against the turn of events. In the interest of the German spirit and the preservation of its own opposition to democratic civilization one might almost wish for this."

In the end, however, Mann conceded that democracy was probably inevitable in Germany. He therefore proposed that the only hope for preserving the German spirit was "the separation of cultural and national life from politics, the complete detachment of one from the other." Mann himself, as we shall see, eventually rejected this dubious wisdom. It was unfortunate for Germany that many of his intellectual colleagues did not.

Meanwhile, the Bavarian government, like that of the Reich, was trying desperately to stay afloat through timely concessions and strategic backpedaling. On 14 October it released Kurt Eisner from prison so he could campaign for one of Munich's Reichstag seats recently made vacant by the retirement of the Bavarian SPD leader Georg von Vollmar. The government hoped thereby to show its goodwill toward the militant Left. It also expected that Eisner would fare badly in the election against his main rival, the moderate Socialist Erhard Auer. Auer, after all, was a native Bavarian of peasant background with ample girth and a folksy manner. How could he be beaten by a skinny Berlin Jew?

Yet Eisner, looking more unkempt than ever, with hair to his shoulders and beard to his navel ("You see me just as Stadelheim released me," he crowed to his supporters), ran a brilliant campaign perfectly attuned to the apocalyptic mood of the times. He conducted, that is, less a political campaign than a crusade for revolution. "There will be no Reichstag elections anyway," he said. "The revolution will come first." Removal of Germany's emperor and all its kings, he cried, was the only way to end the mass murder on the front and the criminal injustice at home. He dismissed Auer as an establishment stooge who would surely keep the troops on the front and the princes on their thrones.

Eisner's audiences grew by the day, yet the Bavarian government remained serenely confident that the people would reject this alien creature. At the same time, the government sought to pacify the citizenry through a hasty series of reforms similar to those instituted in the Reich. Under the "new order" announced in Munich on 2 November, the king could no longer dismiss ministries at will and the upper house could not veto legislation passed by the Landtag. That body would now be elected by proportional representation, and two Social Democrats would become members of the royal cabinet. Bavaria, in short, would have a true parliamentary government.

But the changes came too late. Or, more precisely, they could not achieve the desired impact when people's daily lives were still governed by the chaos of war, which seemed all the more brutal and unbearable now that it was clearly going to be lost. Reform was not very exciting when revolution was in the air.

On 5 November Munich learned that radical sailors at the naval base at Kiel had just seized their ships rather than venture out on a suicide attack against the British fleet. That very evening some of King Ludwig's personal guard made their way to the Theresienwiese to hear Kurt Eisner swear a formal oath "that Munich shall arise in the coming days."

The next day Bavaria's outgoing cabinet met with the new one slated to take power on 8 November. Minister of War Philipp von Hellingrath admitted that there were "restless and unreliable elements even in the Bavarian army" but insisted that the military as a whole was "securely in our hands." He added: "Nothing is going to happen." Ernst Müller-Meiningen, incoming minister without portfolio, was not so sure. He warned that Eisner, "in his embodiment of Christ with long prophet mane," was a dangerous demagogue who should not be underestimated. Yet most of his colleagues, including Auer, who was also to join the new cabinet, still could not take Eisner seriously. "Eisner is out of the picture, you can be sure of that," Auer promised. Then he repeated the war minister's reassuring words: "Nothing is going to happen."

3

Red Munich

IN EARLY APRIL 1919 a British military official who had been sent to Germany to evaluate conditions in that defeated land delivered the following assessment from his base in Munich:

> The greatest danger lies in the fact that the nerves of the German people appear to have broken down. A people of limited political understanding, they imagined, when the armistice was signed, that peace was immediately at hand and the privations of four and a half years were over. Five months have passed, and their exaggerated hopes of a speedy peace, of quick supplies of food and clothing—hopes unduly encouraged by a somewhat reckless press—have been disappointed. Hope deferred has made the German heart sick. From the heights of hope last November—and in spite of the disaster

that had overtaken them the Armistice was hailed with genuine joy in Germany—they have plunged into the depths of despair. And it is this despair which has given Bolshevism its chance.

It is significant that this report was dispatched from Munich, for it was in the Bavarian metropolis that the German despair seemed most pronounced. Munich was the first provincial capital to lose its monarch and the last German city to see order restored in the wake of the upheavals of 1918–1919. The revolution there progressed through stages of escalating radicalism, culminating in the creation of two successive soviet regimes. Ignited by exasperation over the seemingly endless war and by bitter resentment toward the central authorities in Berlin, the revolution in Munich produced excesses of irresponsibility and popular passion that shocked the world.

The One Hundred Days of Kurt Eisner

The weather was unseasonably mild on the afternoon of 7 November 1918, when several columns of restless people converged on Munich's Theresienwiese. They had come at the invitation of both Socialist parties, the SPD and the USPD, to demand an immediate end to the war. The SPD was not enthusiastic about cosponsoring this demonstration but understood it could not hold out for "national defense" without losing followers to Kurt Eisner and his Independents.

The makeup of the crowd, which by late afternoon exceeded eighty thousand, confirmed the Majority Socialists' anxieties. In addition to SPD loyalists from the big industrial unions, there were many radical Saxons from the local Krupp works; mutinous soldiers and sailors who had abandoned their units; rebellious farmers brought in by their leader, the blind demagogue Ludwig Gandorfer; a smattering of Schwabing bohemians; thousands of women and teenagers; and the usual assortment of beer hall rowdies ready to follow any fast talker who promised a little excitement.

Eisner was on hand to offer just such stimulation. He stood on a soapbox and harangued the crowd for more than an hour. When he was done, one of his aides shouted: "Comrades, our leader Kurt Eisner has spoken. There is no reason to waste any more words. Follow us!"

Eisner now led a swelling band of followers toward a school that housed a temporary military barracks and munitions depot. The Munich writer Oskar Maria Graf, who was part of the mob, described the scene:

All at once the howling mass started to move. Like an impatient black wave it rolled, thousands upon thousands strong, down the hill into the streets. We went at a fast trot past closed-up houses with their window shades pulled down. . . . Eisner was pale and looked deadly earnest; he said nothing. Sometimes he seemed as if he himself had been overtaken by the mighty event. . . . He went arm in arm with the broad-shouldered, blind peasant leader Gandorfer. This character moved much more freely and boldly, like a typical Bavarian peasant. . . . There was no opposition. All the police seemed to have disappeared. . . . All along the route people joined our ranks, some of them armed. Most laughed and chatted as if on the way to a party. Occasionally I turned around and looked behind me. The whole city seemed to be marching.

Upon arriving at the school, the mob rushed inside and emptied the arms depot; this was easy, for the guards promptly defected to the revolutionaries. Now the crowd surged across the nearby Donnersberger Bridge and, dividing into smaller units, advanced upon a number of military posts, most of which they took with equal dispatch. Only at the massive Türkenstrasse Barracks did the revolutionaries encounter any opposition, which they quickly put down with tear gas and warning shots. No doubt the situation might have been different had the government troops been willing to employ all their resources against the rebels. But after four years of war they were no longer prepared to put their lives on the line for the Wittelsbachs. Moreover, the civilian authorities were in complete disarray, having underestimated the threat posed by Eisner and his followers.

Another band of revolutionaries descended upon Munich's largest beer hall, the Mathäserbräu, and took over one of the lower floors for an impromptu political meeting. Against a background of drunken cheering, the soldiers established a Council of Soldiers and Sailors. A little later that evening Kurt Eisner presided over the establishment of a Council of Workers. He was elected chairman, the first electoral office he had ever held. He then combined the two groups into a Council of Workers, Soldiers, and Peasants, which dispatched truckloads of soldiers to take control of key buildings. At the same time, the council put up hundreds of yellow posters announcing the advent of the new order. "Down with the Dynasty! Long Live Freedom!" the placards proclaimed.

At about 10:00 P.M. the council members, protected by an armed guard of sixty men, marched from the Mathäserbräu to the Landtag building, where they heard Eisner proclaim the birth of the Bavarian Republic in a high, squeaky voice. "The Bavarian revolution is victorious. It has put an end to the old plunder of the Wittelsbach kings. . . . Now we must proceed to build a new regime. . . . The one who speaks to you at this moment assumes that he is to function as the provisional prime minister."

But what of the old ruler of Bavaria? In the early afternoon of 7 November 1918 King Ludwig III was enjoying his usual walk in the Englischer Garten when a policeman on a bicycle begged him to return to the Residenz; it seemed that a mob was heading toward the Old City. Ludwig returned to find an unruly crowd milling around the main entrance to the palace. After entering through the stable doors, he sat down to dinner with his wife, Queen Maria Therese. At eight two of his ministers arrived and advised him that the situation had become so dangerous that he and his family must vacate the capital at once. His Majesty could not, they warned, count on any troops in the city to defend him. Envisaging nothing more than a tactical retreat, Ludwig instructed his family and a few retainers to prepare themselves for a nocturnal auto journey to Wildenwarth, a Wittelsbach estate near the Austrian border.

The escape began on an inauspicious note, for it turned out that the royal chauffeur had gone over to the revolutionaries. As a replacement Ludwig turned to the owner of a rental car agency who had once driven for his father. "This trip could be dangerous, Tiefenthaler," warned the king. "I'm afraid of nothing," replied the doughty chauffeur. At 9:30 P.M. the royal party climbed into three cars and pulled away from the Residenz. They managed to get out of Munich safely enough but ran into trouble on the dark roads outside the city. With a heavy ground fog obscuring visibility, Tiefenthaler piloted the king's auto into a swampy potato field and got stuck. Setting out on foot across the countryside, he eventually found a farmhouse where, as it happened, two soldiers with horses were overnighting. Unaware that a few hours earlier their monarch had been deposed, they pulled Ludwig's car from the muck. The party drove on to Wildenwarth, where it arrived at 4:30 A.M.

The king expected to stay there only until the trouble in Munich had abated, but the next day he learned that his kingdom had become a republic and that a band of revolutionary soldiers was already on its way to Wildenwarth to arrest him. He therefore resumed his flight, which took him first to Austria and then on to exile in Hungary, where he remained until his death in October 1921.

ON THE MORNING of 8 November Münchners awoke to find red flags flying over the twin towers of the Frauenkirche and yellow posters tacked up all over town. They read:

FELLOW CITIZENS!

In order to rebuild after long years of destruction, the people has over-thrown the power of the civil and military authorities and has taken the regime in hand. The Bavarian Republic is hereby proclaimed. Elected by the citizens and provisionally instituted until a definitive representation of the people is created, the Council of Workers, Soldiers, and Peasants is the highest authority. It has law-giving power.

The entire garrison has placed itself at the disposal of the republican regime. The General Command and the Police Presidium stand under our direction. The Wittelsbach dynasty is deposed.

LONG LIVE THE REPUBLIC!
The Council of Workers and Soldiers
Kurt Eisner

To ensure a peaceful transition to the new era, Eisner's Council of Workers, Soldiers, and Peasants ordered beer halls and taverns to close at 8:00 P.M. and required all civilians to be off the streets one hour later. On the first day of the new republic, only one newspaper, the *Münchener Neueste Nachrichten,* was allowed to appear. It carried Eisner's proclamation of the revolution, along with an appeal to farmers to keep provisioning the cities. The paper also printed a promise that the "Democratic and Social Republic of Bavaria" would muster the "moral force to obtain for Germany a peace that will preserve her from the worst." Cautiously it assured that public order, security of persons, and private property would be guaranteed and that a constitutional assembly would be convoked for which "all men and women of age" would be able to vote. The announcement ended on a characteristic note of high humanism: "In this time of wild murder we abhor all bloodshed. Every human life should be holy. Long live the Bavarian Republic! Long live the peace! Long live the creative work of all labor activity!"

For the most part Münchners passively accepted this sudden change of regimes. To be sure, a few people seized the moment to plunder shops, but the city's Wittelsbach statues and monuments remained standing. Even those appalled by the sudden turn of events did not, at least at first, do anything of consequence to alter the situation. Rather, they grumbled among themselves at their favorite beer halls, and some scrawled anti-Eisner graffiti on buildings. Others, like Thomas Mann, spilled their bile in the privacy of their diaries. Mann's commentary on the new regime is especially noteworthy, for it sounded a theme that was to become increasingly common among bourgeois Münchners as the revolution progressed. On 8 November he wrote:

Both Munich and Bavaria governed by Jewish scribblers. How long will the city put up with that? Incidentally, it is said that Herzog [a member of the ruling council] has already expressed his frustration with Eisner, who is not nearly radical enough for him. Herzog, by contrast, is ultrabolshevistic. . . . [He is] a slimy literary racketeer . . . who let himself be kept by a moviestar, a moneymaker and profiteer at heart, with the big-city piss-elegance of the Jew-boy, who would lunch only at the Odeon Bar, but neglected to pay [the dentist] Ceconi's bill for partially patching up his sewer-gate teeth. That is the revolution!

Thomas Mann and other conservatives feared that the new regime might try to emulate the Russian Bolsheviks, but it soon became evident that Eisner was no Lenin. Unlike the Soviet leader, he was entirely unprepared to advance the revolution by liquidating "class enemies" or by establishing a "dictatorship of the proletariat." Nor, unlike some of the Schwabing bohemians who initially backed him, did he welcome the prospect of anarchy. He was determined to effect an orderly transition to an egalitarian state in which all Bavarians could live harmoniously. Immanuel Kant, not Karl Marx, was his true guiding star.

On the morning of 8 November Eisner asked his old adversary Erhard Auer to help form a coalition government to replace the Council of Workers, Soldiers and Peasants as Bavaria's governing body. Although Auer had little love for the revolution, he accepted the invitation because he saw no way to undo what had been done. That afternoon a new government was formed with Eisner at the head but with SPD men in most of the important ministries. Auer himself took the post of the interior, which controlled the police. Within hours of its inception, it seemed, the Munich revolution had become a model of moderation.

Eisner confirmed this tendency in his speech introducing the new government. He promised a conciliatory course and assured property owners that he had no intention of confiscating their holdings. At the same time, however, he insisted that Germany must abandon its monarchical institutions, for the Allies would negotiate a favorable peace only with republicans. This was a none-too-subtle reminder that Berlin needed to oust Kaiser Wilhelm II just as Munich had ousted King Ludwig III.

Berliners did not need any advice from their southern cousins. On the morning of 9 November thousands of arms factory workers in the capital marched to the city center, chanting, "Peace, Bread, Freedom!" Arriving at the gates of the royal palace, they added the magic word *Republic.* Believing that he might yet save the monarchy by jettisoning the monarch, Max of Baden took the liberty of announcing Wilhelm II's abdication at noon. Max then handed the chancellorship over to the SPD leader Friedrich Ebert, a former saddlemaker who was known to favor a constitutional monarchy. But Ebert's preferences counted for little in the atmosphere of confusion that now gripped Berlin. Shortly after he and his colleague Philipp Scheidemann took the reins of power, word came that the radical Spartacist leader Karl Liebknecht was about to proclaim a Socialist republic on the Bolshevik model. This was precisely what the SPD had been dreading for months. Aiming to undercut Liebknecht, Scheidemann appeared on the balcony of the Reichstag and delivered an impromptu speech, ending with the fateful phrase "Long live the great German republic!" Ebert was furious with his colleague for taking a step that he believed only a constituent assembly could decide. But once the Socialists had proclaimed the republic there was no way to unproclaim it. In their bewilderment they resembled, wrote the novelist Alfred Döblin, a "virgin with her baby."

On 11 November the long-awaited armistice was officially concluded in a railway car at Compiègne north of Paris. While most people in Munich breathed a sigh of relief that the war was finally over, even if it had ended in bitter defeat, the adoptive Münchner Adolf Hitler found nothing to be relieved about. During those crucial days of revolution and surrender, he was pacing the halls of a military hospital in Pasewalk (northeast of Berlin), where he was slowly recovering from the effects of a mustard gassing he had sustained on 14 October near Ypres. He claimed to have been temporarily blinded in the attack, but it is possible that the blindness was largely psychosomatic, as if he could not bear to see Germany go down to defeat. As he tells the story in *Mein Kampf,* one day in early November some sailors arrived at the hospital and "proclaimed the revolution." They were led by "a few Jewish youths" recently released from a "gonorrhea hospital." Hitler hoped, he says, that this "high treason" was just a local affair, and he was able to convince some of his fellow patients, "especially the Bavarians," that this was the case. "I could not imagine that the madness would break out in Munich, too. Loyalty to the venerable House of Wittelsbach seemed to be stronger, after all, than the will of a few Jews." But during the next few days rumors of general revolution reached Pasewalk, and when the empire fell, a hospital pastor confirmed the worst.

Hitler further relates that during the "terrible days and nights" following the armistice, as he ruminated on this awful crime, "hatred grew in me, hatred for those responsible for this deed." With the hatred came knowledge of what his own mission must be. He would wage war on the traitors at home who had thrust the "dagger" in the back of Germany's armies. The struggle would be bitter and merciless, he knew, for there was no "making pacts with Jews." But his own fate was sealed: "I, for my part, decided to go into politics."

As in many other parts of his memoir, Hitler here was playing fast and loose with the truth. In reality he made the decision to "become a politican" only after the Bavarian revolution had been put down. He had no sentimental feelings toward the Hohenzollerns or the Wittelsbachs. He undoubtedly despaired over the revolution and armistice, but his chief concern at the time was over what these developments might mean for him. With the end of the war he had lost the one place in life that seemed perfectly to suit him. He had loved the "comradeship of the trenches" and the purposeful violence of the great crusade. The army had, moreover, provided him with the only sustained employment he had ever known. Now, at age twenty-nine, he could only assume that he would soon have to return to the civilian world, where he had always been a failure.

WHILE HITLER WAS despairing at Pasewalk, Eisner settled into his task of running the Free Republic of Bavaria. The new prime minister still struck many, if not most, Münchners as a wildly improbable ruler. "Eisner gave me the impression of being an old, well-meaning, but uncanny Jew," recalled Frieda Duensing, director of a school for wayward girls. "He seemed without understanding of what he had done or wanted to do. [He was] something of a nutcase—the type who sets a house on fire, enjoys the spectacle, and doesn't think too much about what the future will bring." The folk singer Weiss Ferdl abused Eisner for imagining that he could bring freedom to Germany by shouting slogans and turning everything topsy-turvy. "Revolutilatilutilai! Holaridium! Turn everything around / Bring everything around / And shoot everything up. Boom! Boom! Boom!" Even *Vorwärts,* the Berlin-based SPD paper, ridiculed Eisner's ambitions in Bavaria:

> You are living in a world of sweet delusion if you imagine you can put your confidence in the Bavarian people—you, a literary immigrant from Berlin who never played a role in Bavaria's political life, a man virtually unknown to the public three weeks before taking office. . . . This minister-presidency of yours has nothing to do with the great gravity of our times. It stands in shattering contradiction to them. It is a Punch-and-Judy show in real life, freely adapted from Frank Wedekind by Kurt Eisner, with the author in the title role—homemade theater in the Munich-Schwabing style. In five minutes the curtain will come down, and it will all be over.

Eisner's problem, however, was not just that he was an outsider but that he was an incompetent outsider. He was unable to shift from the world of theatrical journalism and coffeehouse philosophizing to the complex realities of political administration. Moreover, he was excessively tenderhearted for his new responsibilities. With his training in Kantian philosophy, he thought he could persuade old enemies to cast aside their differences in a new "communism of the spirit" that would yield a "Reich of light, beauty, and reason." Politics for him was (as he put it) "a form of self-actualization like poetry, watercolors, or composing string quartets."

Eisner's style as a leader was evident in his first public ceremony as prime minister, the staging, on 17 November, of an elaborate celebration of the revolution. He saw to it that the men and women who assembled in the National (formerly Royal) Theater wore somber business suits and modest dresses rather than the traditional tuxedos and low-cut gowns. The new ministers of state sat scattered around the hall rather than in the boxes because they, like everyone else, had drawn their tickets by lot. Yet the evening's program was as pompous and high-toned as its classics-worshiping impresario could make it. To begin, Bruno Walter led the Munich Philharmonic in Beethoven's Leonore Overture, an ode to political freedom and the triumph of the human spirit. Then Eisner, his hair and beard trimmed at last, delivered an oration promising that Beethoven's emancipatory vision anticipated "the reality which even now we are experiencing." To the crowd he asked: "What do we want?" He answered himself: "We want to give the world an example that finally a revolution, perhaps the first in the history of the world, will *unite the Idea, the Ideal, and the Reality*!" When Eisner finished, a group of actors played a scene from Goethe's *Epimenedes Erwachen,* ending with the call "Upward, Onward, Upward! And the work, will be done!" Next, some singers performed the section in Handel's *Messiah* in which the chorus intones: "The people who wander in the darkness see a great light." Then the orchestra played Beethoven's Egmont Overture. To conclude, the entire audience sang Eisner's own poem, "Hymn to the Peoples," which ended with the invocation "Oh, world rejoice! Oh, world rejoice!" One member of the audience, a theater director, was so moved that he urged Eisner to repeat the performance for Munich's children.

Perhaps Eisner should have done so, for this was the kind of thing he did best, though some citizens wondered, as the *Münchener Neueste Nachrichten* archly put it, why the regime was celebrating freedom when hunger, fear, and misery still gripped the land. In a similar vein Josef Hofmiller, a conservative editor, chastised Eisner for staging "a national celebration in the wake of a shameful armistice and on the eve of what will probably be an equally shameful peace settlement."

Eisner indeed faced a host of challenges crying out for immediate action. Law and order had broken down following the collapse of the traditional organs of public security. Revealingly, Eisner initially dealt with this problem by appointing an unknown lieutenant as commander in chief of the Bavarian Army and by asking workers in the factories to provide "a number of trustworthy, energetic men for the maintenance of order." These steps resulted in massive confusion, as a plethora of ad hoc security patrols, operating out of various factories and beer halls, fought one another in the streets to keep order. Eventually Eisner delegated all security operations to his new minister for military affairs, Albert Rosshaupter, but Rosshaupter was so overwhelmed by the task of feeding and housing thousands of demobilized soldiers that he hardly had time for other affairs.

Some of Eisner's more radical followers urged him to take advantage of the royal collapse to "socialize the economy"—that is, to place large agricultural, industrial, and financial institutions under state ownership. But the prime minister argued that it made no sense to attempt this when "the productive power of the land" was exhausted.

Eisner did not lose much sleep over his government's failings on the domestic front, for he expected to do great things in the realm of foreign policy. In his self-appointed capacity as republican Bavaria's first foreign minister, he promised a just peace for Germany, and in the process he hoped to make Bavaria the moral and political arbiter of the new Reich. Germans and foreigners alike, he believed, must learn to look to Munich, not to discredited Berlin, for leadership and guidance.

Three days after taking power, Eisner sent a telegram to the Allied governments appealing for a lenient peace. The appeal had as its main target President Woodrow Wilson. To improve his chances of influencing Wilson, Eisner secured the services of an American evangelical pacifist and amateur diplomat named the Reverend George D. Herron, whom he incorrectly believed to be a close confidant of the American leader. Herron wrote Wilson that "The members of the new Bavarian Ministry are the best that Germany has to offer," adding, in a bow to Wilson's academic background, "The new Republic is practically constituted by the faculty of the University of Munich." Alas, Wilson ignored both Herron and Eisner, choosing to deal exclusively with the central government.

Undeterred by the silence from Washington, Eisner made another, more controversial effort to speak for the new Germany. On 25

November, during a conference of the German states in Berlin, he published reports from Munich's legation in Berlin documenting the imperial government's support for Vienna's aggressive policy toward Serbia in July 1914. Eisner apparently hoped that such openness about German complicity would facilitate easier peace terms.

The Bavarian prime minister's confession on behalf of Germany's former rulers did not impress the Allies; they did not need this exposé to know that Germany was responsible for the war. The Bavarian leader's own countrymen, meanwhile, were aghast over the move. The *Münchener Neueste Nachrichten* thought it "simpleminded" to cast all blame for the war on German "militarists," since, as any half-wit knew, the French revanchists and Russian Pan-Slavists had also been anxious for war. In any event, confessing guilt would only give Allied hard-liners welcome ammunition. Eisner's Majority Socialist partners, whom he had not bothered to consult regarding his foreign policy initiative, were equally upset, for they had also backed the war.

Another bone of contention between Eisner and the SPD was the Council of Workers, Soldiers, and Peasants. Eisner wanted it to function as a kind of "shadow parliament" that would engage in "constant criticism and discussion of political and social life." The SPD, however, regarded the council as a threat because it challenged the principle of parliamentary government and hindered cooperation between the new regime and the middle-class parties. Under pressure from the SPD, new regulations issued in late November relegated the council to a symbolic role.

Yet another source of dispute within the Eisner government concerned the timing of elections for a new Landtag. Eisner wanted to put off the elections because he feared that the majority of Bavarians were not yet sufficiently "liberated" to vote for his party. The Majority Socialists, however, looked to the Landtag elections as an expeditious way to terminate the Eisner experiment. Reminding the prime minister of his promise of timely elections, they were able, in a cabinet meeting on 5 December, to schedule a Landtag vote for 12 January 1919.

While temporarily pacifying his Socialist partners, Eisner's concessions enraged Munich's radical Left, which saw them as the death knell for the revolution. They believed that "true democracy"—the kind that Lenin had recently introduced in Russia—had nothing to do with parliaments and elections. They knew, as Ernst Toller put it, that the fate of the republic must not be left to "the chance results of a questionable election and an ignorant people." On the night of 6 December about four hundred Munich anarchists, led by Erich Mühsam, occupied the offices of several conservative newspapers. On the presses of one of them, the *Bayerische Kurier,* these self-styled "International Revolutionists of Bavaria" published a special edition urging their comrades to press the revolution forward. Then the group captured Erhard Auer and forced him at gunpoint to draft a letter resigning his ministerial post.

Rushing around Munich in the middle of the night, Eisner was able to put an end to this insurrection. He convinced Mühsam and company to vacate the newspaper offices, and he tore up Auer's dragooned letter of resignation. Yet he refused to punish any of the rebels. "I know you meant well. You acted out of love for me, but it was not a good thing to do," he chided.

This slap on the wrist served only to encourage the radicals to undertake more decisive action. On 11 December a small group of them founded a local branch of the Spartakusbund (Spartacist Association), a Bolshevik-inspired group led by Luxemburg and Liebknecht. They vowed to advance the revolution, with force, if necessary. "Does the government want order or does it want anarchy?" asked the *Münchener Neueste Nachrichten* in response to this ominous development.

A high degree of disorder, in fact, seemed Munich's fate in the first months of peace. The presence of huge numbers of demobilized soldiers swelled the ranks of the city's unemployed. BMW laid off thirty-four hundred workers in a single day in mid-December. Food shortages were as acute as ever because the Allies had not yet lifted their blockade of Germany. Soaring inflation made it difficult to buy the little food that was available. Bread had gone up fourfold, while a bottle of wine previously fetching 1.90 marks had gone up to 5.10. Since 1913 building costs had risen 250 percent. To cope with the inflation, Munich issued an "emergency currency."

Misery engendered demonstrations, some of them violent. On New Year's Eve nine people were killed in street brawls; a week later two more died. Eisner passionately condemned the violence, but he rejected pleas from conservatives, as well as from some Socialists, to set up a *Bürgerwehr* (citizens' militia) to assist the police. Therefore, members of the SPD and the bourgeois parties acted on their own, establishing a Republican Security Force independent of the Eisner regime.

Meanwhile, Munich's hydra-headed Right now launched a concerted drive to rid Bavaria of its hapless prime minister. Local newspapers spread the rumor that Eisner was in reality a Galician Jew. Eisner denied the charge but rejected his advisers' calls for press censorship. "Let them insult me as much as they want. That won't bother me. My entire life is open to the world." But it was Eisner's "life" that now seemed so offensive to the hundreds of Münchners who paraded under his office window shouting, "We want a Bavarian! We want a Bavarian!"

Some wanted a Bavarian king. As Josef Hofmiller put it in his diary:

> Bavaria is simply not ripe for this [revolutionary] development. . . . Monarchical sentiment has run deep in our blood for hundreds of years. . . . The *Altbayer* wants to be ruled by someone with a crown, not a top hat; by someone who wears a uniform and not a black coat; by a man who goes to the Oktoberfest in a carriage pulled by six horses and not in a car. Our ruling house and people grew together over the span of 700 years and cannot be driven asunder today or tomorrow by the well-intentioned bromides of a littérateur.

The most concerted and dangerous opposition to Eisner's regime came from the radical *völkisch* faction. The key player here was Julius Lehmann, the right-wing publisher who had campaigned so assiduously for Germany's racial cleansing during the war. On 10 November Lehmann convinced the Thule Society to establish a secret paramilitary organization to overthrow the new government. Called the Kampfbund Thule (Fighting League Thule), the group procured arms from the army command and hid them in Lehmann's publishing house. The plotters included a number of men soon to become prominent in the Nazi movement: Anton Drexler, Hans Frank, Rudolf Hess, and Alfred Rosenberg. Yet the conspiracy also included a government informer, who exposed the Kampfbund's plot. Lehmann and several other conspirators were arrested and imprisoned.

Lehmann was therefore not present when two of his Thule Society colleagues, Karl Harrer and Anton Drexler, met in a cheap Munich hotel on 5 January 1919 to establish a new rightist grouplet called the Deutsche Arbeiterpartei (German Workers' Party, DAP). The new party embraced only a handful of members, but it had big ideas, including the establishment of a *völkisch* dictatorship. Soon, under the name National Socialist German Workers' Party (NSDAP), it would launch a full-scale crusade to realize that goal.

While Thule and the DAP were plotting their next moves, Munich prepared for the Landtag election scheduled for 12 January. The city was awash in electoral propaganda: Handbills and posters were tacked to every conceivable surface; loudspeaker trucks screamed slogans; and, in a startling novelty, airplanes pelted the populace with leaflets. Hofmiller saw the frantic electioneering as one more sad sign of the changing times: "The placards, in all possible screaming colors, resembled carnival advertisements. . . . The Residenz was plastered top to bottom with red propaganda. . . . A long red flag waved sickeningly from the top of the Landtag. From the concierge's cell protruded a similar red banner, which looked exactly like the red flag that chimney sweeps use to signal when they are burning out a flue."

Hofmiller seemed to notice only the red propaganda, but the conservative parties were just as prominently represented. The Bayerische Volkspartei (BVP—previously the Center) claimed that Spartacus lurked behind Eisner and was impatient to push him aside and turn Bavaria into a Soviet-style state. Hoping to tap into Catholic anxieties, the BVP ran a poster depicting a naked man in a gladiator's helmet ripping apart the Frauenkirche with his bare hands. "Christian people! Will you allow Spartacus to tear down your churches? Give your answer on election day!"

Election day was warm and sunny, and some 86 percent of Bavaria's eligible voters turned out to cast ballots. Among them were newly enfranchised women, who made up 53.4 percent of the total electorate in the state. In Munich long lines of nuns and monks stood outside heavily guarded polling places. The USPD complained that the BVP had scoured every monastery and convent for the "cattle vote" it herded to the polls.

The election turned out badly for the prime minister and his party, which statewide won less than 3 percent of the total and only 3 of the 180 contested Landtag seats. The biggest vote getters were the BVP and the SPD, which won 35 percent (66 seats) and 33 percent (61 seats) respectively. In Munich the USPD did a little better, but here too it was overwhelmed by the other parties, especially by the SPD, which won eleven out of twelve precincts. The BVP took little comfort in the Majority Socialists' success, but it delighted in the humiliation of Eisner. "This Jew should no longer stand at the head of a *Volksstaat* whose voters have just handed him a crushing defeat," declared the party.

But Eisner was not yet ready to step off the political stage. He enjoyed being prime minister, and he believed that he was still needed in the post. In addition to the continuing threat from the far Left, he could point to a new threat from the far Right. Just three days after the Bavarian elections rightist soldiers in Berlin murdered Rosa Luxemburg and Karl Liebknecht. Moreover, closer to home counterrevolutionaries in Munich were distributing leaflets urging the establishment of a right-wing dictatorship. Now more than ever, thought Eisner, Germany needed a humane and civilized spokesman.

Martyr for the Revolution

Determined to fill this role himself, in early February 1919 Eisner attended the first postwar conference of the Second Socialist International in Bern, where he repeated his earlier admission of German war guilt and issued an appeal to German prisoners of war in France to help rebuild that devastated country. This gesture ignited a new storm of indignation. Munich newspapers protested that Eisner wished to press German POWs into forced labor. The *Münchener Post* reminded its readers that he represented barely 3 percent of the electorate. "Even in the Socialist camp," gloated Karl Alexander von Müller, the conservative historian, "Eisner is judged as little more than a charlatan or a criminal." Eisner's close friend the radical poet Gustav Landauer had to agree: "Eisner is the most cursed man in Germany." Hoping to force his departure, Auer announced in Eisner's absence that the Landtag would convene on 21 February; the prime minister would have to resign then, if not before.

While Eisner temporized, the radical Left, aware that the SPD and BVP intended to eliminate the council and cast off the last vestiges of the revolution, sought to regain the initiative. On 16 February the leftists staged a large demonstration on the Theresienwiese, followed by a parade into the Old City. Their message was garbled, however, because a number of Majority Socialists carrying placards supporting parliamentary government participated in the demonstration. Eisner too joined the rally in an effort to give it a progovernment slant. He failed to achieve this, but his appearance gave the Right one more reason to brand him a dangerous radical. On the following day Dr. Herbert Field, a Munich-based representative of the American Commission to Negotiate Peace, recorded in his diary: "All that I meet seem to expect Eisner to be assassinated. I fear bloodshed will come before the week is over."

As it happened, Field was right on target. In the course of the next few days Eisner concluded that he would indeed have to resign, and he decided to make the announcement at the opening of parliament on 21 February. That morning he wrote his farewell speech in his office at the Foreign Ministry and dismissed his secretarial staff. Then, at ten sharp, he set off for the Landtag building accompanied by two aides, Friedrich Fechenbach and Benno Merkle, along with two armed guards. Given the death threats. Fechenbach urged Eisner to avoid his regular route, which was dangerously exposed. Eisner replied, "They can only shoot me dead once," as if this were not enough. Thus the quartet took the regular route, Eisner flanked by Merkle and Fechenbach, with the guards walking a few steps in front.

In a doorway around the corner from Eisner's office stood a young man named Count Anton Arco auf Valley. Born in Austria, Arco had served as a lieutenant in the Bavarian Cavalry in the recent war. Like many officers returning to revolutionary Munich, he had had his rank insignia ripped off by radicals. Hating the revolution, he had applied for admission to the Thule Society, only to be rejected on the ground that his mother was Jewish. His girlfriend meanwhile taunted him as a weakling. Of Eisner, he had written: "He is a Jew. He is not a German." In his passion for revenge, he did not stop to think that the assassination of an isolated and impotent leader might not constitute a brilliant stroke for the counterrevolution.

Arco waited until Eisner and his party had passed. Then he ran up behind the prime minister and shot him point-blank in the head and back. The first shot shattered Eisner's skull, while the second pierced one of his lungs. He collapsed on the sidewalk, a pool of blood forming around his body.

His deed accomplished, Arco started to run, but he managed only a few steps before one of Eisner's guards felled him with a shot in the leg. As he lay writhing on the pavement, the guard pumped four more rounds into him. Nonetheless, he was not dead when soldiers carted him to the hospital, where Germany's foremost surgeon, Ernst Ferdinand Sauerbruch, operated to save his life.

There was no need to operate on Eisner. He was already dead when Fechenbach and the two guards carried him back to the Foreign Ministry. Meanwhile, at the spot where he had fallen, sobbing proletarian women dipped handkerchiefs into the drying pool of blood. A crowd of workers and radical soldiers listened to a man swear that the assassin was a paid agent of Eisner's old rival Auer. Another claimed that the killer was a hit man for the BVP. The writer Oskar Maria Graf gained the impression that if someone had advocated shooting a dozen bourgeois, the mob would have done so with alacrity.

Shortly after the assassination one of Eisner's guards, his uniform spattered with blood, rushed into the Landtag and told the delegates what had just transpired in the street outside. Frau Eisner, present to hear her husband's resignation address, fainted and was carried from the building. Someone in the visitors' gallery shouted, "Revenge for Eisner! Down with Auer!" The session adjourned for an hour. When the deputies returned, Auer delivered a brief eulogy, calling Eisner "a man of the most unsullied idealism."

The SPD leader had no sooner sat down when a man entered the hall, pulled a Browning rifle out from under his coat, and blew Auer out of his chair. Critically wounded, Auer survived, saved by the same Professor Sauerbruch who attended to Arco; for a time the two lay in neighboring hospital rooms, and Auer gallantly sent Arco a bouquet of red roses. Auer's assailant, it turned out, was an unemployed butcher named Alois Lindner. After shooting Auer, Lindner turned on his heels and walked back down the aisle, firing at the BVP benches as he went. At the door a porter tried to disarm him, but Lindner shot him dead and escaped. At the same time, an unidentified man in the visitors' gallery began raining bullets on the deputies. They dived madly under their seats, but one BVP man took a fatal shot in the head.

Horrifying as they were, the bloody events of 21 February served only as a prologue to the agonizing drama that was to unfold in the coming weeks. Overnight Eisner became a martyred saint to many people who had been calling for his ouster, or even for his death, just a few days before. "It is strange," observed a young girl after the killing, "up until now I heard people ask every day, 'Is there no bullet for Eisner?,' but since he's been shot, everyone is beating his breast and cursing his murderer." Eisner's death, agreed Karl Alexander von Müller, prompted the "greatest mood swing" he had ever seen in Munich. Having thoroughly damned the prime minister during his term in office, people were now hailing him "as a hero, messiah, liberator and unifier of the proletariat."

Of course, not everyone became a convert. Eisner's bloody end, even more than his controversial policies, polarized Bavaria. Most of Munich's middle- and upper-class citizens were happy to see him out of the way, and some even welcomed the violent manner in which this was effected. Thomas Mann, who did not approve of the murder, recorded that his son Klaus's schoolmates "applauded and danced when the news came." In the privacy of his diary, Hofmiller made fun of the proletarian women who bloodied their hankies at the assassination scene. How could they have been sure that the stuff they were mopping up belonged to Eisner and not to Arco auf Valley? he wondered. The wife of racist publisher Julius Lehmann declared that she and her friends "breathed more easily" upon learning of Eisner's death since "we held [him] to be an evil spirit."

Perhaps these ladies would not have breathed so easily had they experienced what another bourgeois woman, the writer Ricarda Huch, witnessed on the afternoon of 21 February. Strolling on the Ludwigstrasse with her daughter, she encountered a mob from the proletarian suburbs. "One noted faces that one rarely saw [in this quarter]: angry, inhuman, threatening faces. . . . They stared at our sort with undisguised menace [and] made threatening comments that we were clearly meant to understand."

TOP: *The Feldherrnhalle and Theatinerkirche.* (Stadtarchiv München)
BOTTOM: *Marienplatz, Munich's central square.* (Stadtarchiv München)

ABOVE: *The Prince Regent Luitpold, 1901.* (Stadtarchiv München)

OPPOSITE, TOP: *The Ludwigstrasse, with Ludwigskirche.* (Stadtarchiv München)

OPPOSITE, BOTTOM: *Garden Court at the Hofbräuhaus, 1896.* (Stadtarchiv München)

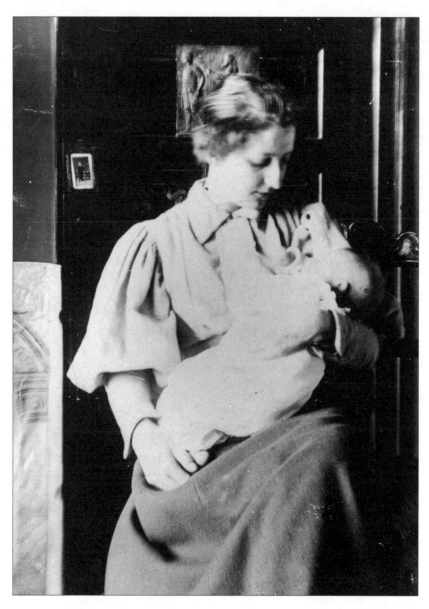

ABOVE: *The "Queen of Schwabing": Fanny zu Reventlow and son, Ralf.* (Stadtarchiv München)

OPPOSITE, TOP: *Fasching Party of the Journalists and Writers' Association, Schwabing, 1905.* (Stadtarchiv München)

OPPOSITE, BOTTOM: *A scene at Café Simplicissimus, one of Schwabing's many bohemian watering holes. The café was named after the famous satirical magazine.* (Stadtarchiv München)

OPPOSITE, TOP: *The Cosmic Circle plus one: (left to right) Karl Wolfskehl, Alfred Schuler, Ludwig Klages, Stefan George, Albert Verwey.* (Bildarchiv Preussischer Kulturbesitz)

OPPOSITE, BELOW: *Bavarian troops marching off to war, 1914.* (Stadtarchiv München)

RIGHT: *General Erich Ludendorff, 1917.*

Prorepublican soldiers in front of the Bavarian Landtag during the revolution of 1918. (Stadtarchiv München)

ABOVE: *Return of the Bavarian Second Infantry Regiment from the front, December 1918.*
RIGHT: *Kurt Eisner, leader of the Bavarian revolution of 1918–19.* (Bildarchiv Preussischer Kulturbesitz)

Heinrich and Thomas Mann. (Bildarchiv Preussischer Kulturbesitz)

LEFT: *Hitler's first residence in Munich: Schleissheimerstrasse 34.* (Library of Congress)

BELOW: *A Nazi speaker addresses the crowd in the Marienplatz during Hitler's Beer Hall Putsch, 9 November 1923.* (Library of Congress)

Determined to keep alive the passions aroused by Eisner's murder, his followers erected a bizarre shrine at the death site. It consisted of a dozen rifles stacked in a pyramid over a pile of flowers; a wreath holding Eisner's picture hung on a wire in the middle. According to an American reporter, women and children constantly added fresh flowers to the pile. Their piety, he suggested, was inspired not just by remorse but also by the knowledge that "in all the well-to-do sections, men and women of property and privilege were saying openly that Eisner ought to have been shot, that he was nothing but a Galician Jew anyway and never a Bavarian." Certainly the Thule Society held this view. One of its members desecrated Eisner's shrine by sprinkling it with the urine of a bitch in heat; soon every male dog from miles around was lifting his leg on the sacred spot.

The "Schwabing Soviet"

Ironically, if Eisner had managed to resign as he had intended, parliamentary government might have been introduced. As it was, power now passed to a new ad hoc revolutionary body calling itself the Zentralrat (Central Council), which consisted of eleven delegates drawn from the left-SPD, USPD, and Communists. The Zentralrat immediately called for a three-day general strike and imposed a curfew on the capital. Revolutionary soldiers patrolled the streets and set up machine-gun posts on prominent corners. Because the university had been a bastion of anti-Eisner sentiment, it was shut down until further notice. The new government also took control of Bavaria's non-Socialist press, forcing the Catholic *Bayerische Kurier* to publish atheistic articles and the national liberal *Münchener Neueste Nachrichten* to run Socialistic pieces. More ominously, the council decreed that members of the Socialist parties would receive arms from army stockpiles, while all bourgeois citizens had to turn in any weapons they possessed. Finally, the new rulers ordered prominent bourgeois organizations to hand over fifty representatives as "hostages" to the state; three of these would be shot for every revolutionary harmed, the regime warned.

On 26 February the mild man whose violent death had brought Munich to such a pass was laid to rest in a state funeral that would have done a Wittelsbach proud. By order of the Zentralrat, Munich's Town Hall was wreathed in black and all its churches flew red flags from their spires. To the sounds of cannon salutes, muffled drums, and tolling church bells—rung, in some cases, by priests at gunpoint—Eisner's cortege made its way through the Old City to the main cemetery east of town. The prime minister's casket rested on an ornate carriage appropriated from the royal house; the driver was a former royal coachman who had changed his political spots but not his uniform, which was Wittelsbach blue and white trimmed with gray fur. At the cemetery Gustav Landauer delivered a eulogy in which he compared Eisner to Goethe, Jesus, Jan Hus, and the prophets of the Old Testament. Like Jesus and Hus, said Landauer, Eisner had been killed by stupidity and greed, and like the prophets, he had "wrestled with weak, wretched human beings because he loved humanity." Heinrich Mann offered another commemoration, declaring: "The hundred days of Eisner's government brought more ideas, more joys of rationality, more intellectual stimulation, than the fifty years that went before."

"The outlook is extremely dark. I expect to see a bolshevist reign installed in the near future," wrote Herbert Field on the day of Eisner's funeral. Again the American was prescient, though it would be a few weeks before Munich witnessed the installation of a Bolshevist-style regime. In the meantime the city seesawed between efforts to extend the revolution and to restore order. That all these measures were undertaken in Eisner's name was a testament to the ambiguity of his legacy.

Following its flurry of radical gestures, the Zentralrat began to backpedal toward a more moderate course. Under pressure from the SPD and the middle-class parties, Ernst Niekisch convinced his colleagues to release their bourgeois hostages and to drop efforts to build a working-class armed guard. Moreover, rather than decree that Bavaria would be ruled by a council system, the Zentralrat convened a Congress of Bavarian Councils to debate whether the councils or the parliament should hold decisive power.

As the congress began its deliberations on 25 February, mobs of radical soldiers and unemployed workers assembled in two of Munich's largest beer halls and demanded the creation of a soviet republic. Rowdy delegations then marched to the congress meeting, determined to press for a soviet regime and a Red Army.

The radicals had an ally within the congress in the person of Max Levien, head of the local Communist Party. Of Huguenot extraction, the Russian-born Levien had run one of Munich's soldiers' councils in the November revolution. An admirer of Lenin, he was more like a Schwabing bohemian than a disciplined Bolshevik. He slouched about in a rumpled uniform, drank heavily, and allegedly rented out his wife as a prostitute. Now he urged a "second revolution"—that is, a permanent enshrinement of the council system in place of parliamentary government. However, when he and Erich Mühsam presented a motion on 28

February—a week after Eisner's murder—calling for a soviet republic, the congress rejected it by a vote of 234 to 70. Clearly, the majority of Bavaria's council members were still committed to the principle of parliamentary government. Indeed, the congress next agreed, by an equally lopsided vote, to recall the Landtag as soon as possible.

News of these decisions prompted new demonstrations of revolutionary outrage in Munich. On 1 March a crowd of several thousand radicals gathered on the Theresienwiese to demand the proclamation of a soviet. However, before matters could go any further, the recently created SPD militia, the Republican Security Force, broke up the rally, killing three men. This timely show of force allowed the congress to finish its deliberations without any more intrusions from the streets.

In its final meeting, on 8 March, the congress stipulated that the Landtag should select a new cabinet and draw up a constitution based on parliamentary principles. Understandably Levien was furious. The congress had "labored and brought forth a mouse," he fumed. The Communist delegates stalked out of the congress, and Levien and some other radicals withdrew from the Zentralrat. The moderates heaved a collective sigh of relief.

Ten days later the Landtag met and appointed a new cabinet. The incoming prime minister was Johannes Hoffmann, who had served as minister of education and culture under Eisner. A tall, handsome man in his early fifties, Hoffmann had originally belonged to the left wing of the SPD, then moved to the center. "Every revolution has two enemies," he liked to say, "one to the right, the other to the left." In order to lead Bavaria safely between Right and Left, he put together a cabinet containing no BVP members or Communists. He launched his new government with the words "The political act which Prime Minister Eisner wanted to undertake on 21 February is now accomplished."

Hoffmann meant by this that parliamentary government was now safely established, but his declaration was premature, for thousands of radicals in the capital still hoped for a second revolution. Their demands might have subsided had the city and state not faced a continuing array of seemingly insoluable socioeconomic problems. Bavaria's economic condition was, as Hoffmann admitted, "wretched," particularly in Munich, where unemployment had now reached almost forty thousand, and municipal debt had climbed to eighty-five million marks. The capital's credit was so bad that state-run agencies like the post office had stopped accepting Munich's emergency currency. As ever, food shortages kept a good portion of the population hungry and (in the opinion of the observant Mr. Field) "mentally unbalanced." Shortages propelled the black market, which remained the chief source of food and fuel, despite escalating prices. Perhaps worst of all, Münchners could not escape their miseries in the traditional pre-Lenten Carnival festivities, for the police had determined that the times were too troubled for such antics.

As if all these woes were not enough, Hoffmann's regime had to contend with a challenge from the Reich in the form of a draft constitution for the new Weimar Republic that would deprive Bavaria of most of its cherished sovereign rights. Under the new system Bavaria could no longer maintain its own military command, diplomatic corps, post and telegraph service, transportation system, and direct taxation arrangements; even its precious beer tax, the source of critical state revenue, was in jeopardy. Some BVP politicians were so incensed by the new constitutional plan that they advocated Bavaria's secession from the Reich. While agreeing that the new system demanded too many sacrifices from Munich, Hoffmann refused to mount a frontal attack on the national government, proposing instead to search for a "middle way" between Bavarian particularism and extreme national centralism. He ruled out secession, insisting that a "Bavaria outside the Reich is a thing of impossibility." Not surprisingly, this stance made *him* a thing of impossibility to militant particularists. In an editorial entitled "Eisner and Hoffmann," the *Bayerische Kurier* grumbled that when it came to standing up for states' rights, even the "Jew from Berlin" had been a better Bavarian than Hoffmann.

Yet it was the radical Left that, at least for the moment, presented the greatest threat to Hoffmann's regime. Despite their setback on 1 March, radical agitators continued to pack beer halls with anti-Hoffmann rallies. Planes dropped leaflets declaring (falsely) that all Bavaria stood behind the radicals. These elements got a powerful boost from abroad when, on 22 March, Communist forces in Hungary overthrew the existing bourgeois government and established a soviet. Budapest's new ruler, Béla Kun, called upon Bavarian radicals to emulate his example. "The news from Hungary hit Munich like a bomb," wrote Mühsam.

Fearing that Munich might go the way of Budapest, Hoffmann announced that the Landtag would reconvene on 8 April, two months earlier than originally scheduled. For Bavaria's radicals, this was yet another act of treachery. Meeting in Augsburg on 3 April, they passed resolutions demanding a Bavarian soviet and alliances with Moscow and Budapest. They dispatched a delegation to Munich with orders to negotiate with Hoffmann, threatening a general strike if he proved intractable.

The prime minister, however, was not available to negotiate. Sensing trouble, he had left for Berlin to confer with the Scheidemann government about the looming crisis in Munich. In his absence a panicky Zentralrat rescinded Hoffmann's recall of the Landtag. No doubt it was influenced by a rally of some four thousand radical soldiers in the Löwenbräukeller. The Munich garrison, for its part, announced that if a general strike broke out, it would side with the striking workers and offer no protection to the government. Someone installed machine guns around the Landtag, presumably to discourage anyone from meeting there.

On 5 April, against this ominous backdrop, the remaining members of Hoffmann's government, along with about 150 representatives from the Socialist parties, the Communists, and the councils, met in the Ministry of Military Affairs to sort out the next steps in the Bavarian revolution. Host for the gathering was Hoffmann's military minister, Ernst Schneppenhorst, a former lumber union official from Nuremberg who was known to distrust the council movement. The leading spokesman for the radicals was a Communist named Eugen Leviné, who had recently arrived from the German Communist Party (KPD) headquarters in Berlin with orders to instill more discipline into the local branch. The new leader, whose real name was Niessen, was a Russian-born Jew who had been educated in Germany, fought in the Russian revolution of 1905, suffered arrest and torture at the hands of czarist police, and eventually returned to Germany to fight in the revolution of 1918. An ugly little man with a high, nasal voice, he was known to be tough, resourceful, and shrewd. Everyone expected a fierce battle between him and the equally determined Schneppenhorst.

As it happened, a battle did erupt, but with the chief antagonists taking positions that no one would have predicted. Like political cross-dressers, the rightist Social Democrat Schneppenhorst urged the proclamation of a soviet, while the Communist Leviné vehemently opposed this action. Schneppenhorst's strategy, it seems, was akin to inviting the bandit into the bank and asking him to run it; presumably he would be tamed by his responsibilities. Unluckily for Schneppenhorst, Leviné saw through this stratagem and was not tempted by it. Like his mentor Lenin, he did not believe that Communists should participate in inept bourgeois governments; they should wait until conditions allowed them to seize power and then rule by themselves. As Leviné put it at the meeting, "We can only take part in a republic of councils if it is proclaimed by the councils—and if the majority of them are communists. We can only participate in a council regime pursuing a communist policy—and only the communists themselves can do that." He added that he understood what Schneppenhorst was trying to do: He was trying to launch a "pseudo-putsch from a smoke-filled room." Livid, Schneppenhorst responded that he would not be insulted by a "Jewish goblin" from Russia.

The delegates watched this exchange with consternation. They were in a dilemma, for if they now proclaimed a soviet, as Schneppenhorst had proposed, they would have to do so without the Communists, and that was like setting up a church without priests. Avoiding a decision, they adjourned for forty-eight hours so that delegates could travel to other Bavarian cities and test the political wind blowing in the provinces.

This allowed Schneppenhorst to attend an SPD conference in his native Nuremberg, where he discovered that the Socialists, not to mention the local bourgeois parties, were vehemently opposed to any radical experiments. He was instructed to withdraw his call for a soviet. He was happy enough to do so, for he had never been comfortable in his red suit, even if he had donned it only as a disguise. He returned to Munich to try to undo the damage he had caused.

But he was too late. Munich was not like Nuremberg. Radicals were running through the streets screaming the Bolshevist slogan "All Power to the Soviets!" These zealots seemed to believe that Munich could do for Germany what Budapest had done for Hungary and Petrograd and Moscow had done for Russia. Radical soldiers were threatening to give military muscle to this enterprise. The local bourgeoisie, having been forced out of the political picture since the war, was cowed and irresolute, waiting behind closed shutters for rescue. Some even entertained the grimly vengeful view that a Communist takeover in Central Europe might not be so bad because at least it would tweak the hated Western powers. As Thomas Mann wrote in his diary on 5 April, "We are on the point of declaring a soviet republic here, to be allied, moreover, with the Hungarian and Russian soviets. I find Bavaria terribly comical, and see all this as little more than mischief, but I would like to see the Allies forced to swallow it, and I almost love communism insofar as it is pitted against the Entente."

The very next evening Bavaria's political drama grew even more amusing, as a ragtag collection of council representatives gathered in the queen's suite of the Wittelsbach Palace to resume the deliberations broken off two days earlier. Ernst Toller recalled the scene in his memoirs: "The great rooms where once maids-in-waiting and powdered lackeys had fawned attendance on their royal masters now rang with the heavy tread of workmen, farmers, and soldiers. Red Guards, couriers, and typists leaned out from the silk-curtained windows of the ex-queen's bedroom."

The meeting was called to order by Niekisch in his capacity as chairman of the Zentralrat, but Gustav Landauer, the gentle anarchist, set the tone. As an old friend of Eisner's, Landauer enjoyed a certain moral authority, buttressed by his reputation as a literary scholar who had translated Walt Whitman. Like Eisner, he resembled an Old Testament prophet, with a bent frame, black hair down to his shoulders, and flowing beard. Philosophically he shared Eisner's commitment to the nonviolent transformation of capitalist society. Unlike Eisner, he emphasized his Jewishness, believing that the Jews had a messianic mission to unite all nations and to effect the spiritual elevation of the world. Now, at the meeting in the queen's bedroom, he argued passionately that the group should, in a "creative revolutionary act," proclaim itself the government of Bavaria in place of Hoffmann, who was still in Berlin. After little discussion his motion carried with one abstention, by Niekisch.

This done, the meeting turned to the business of appointing ministers—or, as they preferred to call them, "people's commissars." Almost immediately Erich Mühsam proposed himself for the post of commissar for foreign affairs. He had, as he pointed out, an excellent reputation abroad and solid leftist credentials. But the other delegates were not convinced. As Niekisch recalled, "He [Mühsam] was an effervescent, witty spirit, a good man, but obviously so much a literary bohemian that no one could imagine him holding a responsible office." After an embarrassed silence Landauer declared that while he respected Mühsam as a person, he could not see him as foreign commissar, a verdict quickly seconded by others, including Toller. The latter, it turned out, had his own favorite for the job, one Dr. Theodor Lipp, whom Toller had brought along to the meeting. No one had heard of Lipp, but Toller assured his colleagues that the gentleman, who sported an impressive goatee and an immaculate suit, was an accomplished diplomat and expert on foreign affairs. Perhaps embarrassed to be unacquainted with so worthy a figure, the delegates promptly voted Lipp in.

Someone then proposed that Niekisch become commissar for education and enlightenment, but he declined, allowing Landauer to put himself forward for the job. There was another embarrassed silence. Eventually a representative from the Farmers' League observed that it would be inadvisable to appoint a non-Bavarian, and a Jew at that, to a post dealing with matters of culture, education, and religion. But just as it appeared that Landauer would be rejected, Mühsam roundly berated his colleagues for harboring sentiments that belonged to a "bygone age." The revolution, he said, demanded a new outlook and new leaders. Those objecting to Landauer on grounds that he was a Jew were nothing but "reactionaries." The Zentralrat members unanimously approved Landauer as commissar for education and enlightenment.

As the delegates were finishing their selection of commissars, Eugen Leviné suddenly appeared on the scene. Most delegates welcomed his arrival, for they still felt uncomfortable about proclaiming a soviet without any genuine soviet personnel and hoped that Leviné was now prepared to endorse their plan. But he was not; he simply wanted to condemn them again for trying to create a new order in collaboration with "soiled" repesentatives of the old one. Some of the delegates were so disturbed by the Communist opposition that they proposed dropping the whole idea of a Bavarian soviet. But the majority was determined to press on, fearful that if they did not, radical soldiers and unemployed workers would do it for them. In his motion for a soviet, Landauer said this would "signal the dawn of a new era of universal peace and noble humanity." The delegates passed Landauer's motion, again with Niekisch's abstention. Even before the final vote was taken, in the early-morning hours of 7 April, telegrams were being dispatched across the land announcing the new order and urging towns and villages to celebrate by ringing church bells.

Most Bavarians were not inclined to ring any bells when they learned that their venerable state, thanks to the machinations of a cabal of radicals in Munich, was now a soviet republic. The mayors of Regensburg, Augsburg, and Rosenheim said they would cooperate with the new regime, but almost all the smaller and medium-size towns registered staunch opposition. So did Bavaria's second-largest city, Nuremberg, home of Schneppenhorst and headquarters of two army corps that were likely to follow his bidding. It was to Nuremberg that Prime Minister Hoffmann traveled after leaving Berlin and before establishing a rival government in nearby Bamberg. The stage seemed to be set for a violent confrontation between Munich and the rest of the state.

But even in Munich itself most residents were anything but enthusiastic about the new soviet, which they immediately dubbed the Schwabing Soviet, the latest harebrained scheme from that nest of coffeehouse dilettantes. This view was aptly summarized by Hofmiller in his diary on 7 April: "I just don't understand why the gentlemen did not [issue their proclamation] a week earlier. [The first of] April would have been a more appropriate date." But there was also fear that this farce might quickly degenerate into genuine tragedy. Thomas Mann, for one, expected "a fourth and totally radical upheaval before reaction sets in." He could not have been more sagacious.

Even the new rulers sensed that they might be operating on borrowed time. On 7 April Landauer wrote a friend: "I am now Commissar for propaganda, education, science, art, and a few other things. If I am allowed a few weeks' time, I hope to accomplish something, but there is a possibility that it will only be a couple days and then it will have been but a dream." Niekisch, who was now chief of state by virtue of his presidency of the Zentralrat, did not want to participate in the dream at all. Hoping to bring Hoffmann back to Munich, he resigned on 8 April. His place was taken by twenty-five-year-old Ernst Toller, who wondered what this latest twist in Bavaria's revolution portended. "What would it achieve? How would it end?" he asked.

Yet there were high expectations in some quarters. President Toller's anteroom was filled with people who, in his words, "believed that the Soviet republic had been expressly created to satisfy [their] own private desires." One woman wanted papers so she could get married; a man wanted to force his landlord to remit his rent; a group of self-professed revolutionaries demanded that Toller arrest their personal enemies. There were also legions of cranks offering advice for the betterment of humanity. Variously, they proposed that the world's evil resided in cooked food, the gold standard, unhygienic underwear, technology, the lack of a universal language, department stores, or birth control. A Swabian shoemaker submitted a voluminous pamphlet proving (in Toller's words) that "modern man owed his moral sickness to the fact that he satisfied his elementary needs in closed rooms and with the aid of artificial paper; whereas if he spent these daily moments out in the woods and availed himself of the natural moss all spiritual poisons would also evaporate into the surrounding air, and he would be at the same time bodily and spiritually purified, returning to his work with a strengthened social conscience and a diminished egoism; true love of humanity would be awakened and the Kingdom of God on Earth would be at hand."

Alas, Toller and his colleagues did not adopt any of these possibly pathbreaking ideas. What they *did* do, however, was outlandish enough to horrify most Bavarians. In a blizzard of decrees the new government set about conjuring up the Socialist millennium. Banks and large industrial concerns were ordered nationalized. Restaurants and cafés were closed, save for the Stefanie, which served as an unofficial headquarters for the revolution. Landauer declared that henceforth the Bavarian universities would be run by the students, and professors would give up their titles. He placed the press under the jurisdiction of a new censorship board composed exclusively of Schwabing literati. He also ordered the end of "legalistic thinking" and required newspapers to print the poems of Hölderlin and Schiller on their front pages. The commissar for justice, taking a leaf from the French Revolution, established "revolutionary tribunals" with the aim of rooting out counterrevolutionary activity. The finance commissar, in an effort to halt the flight of capital, prohibited depositors from removing more than two hundred marks per day from their bank accounts. The agriculture commissar announced plans for a sweeping collectivization of Bavaria's farms. The housing commissar froze all rents, ordered that unused lofts in the city be turned over to artists for studio space, and decreed that henceforth all houses must be built with the living rooms above the kitchen.

In an effort to prevent bourgeois Münchners from hoarding food, government troops sporadically searched homes of the well-to-do. On one occasion a soviet patrol invaded the villa of Professor Erich Marks, noted biographer of Bismarck. Finding the pantry shockingly bare, one of the soldiers whispered to Marks's wife: "Listen, I can give you an address where you can get some things—eggs, butter, and bacon." Amid all this activity, someone in the government found time to decree that henceforth the German name for Bavaria, Bayern, should be spelled with an *i* rather than a *y*.

Odd and unsettling as many of these measures were, they seemed almost ordinary compared with the activities of the new commissar for foreign affairs, Dr. Lipp. In response to a congratulatory message from Soviet Russia's foreign minister, Georgi Chicherin, Lipp sent a telegram to Lenin saying that the proletariat of South Bavaria was "firmly joined together as a hammer" but complaining that the "fugitive Hoffmann took the toilet key to my ministry with him." He went on to say that "the hairy gorilla hands of Gustav Noske [military minister in the Reich government] are dripping in blood" and signed off with references to Kant's plea for eternal peace. In case Lenin was indifferent, he sent a copy of this missive to the pope, whom he addressed as an intimate friend. The pope did not respond, but Lenin, obviously worried about what was going on in Munich, wrote back to inquire about the revolution's specific accomplishments, tactfully ignoring the toilet key crisis.

Learning of Lipp's busy international correspondence, his colleagues did some checking on him and discovered that he had recently been released from an insane asylum. They concluded that he must be removed from office immediately. Toller ordered Lipp to come see him. When he appeared, Lipp asked Toller: "Have you seen the King's bathroom? I tell you it's a scandal. I found a little boat there and the lackey told me that instead of governing King Ludwig used to sit in a hot bath for hours on end playing with his little boat." Exasperated, Toller handed Lipp a copy of the lost privy key telegram and asked him if he was responsible for it. Lipp replied proudly that he had written it with his own hand. Toller then handed him a letter of resignation to sign. Lipp rose somberly from his chair, smoothed the lapels of his frock coat, stroked his Henri IV beard, and signed. "Even this I do for the Republic," he said with a sigh. However, that afternoon he was back in his office dispatching more telegrams, and he had to be "kindly but firmly taken away."

Lipp's dismissal, while obviously necessary, was of little moment, since the Schwabing Soviet was now under heavy attack from all sides. Among the attackers were the Communists, who decided that they could not allow this pack of coffeehouse intellectuals to stay in business. In an abrupt change of tactics, Leviné declared on 8 April that if Munich were to have a soviet, it must be a genuine one. On the following day, at a huge rally in the Mathäserbräu, he tried unsuccessfully to convince Toller to turn over power to him.

The Hoffmann government in Bamberg, meanwhile, was searching for ways to bring down the Munich soviet. Hoffmann rejected an offer of federal troops from the Reich government, fearing that their use even against an unpopular regime would inflame particularist hatreds against the "Prussians." He therefore began to assemble a militia from native stock, and while these forces were gathering for a march on Munich, he did all he could to isolate the capital. Farmers loyal to Hoffmann stopped delivering food; telephone, postal, and rail service was cut; and the central bank in Berlin suspended money transfers to Munich. At the same time, Hoffmann's people made contact with elements inside the capital that were prepared to help overthrow the soviet. Key to Bamberg's fifth column was the Republican Security Force, which maintained an outpost in Munich's central train station. The Thule Society meanwhile was busy recruiting anti-Soviet forces among the right-wing fraternities.

Hoffmann probably could have destroyed the soviet by slowly starving it to death, but with the Reich government demanding a quick solution, he decided to unleash his fifth column. At dawn on Palm Sunday, 13 April, the security force staged a surprise attack on the Wittelsbach Palace, arresting many of the soviet leaders and conveying them to the railroad station. Confident that they would soon receive additional support from Hoffmann, they put up posters declaring that the Zentralrat had been overthrown and the legitimate government reinstated.

Like so many ambitious pronouncements in those chaotic days, this decree expressed a wish rather than a reality. The Palm Sunday Putsch had indeed eliminated the Schwabing Soviet, but this simply opened the way for the Communists to make their own grab for power. After gathering at the Theresienwiese, heavily armed soldiers loyal to the KPD marched into the Old City. Sunday strollers ducked for cover as bullets started whizzing around the Marienplatz. A sailor playing pool in a restaurant took a fatal shot in the head; several other people were wounded.

Then the leftists attacked the security force barricaded in the train station. According to a witness, the opposing forces exchanged sporadic machine-gun bursts, small-arms fire, and grenades for several hours; the large metal train schedules were riddled with holes. By 9:00 P.M., with their ammunition exhausted and no relief in sight, the security force fled the building through the rear by rail.

While the train station firefight was still in progress, Eugen Leviné was presiding over a meeting at the Hofbräuhaus. The men to whom he spoke, all veterans of the Council of Workers, Soldiers, and Peasants, agreed to establish themselves as the "legislature" of a new Bavarian soviet, this time a real one under the leadership of a four-man Vollzugsrat (Executive Committee) controlled by the Russian-born Communists Leviné, Levien, and Towien Axelrod. Leviné declared that the new regime would represent "the genuine rule of the proletariat" and that it would carry on its "unavoidable struggle like its Russian brothers."

"We Bavarians Are Not Russians!"

Munich's Communist-dominated soviet began with brave words, but its situation was bleak. Talk of fraternal ties to Russia and Hungary notwithstanding, the new rulers could expect no support from either of those places, since Russia was racked with civil war and the Hungarian soviet was collapsing. Furthermore, the Reich government and most of the rest of Bavaria resolutely opposed Munich's latest and most alarming political experiment.

Aware of the hostility surrounding them, but confident that the wheels of history were rolling irrevocably in their direction, the soviet leaders immediately took steps to extend and protect the revolution. They proclaimed a general strike of indefinite duration and threatened to shoot anyone who did not abide by it. They disarmed the Munich police and distributed weapons among workers who pledged loyalty to the new regime. To ward off attacks from outside, they began building a Red Army composed of demobilized soldiers, radical trade unionists, and some leftover Italian and Russian prisoners of war. Commandant of the Red Army was one Rudolf Egelhofer, a twenty-six-year-old North German sailor who been active in the naval mutiny in Kiel in November 1918. An admirer described him as "a comet in the revolutionary sky." But he was a dark star, fond of complaining that there were as yet no lampposts in Munich with reactionary generals hanging from them.

It was one thing to recruit a new army, quite another to feed, equip, and pay for it. Isolated as it was, the new regime was virtually without material resources. To get what it needed, the Vollzugsrat decided to shake down the bourgeois population of Munich. Soldiers combed the wealthier parts of town, collecting foodstuffs, linens, clothing, and silverware. Fearing that his own house would be hit, Thomas Mann practiced what he would say to potential looters: "Look, boys, I am not a Jew, or a war-profiteer, or anything else that's bad. I'm just a writer who built this house with money earned from intellectual labor. I have 200 marks in my desk drawer, which I'll give you. Divide it among yourselves, but don't take away my furnishings and books."

Not content with informal plundering, the Vollzugsrat also required citizens to turn over all their cash in exchange for credit slips. When people showed little interest in emptying their pockets for the regime, they were ordered to open their safety-deposit boxes and private safes. Of course, Münchners balked at this too, and these measures netted only about fifty thousand marks. Thus the new government resorted to the dangerous tactic of its predecessors: It ordered a printing firm to turn out millions of marks in "emergency currency."

Since the Bavarian soviet was to be a "dictatorship of the proletariat," the new regime openly encouraged class warfare. It put up posters in the poorer districts saying, "Come out of your slums! Flats are available! Help yourselves!" It promised to distribute food confiscated from bourgeois and aristocratic hoarders. In one much-celebrated instance Red guards handed out a bathtub full of eggs that they had commandeered from a countess. But because the Red Army had priority access to all confiscated items, Munich's poor got little of the takings.

Indeed, food shortages had become more acute than ever, as Munich was effectively blockaded by the Hoffmann government and hostile peasants. The soviet nominally controlled some farming regions in the immediate vicinity of the city, but the farmers ignored injunctions to deliver food to the "Red swine." Milk was in particularly short supply. When dairy deliveries fell to one tenth of normal, the Vollzugsrat declared that churning milk into butter or cheese was "sabotage of the Soviet Republic" and punishable by death. Next, the regime outlawed the consumption of milk by anyone but small children who were certified by a doctor to be in immediate danger of death from malnutrition. Leviné, however, was not overly distressed by the milk crisis because he saw it as a long-term gain for the revolution. "What does it matter if for a few weeks less milk reaches Munich?" he asked. "Most of it goes to the children of the bourgeoisie anyway. We are not interested in keeping them alive. No harm if they die—they'd only grow into enemies of the proletariat."

Horror stories from Munich about hungry children and plundering soldiers put the Hoffmann government in a bind. The soviet's days were clearly numbered, but given the brutality of Leviné and company, the collapse might not come until after many innocent citizens had starved. It was imperative, therefore, to employ armed force against the soviet and to do so on a scale large enough to accomplish the task in short order. Yet Hoffmann still hoped to keep this operation Bavarian, or at least South German, so his enemies could not play the ever-effective anti-Prussian card. Thus he urged his fellow Bavarians to join one of the many paramilitary Freikorps (Free Corps) units that were being organized to march on Munich. He also accepted neighboring Württemberg's offer of Free Corps volunteers. The appeals his government issued deserve quotation for their nativist tone. "Russian terror reigns in Munich," declared Transportation Minister Heinrich von Frauendorfer. "Led by alien insurgents, Communists have seized power. . . . If we do not want to experience the fate of Russia, we must protect our threatened Bavarian land to the last man. Volunteers from all parts of the state must report immediately to assembly points and gather weapons. Not an hour of hesitation!" On the following day Hoffmann himself added an appeal:

> Bavarians! Countrymen! In Munich there rages a Russian terror, directed by alien elements. This insult to Bavaria cannot be allowed to last another day, another minute. All Bavarians must do their part, irrespective of party. . . . You men of the Bavarian mountains, Bavarian plains, Bavarian forests, rise up as one, gather in your villages with weapons and equipment, select your leaders. . . . Munich calls for your aid. Step forward! Now! The Munich disgrace must be wiped out. That is the honorable duty of all Bavarians!

Honorable, perhaps, yet also highly problematical, for the Free Corps units Hoffmann was gathering were not just fiercely anti-Communist but also, for the most part, militantly antidemocratic and racist. Their ranks were filled with ex-soldiers who had served on the front, as well as with younger men who yearned for military experience. The most important of the Bavarian Free Corps was led by Franz Ritter von Epp, a former commander of the Bavarian Life Guards, who despised the new Weimar Republic and dreamed of bringing back the monarchy. Epp's right-hand man was Ernst Röhm, a swashbuckling army captain who was soon to gain notoriety as chief of Hitler's storm troopers. Like many of the other Free Corps units, Epp's group had ties to the Thule Society, which smuggled money and men out of beleaguered Munich to the forces massing in the hinterlands.

While the various Free Corps and militia groups were gathering for the assault on Munich, conditions in the city became ever more desperate. There was now no food in the stores, nor gas or coal to be had. Berlin's representative in Munich reported that even the local workers were becoming fed up with the constant strikes and military maneuvers. On 10 April Munich's moribund city council sent a secret missive to Bamberg complaining that the soviet was running the city into the ground and brutalizing the citizenry. It promised a rebellion from within if Hoffmann would send soldiers.

On 14 April a skirmish broke out between a unit of the Red Army and some Hoffmann troops deployed around Dachau. Commanding the Red forces was Ernst Toller, who had decided to ally himself with the new soviet despite some serious reservations about its Russian leaders. Toller's outfit managed to win this engagement, but only because the enemy forces were even more incompetent and ill led. This minor Red victory was sufficient to convince Hoffmann that he needed a more effective force to liberate the capital. Breaking his vow to do without Reich assistance, he requested federal troops from Berlin's military minister, Gustav Noske. The latter promptly promised twenty thousand men, including several thousand Prussians. But he insisted as a condition that overall command of the assault force must rest with General Ernst von Oven, a Prussian. Hoffmann's acceptance of this condition signaled a new humiliation of Bavaria by Prussia. In fact, one might say that Noske achieved following the defeat of 1918 what Bismarck had not risked after the victory of 1871; his intervention in the old Wittelsbach realm crowned the work of the Iron Chancellor.

As the vise around Munich continued to tighten, divisions split the ranks of the town's defenders. While the Communist leadership grimly adopted a siege mentality, some of the other soviet leaders, notably Ernst Toller, developed second thoughts about greasing the wheels of history with massive quantities of blood. Toller had already gotten himself in trouble with Leviné and Egelhofer by refusing to bombard Dachau and by protesting the gang rape of a young girl by thirty Red soldiers. He had also gone out of his way to prevent his colleagues from adding Thomas Mann to their cache of bourgeois hostages. Now, with the Whites closing in, he argued that "We had no right to call the workers to battle when the only prospect was certain defeat; no right to call the workers to shed their blood for no purpose at all."

Toller found some allies within the Council of Workers, Soldiers, and Peasants, which had continued to meet daily in the Hofbräuhaus. A young bank clerk who had been made to serve as the regime's finance minister charged that the confiscation of private goods and bank accounts was "political theft." At a council meeting on 26 April the clerk and Toller accused the Communists of using their Russian revolutionary credentials to intimidate the local radicals. "The great feat of the Russian Revolution lends to these men a magic luster," said Toller. "Experienced German Communists stare at them as if dazzled." Determined, at this late hour, to break free of the Russian spell, the council passed a vote of censure against the Vollzugsrat and formed a countergovernment of its own. It justified its action with the stirring declaration *"We Bavarians are not Russians!"*

Yet the council's liberation was purely rhetorical, for the Vollzugsrat refused to recognize its coup and promptly placed Munich under the direct control of the Red Army. The Reds set about barricading the city for the coming Armageddon, tacking up posters warning that if the "Prussians" were allowed to triumph, the streets would run in blood.

By 30 April an unnatural quiet reigned in the city, broken only by occasional alarm bells ringing in comandeered church towers. Munich's bourgeoisie stayed off the streets in hopes that their deliverers would soon appear. In their impotence people quietly cursed the "aliens" who had taken over their city. They also cursed Jewish fellow citizens who allegedly aided the Soviets. Rumor had it, noted Hofmiller in his diary, that an anti-Soviet strike by civil servants could not be carried out because Jewish lawyers and judges would continue to serve the regime. Jewish doctors would also continue to work, "allegedly out of reasons of humanity, but actually to steal the patients of non-Jewish colleagues." Hofmiller was unsure if these rumors were true, but he was certain of one point: The *Galizier* (Eastern Jews) who had "corrupted our workers" deserved to be summarily shot. Thomas Mann agreed: "I hope those scoundrelly heroes of the 'masses' . . . can be seized and given over to exemplary judgment."

White Terror

The reckoning that came over the next few days was as bloody as even the most fervent anti-Communists could have wished. It was animated by thirst for vengeance; racial, religious, and class hatred; and an atavistic love of butchery. The mentality that governed it was perhaps best summed up by the Free Corps officer Manfred von Killinger, who wrote in his memoirs: "Munich was under the rule of the Red hordes. Levien, Leviné-Niessen, Mühsam, etc., what kind of people were these? Were they Bavarians? No! Jewish, internationalist riff-raff, Schwabing intellectuals. . . ."

On 30 April the Munich suburbs of Starnberg and Dachau fell to the

Whites. At Starnberg the Free Corps massacred twenty medical orderlies, and at Dachau they executed eight unarmed Red soldiers. When news of the killings reached Munich, soldiers of the First Red Infantry Division asked permission from Egelhofer to exact revenge by executing some of the hostages they were guarding in the Luitpoldgymnasium, a local high school. The prospective victims included two Prussian hussars who were said to have participated in the murder of Liebknecht and Luxemburg in Berlin, seven Thule Society members, and a Jewish painter who had torn down a revolutionary poster. After personally interrogating the hostages, Egelhofer consented to their execution. In pairs the victims were taken into the school courtyard, placed against a wall, and shot.

News of the *Geiselmord* (hostage murder) inspired horror and revulsion throughout Munich, even among non-Communist officials of the soviet. As soon as he learned what had happened, Toller rushed to the Luitpoldgymnasium to prevent more loss of life. He was able to liberate six hostages who were cowering behind a locked door, and he ordered that the ten bodies he found piled in a shed be taken away and buried. "The very sight of them would be enough to lash the Whites into an orgiastic frenzy of revenge," he knew. His order to bury the bodies, however, was not carried out; the corpses were left where they lay, next to garbage cans containing parts of slaughtered pigs. This led to the assertion, splashed across Munich newspapers after the liberation, that the Reds had hacked off their victims' penises and thrown them in the garbage.

As it turned out, the Whites did not need to see the results of the *Geiselmord* be be whipped into a frenzy for revenge. Reports about the murder induced their leaders to move up their attack on Munich from 2 May to May Day, the traditional workers' holiday. They expected to encounter a staunch and well-coordinated defense. But the Red Army, contrary to its own propaganda, was in no position to put up effective resistance. It numbered only about two thousand men, of whom only a few hundred were actually prepared to fight. The *Geiselmord,* moreover, unnerved the Reds as much as it enraged the Whites. According to one Red officer, "panic and revulsion spread through the ranks; men threw down their weapons, and morale collapsed entirely."

The result was that most White units encountered little or no opposition as they entered the city on the morning of 1 May. When they marched into Schwabing, people cheered and showered them with presents. Along the Maximilianstrasse, residents displayed blue and white cloths (the Bavarian colors) to welcome their liberators. On the Ludwigstrasse swastika-helmeted members of the Ehrhardt Brigade, a notoriously brutal Free Corps unit, marched to the Feldherrnhalle singing "Swastika on helmet, black-white-red [the old imperial colors] band. . . ." The troops were "good-looking and well disciplined," observed Thomas Mann.

There were, however, a few places where Red soldiers, aided by civilians, put up a spirited, if doomed, fight. In the Karlsplatz some Reds fought on for several hours before being burned out of their positions by Prussian flamethrowers. The nearby Mathäserbräu became a battlefield when Red soldiers who had been defending the adjacent Palace of Justice took refuge there among the heavy tables and wooden kegs. When that bastion fell too, the Reds made their last stand in the central train station, holding out until the next morning. Among the survivors of that battle was Commandant Egelhofer. Captured, he was taken away for interrogation and summarily shot.

The relative ease with which the anti-Soviet forces took Munich allowed Free Corps men like Manfred von Killinger to have the sport they had been hoping for. When Killinger's boys encountered a young woman—"a typical Schwabing painter-bitch"—who dared insult them, Killinger ordered her stripped and beaten with a riding crop "until there was not a white spot left on her backside." Taking over the tattered Residenz, Killinger railed at the "Spartacist pigs" who had defaced an ornate table by putting a machine gun on it. However, the Free Corps leader could only laugh indulgently when his group's mascot, a dog named Putsch, soiled the throne of the Wittelsbachs.

There was nothing comical or sporting about the fate suffered by Gustav Landauer, Whitmanesque poet of nonviolent revolution. Though he had not been a member of the second Munich soviet, he was seen as a major criminal by the government troops who found him hiding in the home of Eisner's widow on May Day morning. He was taken to Stadelheim Prison, where someone had scrawled: "This is where we make sausages of Spartacists." After being made to run a gauntlet of soldiers slapping him and shouting, "Smash him to a pulp!" he was knocked to the floor by an officer's riding crop. Then some of the soldiers kicked him and hit him with rifle butts. Finally, one of the officers fired several rounds into his prostrate body. The corpse was stripped and thrown into a washhouse.

"The Munich communist episode is over," wrote Thomas Mann in his diary on the evening of 1 May. "I, too, cannot resist the feeling of liberation and cheerfulness. The pressure was abominable." The papal nuncio in Munich, Eugenio Cardinal Pacelli (later Pope Pius XII), declared that the "bestial hostage murder" demanded harsh retribution.

The federal troops and Free Corps now in control of Munich needed no such encouragement to clean out "the Red nest." Operating under martial law, the troops summarily shot 142 prisoners, among them 55 Russian POWs. Another 186 were executed after lightning-fast court-martial proceedings. The Free Corps, for its part, simply killed at random. On 5 May the Freikorps Lützow murdered 12 workmen who had been denounced as troublemakers by a local priest. Another group killed a chimney sweep caught carrying the red flag of his profession.

Now that it was safe to do so, many Munich burghers also joined in the "cleansing" of their city. They formed a Munich militia for this purpose. Oskar Maria Graf described them at work: "Suddenly the burghers came out of hiding and ran around importantly with rifles slung over their ... shoulders and militia armbands on their coats. They searched eagerly for prey, and when they found one, they bawlingly sprang on him, spit on him, punched him like wild men, and proudly carried their half-dead victim to the soldiers."

Arrests often occurred because of anonymous denunciations, and it is significant that one of the denouncers was Adolf Hitler. The future Führer had been in Munich since late February, attached to the Second Infantry Regiment. Contrary to his assertion in *Mein Kampf* that he had avoided arrest in late April by scaring off some Red "scoundrels" with his leveled carbine, he had done nothing to attract attention to himself during the entire time the revolution swirled around him. A few days after the suppression of the soviet he was called before a military commission to report on the activities of his regiment during the revolution. Asked to identify soldiers who had sided with the leftists, he fingered a number of his comrades.

By 6 May Munich was quiet enough for middle-class citizens to walk freely through the streets. A military band played waltzes in the Lenbachplatz. But some of the Free Corps were still in a mood to kill. That evening a group of them, thoroughly drunk, raided an alleged Spartacist gathering, herded thirty prisoners into a cellar, and proceeded to shoot, trample, and bayonet twenty-one of them to death. It turned out, however, that the "Spartacists" in question were members of the St. Josef Society (a Catholic workers' club affiliated with the BVP), who had gathered for a theatrical performance. Even revenge-hungry Münchners were sickened by this episode, which posters around town blamed on "the Prussians."

It now remained only to try to punish the revolutionary leaders who had as yet escaped judgment. Max Levien managed to flee to Austria, but his colleague Eugen Leviné was quickly captured and put on trial.

Convicted of high treason, he was executed on 5 June as "an alien infiltrator who had pursued his aims with total disregard for the welfare of the population." His sometime rival Ernst Toller evaded capture for a time by hiding out in Schwabing. In searching for him at his apartment, the authorities found copies of poems by Rilke, which caused them to search Rilke's flat as well. The poet fled Munich, never to return. Toller, however, was captured after five weeks and thrown into Stadelheim Prison, where he was manhandled by his guards. In his subsequent trial for treason the prosecutor was careful to note that though he claimed to be "confessionless," he had Jewish ancestry. Toller might have shared Leviné's fate had not a number of prominent literary figures, including Thomas Mann, sent in testimonials on his behalf. He was sentenced to five years in prison, without parole.

As the White Terror finally waned, Munich returned to a superficial normality. The period of extraordinary revolutionary chaos, however, had left the city a simmering kettle of bitterness and fear, ready to boil over at the slightest provocation. And it would soon become evident that there were plenty of agitators anxious to light fresh fires under the pot. Among them were Adolf Hitler and the angry young men who began flocking to his side in the early years of the new republic. Hitler's skill at manipulating the revolutionary legacy prompted contemporary observers to expound the simple shorthand "Without Eisner, no Hitler." This view is far too facile, for it vastly simplifies Hitler's rise to power and ignores the importance of developments preceding the revolution. It is also too simple to assert, as has the historian Georg Franz, that the radicalism and violence of the Munich revolution meant that "nowhere could and must the counterswing of the pendulum be more violent than in Munich." Historical developments do not necessarily unfold according to the physics of pendular motion, and Munich's postrevolutionary political development was not a simple yin to the soviet yang. Nonetheless, the duration and intensity of the revolutionary experience in Munich made many of those who felt victimized by it especially receptive to the politics of hatred served up by rightist agitators like Hitler. More than ever, traumatized Münchners found reasons to distrust "aliens" and to place blame for continuing tribulations on convenient scapegoats. More than ever, they regarded liberal cultural and political ideals as sources of potential disruption. In the end, therefore, the revolutionary experience did indeed serve as a crucial milestone on Munich's road to the Third Reich.

4

Birthplace of Nazism

"ONCE, THE HANDSOME and comfortable city attracted the best minds of the Reich. How did it happen that they were now gone, and that in their place everything that was rotten and unable to maintain itself elsewhere was magically pulled toward Munich?" So asked Lion Feuchtwanger in his roman à clef of Munich in the early twenties, *Erfolg* (1930). A Müncher himself, Feuchtwanger was appalled that his native city, in the first years of the Weimar Republic, became a haven for right-ist agitators and *völkisch* organizations. Whereas Berlin emerged as one of the world's most cosmopolitan cities, Munich embraced virulent national-ism, racism, and provincialism.

Of course, conservative Münchners had their own bohemian and rad-ical past to react against, and the vehemence with which they embraced authoritarian solutions in the postrevolutionary era stemmed in part from a desire to bury all remnants of this troubling legacy. As we have seen, however, Munich's bohemian culture itself harbored darker admixtures of racism, insularity, and hero-worship. Now war and revolution had generated a climate of hatred and anxiety in which the darker dimensions of Munich's prewar culture and society could come to the fore.

Among the welter of rightist groups that jockeyed for influence in postrevolutionary Munich, one eventually grew powerful enough to deliver on its promise to change the world: the Nazi movement. Unlike some of its competitors, the fledgling Nazi Party was homegrown, "made in Munich." While it seemed at the time of its birth a distinctly unlikely candidate for future prominence, after about three years it had emerged as the most credible of all the *völkisch* groups in the city, and some local journalists were already calling its leader, Adolf Hitler, the king of Munich. How did a party that began so inauspiciously move so rapidly to the front of the pack? How did Hitler go so quickly from being an unknown corporal in the Bavarian Army to a serious contender for power in Bavaria's capital? The answers must be sought in the politically charged milieu in which the party was born and experienced its first crucial growth.

Versailles and Weimar: A Double Indemnity

On 9 May 1919, three days after the Munich soviet was suppressed, the Western Allies announced the terms of the Versailles Treaty. Expecting bad news, Germans were nonetheless horrified at the harshness of the provisions. Germany was to lose all its colonies, 13 percent of its home territory, and 10 percent of its population. The easternmost province of East Prussia would be cut off from the rest of the Reich by the Polish Corridor. These territorial sacrifices were aggravated by military and economic concessions. Germany's new army, the Reichswehr, would be limited to one hundred thousand officers and men, all volunteers. Germany's famous General Staff was to be eliminated, and its officers' schools were to be closed. To guarantee fulfillment of the military provisions, the Reich's westernmost territory, the Rhineland, was to be occupied by Allied forces for ten years and kept "demilitarized" indefinitely after that. On the economic front, Article 231 of the treaty stated that Germany and its allies bore responsibility for all the losses and damages incurred by their enemies during the war. As the guilty party Germany would have to pay reparations and hand over for trial those of its citizens whom the

Allies suspected of having committed acts in violation of the laws and customs of war.

Germans everywhere screamed in rage, but the outcry was especially loud in Munich. Bavarians complained bitterly that the Rhenish Palatinate, Bavaria's outpost on the Rhine, would be occupied by French troops. They protested that it was unfair that Crown Prince Rupprecht, a "peace-loving man," was being lumped together with "militaristic Prussians" as a candidate for Allied punishment. But most of all, they protested that the Allied demands for reparations in kind, such as dairy cattle and timber, fell disproportionately on an agricultural state like Bavaria.

Munich's politicians, press, and leading cultural figures lashed out at the Entente powers. The city council passed a resolution condemning the treaty. *Simplicissimus* insisted that President Wilson had engineered a peace settlement from which only capitalist America would profit. By contrast, *Simpl*'s sometime contributor Thomas Mann focused his hatred on France's Georges Clemenceau, behind whose anti-German policy he presumed a deep-seated ethnic hatred. He wrote to a German friend on 12 May 1919: "About the Entente peace there's little to say. It reveals the godly blindness of the victors. That poisonous antique [Clemenceau] who concocted the treaty in his insomniac old-man nights has *slant* eyes. Perhaps he has the right-by-blood to dig the grave of Western civilization and bring about the triumph of *Kirgistentum* [Mann's term for the Slavic East]."

Bavarian conservatives were also highly critical of the Socialist-dominated government in Berlin for agreeing to the terrible terms. They persisted in this charge despite their own admission that resistance would have been futile. Meanwhile, some particularists held the Hoffmann regime in Munich accountable for yet another "disgrace": the newly announced Weimar Constitution, which significantly reduced Bavaria's autonomy within the republic. Hoffmann's representatives at the constitutional negotiations, the particularists charged, had made no concerted effort to protect Bavarian rights because they were centralists at heart. The opprobrium with which the Hoffmann government was saddled severely undermined its legitimacy in the chaotic aftermath of the 1918–1919 revolution.

The Civil Guards

While Münchners seethed over the Versailles Treaty and the Weimar Constitution, the streets of their city continued to resemble an armed camp. With Hoffmann still in Bamberg (the cabinet and parliament did not return until 17 August 1919), control over the capital remained with General von Oven and his Prussian troops, assorted Free Corps units, and the Bavarian branch of the Reichswehr (Group Command Number 4) under General Arnold von Möhl. But the presence of troops was not enough to reassure bourgeois Müchners that their lives and property were safe. The army, after all, was in a state of flux as it began to reduce its ranks to the ceiling established by the Entente. Some of the Free Corps units were breaking up or were being diluted by new members who, in the words of Ernst Röhm, had "watched the [anti-Communist forces'] entry into Munich from their windows in their nightshirts."

Against this backdrop, some middle-class citizens decided to take "law and order" into their own hands. They joined units of Einwohnerwehren (Civil Guards), established to avert a possible resurgence of communism. The Civil Guards had the blessing of the Hoffmann government but were accountable only to their own leaders. Funded primarily by private donors, they obtained arms and munitions from war surplus stockpiles made available by the Reichswehr. The Bavarian Einwohnerwehr's head-quarters in Munich's Ring Hotel resembled a fortress, complete with artillery and armed patrols. The group's commander, a forestry official named Georg Escherich, presided over an organization that within a year of its founding embraced almost three hundred thousand men, thirty thousand of them stationed in Munich.

While the Bavarian Civil Guards often claimed to be nothing more than a nonpolitical peacekeeping agency, they were in reality as ideologically motivated as the Free Corps units they largely supplanted. They were militantly anti-Socialist and antidemocratic and pined for the revival of an authoritarian regime. They institutionalized Bavaria's rejection of the Versailles settlement and its hatred for the Weimar Republic. Above all, they despised Berlin as Germany's new mecca of left-wing politics, multiethnic society, and avant-garde culture.

By reaching out to similarly inclined groups elsewhere in Germany and in neighboring Austria, the Bavarian Einwohnerwehr created a large counterrevolutionary network with Munich at its center. Escherich headed an umbrella association called Orgesch, which included Civil Guard formations in central and northern Germany. His aide Rudolf Kanzler set up another association, called Orka, which embraced self-defense groups in western Austria and maintained close ties to rightist factions in Hungary and the Ukraine. Taken together, these organizations amounted to a kind of White International, the militant Right's answer the Red International based in Moscow.

"I Could Speak"

In spring 1919 the Bavarian Reichswehr established a military intelligence bureau in Munich called Abteilung I b/P. Its main job was to monitor morale among the troops and to expose any hints of subversive activity. It also had the task of infiltrating the more than fifty political organizations that had sprouted up in the Bavarian capital since the end of the war.

Commanding this unit was Captain Karl Mayr. On Mayr's initial list of "political education agents," compiled in late May 1919, stood the name Hittler, Adolf (*sic*). It is probable that Hitler made the list on the basis of his earlier work as a political snitch. However, in an article he wrote in 1941 for an American magazine, Mayr maintained that he had selected Hitler partly out of pity. "When I first met him he was like a stray dog looking for a master," he recalled. The future Führer, Mayr claimed, was "ready to throw in his lot with anyone who would show him kindness" and "would have worked for a Jewish or a French employer as readily as for an Aryan." Whether or not this assessment is accurate, Hitler undoubtedly welcomed his new job because it allowed him to postpone returning to civilian life.

Hitler and his fellow agents were enrolled, as part of their training, in a special indoctrination course at the University of Munich in summer 1919. According to the Reichswehr leadership, the course would give its participants understanding of the basic political ideas of the era and help them develop trust and confidence in the nation. Teachers included the conservative editor and diarist Josef Hofmiller; Karl Alexander von Müller, the nationalist historian; and Müller's brother-in-law Gottfried Feder, a self-taught economist who lectured on the evils of "interest slavery."

In *Mein Kampf* Hitler described this university course as another crucial milestone on his road to becoming a politician. "For me the value of the whole affair was that I now obtained an opportunity of meeting a few like-minded comrades with whom I could thoroughly discuss the situation of the moment." In addition to encountering such colleagues, Hitler received his first sustained education in economics from Feder, who illuminated the differences between capital based on "productive labor" and that generated by speculation and interest, which the lecturer insisted was the province of the Jews. "Right after listening to Feder's first lecture," wrote Hitler, "the thought ran through my mind that I had now found the way to one of the most essential premises for the formation of a new party."

In fact, there is no evidence that Hitler was thinking of starting a new party at this point, but Feder's lectures, and those of Hofmiller and Müller, did present him with some of the phrases and ideas that he soon employed in his political work. They helped him to crystallize his thinking, to harden inchoate anti-Semitic and anti-Marxist impulses into an all-embracing conspiracy theory and crusading ideology. At the same time, the courses gave him the confidence to speak his mind to his fellow students and to hone his famous oratorical skills. When another student dared to speak on behalf of the Jews, Hitler rebuffed him and (at least according to his own account of the incident) convinced "the overwhelming majority of the students."

Hitler's forensic abilities caught the attention of Professor von Müller. One day the professor noticed a group of students engaged in spirited discussion. As he recalled in his memoirs, "The men seemed spellbound by a man in their midst, who railed at them uninterruptedly in a strangely guttural yet passionate voice. I had the unsettling feeling that their excitement was his work and simultaneously the source of his own power. I saw a pale, thin face under an unsoldierly shock of hanging hair, and striking large light blue eyes that glittered fanatically."

After the next lecture Müller waited to see if this strange man would raise his hand to ask a question, but he did not. Still, the professor's interest was piqued. "Do you know that you have a natural orator among your group?" he asked Mayr. Upon learning whom the professor meant, Mayr said, "Oh, that's our Hitler from the List Regiment." Twenty-five years later Müller commented: "I could not have known that here I was face-to-face with the bloody man of destiny who would soon mesmerize an entire people for two decades with his obsessive oratory, pulling them through a maelstrom of sacrifice, heroism, hopes, crimes, and endless misery into a horrific collapse, compared to which the upheaval and destruction we had previously experienced seemed a harmless prelude."

In July 1919 Captain Mayr assigned Hitler to lecture in the barracks around Munich. Excited to have a captive audience, Hitler enlightened the soldiers on the manifold evils of the international Marxist–Jewish–big-capitalist conspiracy. Enthusiastic responses from the troops convinced him that he was indeed an effective orator, especially before large groups. "[The] thing that I had always presumed from pure feeling without knowing it was now corroborated: I could 'speak.' "

Mayr next sent his prize speaker on a mission to a military transit camp outside Munich, where soldiers were waiting to be discharged. Hitler's job was to turn these men, many of whom had become radicalized, into good patriots. He went about this task by giving them new targets for their anger. Rather than the former kaiser and his generals, they should learn to hate the "November criminals" who (in 1918) had "stabbed the German army in the back." It is impossible to know how many soldiers

Hitler actually converted, but his superiors were again impressed. The commander of the transit camp wrote: "Herr Hitler, if I might put it this way, is the born people's speaker, and by his fanaticism and his crowd appeal he clearly compels the attention of his listeners, and makes them think his way."

Hitler returned to Munich in late August and promptly took another important step toward a career in politics: He wrote his first position paper. The occasion was a request from Mayr to reply to a letter he had received from a former army agent named Adolf Gemlich regarding "the Jewish question." Why were the Jews such a curse? In his response Hitler argued that the Jews represented more than a social, economic, or religious problem; they were a "race tuberculosis." They must be combated with a "methodical legal struggle" culminating in their "deliberate removal." Because the current government in Berlin could not be expected to carry out such a policy, Germany needed a new "government of national strength" led by "national personalities possessing leadership and profound inner feelings of responsibility."

At about the time that Hitler wrote this revealing letter—mid-September 1919—he was ordered by Mayr to shift his focus from investigating internal military matters to monitoring the political scene in Munich. The army leadership wanted to keep watch on the welter of new organizations in the Bavarian capital. These ran the gamut from the Society of Communistic Socialists to the radical rightist Schutz- und Trutzbund (League for Defense and Attack). Some of these groups, the army reasoned, merited encouragement; others might have to be undermined or suppressed.

On 12 September Hitler was sent by Mayr to investigate one of the least imposing of the new parties, the Deutsche Arbeiterpartei (German Workers' Party), which we recall had been founded in January 1919 by Anton Drexler and Karl Harrer. Since then the party had not made much progress. Even now it had only a few dozen members and no significant financial backing. Yet who knew? It might eventually amount to something.

The DAP meeting that Hitler attended was held in a dingy back room of the Sternecker brewery. He arrived in a baggy suit rather than his military uniform, and he had trimmed his drooping mustache to the tidy little patch that became his trademark. He did not, however, try to hide his army affiliation, truthfully signing the guest book as Lance Corporal Adolf Hitler, Second Infantry Regiment.

The main speaker that evening was Feder. As usual, he belabored the evils of unproductive capital and interest slavery. More interesting for

Hitler was the discussion that followed. He was supposed to monitor this carefully for clues to the nature and potential usefulness of the little party. But Hitler could not simply sit back and take notes. When one of the discussants, a professor from the university, argued that Bavaria should secede from Germany and form a union with Austria, Hitler (according to his account in *Mein Kampf*) demanded the floor and gave "the learned gentleman my opinion on this point." Bavaria, he contended, must remain an integral part of the Reich and help lead it out of its current predicament. Hitler conveyed this message so effectively that Anton Drexler, sitting on the platform, whispered to one of his colleagues, "This one has a big mouth! We could use him!" Before Hitler left, Drexler made sure that the visitor picked up a copy of his pamphlet *My Political Awakening,* which related how he had seen through the subterfuges of Marxism and awakened to the dangers of Jewish financial manipulation. The pamphlet also urged class reconciliation in the name of national revival and called for an authoritarian government to replace the parliamentary regime in Berlin.

Hitler read Drexler's little work with interest, for the mechanic's awakening seemed to mirror his own. He was also intrigued by Drexler's "national Socialist" mixture of anticapitalist and nationalistic motifs. The notion of winning over the workers for the nation was something that Hitler was also coming to see as imperative. On the other hand, Hitler was not overly impressed by the DAP; it was just "a new organization like so many others."

He was therefore taken aback when, about a week later, he received a postcard saying that he had been "accepted" for membership in the DAP and requesting his presence at a leadership committee meeting a few days hence at a tavern called the Altes Rosenbad. What a way for a party to win new members! he said to himself. Nonetheless, he decided he would take a closer look at the party.

At the Altes Rosenbad Hitler found conditions even worse than he had expected. Drexler and the other men were sitting in a shabby room under "the murky light of a broken gas lamp." Drexler introduced Hitler to Harrer, a clubfooted sportswriter who described himself as "chairman of the national organization." From the minutes of the previous meeting Hitler learned that the party had a total of seven marks and fifty pfennigs to its name. As the meeting progressed, he also discovered that the DAP had no formal program, no printed propaganda (save Drexler's little book), not even a rubber stamp.

Yet Hitler began to sense that the very weaknesses of this group offered him opportunities for advancement. As he recalled in *Mein Kampf,* "This absurd little organization with its few members seemed to me to possess the one advantage that it had not frozen into an 'organization' but left the individual an opportunity for real personal activity." Thus, instead of throwing Drexler's invitation back in his face, he formally confirmed his membership on 19 September 1919. "It was," he later wrote, "the most decisive resolve of my life."

Hitler's description of this moment failed to mention that he had to obtain special dispensation from Captain Mayr to join the DAP since Reichswehr personnel were not supposed to become members of political parties. In his 1941 memoir Mayr claimed that he made an exception in Hitler's case to please General Ludendorff, who had recently returned to Germany from exile in Sweden. Ludendorff and his allies, wrote Mayr, were shopping around "like Hollywood scouts" for somcone who had the talent to win over the German masses for the nationalist cause. At first they were thinking along the lines of a "German Joan of Arc" and "hunted diligently through the Bavarian mountains for a red-headed peasant girl who could be sold as a goddess, a divine messenger sent straight from Valhalla to wake up the Germans and save them from their bondage by leading them to victory and everlasting glory." But finding no such creature, they turned to Mayr for help. He concluded (so he says) that his own Adolf Hitler, the little corporal with the big mouth, might do nicely in this role. He could certainly incite fanatical passions, and he was lowly enough to be held in check by his masters. Mayr therefore gave Hitler his blessing to join the DAP, along with a stipend of twenty gold marks per week to be used to help the little party get on its feet.

Although the imagery is pleasing, it is highly doubtful that Mayr offered his prize speaker to Ludendorff as Germany's best answer to Joan of Arc. At this time Ludendorff was still in Berlin and not in regular contact with Mayr. The captain's account was clearly aided by hindsight and a lively imagination, not to mention a desire to inflate his own importance as "Hitler's boss." The reality is that Mayr and the Bavarian Reichswehr command were anxious to slip Hitler into the DAP because their intrepid investigator—his self-serving account in *Mein Kampf* notwithstanding—had made the group sound like something the army ought to further in its effort to influence the political climate in Munich.

Munich's "Wolf"

As Hitler was making his momentous decision to join the DAP, the city in which the fledgling party was headquartered continued to toss about on the rough waters of economic misery and political anxiety. In mid-July General von Oven and his troops left the city, on 1 August martial law was lifted, and shortly thereafter the state government returned to Munich. But these outward signs of normality did nothing to diminish popular anxieties about public security. The Civil Guard movement grew apace, padding its ranks with such pillars of the community as Müller, Spengler, and Thomas Mann.

Bourgeois insecurity was heightened by economic distress and social dislocation. Food costs continued to soar. In early summer a police report expressed alarm over the "fantasy prices" for many items, especially the fresh fruit sold by "unscrupulous street peddlers." In August the food office warned that there was only enough corn and wheat on hand for another fourteen days. A little later Thomas Mann's wife, Katia, reported a "depressing air of crisis in town" as the result of a doubling of the price of bread and a decline of the value of the mark. Of course, all Germany was having to cope with high inflation, but Munich was especially hard hit because it had a high percentage of the most vulnerable groups: small producers and retailers, civil servants, white-collar employees, and retired people living on fixed pensions.

Escalating socioeconomic miseries generated a wave of anti-Semitic agitation. A police report of 22 November 1919 spoke of *Judenhetze* (attacks on Jews) attributable to the belief that this group was behind the "increased usury, profiteering, and smuggling." At the turn of the year factory workers distributed flyers proclaiming: "Our misery is due entirely to the Jews who have infested our fatherland. They should be summarily expelled. On Silvester [January 1], Munich's work force will make good on its threat—'Out with the Jews, or Down with the weak-willed government.' " This threat turned out to be beer hall bravado, but it illustrated that in allegedly "classless" Munich one thing really *was* classless: militant anti-Semitism. The number of anti-Semitic incidents, moreover, continued to mount with the inflation curve. In early 1921 a Jewish synagogue on the Rudolfstrasse was vandalized, and members of a Jewish club were attacked and beaten. The Bavarian Ministry of the Interior pleaded with the Munich police to take a firmer line against the perpetrators of racist attacks, "so as to dampen the impression that the authorities take less seriously outrages committed by anti-Semites than those committed by the Left."

One of the realities of life in Munich, in fact, was that the authorities were severe with offenders having left-wing credentials, while practicing benign neglect when it came to offenders from the Right. The trials of the Reds accused of participating in the Luitpoldgymnasium hostage murders took place in fall 1919. The six defendants were found guilty and immediately executed. Alois Lindner, the would-be assassin of Erhard Auer, was arrested in Austria and extradited to Munich on condition that he would not be sentenced to death. Convicted of attempted murder and manslaughter, he was sentenced to fourteen years' imprisonment (five of which he served before he died). All in all, Bavarian courts handed down some 1,809 prison sentences in connection with the revolution; the prisoners on average served three quarters of their terms. By contrast, none of the Free Corps men who had committed murders or other atrocities during the "liberation" of Munich had to pay for their crimes, and the police habitually turned a blind eye to the ongoing attacks against Jews or members of leftist organizations. Indeed, the Munich police president called for the wholesale expulsion of Eastern Jews and the "internment" of radicals, especially "intellectual, academic trash."

Another telling index of official sensibility was the judicial fate of Count Arco, the murderer of Kurt Eisner. His trial took place in January 1920. Because he did not refute the charges against him, the court had no choice but to convict him of first-degree murder and to sentence him to death. The judges, however, passed this sentence knowing it would be revised. Indeed, on the very next day the Bavarian Landtag commuted Arco's sentence to life imprisonment, with the possibility of further revisions later on. Justifying its intervention, the parliament argued that Arco had acted "out of patriotic motives" and was free of any "personal feeling of hatred" toward his victim.

Arco was sent to Landsberg Fortress, where he enjoyed a comfortable suite of rooms, the opportunity to entertain guests, and the freedom to take walks in town. But he did not have to endure even this comfortable confinement for long. On 13 April 1924 the Bavarian government pardoned him and allowed him to return to Munich, where he became active in Nazi politics.

As Arco was beginning his sentence in Landsberg, Adolf Hitler was busy trying to turn the little party he had just joined into something more formidable than an obscure coterie of beer hall malcontents. The first order of business, he decided, was to make the group better known to the public. In early November he convinced his colleagues in the DAP's leadership committee to advertise an upcoming meeting in the press, instead of relying merely on posters and word of mouth.

The meeting in question was held in a basement room of the Hofbräuhaus that could hold 130 people. To the party's delight, 111 appeared. This was the largest crowd the DAP had ever attracted, and it seemed to prove that Hitler knew what he was doing. A few days later, at the Eberlbräukeller, he harangued some 300 people about the Versailles Treaty, which he called an iron yoke that could be broken only by German iron.

By all accounts, his speech was effective, but the DAP meetings held biweekly during the next month did not fill the halls Hitler had rented. Harrer became nervous about the costs, accusing Hitler of overextending the party in his drive for public attention. Hitler, for his part, saw Harrer as an "eternal doubter" whose caution was holding the party back. With the support of the new members he was bringing in, Hitler managed to force Harrer out of the party leadership in December 1919.

At about the same time Hitler secured a headquarters for the party in a room at the Sternecker brewery, where he had witnessed his first DAP meeting. For its shabby quarters the party paid fifty marks a month, or about one dollar at the steadily decreasing rate of exchange. To meet this and other expenses, including a typewriter and some rubber stamps (finally), the party collected modest dues.

To judge from Munich newspapers and police records, the DAP in late 1919 was still an obscure bunch. By far the largest force on the right was the Einwohnerwehr, which paid little attention to the DAP. The most prominent *völkisch* organization was the Schutz- und Trutzbund, which was rich enough to rent the largest beer halls for its meetings. Hitler was sometimes invited to these meetings, but he was never the principal speaker. When he did speak, he tried to make himself stand out by drawing distinctions between his own position and that of his hosts. For example, addressing the "Jewish question," he declared that "the greatest scoundrels" were not the Jews themselves but "Germans who place themselves at the disposal of Jews." He also emphasized the DAP's radicalism, declaring, "We fight the Jews because we fight big capitalism."

A little later, in a more systematic effort to give the DAP a coherent image, Hitler and Drexler drew up a party platform consisting of twenty-five points. Among other issues the program demanded that "incomes unearned by work" be eliminated; all war profits be confiscated and business trusts nationalized; and large industries be made to share profits. To help maintain a "healthy middle class," the platform advocated turning over department stores to small retailers and granting most state contracts to little producers.

Shortly after the new platform had been drawn up, the DAP, at Hitler's urging, changed its name to the National Socialist German Workers' Party (NSDAP)—in popular parlance, Nazis. The new name, with its inclusion of the term *national*, was meant to show that the group's radicalism must not be confused with Marxism. This was to be a

Germany-first enterprise, totally hostile to traditional leftist internationalism.

The Twenty-five Points and the new name were announced at a meeting in the Hofbräuhaus on 24 February 1920, three days after leftists in the city had commemorated the first anniversary of Eisner's death. This time Hitler had rented the hall's huge banquet room. Worried about filling this cavernous space, he had covered Munich with posters printed in brilliant red, a provocation both to the Marxist Left and to the traditional "black" Right. But the tactic proved a good one, for the meeting drew more than two thousand people. Not all of them, however, were there to cheer. As Hitler began to speak, some in the audience began to throw their beer steins at him, a traditional Munich way of expressing disagreement. Deftly ducking the steins, Hitler paused to allow his hardier supporters to attack the protesters with rubber truncheons, whips, and steins of their own. Eventually he was able to resume his speech and announce the party platform, which brought warm applause.

As he called the meeting to a close a little later, Hitler had reason to feel satisfied. The unprepossessing outfit he had joined four months previously now had an ambitious program and a new name; it had staged its first "mass meeting" and showed that it could defend itself in the stein wars. The large turnout suggested that it was beginning to make a mark in Munich. Later Hitler could write with some justification: "When I finally closed the meeting, I was not alone in thinking that a wolf had been born that was destined to break into the herd of deceivers and misleaders of the people."

The Kapp Putsch

Of course, Munich was not the only city in Germany to harbor groups of embittered men who could not reconcile themselves to the new republican system. The national capital itself had its share of dedicated counter-revolutionaries. In winter 1919–1920 a number of local rightists formed an organization called the Nationalist Association, whose goal was to destroy the democratic order. Leaders of the group were Walther von Lüttwitz, commander of the Berlin Military District, and Wolfgang Kapp, a Prussian government official and veteran of the wartime Fatherland Party. The association's patron saint was General Ludendorff, who after returning to Germany from his brief Swedish exile was holding court in Berlin's opulent Hotel Adlon for a motley circle of rightist desperadoes.

The Nationalist Association's frustrations reached a boiling point in February 1920, when the central government ordered the demobilization of sixty thousand soldiers to accommodate the Allies' demilitarization edict. Among the units to be disbanded was the Second Naval Brigade under Captain Ehrhardt, which in an earlier incarnation had helped suppress the Munich soviet. After being absorbed into the provisional Reichswehr, the brigade had set up headquarters at Döberitz outside Berlin, where it impatiently awaited a new call for action. When the order to disband came instead, Ehrhardt and his allies tried to persuade Defense Minister Noske to rescind it; when that proved fruitless, they decided to move against the regime.

On the night of 12 March the Ehrhardt Brigade marched into Berlin preceded by an assault company of heavy artillery. The men wore their trademark swastika helmets and chanted: "Worker, worker, what's to be your plight / When the Ehrhardt Brigade's ready to fight? / The Ehrhardt Brigade smashes everything to bits / So woe, woe, woe to you, you worker son of a bitch!"

Learning of the brigade's approach, the central government appealed to the army leadership to defend the republic, but General Hans von Seeckt, chief of the Reichswehr Truppenamt (the new equivalent of the outlawed General Staff), responded that "troops do not fire on troops. . . . When the Reichswehr fires on Reichswehr, then all comradeship within the officer corps has vanished." Deprived of military support, the cabinet fled to Dresden and later to Stuttgart. As the government was leaving, Ehrhardt's men marched through the Brandenburg Gate to be greeted by Ludendorff, Lüttwitz, and Kapp, who was decked out in top hat and tails as the titular head of the new regime. From all appearances, the Kapp Putsch was a resounding success.

In fact, however, like so many putschists before and since, Kapp and his allies were unprepared to govern what they had so boldly seized. The first sign of confusion was their inability to find anyone to type the manifesto announcing their seizure of power. Eventually, after two days had been lost, Kapp's daughter consented to do it. Other necessary paperwork was held up because President Ebert's officials, in a cruel but brilliant act of sabotage, had hidden all the rubber stamps before fleeing. The new rulers also had no money to pay their troops. Kapp instructed Ehrhardt to take the necessary funds from the State Treasury, but the latter refused on the ground that he was "an officer, not a bank robber." Most of the governmental bureaucracy stayed loyal to Ebert, resolutely ignoring the putschists. Seeckt, though unwilling to mobilize troops against the coup, also refused to work for it.

While the Kappists wallowed in ineptitude and Seeckt sat warily on the fence, the workers of Berlin took matters in hand by staging the most effective general strike in German history. Trams stopped running; factories emptied; stores closed; waiters took off their aprons. A regime that had difficulty typing its own manifestos could hardly stay afloat in such circumstances, and after just four days of chaos and irresolution Kapp decided to call it quits. Grandly announcing that he had accomplished all his aims, he hopped on a plane bound for Sweden, Ludendorff's refuge in 1918. As for the latter, he felt obliged to flee once again, but this time he headed south: to Bavaria.

Ehrhardt's disgruntled soldiers marched back to Döberitz but not before venting their frustration on the Berliners. As they were leaving, a young boy mocked them. Two of the men broke ranks and clubbed him to death. A crowd assembled to protest, whereupon the soldiers fired point-blank into the mass of people, killing and wounding more than a dozen.

The putsch attempt was also causing bloodshed in other parts of the republic. In the Ruhr area, Germany's most industrialized region, a "Red Army" cited the danger from the Right as an excuse to wage pitched battles with the Reichswehr. In industrial Saxony a short-lived "soviet" threatened to slaughter the middle classes. These events were an ugly foretaste of things to come. As the sharp-witted Berlin journalist Kurt Tucholsky surmised at the time, the Kapp Putsch was an "unsuccessful dress rehearsal" for a drama whose opening night was merely postponed.

In Munich the opening night came sooner. Expecting to liberate not just Berlin but the entire Reich, the Kappists had made contact with rightist elements throughout the country, including Munich. Lüttwitz maintained ties to Möhl, while Kapp was close to Julius Lehmann and the racist publicist Dietrich Eckart (about whom more below). Nevertheless the northerners had failed to inform the southerners of their exact plan of action, and the putsch caught Munich by surprise.

Once they had learned of the takeover in Berlin, however, rightist forces in Munich were quick to voice their support. Some army officers and Civil Guards called for an extension of the coup to Bavaria. To preempt any such action, Munich's Socialist workers staged a general strike. General von Möhl, though in sympathy with some of the Kappists' ideals, was unwilling to see Munich taken over by the northern rebels. He declared that the Bavarian Reichswehr would protect the Hoffmann government if the Kappists tried to move south.

Yet if the Kappists were warned away from Munich, some of the local counterrevolutionaries saw that the tumultuous events in Berlin provided an opportunity to rid Bavaria of its Social Democratic government. In the early hours of 14 March a delegation consisting of Civil Guard leader Escherich, Munich Police Chief Pöhner, and Dr. Gustav von Kahr, president of the Upper Bavarian government, paid a call on General von Möhl at Reichswehr headquarters. The men told Möhl that he must declare martial law and take over the government; otherwise a bloody civil war would erupt. Möhl understood this to mean that if he did not take action to guarantee "law and order," the Civil Guards might try to do so themselves. Acquiescing, he accompanied the men to see Minister President Hoffmann, who was told that the security forces could not keep the peace unless he turned over all power to the military.

Unwilling to participate in this charade, Hoffmann resigned, just what his callers had wanted him to do. His cabinet, thoroughly cowed by the military and Civil Guards, voted to give Möhl the powers he asked for, then resigned en masse. Two days later, on 16 March, the Landtag appointed Gustav von Kahr Bavaria's new premier. He took over with the promise that his government, backed by the army and guards, would ensure that tranquillity reigned in Bavaria. Thus, whereas the Kapp Putsch was a fiasco in Berlin, something like it succeeded in Munich. The Bavarian capital, famous a year earlier as the center of Communist subversion, now could hold itself up as a model of conservative order.

Adolf Hitler had voiced his support for the Kappists as soon as they announced their putsch. But when credible information about the coup's further progress failed to reach Munich, Captain Mayr, who also supported the putsch, asked Hitler to go to Berlin to see what was happening. Hitler immediately agreed. Indeed, he was so eager to undertake this mission that for the first time in his life he flew in an airplane. Lamentably for him, the craft in question was a tiny biplane that pitched about violently throughout the flight, making him repeatedly sick.

Accompanying Hitler on the trip was Dietrich Eckart, a well-known poet, playwright, and man-about-Munich. In looks and mannerisms, Eckart fitted the stereotype of the earthy Bavarian. Totally bald, he had an enormous paunch that bespoke many happy hours in the beer halls. He was always ready with bawdy jokes and whacks on the lederhosen. But equally true to type, he was a great hater. His "sworn enemies" were Jews and Marxists, whom he blamed for Germany's plight, as well as for the bad reviews he received for his plays and poems. He vented his hatreds in a racist sheet he published called *Auf gut Deutsch* (In Plain German). Here he expressed the hope that a "German savior" would soon appear on the horizon. The savior would have to be a "man of the people" as well as a bachelor. "Then we'll get the women!" predicted Eckart, a ladies' man.

When Eckart met Hitler in late 1919, he seems to have thought that the Austrian visionary might be the redeemer he had in mind. Hitler, for his part, saw that he could profit from an association with Eckart, who had many influential friends in Munich. He also had substantial funds at his disposal from patrons like Kapp and Mayr and from his well-known translation of Ibsen's *Peer Gynt*. He was happy enough to spend a few marks on his new friend, taking him around to restaurants and buying him a trench coat. Eckart was the first of many well-placed Münchners who tried to make the unsophisticated Hitler a little more worldly.

On their trip to Berlin Eckart hoped to introduce Hitler to the Kappists, some of whom he knew personally. Alas, the men landed in Berlin just as the putsch was collapsing and the leaders were fleeing. Hitler would have liked to stay in town for a while, but Eckart insisted upon returning immediately to Munich. Hitler's only consolation was that he was able to return by train.

"Traitors Fall to the Feme!"

Gustav von Kahr, Bavaria's new premier, liked to contrast himself with Kurt Eisner, and indeed, the two seemed polar opposites. The scion of a Protestant family that for generations had advised Bavaria's Catholic kings, Kahr was a short, powerfully built man with rough facial features, close-cropped hair, and a prim goatee. He favored black suits and old-fashioned high-collared shirts. Full of pious rectitude, he lacked imagination, striking contemporaries as "colorless." His goal, however, was not to be exciting but to render Munich and Bavaria safe once again for people of his tastes and values. Like many conservative Bavarians, he also hoped that his capital might become the springboard for a monarchist revival throughout Central Europe. His tragedy was that in trying to make Munich a bastion of conservative order, he helped further the rise of the radical Right.

Following the Kapp Putsch, extreme right-wingers and disgruntled nationalists from all over Germany descended upon Munich as if, as Feuchtwanger proposed, it possessed some "magical" attraction. Munich's allure for counterrevolutionaries was not, however, very mysterious: Because of the influence of Prime Minister von Kahr, Police Chief Pöhner, and the local Reichswehr command, rightist agitators and putschists on the lam from the law could operate openly on the banks of the Isar.

Among the first to find refuge in Munich was Captain Ehrhardt, wanted by the Berlin police for his part in the Kapp affair. Invited to the Bavarian capital by Pöhner, Ehrhardt established a new headquarters on Franz-Josef-Strasse. Through the good offices of Julius Lehmann and the Thule Society, he was able to find seasonal employment for members of his demobilized Naval Brigade in farms outside town. To keep their military skills intact, Ehrhardt's men joined the Einwohnerwehr or the more radical Bund Oberland, an outgrowth of the Freikorps Oberland, which had fought against the Munich soviet.

Another Kapp refugee was Dr. Max Erwin von Scheubner-Richter, a prissy little man who wore a pince-nez and immaculately tailored suits. A native of the Baltic region, he became the liaison between Munich's *völkisch* leaders and its large community of White Russians. While the native rightists plotted the downfall of the Weimar system, the expatriate Russians dreamed of expelling the Bolshevists from their homeland.

The major figure among Munich's burgeoning community of rightist refugees was General Ludendorff, who, as we noted, had come south as soon as the Kapp adventure turned sour. He took up residence in a villa in the Munich suburb of Ludwigshöhe. His new quarters became a kind of *völkisch* Lourdes, with rightist pilgrims hastening there in search of inspiration. Among them was Adolf Hitler, who was now a private citizen, having been released from the army on 31 March 1920. Ex-Corporal Hitler was overjoyed to meet Ludendorff face-to-face. He became convinced that he and the general must work together to save Germany.

Some of the men who congregated around Ludendorff and Ehrhardt in Munich established a shadowy outfit called Organisation Consul (the name derived from an alias, Consul Eichmann, used by Ehrhardt), which dedicated itself to a brutal terror campaign against "enemies of the Reich." Headquartered in Ehrhardt's offices on Franz-Josef-Strasse, the OC was made up primarily of ex-Naval Brigade personnel and Oberland veterans. The group's unofficial leader was Manfred von Killinger, the ex-Freikorps thug who had taken such delight in the suppression of the Munich soviet. Members of the OC took oaths of secrecy and pledged their loyalty unto death. Any member who betrayed the organization could count on being murdered himself. Their motto was "Traitors Fall to the Feme," Feme being the code word for the hit squad attached to the group.

Although obsessed with secrecy, the OC did not have to worry that the authorities in Munich would give it much trouble. It enjoyed support and protection from Police Chief Pöhner, who provided its members with fake identification papers and allowed them to use his own office for especially sensitive business. The army too provided support, as it did for many of the radical rightist organizations in Munich.

The OC's plans called for the assassination of the republic's top officials, but as if warming up for this task, it began its murder campaign with smaller fry in its own backyard. In October 1920 the OC murdered a young servant girl named Marie Sandmeier, who had apparently informed the Allied Disarmament Commission that a former employer was hiding illegal arms on his estate. Just after she turned over this information, a man describing himself as a member of the commission called on her and (according to one of her housemates) asked her to go for a walk in Förstenried Park to discuss her revelations. Her strangled body was found in the park under a sign saying: "You lousy bitch; you have betrayed your Fatherland. The Black Hand has judged you." Shortly thereafter a waiter named Hartung who had worked for the Civil Guard as a spy made the mistake of threatening to expose a guard arms cache if he did not get a higher salary. Instead he got a trip to the bottom of the Isar with stones tied to his legs and eleven holes in his head.

The Munich police learned the identity of the murderers of Sandmeier and Hartung from Civil Guard members, who boasted of having enlisted the OC to get rid of these "traitors." A conscientious detective planned to arrest the killers, but Police Chief Pöhner delayed the investigation long enough for the men to flee the country. Thereafter he automatically gave the OC the names of citizens who brought compromising information about its activities to the police. When one citizen came to Pöhner and asked if he was aware that there were "political murder gangs" operating in Munich, he replied, "Yes, but not enough of them."

Emboldened by its apparent license to kill, the OC next gunned down the leader of the Independent Socialists in Bavaria, Dr. Karl Gareis. He had dared call for a crackdown on political terror. In celebration of his murder, rightist thugs strolled through Schwabing, where Gareis had been killed, singing, "O hero brave whose shot made Gareis fall / And brought deliverance to all / From the Socialist swine. . . ."

In August 1921 Munich's OC moved farther afield and sent two of its killers to southwestern Germany to assassinate the prominent Center Party politician Matthias Erzberger, who was vacationing in the Black Forest. Erzberger was seen by the Right as one of the prime "November criminals" because he had signed the armistice agreement in 1918. Hitler had demanded that he be hanged, since shooting was too "honorable" for him. Unconcerned with such fine points, the OC assassins dispatched their man by pumping twelve bullets into him as he was taking a stroll.

The police in Baden were soon able to establish the identities of the killers as Heinrich Tillissen and Heinrich Schulz, both former members of the Ehrhardt Naval Brigade. They also learned that the men had returned to Munich after the murder. But when officials of the Baden police traveled to the Bavarian capital to arrest the killers, they discovered that their quarry had taken flight to Hungary. It seems that Pöhner himself had provided them with false passports. The only figure to be arrested in connection with the assassination was Manfred von Killinger, accused of masterminding the plot. Tried for murder in Munich by sympathetic judges, he was acquitted of the charge and set free. Among the first to congratulate Killinger was Hitler, who saw to it that the old freebooter found a new political home in the Nazi Party.

The Erzberger murder focused national attention on Munich as a breeding ground of right-wing terrorism. A Baden newspaper fumed that the Bavarian authorities were so primitive that in comparison with them "niggers in the bush seemed like carriers of high civilization." Leftist and liberal groups all over Germany demanded that the central government in Berlin do something to combat the "reactionary tide" emanating from Bavaria. In response the republican regime appealed to Kahr to impose some checks on the rightist groups congregating in Munich. Kahr, not surprisingly, rejected this appeal as "interference" in Bavarian affairs. He proposed that Berlin could learn by Munich's example and purge its own house of subversive and unpatriotic elements.

Munich versus Berlin

The troubled relationship between Munich and Berlin was further strained by a prolonged battle over the fate of Bavaria's Civil Guards. At the Spa Conference in July 1920 the Allies demanded the dissolution of Germany's paramilitary self-defense groups on the ground that they could facilitate mobilization. Most of the units were disbanded over the next few months. Aware of how sensitive this issue was in Bavaria, however, the central government tried for a time to persuade the Allies to make an exception for that state. When these efforts failed, Berlin joined the powers in demanding the dissolution of the Bavarian units. Kahr, prodded by Escherich, refused to comply. The Allies therefore threatened to send troops into Germany. Determined to avoid such an intrusion, Berlin issued a new ultimatum to Munich: Disband the guards or face occupation by military forces from the North. Escherich declared that he would not bow to force and bragged that the Einwohnerwehr was so strong that no one would dare thwart it. Referring to the news that Prussian troops might help disarm the local Civil Guards, he warned that any Prussian who tried this had better have made out his will. Kahr offered his "personal protection" to guard members who disobeyed the disarmament edict. Hitler, for his part, declared that without its Civil Guards Bavaria would be "defenseless" against enemies from within.

In the end, however, Kahr was not foolhardy enough to plunge Bavaria into a military conflict with Berlin. Nor was the Bavarian Reichswehr anxious to take on its northern counterparts. In late spring 1921 the premier put pressure on Escherich to comply with the dissolution order, at least outwardly. The Civil Guard leader, for all his bluster, could not resist this pressure, since behind it stood the Reichswehr. On 4 June 1921 the Bavarian Einwohnerwehr, the largest of postwar Germany's self-defense organizations, was officially dissolved.

The dissolution, however, was only superficial. Most Civil Guard members hid their guns rather than turn them in to the Allied Disarmament Commission. Many others simply switched over to other paramilitary groups that continued to operate in Munich—most notably the Bund Bayern-und-Reich, which, like the Civil Guard, combined regionalist and nationalist motifs. Still others drifted into radical groups like the Nazis' new party army, the Sturmabteilung (SA). The Einwohnerwehr's dissolution in fact turned out to be a windfall for Hitler because in addition to bringing him new personnel, it somewhat reduced the competition for influence in Munich's cluttered right-wing scene.

For Kahr, the necessity of giving in to Berlin was a humiliation, and he suffered another one shortly thereafter, when the republican government successfully forced Munich to terminate the martial law arrangements under which local officials were disregarding citizens' civil rights. Losing the backing of the Bavarian parliament and his own party, the BVP, Kahr resigned in September 1921. Pöhner too stepped down but in compensation was allowed to become a judge on Bavaria's highest court. Not long thereafter he also found his his way into the Hitler camp.

With the departure of Kahr and Pöhner, and the advent of a less stridently confrontationalist Bavarian government under Count Hugo von Lerchenfeld, tensions between Munich and Berlin relaxed somewhat. Popular sentiment in the Bavarian capital, however, remained bitterly anti-Berlin. Extreme particularist factions like the Monarchist Party agitated for secession from the republic. Munich's top religious leader, Archbishop Michael von Faulhaber (who was promoted to cardinal in October 1921), admonished his fellow priests to keep their "consciences clean and free relative to the republic," which he said was born out of the "sin of the revolution" and stood "under the curse of God."

No one in Munich, however, shouted the antirepublican message louder than Adolf Hitler. In speech after speech he railed about the "Berlin

Asiatics" who were bent on making Bavarians do their bidding. By no means a Bavarian particularist, not to mention a separatist, Hitler nonetheless understood that in Munich hatred of the republic was intimately connected with hostility toward Berlin and its centralizing bureaucrats. As long as Germany was ruled by the *Saupreussen,* he was eager to project himself as a Son of the South.

Soon Hitler was also feeling confident enough to challenge Munich's best-known rightists on questions of strategy. On 14 June 1922 the Nazi leader attended a meeting with Ludendorff, Kahr, Epp, and Georg Pittinger, who headed the Bavarian Bloc for the Maintenance of Public Order. When some at the meeting suggested that strategic compromises with the Berlin government offered the surest route to German revival, Hitler protested vehemently, insisting instead on a tactical alliance with the Communists "for the purpose of delivering them from the hands of the Jews and of making use of them later to get the power into our own hands." Hitler's heretical suggestion provoked his expulsion from the meeting. Before storming out, he shouted, "You will live to regret the treachery which you are committing against the German race today; you will recognize too late what a power I have behind me."

Hitler was getting ahead of himself here—his "power" was not yet all that evident—but his behavior at the meeting showed that he was already restless under the tutelage of his more established colleages and was willing to stand up against all of them—even the exalted Ludendorff. Yet Hitler's go-it-alone bravado was also partly bluff; he knew that he could not make genuine headway on the national scene without help from Munich's influential community of conservative nationalists.

In June 1922, shortly after Hitler's stormy confrontation with Kahr and company, President Ebert paid an official visit to Munich. The president had been scheduled to come a month earlier to open the German Trades Exhibition but had canceled his appearance at the last moment because of a scandal over political symbolism. To honor his visit, the Lerchenfeld government had agreed to fly the flag of the republic at the train station and exhibition building. However, rioters had torn down and burned the first banner, while the second one, in the words of a local newspaper, had been blown down by "the patriotic wind of Bavaria." When, after promises of enhanced security, Ebert announced he would come to Munich after all, Hitler issued a proclamation declaring that the visit was "an insult to Bavaria," and he threatened to use force to disrupt it.

In the end Ebert was able to make his visit without being attacked, but he could hardly have enjoyed his stay. As the British consul general reported, "The President arrived yesterday morning and was given a chilly reception . . . . He had the unpleasant experience of being hooted at wherever he went. There was no display of troops or bunting in the President's honour, and probably most foreign tourists here were entirely unaware that the head of the German State was visiting Munich."

On 24 June 1922 Germany was shaken by another political assassination, that of Foreign Minister Walther Rathenau. As a Jew and as one of the officials responsible for fulfilling the terms of the Versailles Treaty, Rathenau was a prime target for the right-wing hit squads. The killers came from the Berlin cell of the OC and carried out their bloody mission in the republican capital itself. It was an especially brazen affair: The murderers pulled up alongside Rathenau's open car as he was driving to work and sprayed him with machine-gun fire, then finished him off with a grenade.

The Rathenau murder galvanized the Bavarian capital as much as any city in the republic. The Munich City Council sought to pass a resolution condemning the killing; it was unable to do so, however, because the SPD and BVP delegates could not agree on appropriate wording. The Socialists' text called on the central government to adopt tough new measures aimed at preventing further attacks on republican officials. The conservatives merely urged that "responsible authorities" do all they could to combat "efforts to disturb law and order, from whatever direction they might come." While the Socialists sponsored a rally honoring the murdered minister, the Nazis distributed flyers saying, "Rathenau, now he's dead!! Ebert and Scheidemann, however, are still alive. To the gallows with the Jew government!"

Hitler was not among the Nazi demonstrators, for he was in Stadelheim Prison serving a month's sentence for breach of the peace. It seems that he and his followers had been a little too forceful in breaking up a rival political rally. The Lerchenfeld government wanted to show that even rightists had to respect the law. Hitler's sentence, however, was ridiculously light, and he received many privileges in jail, including a private toilet. While he welcomed the Rathenau murder, he had no illusions that a few assassinations would substantially change the picture. He was working for the day when the courts themselves would execute "10,000 of the criminals responsible for the November treason."

As the Munich Socialists hoped, the Reichstag hastily passed a Law for the Protection of the Republic, which contained restrictions on antirepublican groups and new penalties to be imposed on those who urged violence against the republic or its officials. One of its provisions required that all cases of treason and political murder be tried in a new central court in Leipzig. Bavarian conservatives opposed this measure because it undercut their state's own People's Courts. Thus, on 24 July 1922, three days after the Reichstag's law was published, the Bavarian Landtag passed a Decree for the Protection of the Republic, which would "replace national law" in instances of political transgressions.

Bavaria's rightists backed up their government's stand on states' rights with a massive demonstration on Munich's Königsplatz. The sponsors were a loose coalition of right-wing groups calling themselves the Fatherland Front. Among the speakers was Adolf Hitler, recently released from jail. Addressing the largest crowd he had ever faced, some fifty thousand people, he declared that Bavaria was "the most German land in Germany!" The "November criminals in Berlin," he said, must not be allowed to invade sanctuaries of patriotism in their efforts to persecute the true defenders of the national cause. He urged the assembled masses to take an oath "to save Germany in Bavaria from Bolshevism." According to one witness, Hitler's words were electrifying, his "magnetism holding these thousands as one."

A Raw and Brutal Bunch

Now calling himself a "writer" and living in a flat near the Isar River, Hitler saw to it that hardly a week went by without a Nazi meeting or rally. According to Munich police reports, by June 1920 the NSDAP counted eleven hundred members. A few months later Mayr could brag to the exiled Kapp about the progress the Nazis were making under Hitler:

> The nationalist workers' party is the basis for the strong commando troop we lead. Its program is still a little awkward and fragmentary, but we will amplify it. The fact is that under this flag we have won quite a few supporters. Since July of last year I've been trying to strengthen the group. . . . I've managed to bring some very competent young people to the fore. A Herr Hitler, for example, has become a dynamic force, a people's tribune of the first rank. In the local Munich chapter we now have over 2,000 members, while in September [i.e., a year earlier] it was only 100.

However, while the party continued to grow, the progress was not substantial enough to satisfy Hitler. What the group needed, he believed, was a more effective advertising vehicle. Thus when he learned in December 1920 that the *Völkischer Beobachter* (formerly the *Münchener Beobachter*) was for sale, he set out to buy it. To procure the 120,000-mark asking price, he turned to Dietrich Eckart, who squeezed half the necessary sum from Ritter von Epp and the Reichswehr, the other half from friends.

Hitler was also convinced that his fledgling party needed more effective ways of defending itself in the volatile atmosphere of postwar Munich. Many of the parties, especially those on the Left, maintained bands of toughs to protect their rallies and to rough up opponents. Determined that the Nazis would not be outdone in this area, Hitler set out to organize a paramilitary force that could put rival thugs to shame.

The resulting Storm Troop, or SA, grew out of a "gymnastics and sports" section established in the DAP soon after Hitler joined the group. Its first leader was a twenty-three-year-old watchmaker named Emil Maurice, who also served as Hitler's chauffeur. Maurice was soon succeeded by Hans Ulrich Klintzsch, a veteran of the Ehrhardt Brigade and a member of the OC. In its early phase the group was dominated by demobilized soldiers and ex-Freikorps men, along with nationalistic students, artisans, and white-collar employees. Most of the men were young and rowdy since the outfit's purpose was to fight, not to discuss fine points of party dogma.

And fight they did. Starting in fall 1920, the "gymnastic section" was on hand at every Nazi rally, bouncing hecklers with use of their "life preservers"—rubber truncheons and wooden clubs. They also broke up rival rallies and attacked opponents in the streets. Not surprisingly, they were especially keen on beating Jews. As they marched through the streets looking for victims, they sang: "The Jew with flat feet and hooked nose and crinkly hair / He dare not breathe our German air? Throw him out!"

Munich's police did little to deter the SA from its brutal business. Maurice bragged that "despite the presence of six policemen," his SA boys beat senseless a man in the train station who had dared call them "fresh fellows." According to one of Hitler's aides, Police Chief Pöhner's "tolerance" was absolutely crucial, for without it the SA might have been banned before it could properly establish itself. Hitler himself was aware of the importance of staying on the police's good side. He instructed his thugs not to call the cops "Jew lackeys," for "they hate the Jews too." He promised that if the SA kept its "discipline," it would soon have the run of Munich. Yet Hitler was also well aware that the SA could not be too fastidious if it was effectively to terrorize the party's enemies. His desire was for controlled and orchestrated violence, not for genuine restraint.

Indeed, to symbolize his commitment to radical, racist politics, Hitler adopted the red-white-black swastika flag as the official emblem for the party and its fighting arm. Explaining this choice at an SA meeting, he said, "Our flag is red, because we are 'social,' the circle is white, because we are 'national,' and the swastika means that we are anti-Semitic." The Nazis' colors and menacing hate symbol now became commonplace in the streets of Munich.

Hitler soon had cause to be thankful for the ready fists of his bullyboys. On 4 November 1921, during a Nazi rally in the Hofbräuhaus, the SA, now some three hundred strong, rose to defend their leader when he came under attack by some leftists. According to Hitler's later account, his storm troopers threw themselves "like wolves in packs of eight or ten again and again on their enemies, and little by little thrashed them out of the hall." In reality it was the Munich police who cleared the hall, though the SA split some heads and thus proved its reliability.

After the Hofbräuhaus imbroglio Hitler told an assembly of SA men: "We have won a major battle. You have survived a baptism of fire despite being outnumbered." He exulted in the fact that Münchners were calling the SA a "raw and brutal bunch who are afraid of nothing." He also announced proudly that he had recruited the "master boxer Haymann" to give boxing lessons to selected SA members. By the next spring he hoped to have sixty to eighty trained boxers in the SA ranks, "so that the opposition parties will fill their pants whenever they hear the SA name."

For all his tough talk and pugilistic fantasies, however, Hitler knew that the SA could not become a credible force without assistance from the Reichswehr, which had indicated a willingness to help support paramilitary groups at a time when its own numbers were held in check by the Versailles Treaty.

The key figure here was Ernst Röhm, who took over from Captain Mayr as the Bavarian Reichswehr's chief liaison with the *völkisch* community. A decorated war veteran, Röhm thought of himself as the soldier's soldier. "I am a soldier," he wrote in his memoirs. "I look at the world from my perspective as a soldier. A soldier cannot compromise. All my activities must be seen from this standpoint." The captain's military experience was written in his face, which featured a nose that had been partly shot away and a cheek deeply creased by a bullet scar. Since the end of the war he had put a lot of flesh on his short frame, the result of doing his politicking over endless steins of beer. He had joined the DAP in late 1919 and was providing it with small subsidies from a secret Reichswehr fund at his disposal. When the DAP grew into the NSDAP and created its SA, Röhm took the fighting group under his wing, sending regular subsidies its way, along with demobilized officers, Freikorps acquaintances, and even some active-duty soldiers. Röhm and Hitler, fellow former trench rats, became such fast friends that they used the intimate Du form of address, something the stiff Hitler did with very few people.

Whether Hitler knew then that his new friend was a homosexual is unclear; if he did, he did not let it impede what was obviously an invaluable relationship.

Hitler's Munich Helpers

With support from the regular army, Hitler's party was able to make its presence felt on the Munich scene, but it could not have elevated itself over competing *völkisch* groups had it not been able to grasp other helping hands in the Bavarian capital. Hitler himself would undoubtedly have remained a minor rabble-rouser without a little help from his friends.

Perhaps the most important lift came from elements of Munich's social and business elites. It may seem surprising that some wealthy citizens wished to associate with a bunch of brawlers like the Nazis. Yet it was precisely the Nazis' reputation for brutality that made them attractive to people still terrified of the radical Left. As for Hitler, his very marginality, his redolence of the seamy underside of life enhanced his appeal to bored socialites anxious to spice up their lives with the whiff of danger.

Hitler's contacts with members of Munich's elites did not come immediately. In the first year or so after the NSDAP's foundation, he had no relationship with Bavaria's industrial and business circles because his rhetoric sounded too radical. As we have seen, as late as June 1922 he could propose a tactical alliance with the Communists. But by this time, with his growing party in need of new sources of funding, he was trying to make his message more suitable to people of wealth and standing. In an address to the conservative National Club of Berlin in May 1922, he focused on the need to fight Bolshevism, claiming that only the NSDAP was capable of wooing workers from Marxism. Among his audience was a malt coffee maker from Munich named Hermann Aust. Upon his return to Munich, Aust arranged for Hitler to meet members of the League of Bavarian Industrialists and the Herrenklub, Munich's most fashionable men's club.

These meetings led to an invitation to address an audience of prominent businessmen in Munich's Hall of Merchants Guild. Hitler must have impressed his listeners, for after the talk a number of them gave money to Aust with the request that he pass it on to the Nazi leader. However, the sums in question were relatively small. One cannot speak, as some leftist journalists were doing, of Hitler's supping copiously at the well-laid table of "Big Business." Munich was simply not the place where this kind of largess would have been forthcoming; despite its industrial growth, the city still lacked a commercial establishment on the scale of Berlin or the Ruhr, and the business barons who resided there were notoriously frugal with their political donations. Hitler himself later complained that Munich was dominated by a "stingy petite-bourgeois mentality." Nevertheless, these modest contributions were important, for they enabled the Nazis to stay afloat when some of the other *völkisch* groups were sinking.

Hitler next managed to penetrate some of Munich's most exclusive private homes and salons. The ex-corporal could not have waltzed unintroduced into the inner precincts of Munich high society; he needed go-betweens to drop his name and smooth his path. Hitler's first contacts in this realm were facilitated by Dietrich Eckart, who took the young Austrian to meet his friends in the local artistic and literary community. But an even more useful social cicerone was Ernst F. Sedgwick ("Putzi") Hanfstaengl, perhaps the most colorful personality to lend the Nazi leader a patrician hand.

Tall, lanky, and lantern-jawed, Putzi Hanfstaengl descended on his father's side from well-heeled Bavarian art patrons and on his mother's from illustrious German-American stock. Hanfstaengl senior was heir to the family's Munich-based art reproduction business, which maintained branches in Rome, Paris, Berlin, London, and New York. To prepare Putzi to take over the business, his father sent him to Harvard, where he joined the Hasty Pudding, rowed crew, and played piano at college parties. After graduating from Harvard, he ran his family's art shop on Fifth Avenue, but the upsurge of anti-German sentiment during World War I convinced him to return to Germany. In 1921 he was back in Munich, working as a partner in the family business. According to his (not always reliable) memoir, *Unheard Witness,* Putzi met Hitler about a year after his return to Munich. As he tells the story, a former Harvard classmate serving as a senior official in the American Embassy in Berlin called to say that he was sending down the embassy's military attaché, Captain Truman Smith, to reconnoiter the political scene in Munich. Putzi agreed to show Smith around "in spite of the fact that the captain was a Yale man." He gave Smith letters of introduction to Kahr, Ludendorff, and Count von Lerchenfeld. But Smith cast his net wider than this: One day he called Putzi to say he had met "a most remarkable fellow" named Adolf Hitler and asked if Putzi could "have a look at him." Putzi duly went to hear Hitler speak at the Kindl beer hall and was, as he put it, "really impressed beyond measure." He was so impressed indeed that he pledged one dollar (then worth about six thousand marks) a month to the Nazi Party and a little later turned over fifteen hundred dollars to the party from his share of the proceeds generated by the family art shop in

New York. The money was used to buy a rotary press for the *Völkischer Beobachter,* allowing the paper to appear on a daily rather than weekly basis.

Soon Putzi was an integral part of Hitler's small circle of cronies in Munich. In addition to supplying much-needed cash, he ingratiated himself with Hitler by pounding out passages from Wagner's operas on the piano; Hitler was so smitten with Wagner than even Putzi's rough renditions sent him into ecstasy. Hanfstaengl also claims to have taught Hitler some Harvard fight songs and cheerleading drills, which allegedly so enthralled the Nazi leader that he ordered the SA to adopt them for its own use. " 'Rah, rah, rah!' became 'Sieg Heil, Sieg Heil!' " boasted Putzi, no doubt somewhat fancifully.

The SA hardly needed Putzi Hanfstaengl to learn to march, and the young Harvard man's value to Hitler and the party was less as a direct influence (all his efforts to enlighten the untraveled Austrian on the realities of life in the United State fell flat) than as an intermediary. In 1922 he helped Hitler break into Munich's circle of wealthy Wagnerians by putting him in contact with the Bechstein and Bruckmann families. Edwin Bechstein headed the great piano firm, while his wife, Helene, presided over fashionable salons in both Munich and Berlin. Hugo Bruckmann was a publisher whose authors included Wagner's son-in-law, Houston Stewart Chamberlain. His wife, Elsa, was a Romanian princess who spent much of her time looking down her nose at Helene Bechstein.

With his intimate knowledge of Wagner, Hitler tremendously impressed his society hosts. Frau Bechstein was so taken by the young man that she tried to get him to marry her daughter, Lotte. Hitler politely demurred, believing (with Eckart) that men with political ambitions should remain single. Unable to snare Hitler as a son-in-law, Helene treated him like a needy son, showering him with affection, food, and advice. On one occasion she also gave his cause a generous material shot in the arm. At a dinner party she threw for Hitler and Putzi, the latter tactlessly observed that the Nazi movement could survive for several months just on the jewelry she was wearing that evening; taking the hint, she gave Hitler some valuable objets d'art. As for motherly advice, she convinced him that an up-and-coming politician could not go around without a dinner jacket, broad-brimmed hat, and patent leather shoes, all of which she procured for him. Hitler was now suitably attired for the Bechsteins' salons, where he could rub shoulders with the "artistic" elements of Munich's reactionary high society. Here, to his great joy, he met Richard Wagner's son, Siegfried, and his English-born wife, Winifred.

Both (especially Winifred) were to become strong backers, giving him and his movement valuable cultural respectability.

As if aware of his growing social cachet, Hitler did not confine himself to the Bechsteins' embrace but allowed himself to be courted by their bitter rivals, the Bruckmanns. He dropped in at Elsa Bruckmann's salon, which had once been graced by Nietzsche and Rilke but now attracted *völkisch* zealots like Rudolf Hess, Alfred Rosenberg, and Baldur von Schirach (the Nazis' future youth leader). Another regular guest was Alfred Schuler, formerly of the Cosmic Circle, who enjoyed holding forth on the sexual symbolism of the swastika.

While Herr Bruckmann helped Hitler with (probably modest) financial contributions, Elsa Bruckmann, like Helene Bechstein, took it upon herself to make him *salonfähig,* fit for high society. Noticing, for example, that he had no idea how to eat an artichoke or a lobster, she instructed him in these gastronomical mysteries. Seeing his awkwardness upon meeting women, she taught him how to kiss a lady's hand. Again like her rival, Elsa outfitted Hitler in smoking jackets and fancy shoes.

Perhaps inevitably Frau Bruckmann and Frau Bechstein fell into bitter dispute in their simultaneous efforts to housebreak Hitler. Each claimed to be the primary influence; each swore that he cared only for her. Thus Frau Bruckmann became livid over reports that Frau Bechstein had given Hitler the leather dog whip he carried on his rounds. *She* had given him the whip, she said. The truth was that both ladies had presented Hitler with whips, and he had cavalierly allowed each patroness to assume that she was his sole benefactress.

Comical as such situations could be, they were part of a social makeover whose importance should not be underestimated. Through the solicitous instruction of his society backers, Hitler learned to move more comfortably in fashionable circles. This skill proved invaluable as he began to expand his influence beyond his original coterie of Bavarian lowbrows. One might say that Hitler's path to power was paved not only with broken heads and fiery speeches but also with properly eaten artichokes.

Another important, though less socially prominent collaborator was Heinrich Hoffmann, a photographer and amateur painter. Hoffmann's father had been court photographer to Prince Regent Luitpold and King Ludwig III; the son became court photographer to Adolf Hitler, and no modern prince could have wished for a more skillful Velázquez. Hoffmann began taking studio photos of Hitler in late 1922, placing him in poses designed to suggest a many-sided personality: brooding deep thinker; nature lover; fiery orator; SA brawler; even dashing charmer in lederhosen beefcake. Hitler actively disliked some of these shots, forbidding their use for propaganda purposes. Yet on the whole Hoffmann's work was instrumental in at once glorifying and humanizing Hitler. One of the portraits, printed on millions of postcards, became a valued icon among the faithful.

Flattering photography, however, was not the only service that Hoffmann rendered to Hitler. He welcomed the Nazi leader into his comfortable home in Schwabing, where Hitler could chat with the photographer's many friends, including Ernst Röhm and an ex-Jesuit priest named Bernhard Stempfle, who edited a scurilous racist rag called the *Miesbacher Anzeiger*. According to Hoffmann, Hitler was at first suspicious of Stempfle, thinking he might be a "spy of the church party." However, Stempfle gradually gained Hitler's confidence and was allowed to instruct him on the inner workings of the church.

Stempfle was a sometime professor at the University of Munich, whose faculty and student body constituted another important repository of support for Hitler in the early 1920s. Having emerged in the previous century as one of Germany's leading centers of learning, the university was increasingly falling victim to racist bigotry, nationalistic mania, and intellectual provincialism. Although Munich was hardly unique among German universities in showing these tendencies, it had the reputation for harboring the most decidedly *völkisch* professors and students in the republic. The signs of the times were abundant at the institution's sprawling Schwabing campus. In 1920 the great sociologist Max Weber was driven from his classroom for objecting to the clemency for Eisner's killer, Count Arco auf Valley. In the same year university officials canceled a guest lecture by Albert Einstein because of threatened "anti-Jewish demonstrations" by the students. Meanwhile, the association of fraternities voted overwhelmingly to exclude Jewish groups from their federation.

With rising anti-Semitism and extreme nationalism came open declarations of enthusiasm at the university for Hitler. Karl Alexander von Müller pushed his cause among the historians and social scientists; Stempfle rallied the theologians; Max von Gruber (of the Institute for Racial Hygiene) led an avid coterie of doctors and scientists; and Karl Escherich, brother of the Einwohnerwehr leader, took his entire Forestry Institute to hear Hitler's lectures. What impressed the professors was the Nazi leader's ability to articulate his message to ordinary people, a common touch that most of them lacked. Later Professor von Gruber (who became somewhat wary of the Nazis) commented: "We of the middle classes were grateful for Hitler's ability to find a following among the little people and thus to undermine the Social Democrats; in our enthusiasm, we overlooked the dangers inherent in his demagogy. We drove out the devil with Beelzebub."

Another key Hitler supporter among the Munich professoriate was the geographer Karl Haushofer. A former military officer who became a professor in 1921, Haushofer was known for his theory of Lebensraum. Put simply, this theory argued the life-or-death necessity of physical expansion by culturally dominant but "land-starved" states. The geographer insisted that Germany's destiny lay in expansion to the east. Haushofer's ideas came to Hitler's attention through the professor's student assistant, Rudolf Hess, who brought the two men together in 1922. After that Haushofer became one of Hitler's informal advisers on foreign affairs, and his theories, much watered down and vulgarized, found their way into *Mein Kampf.*

Much as Hitler profited from his association with professors and high society types, he did not really enjoy their company and tended to spend more of his time with people whose tastes and backgrounds were closer to his own. As one of his confidants wrote: "Hitler's associates were for the most part simple souls from the most modest homes, like his own, men who knew nothing of the great world beyond their own towns, but were enthusiastic, loyal, looking upon Hitler as not only a genius but an inspired prophet." It was tempting for Hitler's more sophisticated followers to dismiss these men—as Hermann Göring later did—as "a bunch of beer-swillers and rucksackers with a limited, provincial horizon." Yet that very provincialism could be an asset in the early 1920s because it helped Hitler plant a firm footing in the local soil. Sitting night after night in the Café Neumayr with cronies who hung on his every word, Hitler gained a stronger sense of mission. These men were the "backbone of Munich"; if he could conquer them so readily, why not the entire town? And then why not Germany?

Aside from their collective influence as a group, several members of Hitler's original inner circle performed key tasks for their leader and the party.

For personal protection, Hitler could rely on his chief bodyguard, Christian Weber, whom another confidant described as "a typical Munich roughneck, good-hearted and naive, but of colossal nerve and strength in the Nazi cause." A prodigious beer drinker, Weber was what the Germans call a "flesh mountain," almost broader than tall, and a frightening figure when seen pitching down the street in his bulging lederhosen and Tyrolean hat. With Weber by his side, Hitler could move around Munich with the swagger of a small-time gangster.

While Weber was fast with his fists, Hermann Esser was talented with mouth and pen. The twenty-two-year-old journalist had an instinctive feel for the moods and aspirations of ordinary Münchners. In knowing exactly which hot buttons to push, he kept the Nazis in the news and effectively spread the word that Hitler was the last best hope for Germany. With his fine sense of the local terrain, Esser also had the job of personally meeting with individual Nazis throughout the city to explain why it was necessary for Hitler to assume sole leadership over the party. He elucidated the new *Führerprinzip* (leadership principle), which held that (as Hitler put it) "The best organization is not that which inserts the greatest, but that which inserts the smallest, intermediary apparatus between the leadership of a movement and its individual members." Esser was so effective at this task that by the summer of 1921 Hitler was unquestioningly accepted as sole Führer by all the Munich cadres.

Another member of the inner circle who helped Hitler consolidate his control over the fledgling movement was Max Amann, who had been Hitler's sergeant in the war. He retained his sergeant's mentality, which came in handy in his efforts to impose a modicum of efficiency on the undisciplined Nazis. Hitler had given up none of his bohemian ways, and Amann had to summon all his drillmaster skills to get him to show up on time at meetings and appointments.

Hitler found a devoted personal helpmate and amanuensis in young Rudolf Hess, the Munich University student who introduced him to Haushofer. Like his future master, Hess had served in World War I, rising to corporal and winning the Iron Cross, Second Class. During the revolution he had fought against the Munich soviet and had narrowly escaped being grabbed as a hostage by the Reds. After the revolution he had met Eckart, who led him to Hitler. A born follower, the tall, buck-toothed, and morbidly shy Hess decided then and there to devote himself to Hitler's cause, a vow that he doggedly kept throughout his long life.

Another young intellectual who significantly helped Hitler in the early days was Alfred Rosenberg. He was a Baltic German who had fled to Munich at the time of the Russian Revolution. Like Hess, he had joined the Thule Society and befriended Dietrich Eckart, for whose journal *Auf gut Deutsch* he contributed prolix pieces about race and art. He had also translated "The Protocols of the Elders of Zion," an infamous forgery concocted by the czar's police to prove that the Jews were engaged in a vast conspiracy to enslave the world. A perpetually glowering, arrogant, and surly young man, Rosenberg soon alienated many of his colleagues. His unfortunate personality, along with his failure to understand that Nazism was more about power than "philosophy," eventually pushed him to the sidelines of the Nazi movement. In the early days, however, he made his mark on Hitler by aggressively arguing that Russia was an arch-foe that Germany needed to conquer in order to acquire necessary living space. Rosenberg may have been, as one commentator has noted, a "man of profound half-culture," but it was precisely this quality that qualified him for his unofficial title as "Hitler's co-thinker."

Years later, after Hitler had assumed power in Germany and moved to Berlin, he liked to reminisce about the early days of the party in Munich. He considered these days among the best in his life. They heightened his affection for the Bavarian city because he believed that Munich's political and cultural atmosphere had been crucial for his own ideological formation and the growth of the Nazi movement.

For once the historian can only agree. Hitler's real political education began after the suppression of the Bavarian soviet. He had been exposed to various right-wing dogmas and doctrines before coming to the Isar city in 1913, but he did not weave these notions into a coherent Weltanschauung until he started grappling with the demands of his new political vocation amid fellow *völkisch* agitators in postrevolutionary Munich. It was also in this heady environment that he first discovered and honed his famous "voice," his ability to sweep away mass audiences in a cascade of words.

In its earliest manifestation Hitler's chosen political vehicle was essentially a Munich phenomenon, with smaller offshoots elsewhere in Bavaria. The fledgling Nazi movement enjoyed crucial protection from local authorities, who, if not members of the group themselves, looked favorably on its aspirations. As Munich Police Chief Pöhner later explained, "[We] were convinced from the start that [the Nazi movement] was the one most likely to take root among workers infected with the Marxist plague and win them back into the nationalist camp. That is why we held our protecting hands over the National Socialist Party and Herr Hitler."

Hitler understood that if he could mobilize the rightist forces in Munich under his own banner, he would have a tremendous advantage not only over the leftists but also over right-wing groups elsewhere in the Reich. The Nazis would have a base of operations from which they could expand across the nation and to which they could repair and regather their strength if the need arose. As he put it, Munich would be the Nazis' "Mecca or Rome," the physical and spiritual representation of their "inner unity."

5

To the Feldherrnhalle

IN DECEMBER 1922 Adolf Hitler told the Bulgarian consul in Munich that parliamentary government was finished in Germany because it had no following among the people. A dictatorship would soon be installed; the only question was whether it would come from the Left or the Right. If that decision were left up to the German North, continued Hitler, a leftist regime would inevitably result, for the large northern cities had fallen under the sway of Socialists and Communists. But in Munich conditions were different; there the Nazi Party had been growing steadily and was "on the verge of taking power." The Reich's rescuers must therefore come from the healthy South, not from the corrupt North. Holding a wetted finger to the political winds, Hitler was confident that the moment was drawing nigh for him to step forth from his "city of destiny" as the savior of Germany.

"Egyptian Darkness"

In a report on the atmosphere in Munich during the Carnival season of 1922, William Dawson, the outgoing American consul, noted that there was much "wanton extravagance in food and drink." The debauchery, he said, was "very characteristic" of the Münchners, who had "always been noted for their love of pleasure and the whole-hearted manner in which [they] plunge into the Carnival gaieties." The consul's assessment was true enough, but the celebration this season was forced. Like the rest of Germany, Munich was caught up in a dizzying spiral of inflation. The mark had been losing value since the war, but the decline accelerated dramatically in the summer of 1922 following the assassination of Foreign Minister Rathenau. A week after the murder the mark stood at 401 to the dollar; ten days later it was 527. In September a Munich professor wrote that "things political and economical here are in a bigger mess than ever, the future wrapped in Egyptian darkness. As money is daily debased and sinking, no one is inclined to save, for 10,000 marks saved in April will only be worth 2000 marks in September. So you have an artificial and unhealthy spending of money; and to the superficial spectator it might seem as if most people were rolling in wealth." An important symbolic watershed was reached at the end of the year, when the largest bill then in circulation, the thousand-mark note, plunged to the point where it barely sufficed to cover a tram ticket. "With the belief in this venerated symbol of wealth and security," wrote Franz Schoenberner, editor of *Simplicissimus,* "the whole moral order of the little bourgeois had broken down."

But in truth the crumbling was only beginning. In the following year the currency lost value so fast that by autumn it was hardly worth the paper it was printed on. The Berlin Dadaists Kurt Schwitters and László Moholy-Nagy used billion-mark notes to make collages of the national symbol, the eagle, which they turned into a vulture.

This hyperinflation was ignited by Germany's response to the Franco-Belgian occupation of the Ruhr district in January 1923. In protest against the measure, taken because Germany had defaulted on some reparations payments, workers walked out of the factories. Berlin supported such "passive resistance" by covering lost wages and social benefits, which required cranking up the printing presses as never before. Soon more than thirty mills and some two thousand presses were working around the clock to produce paper bills that appeared in ever-higher denominations. In September 1923 the Reichsbank issued a 50-million-mark note; in October it followed with 1-, 5-, and 10-billion-mark bills; on 2 November a 100-trillion-mark note. By early November the mark had fallen to a value of 320,000,000,000 to the dollar; by the end of that month it stood at 4,210,500,000,000. The new American consul in Munich, Robert Murphy, recalled that playing poker that autumn was a heady experience: "It was quite a thrill to raise a trillion."

Most Münchners had no time to play games; all their efforts went into securing the necessities of life. In November 1923 the shortest tram ride cost 250 billion marks; an egg came to about 80 billion; a glass of beer 150 billion; and a sour pickle 4 billion. Prostitutes were able to command 6 billion marks and a cigarette for the "mistress-slave perversion." Everyone got rid of cash quickly, for it was likely to lose much of its value in the time it took to cart it (people actually used handcarts and wheelbarrows) from pay window to store. There were other dangers as well. A woman waiting in line to pay for groceries with a basket of money turned her back to chat with a neighbor; when she turned around, she discovered that someone had tipped out the money and stolen her basket.

The disintegration of the mark put tremendous strain on state and municipal governments. In Munich twelve supplemental budgets totaling nine times the original outlay had to be passed during the fiscal year 1922. Beginning in October 1923, at the height of the inflation, a mechanism was introduced to adjust spending to currency hikes on a daily basis. In that month the city budget totaled 35 million billion marks; dozens of extra clerks had to be hired simply to keep track of the twenty-two-zero sums. The city's Chamber of Commerce reported dolefully: "The fake blossoming of our economy has long since wilted, leaving behind nothing but dead leaves of paper."

Of course, as is always the case in socioeconomic catastrophes, some lucky or clever souls managed to profit from the disaster. People with access to foreign currency or gold could live like kings amid the destitute multitudes. *Simpl*'s Schoenberner recalled how some friends of his lived for many weeks in a fashionable Munich hotel on the proceeds from a deceased grandmother's golden denture.

The social tensions attending the Great Inflation were especially severe in Munich because the city's proximity to a rich agricultural hinterland had traditionally guaranteed relatively plentiful and inexpensive foodstuffs. Now, however, the lure of huge gains caused farmers to deal only on the lucrative black market, as they had in the war. Once again city folk were pillaging farms. Observing this development, the Saxon delegate in Munich thought he detected a degree of selfishness and rapaciousness that went beyond the general level of German nastiness. "One can understand why officials here are uneasy," he wrote, "when one considers the psychology of the Southern Bavarians, who are absolutely unwilling to suffer and to cope as the rest of the German population has to do."

An important concomitant of the Great Inflation was an invasion of tourists, flaunting their hard currency. Munich, always one of Germany's most popular destinations, experienced an influx of visitors in the early 1920s. "Munich is acquiring again much of the old-time charm and is of all the German cities the favorite for visitors to the fatherland. And the beer has the same old-time charm, too," wrote a local booster in 1922. The tourists, however, encountered not just good beer and old-fashioned charm but sullen resentment and opportunistic gouging. The American consul lamented:

> Persons recognized as foreigners by language or dress are frequently the object of hostile glances and may occasionaly be apostrophized in an insulting manner on the street or in public places. In a number of local hostels and restaurants, foreigners appear to receive less favorable treatment and less courteous attention from the management and employees than do German guests. A considerable number of local stores collect a so-called "Valutaufschlag" or extra charge on account of currency from nationals of countries possessing a high exchange, while a few merchants have been known to refuse to sell to foreigners. Munich physicians have entered into an agreement to charge for services to foreigners in the currency of their respective countries and in certain cases have presented to American patients bills which even in the United States would have been considered exorbitant.

The Münchners did not confine their discrimination to foreign nationals; they also targeted German visitors from outside Bavaria. The Berlin journalist Kurt Tucholsky complained that the Munich authorities applied special restrictions and fees to non-Bavarian travelers. "They impose upon travelers onerous rules and punishments, require entry and registration documents that are harder to come by than a visa to Nicaragua, and harass [non-Bavarian] Germans in unbelievable ways. Anyone who does not have a national beer belly of Bavarian provenance is a 'foreigner.' . . . What one finds down there is stupid Prussian bashing and a political narrow-mindedness of the worst sort."

A "German Mussolini"?

The despair generated by the Great Inflation proved a political godsend for Adolf Hitler and his young Nazi movement. "Things are so bad," admitted a member of the liberal Bavarian Democratic Party, "that thousands of decent and honest people are streaming to the Nazis." In his speeches Hitler harped on the horrors of the economic collapse, which he laid directly at the feet of the government in Berlin. The terrible "distress of the small rentier, pensioner, and war cripple," he cried, "stems from the policies of this weak republic, [which] throws its pieces of worthless paper about wildly in order to enable its party functionaries and like-minded good-for-nothings to feed at the public trough." The only salvation, he said, was a "patriotic dictatorship" that would rule in the interest of the hard-working German people and not kowtow to foreigners. "Already," he added, "millions feel that redemption is to be found in our movement. That has already become almost a new religious belief."

But how might that belief be translated into the reality of power? Fortunately for Hitler, there was a model ready to hand: Benito Mussolini, who had come to power in Italy in October 1922 after his Blackshirts' successful March on Rome. Impressed by the Duce's accomplishment, Hitler began to cast himself as a German Mussolini, ready to make his own march on the national capital. Speaking at a Nazi rally in mid-November 1922, he declared: "Mussolini has shown what a disciplined minority can do, if well organized, and if supported by the holy feeling of patriotism. In our country we shall have to do the same if we want to avoid ruin." Hitler's colleague Hermann Esser echoed dutifully: "What a band of courageous men was able to do in Italy, that we can do in Bavaria also. We, too, have [a] Mussolini. His name is Adolf Hitler."

The Nazis' threat to emulate the Italian Fascists brought the party added prominence, along with a new influx of young men anxious to break heads for Hitler. Yet the Bavarian authorities remained complacent. The state's new premier, Eugen von Knilling (BVP), told Consul Murphy in November 1922 that he did not feel that Hitler "is of large enough calibre to advance beyond the point of popular agitator. He does not partake of the qualities of a Mussolini, nor will he attain the measure of success of Kurt Eisner. He has not the mental ability and furthermore the government is now on guard as was not the case in 1918."

The authorities' underestimation of Hitler was all the more problematic because sociopolitical developments all seemed to be conspiring in his favor. France's occupation of the Ruhr, in addition to stimulating hyperinflation, engendered a new wave of aggressive self-pity in Munich.

Thomas Mann reported to his brother Heinrich that the "anger here is terrible—deeper and more unified as that which brought Napoleon down. It is difficult to say what the future will bring." The immediate future brought attacks on the French Consulate, which had to be guarded around the clock by Bavarian police.

Hitler was quick to respond to France's move. On the first evening of the occupation he told an overflow crowd in the Zirkus Krone: "France thinks less of Germany than she does of a nigger state." Yet he devoted most of his speech to an attack on the central government, not France. He insisted that Paris would never have dared to march into the Ruhr had not the "treacherous Jewish-Marxist regime in Berlin" so weakened the country that it was vulnerable to every act of extortion. Rather than waste time denouncing the French, he cried, the Germans should run the "November criminals" out of Berlin.

While Hitler ranted about the November criminals in Berlin, a number of conservative groups organized an anti-French rally in the Königsplatz from which the Nazis were excluded. They were kept out because local conservatives were beginning to believe that Hitler might be dangerous to Bavarian regional interests. The influential Christian Peasants Union worried that if he ever came to power, he would bully the states and impose price and production controls on agriculture. The Nazi leader was also chastised for proposing that Italy's postwar annexation of the Austrian South Tyrol (which was culturally close to Bavaria) should be accepted in the interest of smooth relations with Rome. Bavarian clericals feared (rightly, as it turned out) that he might not be a friend of the church. "In a word," wrote the British consul, "Hitler is no longer considered a Bavarian."

Hitler insisted that he was not offended by his exclusion from an event that seemed to him a worthless farce. "Protests by a defenseless people are completely useless," he told a Nazi meeting at the Café Neumayr on 15 January. "If a nation cannot accompany its protests with the flash of its sword, then the protest is merely a flash in the pan." The French would be a lot more impressed, he went on, if they were to learn that the German people, instead of shouting harmless slogans, were "hanging their traitorous leaders one after another." Only the Nazis, he concluded, were prepared to take such drastic measures, and they would do so alone if necessary. "We are powerful enough to proceed by ourselves. One can exclude us from the Königsplatz but that will only speed up the day when we make Munich our own."

Hitler's expression of go-it-alone bravado brought in a wave of fresh recruits. So many young men now wanted to join that the Nazi business office had to close down for a few days to process the applications. As rewarding as this development was for Hitler, however, it also carried a danger: Expecting him to deliver quickly on his promises of violent action, the new recruits were likely to grow restless if he dithered. As the British consul shrewdly observed, "[Hitler's] followers are rapidly getting out of hand; he will find it imperative to justify himself somehow, and the temptation to let himself be rushed into violent action will be hard to resist."

When Hitler announced in mid-January that the Nazis would hold a Party Day rally in Munich at the end of that month, many thought that the moment of reckoning had already come. According to the scenario, Nazis from all over Germany, as well as Austria and Czechoslovakia, would converge in the Bavarian capital for a weekend of meetings and marches. There would be an SA maneuver and rallies at every major beer hall. "The general expectation," cabled the British consul, "is that Sunday [28 January] will see a National Socialist outbreak."

The Bavarian government certainly harbored this fear, and its unease was compounded by news that the Social Democrats would stage a rally of their own to coincide with the Nazi demonstration. The Nazis could be counted upon to show their manhood by attacking the Socialists; moreover, they might even use the Red rally as the pretext for a coup. Determined to avert such a possibility, the Knilling government declared a state of emergency and banned both rallies.

Hitler learned of the ban just two days before the Party Day was set to begin. He told Police Commissioner Eduard Nortz that the rally would go on regardless of the prohibition. If the police decided to shoot when the storm troopers marched, he, Hitler, would "place himself at the head of the group, and they could shoot him down." But the first shot "would unleash a red flood," and two hours later "the government would be finished."

Despite such bloodthirsty rhetoric, Hitler did not want an armed confrontation with the government at this point; he sensed that his undisciplined forces would be no match for the police and army. At the same time, he believed that his rally must go on as advertised, or he would lose credibility with his own people. He therefore turned to some of his friends in high places for help in getting the ban reversed. With the assistance of Ernst Röhm he managed to secure an audience with General Otto von Lossow, chief of the Reichswehr garrison in Munich. During their meeting Hitler gave his "word of honor as a former soldier" that he would not attempt a putsch. A number of military officers, including Ritter von Epp, also vouched for Hitler, assuring Lossow that the Nazi leader was as good as his word. Röhm then took Hitler to see Gustav von Kahr, the former premier who now served as president of the government of Upper Bavaria. Hitler made the same promises to him.

Neither Lossow nor Kahr fully trusted Hitler, but both believed that the Nazis could be more effectively controlled if allowed to hold their rallies under the watchful supervision of the police. Moreover, both men frankly shared many of Hitler's sentiments, especially regarding the evils of Marxism and the perfidy of the central government in Berlin. They therefore agreed to intercede on Hitler's behalf with Premier von Knilling. In a matter of hours the prohibition was rescinded, with the proviso that there be only six beer hall meetings, no outdoor rallies, and no marches through the center of town.

Although Hitler had accepted the government's conditions, once the Nazi Party Day got under way on 27 January he reverted to his original plan of action. During the next three days the Nazi Party essentially took over Munich. It rented twelve of the largest beer halls for rallies, and it commandeered the Marsfeld (Field of Mars) for a ceremonial "consecration" of the swastika flags carried by its new SA units. The streets of the city reverberated to the sounds of Nazis marching, singing, and chanting. Hitler himself seemed everywhere at once, speeding from event to event in a new red Mercedes convertible.

In his speeches–he spoke at every one of the meetings–Hitler ridiculed the Knilling government, mocking its fears of a Nazi putsch. "Yes, Herr Minister, how do you know that we National Socialists want to make a putsch?" he jeered. "Oh, the milkmaid told you so! A streetcar conductor said so, a telephone operator heard it, and it is written in the *Münchener Post*!" The Nazis, he said, had no fear that the Knilling cabinet might cause them any difficulties: "The gentlemen of the government cling too tightly to their ministerial chairs to take the responsibility for firing on defenseless men. . . . This evening shows us that we have triumphed. Despite the exceptional law and state of siege our rallies take place, and our flag dedication will be held tomorrow."

Karl Alexander von Müller, the conservative historian, attended one of the Party Day rallies in the Löwenbräukeller on the Stiegelmayer Platz. In his memoirs he described the scene on that fevered night. "I had witnessed a lot of political rallies in this hall, but neither in war nor in revolution did I, upon entering the place, encounter such a hot breath of hypnotic mass enthusiasm. It went beyond the overcharged tension of these weeks, these days." Müller was impressed by the fact that the Nazis had their own "special battle songs, their own flags, symbols, and greetings" (the thrusting right arm salute, a variation on the Italian Fascists' greeting, had just been introduced). Müller saw "military-style ushers, a forest of bright screaming red flags with black swastikas against a white background." He experienced "a strange mixture of the soldierly and the revolutionary, of nationalist and socialist." The audience—"primarily downwardly mobile middle classes in all their variety"—seemed fully swept up in the spirit of the moment. Would they, he wondered, "be fused together permanently" by this movement?

Like rock concert fans sitting through interminable warm-up acts, the crowd waited impatiently for the headline event, an appearance and brief speech by Hitler. Finally he materialized at the main entrance and made his way toward the podium. "Every one of us," recalled Müller, "jumped up and shouted, 'Heil!' " Down through the middle of the shouting masses came the Nazi leader with his entourage, stepping briskly, his right arm raised stiffly in salute. "He passed very close to me," gushed the professor, "and I saw that this was a different person from the one I had met here and there in private houses: his narrow, pale features were concentrated in wrath, cold flames leaped from his piercing eyes, which seemed to search right and left for possible enemies, as if to cast them down. Was it the mass audience that gave him this uncanny power? Or did he empower the audience with his own inner strength?"

Hitler indeed knew just what these excited people wanted to hear, knew that they needed to be told that their moment of glory and triumph was nigh. At the same time, however, he sought to discourage aspirations for an immediate coup. "We are a movement that lives and grows," he declared. "We can allow ourselves to be a little patient. We grow each week in numbers and power. One day soon our moment will certainly come–the moment when we make a putsch? No, not a putsch, but rather a trumpet blast, and then the walls will come crumbling down."

On the following day Hitler presided over the consecration of the swastika flags presented to the party's four new SA regiments. The banners hung Roman style from long poles and featured the phrase "Germany Awaken!" coined by Dietrich Eckart. The SA men standing in review wore old military uniforms or the alpine outfits of the Freikorps Oberland (the trademark brown shirts would come later). All sported swastika armbands and gray ski caps, which made them look as if they were about to embark on a jolly winter outing. But, of course, their purpose was much more solemn, as Hitler made clear when handing them their precious flags. "No member of that race which is our foe and which has led us into this most abject misery, no Jew shall ever touch this flag," he intoned. "It shall wave before us throughout all of Germany in the march to victory, and pave the way for the flag of our new German Reich."

The Munich authorities noted full well that Hitler had violated the conditions under which he had been allowed to hold his Party Day rally. However, in their relief that the event had passed without significant violence (the ban on the Socialists' counterrally had remained in force), they did not call the Nazis to account. Their passivity was reminiscent of the royal regime's behavior in the face of Kurt Eisner's assault on the monarchy in November 1918. Once again the authorities failed to respond decisively to a brazen challenge. As Carl Moser von Filseck, neighboring Württemberg's delegate in Munich, aptly observed, "The dominant view here is that the government has been made to look foolish; as a result its prestige has suffered a considerable blow, as seen both by the Left and the Right."

"A War Ace with the Pour le Mérite"

In the excitement of Party Day Hitler was again overreaching himself: the swastika flag could not wave over Germany until it waved over Munich, which, despite the Nazis' gains, was still controlled by a conservative government that was unlikely to line up dutifully behind him when he finally gave the signal to march on Berlin. One of the later Nazi fighting songs proclaimed "Today Germany, Tomorrow the Whole World." In mid-1923 a more appropriate slogan would have been: "Today Munich, Tomorrow Germany."

As part of his efforts to strengthen the Nazis' position in Munich and Bavaria, Hitler sought to beef up the SA, which for all its bright new banners remained an undisciplined band of roustabouts. Leadership was a particularly pressing problem, for the head of the group, Hans Ulrich Klintzsch, was not a commanding figure. Hitler was determined to replace him as soon as a suitable candidate could be found.

It was "a stroke of fate," Hitler later said, that just as he was casting about for a new SA head, a young man named Hermann Göring walked into Nazi headquarters and offered his services. Twenty-seven years old, Göring already had a colorful and varied life behind him. He had spent part of his childhood with a foster family in Fürth, near Nuremberg, while his parents went off to Haiti, where his father was stationed as a consular official. Later his mother became the mistress of a flamboyant physician named Hermann Ritter von Epenstein, who had been ennobled by Kaiser Wilhelm II. Epenstein installed the Göring family in an opulent castle north of Nuremberg. Hermann came to idolize Epenstein so thoroughly that he chose him when asked to write a school essay on "The Man

I Admire Most in the World." Only when the essay was returned with the comment that one ought not write in praise of Jews did young Hermann learn that his godfather was Jewish. Although shocked, he remained loyal to Epenstein and got into fistfights with classmates who taunted him. Determined to become a soldier, he fled as soon as he could, undertaking military training in Karlsruhe and then in the Prussian cadet school at Gross Lichterfelde near Berlin.

At the outbreak of World War I Göring was a lieutenant in the infantry, but he soon left that branch to join the air corps, whose aviators jousted like latter-day knights high above the trenches. He soon established himself as one of the great aces of the air war, claiming twenty-seven kills. So skilled was he that he was appointed to succeed Manfred von Richthoven as commander of the Flying Circus squadron when the legendary "Red Baron" fatally crashed behind enemy lines in April 1918. Like Richthoven, Göring won the coveted Pour le Mérite, Germany's highest award for valor.

Göring's honors and fame, however, were more a liability than an asset in the revolutionary atmosphere of postwar Germany. Moving to Red Munich, he ran afoul of the city's revolutionary leaders. He was saved from arrest (and possible execution) by a British member of the Allied Disarmament Commission whom he had chivalrously befriended during the war.

Disgusted by the turn of events in Munich and Germany, Göring decamped for Scandinavia in the spring of 1919. There he worked as a stunt flier, Fokker airplane salesman, and pioneering commercial pilot. His work was poorly paid, but to the young adventurer it was the next best thing to aerial combat.

When flying a charter route in the far north, Göring was forced to make an emergency landing near a castle in the Swedish countryside. Entering the castle, which was decorated with hunting trophies and Nordic battle scenes, he encountered a tall blond woman who might have stepped out of the Nibelungen Saga. She was Carin von Foch, sister of the castle owner's wife. Hermann was immediately smitten by her, and she by him. Alas, Carin was married to a Swedish army officer and had an eight-year-old child. For a time she and Göring carried on a clandestine affair, but soon they decided to marry. While Carin set about arranging a divorce, Hermann enrolled at the University of Munich, hoping to learn a profession that was more lucrative than barnstorming. As soon as Carin's divorce came through, she joined him in Munich, and they married.

In the bleak, inflation-ridden winter of 1922, Hermann found himself together with Rudolf Hess in Karl Alexander von Müller's German history class. The professor later recorded the following description of the future second-in-command of the Third Reich: "He was not yet corpulent or possessed of that strange Neronian femininity that marked his later years; on the contrary, he had the taut body of a combat flier, with a massive chest that jutted out like a knight's breastplate over the tiny classroom desk. . . . Compared to the earlier officers, he was like an exuberant farmhand. When he said something, it was decisive, intelligent, often not without humor, and almost invariably overemphatic."

Despite the adulation of nationalist professors, Göring did not enjoy his historical studies, for he was by nature a man of the sword (or the joystick), not of the pen. Increasingly he cut class and started investigating the political gatherings around town, window-shopping for a purpose in life.

On one occasion he wandered into a Nazi meeting at the Café Neumayr—in fact, into the very meeting where Hitler blasted the Bavarian conservatives for not being prepared to put their guns where their mouths were in their response to the French occupation of the Ruhr. "That was the kind of talk I wanted to hear," said Göring to himself; "that's the party for me! Down with the Treaty of Versailles, God damn it! That's my meat!" Yet it was not just tough talk that attracted him to the Nazis. Like Hitler, he gravitated to the group because it was still small and inchoate enough for him to become, as he put it, "a big man in it."

When Göring presented himself at party headquarters, Hitler was ecstatic: here, amid the beer bellies and trolls, was someone who looked the way Nazis were supposed to, who was a decorated war hero, and who, to make matters perfect, was married to a Nordic beauty with a large fortune. "Splendid, a war ace with the Pour le Mérite!" cried Hitler. "Excellent propaganda! Moreover, he has money and doesn't cost me a cent." The Nazi leader immediately put his new acquisition in charge of the SA with orders to pound some discipline into the outfit.

"You Have Mighty Things to Accomplish"

Not long after Göring took over the SA, Hitler thought he saw a new opportunity to flex the Nazi Party's muscles. Learning that the Bavarian government had given permission to Munich's leftists to hold their traditional May Day march in Munich, Hitler threatened to attack the parade if the government did not ban it. The leftist celebration, he explained, would be "an insult to the overwhelming majority of the city, who saw in the red flag of 1 May the blood of the hostages of 1919 and the painful symbol of the collapsing fatherland." This date, moreover, also had become sacred to the Right, since it was on 1 May 1919 that the Freikorps had "liberated" Munich from soviet control. Hitler further claimed that the leftist parties intended to use the march to launch a coup. When the government nonetheless refused to ban the leftist festival, Hitler ordered his SA to redouble its training in preparation for a showdown.

As the Red holiday dawned, SA units and various armed bands belonging to the recently established Task Force of Patriotic Combat Groups assembled at the Oberwiesenfeld north of the city. Aside from the SA, there were units of the Reichskriegflagge (Reich War Flag, a paramilitary outfit run by Ernst Röhm), the Bund Oberland, and the Bund Wiking, a successor to the disbanded Organisation Consul. Their total numbers were estimated from between twelve hundred and two thousand, and they were equipped with rifles, machine guns, and a few horse-drawn cannon. In preparation for their anticipated confrontation with the Reds, they staged military maneuvers and practiced assault tactics.

All the while, however, elements of the Bavarian State Police, backed up by the Reichswehr, were surrounding the Oberwiesenfeld. Having been humiliated by Hitler during the recent Party Day rally, the government was determined to show him who ran Munich. It had no desire, moreover, to allow the Nazis to turn the May Day festivities into a bloody civil war.

Alerted about the government's actions, Hitler was at once outraged and indecisive. Wearing a steel helmet and his Iron Cross, he stalked around the field, trying to figure out what to do. As his colleague Otto Strasser described the scene: "The sun climbed into the sky—eight o'clock . . . nine . . . ten . . . eleven. . . . Adolf Hitler paced a jittery path before his lieutenants, occasionally removing his steel helmet to wipe the rivulets of perspiration from his face and forehead, gazing long and often toward Munich, the scene-to-be of his great triumph."

Shortly after eleven o'clock a detachment of Reichswehr troops marched onto the field, flanked by units of the state police. Röhm, who had tried unsuccessfully to win the army over to the Nazi cause, was with the troops. The military unit's commander demanded that Hitler and his allies surrender their weapons and disperse immediately. Some of Hitler's colleagues urged him to fight rather than submit to this humiliation, but the Nazi leader, aware that violent resistance might mean the quick and bloody end to all his dreams, rejected their pleadings. "He sulked, taciturn and glowering, but he wouldn't listen to those of his leaders who favored a pitched battle," reported Strasser disappointedly.

After a few minutes of tense standoff, the would-be saviors of Munich handed over their weapons and retreated from the field. Marching through Schwabing, Hitler and some SA men encountered a pair of Communists with a red flag, which they confiscated and burned. Hitler declared that this was but a small token of the fires to come. But there was no serious fighting that day between the rightists and the Reds, who celebrated peacefully on the Theresienwiese. According to the Left, this proved that the streets of Munich were not the exclusive possession of the Nazi hordes, whatever their claims.

Hitler tried to put the best face on the May Day fiasco. As his men were handing over their weapons, he assured them that since the city was apparently calm, no action was needed anyway. He even tried to claim that the Nazi mobilization had effectively intimidated the Reds. To cheer his troops further, he promised defiantly: "Our day will come soon."

His defiance rang hollow to some observers, who saw the May Day defeat as the beginning of the end for Hitler. Consul Murphy, for one, cabled Washington that the Nazi movement was "on the wane," because young radicals were tired of an enterprise that seemed to offer nothing but rhetoric, while the rowdy conduct of his men had antagonized "order-loving members of the community."

For a time after the May Day debacle. Hitler himself seemed discouraged about his prospects. He spent several weeks in seclusion in the alpine town of Berchtesgaden, southeast of Munich, living under the name Herr Wolf in a humble pension. He blew off steam by regaling the pension owner's wife about the evils of Berlin, decrying its "luxury, perversion, iniquity, and wanton display of Jewish materialism." Evoking Christ's encounter with the money changers in the temple, he promised one day to drive out these worshipers of the Golden Calf. For the moment, however, he seemed content to enjoy the beauty of the landscape. Later he was to build his own retreat in this region and, like a latter-day King Ludwig II, escape to it whenever he could.

While Hitler licked his wounds and planned his next moves, the city from which he hoped to launch his cleansing crusade seemed itself in need of a purge. The galloping inflation was bringing out the worst in everybody. Bands of young toughs roamed the streets, rolling old folks for their watches and rings. A journalist called the city "a witches' cauldron of conspiracy, terror, and treason." In such an atmosphere it seemed only appropriate that the Residenztheater premiered Bertolt Brecht's *Im Dickicht der Städte* (*In the Jungle of Cities*) in May 1923. Albeit set in Chicago, the play struck many Münchners as a commentary on their own city in its hour of disorder.

The atmosphere in Munich became even nastier in the early fall when the Reich government, under newly appointed Chancellor Gustav

Stresemann, decided to abandon the costly policy of passive resistance to the French occupation of the Ruhr. In Bavaria and Munich, as indeed throughout Germany, this concession was denounced as a craven submission to foreign pressure.

Hitler, having in the meantime returned to Munich and the political fray, led the crusade against the Stresemann regime. In weekly speeches at the Zirkus Krone he branded the new government traitorous successors to the "November criminals." Again he urged a Mussolini-style solution to the German problem: a march on Berlin. From the size and enthusiasm of his audiences, it seemed that thousands of Münchners agreed with him.

Hoping to undercut Hitler's appeal and to discourage any attempts at a coup, Knilling's government declared a state of emergency based on Article 48 of the Weimar Constitution. (This was technically illegal, for that article gave the right to issue emergency decrees to the national government, not to the states.) In addition, on 26 September Knilling called on former Premier Gustav von Kahr to serve as "general state commissar" of Bavaria. Kahr's new office was vaguely defined, but he was assured that he would have a "free hand in the exercise of executive power."

Because Kahr was widely detested for his earlier repressive policies as premier, this was a provocative move. Recalling Berlin's feud with Kahr over the Civil Guards, Stresemann's government rightly sensed new trouble in the wind. It worried that under Kahr the southerners might even attempt a coup against the Weimar system. But if that should happen, Stresemann promised, he would not flee Berlin as the Socialist-led government had done during the Kapp Putsch. The putschists could "shoot me down right here, in the place where I have every right to sit," he declared. Kahr's old enemies at home were also horrified to see him back at the helm. Commenting on his appointment, the *Times* (London) observed that it was "not calculated to maintain peace in Bavaria, where his party has done as much as any to inflame the political passions and anti-Semitism. . . . Not only the Communists, but the Socialists and even the Republican Democrats, are among his bitterest enemies, and his own fanatical supporters will be unappreciative should he hold the balance at all fairly." The Nazis and their allies were also unenthusiastic about the monarchist Kahr; they regarded him as among the worst of the old-fashioned "high collar politicians."

Kahr's supporters need not have worried that he would show balance or fairness in his dealings with the various political factions contending for power in Bavaria. True, he banned some mass meetings planned by the Nazis, but he was much harder on the Left, dissolving the paramilitary organizations of the SPD and KPD and forbidding all strikes. More ominously, he launched a crusade against foreign-born Jews as part of an ostensible effort to improve the economy. More than one hundred Jewish immigrants who had been charged (though not convicted) of usury or war profiteering were given fourteen days to get out of Bavaria. Kahr justified this action on the ground that "the Jewish element [was] responsible for much of the German misfortune and economic distress since the war." This, of course, was an old story, and Kahr hoped to consolidate his new regime by dipping into the deep well of popular anti-Semitism.

The crackdown on foreign Jews caused Kahr no difficulties with the central government, but the Bavarian commissar soon found himself at war with Berlin on other issues, above all on his handling of the always troublesome Nazi Party. Shortly after Kahr's appointment the Nazis' *Völkischer Beobachter* ran some vituperative attacks on Stresemann and Reichswehr General Hans von Seeckt. The latter, said the paper, did not enjoy the support of the army because he (like Stresemann) had a Jewish wife who influenced him politically.

Seeckt, the ultimate bemonocled Prussian general, was not used to this kind of gutter attack and immediately ordered the Reichswehr chief in Munich, General Otto von Lossow, to suppress the Nazi paper. Concerned that if he obeyed this order, the streets of Munich might erupt in violence, Lossow turned to Kahr for advice. The commissar was no friend of the Nazis, but he was always anxious to display Bavarian independence vis-à-vis Berlin. He therefore instructed Lossow to defy Seeckt's order, as the former proceeded to do. Once again Munich stood toe to toe against its northern rival.

Adolf Hitler was delighted to be the immediate cause for this latest flare-up in the old antagonism between North and South. There was a certain irony here, for the Nazi leader was at heart an archcentralizer who had no use for Bavarian particularism. But as we have noted before, he also understood that he could manipulate Bavarian hatred of the central government to solidify his own standing in the South. Indeed, he now believed that the rift between Munich and Berlin was so severe that he might garner support from local conservatives, perhaps even from Kahr and Lossow, for his long-promised putsch against the Weimar order.

To fortify himself spiritually in this sharpening test of wills, Hitler went to Nuremberg on 30 September for a German Day celebration marking the anniversary of the Prussian victory over France in 1870 at Sedan. The Nazi chief joined other nationalist leaders in forming a new coalition called the Kampfbund (Battle League), which was meant to bring more coherence to the patriotic camp. Speaking before a mass audience at the beginning of the rally, Hitler again raised his followers' hopes for quick and decisive action. "In a few weeks the dice will roll. What is in the making today will be greater than the World War. It will be fought out on German soil for the whole world."

As soon as the Nuremberg rally ended, Hitler drove to nearby Bayreuth, the small Franconian town in which his idol Richard Wagner had spent his last years and built his famous festival theater. Stopping in at Wahnfried, the imposing Wagner villa, Hitler was received by the composer's widow and heirs: eighty-six-year-old Cosima, her son, Siegfried, and her daughter-in-law, Winifred. He then spent some time standing alone at Wagner's grave in the backyard, no doubt soliciting support from the Master's spirit. Finally, he went across the street to see Houston Stewart Chamberlain, who was now partially paralyzed and unable to speak. This was just as well, for it gave Hitler the chance to expound without interruption his plans for building a new Germany. Chamberlain must have been impressed, for after Hitler's return to Munich he sent him a letter saying that the visit had "changed the state of my soul" and given him new hope for Germany. "You have ahead of you tremendous things to accomplish," he declared.

Nothing that transpired in Munich over the course of the next few weeks altered Hitler's conviction that he was a man of destiny, but he also became increasingly aware that he must act soon. Shortly after his return to the capital in early October, he was told by Wilhelm Brückner, chief of the Munich SA, that the storm troopers were getting restless for lack of serious action. They had expended their "last ten pfennings on SA training" in the expectation that through a successful putsch they could be taken into the regular army "and be out of the entire mess." He added: "If nothing happens now the men will sneak away."

At the same time, the political confrontation between Munich and Berlin took on added urgency when General von Seeckt, losing his patience over Lossow's failure to ban the *Völkischer Beobachter,* ordered him to resign his position as head of the Bavarian Reichswehr. Torn between his duty to obey Seeckt and his loyalty to Bavaria, Lossow again turned to Kahr for guidance. The latter not only insisted that Lossow retain his command but also ordered the Reichswehr's Seventh Division, stationed in Bavaria, to take an oath of allegiance to that state.

This was open rebellion against the framework of national unity devised by Bismarck and confirmed by the Weimar Constitution. Old-line Bavarian particularists toasted Kahr as the next best thing to a Wittelsbach king. Members of the Infantry Cadet School in Munich showed their contempt for Berlin by wearing the cockades on their hats reversed, which, according to Putzi Hanfstaengl, was the accepted formula for saying "Kiss my ass!" Other Münchners demonstrated their feelings by pasting stamps of President Ebert upside down on envelopes.

Kahr himself, however, did not seem to know whether he wanted to lead Bavaria into some kind of regional autonomy or to remake the German nation in the image of "healthy Bavaria." Popular sentiment in Munich was also divided between those screaming *"Los von Berlin!"* (Break away from Berlin!) and those demanding *"Auf nach Berlin!"* (On to Berlin!)

To confuse the situation further, just as Kahr was thumbing his nose at Seeckt and the central government, he was also making life more difficult for the Nazis in Bavaria. On 5 October he closed down the *Völkischer Beobachter* for ten days because it had run an SA recruiting ad that sounded like an invitation to a putsch. So no one would get the wrong idea, however, he made it clear that this ban had nothing to do with the Reich's request for action against the paper. But as far as Hitler was concerned, anti-Nazi measures from Kahr were more dangerous than decrees from Berlin. If Kahr could consolidate his power by simultaneously defying the Reich and holding the Nazis at bay, then *he,* not Adolf Hitler, would most likely be the one to define how the conflict with Berlin found its resolution.

Hitler could not afford to acquiesce, but he also had to be careful not to alienate Kahr and his key lieutenants, Lossow and State Police Chief Hans von Seisser. For a time he tried to wean Lossow and Seisser from Kahr by promising them high offices in the new national dictatorship he planned to establish. But the two officials had more faith in Kahr than in Hitler and kept their distance from the Nazi leader. Kahr and his lieutenants, moreover, now began holding private meetings with various rightist figures in Munich, while pointedly excluding Hitler. On 6 November the Bavarian triumvirate conferred with Kampfbund leaders about a possible move against the national capital. They made no concrete plans for such action, however, and the Bavarian leaders stated their opposition to any independent ventures on the part of the radical nationalists.

Hitler immediately got word of this meeting, as he was meant to. The message he drew from it, however, was not what Kahr had intended. Instead of concluding that he would have to wait until the Bavarian officials were ready to act, he decided he must move on his own and pull the others along. He must grab power in Munich and then invite his rivals to accompany him to Berlin. *"Wir müssen die Leute hineinkompromittieren"* (We must coax these people into complicity) was the way he put it. He seems to have believed that when presented with a successful coup in their own backyard, the Bavarian leaders would have no choice but to go along with it.

This was the word he communicated to his top aides at a hastily convened meeting in the evening hours of 6 November. The Nazis could delay their strike no longer, he said; they would move as early as 11 November, the fifth anniversary of the armistice ending World War I. A Nazi victory in Munich would be the first step in reversing that humiliation. This historic day had the added advantage of falling on a Sunday. Hitler explained to Putzi Hanfstaengl that the only time to launch a putsch was over a weekend. "All the people in the administration are then away from their offices and the police are only at half strength. That is the time to strike."

Beer Hall Baby

No sooner had the Nazis settled on their Sunday putsch than they were obliged to alter their plans. News arrived at party headquarters that General Commissar von Kahr would host a meeting in the Bürgerbräukeller on the evening of 8 November to outline his political agenda for the immediate future. The suddenness of the announcement led Hitler to suspect that what Kahr really had in mind was a preemptive strike of his own, probably the proclamation of a Wittelsbach restoration under Crown Prince Rupprecht. This was a frightening prospect, for a successful restoration would undoubtedly dash Hitler's hopes of making Munich the springboard for his "national revolution." He decided that he could not risk allowing Kahr to have his say; he would make his move at the same gathering, where he could not only outflank Kahr but, if necessary, arrest him and the entire Bavarian government. Fortunately the date 8 November also had symbolic significance, for it was the anniversary of Eisner's proclamation of the Bavarian republic, another humiliation Hitler hoped to reverse.

Because Hitler made his decision to strike so precipitously, he had little time to prepare his move. He also had to be careful not to alert the government to his intentions. He therefore began mobilizing the SA, along with other paramilitary units belonging to the Kampfbund, without telling the men exactly what was afoot. The troopers were called to their assembly areas via white notices, which indicated mere training sessions, rather than with red ones, which signaled a serious action. As it happened, the mobilization was not so unobtrusive as to go unnoticed by the Munich police, but Kahr and Seisser decided not to order any special security measures. Paramilitary maneuvers and mobilizations, after all, were by now a commonplace on the Munich scene, and in any event Kahr did not want to give the impression that he feared his own citizenry.

The Bürgerbräukeller, site of the scheduled meeting, was east of the Isar River about a mile from the city center. Like the more famous Hofbräuhaus, it had a number of dining rooms serving the inevitable oxen flanks and pigs' feet, as well as a vast banquet hall that could be used for political gatherings and other ceremonial purposes. The hall was packed that evening of 8 November, mostly with prosperous-looking burghers in suits and furs. One observer got the feeling, however, that some in the audience had not been invited, and indeed, there were quite a few Nazi gate-crashers sprinkled among the crowd.

At about eight Kahr mounted the podium and began to deliver a speech about the evils of Marxism; his pedantic oration seemed designed more for a university lecture hall than a beer hall. The performance was so boring that many in the audience, already well sedated with meat and drink, fell off into merciful slumber.

While Kahr droned on inside the hall, a red Mercedes pulled up outside. Hitler, dressed in his ubiquitous trench coat, stepped out and entered the lobby, where a small group of his supporters waited impatiently. "Minutes seemed like hours. After all, we were all aware that a fateful moment was at hand, which would spell either victory or jail," recalled Johann Aigner, an aide to Scheubner-Richter. To help kill time, Putzi Hanfstaengl handed out beers. "I remember that they cost a billion marks apiece," he wrote later. "I took a swig at one myself and handed the others to our group; Hitler took a thoughtful draught. In Munich, I thought, no one will suspect a man with his nose in a stein of beer of having sinister motives."

After a few more minutes a number of trucks arrived and unloaded their cargo of heavily armed SA men. They surrounded the building and blocked all the exits. Shortly thereafter, according to Putzi, the "front door burst open and in tumbled Göring, looking like Wallenstein on the march, with all his orders clinking, plus about twenty-five brownshirts with pistols and machine guns. What an uproar." Within seconds Göring's men had mounted a heavy machine gun in the doorway of the main hall, pointed directly at the audience. "The philistines got quite a shock at the sight of the machine gun and other weapons," recalled Aigner.

Hitler and his band now started to plow through the crowd, knocking over tables as they went. Karl Alexander von Müller, sitting near the middle of the hall, recalled what happened next:

Steel helmets became visible above the crowd. People jumped up on benches to see what was going on. Suddenly, right in front of me, I saw Adolf Hitler heading down the main aisle toward the podium, bent over, face pale, dark strands of hair hanging down. On either side of him came storm troopers with red armbands, holding pistols above their heads. To the left of me and about ten paces in front of Kahr, Hitler stopped, climbed on a chair, and gave the man to his right a sign. A shot rang out and ripped a hole in the ceiling. "The German revolution has broken out!" he screamed in the sudden quiet. "This hall is surrounded!"

Despite his theatrical bravado, Hitler did not seem very impressive at this moment. Many in the audience were shocked by his crude interruption of their evening. Shouts of "South America" and "Mexico" rang through the hall. Hitler stripped off his trench coat to reveal a cutaway; in the words of one witness, he looked like "a cross between Charlie Chaplin and a headwaiter." Yet it would not do to mock him, for he clearly had the firepower on his side.

Hitler got down from his chair and strode to the speakers' platform, where Kahr, Lossow, and Seisser stood motionless. The Nazi leader demanded that the three men accompany him to a side room, where he asked their forgiveness for proceeding in such a fashion. "It is done and cannot now be undone," he mumbled, as if contrite. Then he told the triumvirate that he was creating a new Bavarian government in preparation for an assault on Berlin. Each of the men would have to accept the post assigned him in the new order. Brandishing a pistol, he declared that if his plan failed, he would shoot the "traitors" and himself.

Despite Hitler's histrionics, Kahr, Seisser, and Lossow did not immediately promise their support. Instead they forced him to spend a good quarter hour lecturing them on their patriotic duty. Back in the main hall, meanwhile, the audience was becoming restless. Some tried to leave but were turned back at gunpoint by SA men. To restore order, Göring mounted the podium and fired a second shot into the ceiling. He told the crowd that Kahr and company were not in danger and that everyone must be patient while a new Germany was being born. "And anyway," he added, "you've got your beer. What are you worrying about?"

Eventually Hitler returned to the podium. He still seemed unsure of himself, demanding attention with yet another shot into the ceiling. As he began to speak, however, he recovered his form. According to Müller, his performance was an "oratorical masterpiece, which any actor might envy." He said that a new government was being formed in which Bavaria's present leaders would all have a place. General Ludendorff would take over the army and return it to its former glory. The goal of the provisional government would be "to begin the march against Berlin, that sink of iniquity, with all the might of this state and the accumulated power of every province of Germany."

His words had an electrifying effect. Müller reported that within a few minutes the audience, originally surly and suspicious, "had fully reversed itself. Hitler had turned them inside out, as one turns a glove inside out, with a few sentences. . . . Loud approval roared forth, no further opposition was to be heard."

Once he had the crowd securely in his hands, Hitler announced dramatically: "Outside are Kahr, Lossow, and Seisser. They are struggling hard to reach a decision. May I say to them that you will stand behind them?" "Yes, yes!" roared the crowd. Part of their enthusiasm, however, undoubtedly derived from the magic of that moment, from the sense, skillfully encouraged by Hitler, that they were present at the creation of a new Germany. Once away from the excitement, many in the crowd would have second thoughts about what they had so heartily approved.

In the meantime, Hitler still faced the task of parlaying the crowd's approval into an endorsement of his plan on the part of the Bavarian triumvirate, who remained sequestered in the side room. When he related to them what had happened in the main hall, they continued to resist his blandishments. He was fast losing patience with them when Ludendorff and former Police Chief Pöhner showed up and added their entreaties to those of Hitler. Their intervention was crucial, for they carried much more credibility with the Bavarian leaders. Finally, after another quarter hour or so of arguing, Lossow and Seisser agreed to join the enterprise. A little later Kahr also gave in, although he insisted upon interpreting the action as preparation for a restoration of the Wittelsbach dynasty. Hitler was happy enough to allow Kahr his little illusion; *he* knew that this putsch had nothing to do with the restoration of a discredited monarchy.

Having reached their ostensible agreement, Hitler and his new partners went back into the main hall and jointly mounted the podium. Kahr announced that he would serve as Bavarian regent pending a monarchical restoration, while Lossow and Seisser also registered their endorsements. Hitler shook hands repeatedly with the three men as the crowd once again roared its approval.

The prevailing atmosphere of harmony in the Bürgerbräukeller did not, however, prevent Hitler and his men from behaving like the renegades they were. Even while the Nazi leader was negotiating with Kahr and company, an SA troop under Scheubner-Richter was rounding up members of Knilling's cabinet who were present in the hall and packing them off to house arrest in Julius Lehmann's villa. Another band of SA men under Rudolf Hess spirited some officials into the mountains and repeatedly threatened them with hanging. Yet another SA contingent broke into the offices of the Socialist *Münchener Post* and smashed everything in sight, including doors, desks, and typewriters. The group then went to the apartment of the *Post*'s editor, Erhard Auer, in hopes of smashing him too. Finding him not at home, they ransacked the place and terrorized his family.

Not surprisingly the Nazis also took this opportunity to go after Munich's Jewish population. A number of Jews among the crowd at the Bürgerbräukeller were singled out through an identity check and detained in the basement after the rest of the audience was allowed to leave. At the same time, SA thugs combed the city for Jews and arrested them in the name of the new Reich. Most of them, including men and women in their seventies, were marched to the Bürgerbräu and locked in the basement with their compatriots. Some were badly beaten. Göring prevented an overly zealous SA man from summarily executing the captives by barking: "We do not have the right or authority to execute—yet." In another part of town a detachment of SA men looted a Jewish-owned printing press of some 14,605 trillion marks. The money was later distributed to the SA men in the Bürgerbräukeller, each of whom got the equivalent of about two dollars.

After a shaky beginning the putsch seemed to be proceeding well enough for Hitler to conclude that he could leave the Bürgerbräukeller to deal with other matters relating to his national revolution. As a precaution, however, he ordered that the Bavarian triumvirate be held in the hall. General Ludendorff took the responsibility for guarding them.

No sooner had Hitler left than the men asked Ludendorff if they could depart. They gave him their word of honor that they would do nothing to thwart the enterprise, which they again claimed to support. This was good enough for Ludendorff, since two of the men were fellow officers. He let them go.

While the Bürgerbräukeller remained the focal point of the putsch that evening, another beer hall across town, the giant Löwenbräukeller, served as the staging ground for a second band of rebels under the command of Ernst Röhm. With Röhm were troops of the Reich War Flag, an SA detachment, and a few Reichswèhr soldiers who had decided to join with the mutinous captain. Their task (at that point known only to Röhm) was to keep themselves amused with drink and speeches until word came from the Bürgerbräukeller that Hitler had accomplished his part of the coup; then they were to take control of the District Military Headquarters on the Schönfeldstrasse.

After what seemed to Röhm an eternity, a coded message came through from Hitler. It said: *"Glücklich entbunden"* (Child successfully delivered). Röhm announced to his now well-oiled followers that the national revolution had begun and that Adolf Hitler had taken power in Munich. The hall exploded in joy.

One of the most excited members of Röhm's entourage was an inoffensive-looking fellow with a spindly frame, no chin, a round face, and bottle-bottom glasses; this was Heinrich Himmler, future leader of the SS. Then twenty-three and the assistant manager of a fertilizer company, Himmler was the son of a high school teacher who had served as tutor to Prince Heinrich of Bavaria, after whom young Himmler was named. Heinrich's life, while secure and comfortable, had been a series of disappointments in terms of the nationalist creed he embraced. He had entered the army too late to see fighting in World War I, had failed to gain a commission, and had missed out on the liberation of Munich. His rightist colleagues often made fun of his physical ineptitude and unathletic body. Desperate to show that despite his failures and infirmities, he was a member in good standing of the master race, Himmler had become an avid follower of Captain Röhm, apparently unaware that the captain himself was no model of Aryan manhood. At any rate the young man now had the chance to make up for all the slights and miseries, for he was given the honor of carrying the Reich War Flag behind Röhm as the troopers set out for the military headquarters.

Once they arrived at their destination, Röhm and his men confronted the resident commander with news of the putsch and ordered him to surrender the building. Thoroughly intimidated by the famous captain, the man did as he was instructed. Without having to fire a shot, the rebels occupied the building and surrounded it with barbed wire. It appeared as if all Munich would soon be in Hitler's hands, just as Röhm had claimed.

But the takeover of the military headquarters proved an anomaly. At other Reichswehr installations the putschists found a much different reception. Röhm himself was unable to make any headway at the Stadtkommandantur (City Command), where the officer in charge threatened to shoot the captain if he tried to gain entry. Röhm did not press the point. The putschists were also thwarted at the city's various barracks complexes, above all at the home of the Nineteenth Infantry Regiment, which became one of the command posts of the government resistance. In all these cases rebel troopers proved reluctant to launch full-scale assaults because most of them hoped one day to be taken into the

Reichswehr, a goal not likely to be furthered by firing upon Reichswehr soldiers. The one barracks where the putschists had success belonged to the infantry officers training school. The young cadets had fallen under the influence of a swashbuckling former Free Corps officer who sided with Hitler. Under his leadership, the whole unit marched smartly to the Bürgerbräukeller, where Ludendorff welcomed them as heroes of the new Germany. The enthusiasm of the cadets, however, was hardly enough to counterbalance the putschists' obvious inability to bring the rest of the Reichswehr behind their revolution.

Just as fatal to Hitler's plan was the rebels' failure to capture most of the key governmental, communication, and transportation centers. Despite the efforts of ex-Police Chief Pöhner, the Police Directory on the Ettstrasse did not support the cause. On the contrary, Pöhner himself was arrested and locked up in the building he had once controlled. Jailed with him was his former aide Wilhelm Frick (later the Nazis' minister of the interior). A band of infantry school cadets tried to take over Kahr's offices in the Upper Bavarian government building but dispersed upon encountering a cordon of state police with orders to shoot. Strangely enough, none of the putschists made an effort to occupy the telephone office and the railroad station, which should have been among their earliest targets. Instead they wasted time spinning plans to sell off Munich's art treasures to finance their invasion of the North.

The beer hall putschists, in other words, were quickly revealing themselves as poor practitioners of the art of insurrection. Certainly they seemed less adept than the followers of Kurt Eisner, whose 1918 revolution they had meant to reverse. Indeed, their operation was beginning to look like an inglorious repeat of the Kapp Putsch three years earlier.

Bumbling as the putschists were, however, they might have had more success had it not been for Ludendorff's fateful decision to let the Bavarian triumvirate leave the Bürgerbräukeller in the early hours of the action. As soon as they had gained their freedom, Lossow and Seisser started to work against the putsch, issuing calls for reinforcements from outside the city and coordinating resistance at the various military and police installations. They made clear from the outset that their promised complicity with Hitler meant nothing since it had been gained at gunpoint.

Kahr, for his part, took somewhat longer to adopt any antiputsch measures; the probable reason is that contrary to his later assertions, he had not been entirely faking his declaration of support at the Bürgerbräu. He seems really to have believed—at least for a time—that he could use Hitler's initiative to bring about his cherished Wittelsbach restoration. However, he learned shortly after his release that Crown Prince

Rupprecht wanted nothing to do with the putsch and would never accept a restoration under its auspices. Cardinal Faulhaber too instructed Kahr on the folly of trying to work with Hitler. Pressured by these influential men, Kahr agreed in the middle of the night to issue a proclamation condemning the putsch. Appearing on posters that went up around the city, Kahr's announcement said that all "agreements" attested to at the Bürgerbräukeller had been extorted by force and were invalid.

Hitler, meanwhile, was back in the Bürgerbräukeller, livid at Ludendorff for letting the triumvirate go but still trying to believe that he could prevail. Most of his men also remained keen on the enterprise, partly, no doubt, because they had plenty to eat and drink. The Bürgerbräu management later presented the Nazi Party with a huge bill for its activities that evening. In addition to charges for heroic quantities of beer and food, the statement demanded compensation for the breakage or disappearance of 143 steins, 80 glasses, 98 stools, 2 music stands, and 148 sets of cutlery. (Oddly, there was no mention of the holes in the ceiling.) A trivial document, perhaps, but one that tells us quite a bit about the men who were planning to become the new rulers of Germany on that cold November night.

Getting drunk in a beer hall was ultimately no method for taking over Germany, and as the night wore on with no orders to move out, Hitler's men started to become restless. So did Hitler himself, for as news of Kampfbund failures elsewhere in Munich reached him back at the beer hall, he knew he had been "betrayed." Again he talked of shooting himself. But at other moments he allowed himself flashes of hope. He insisted that his enterprise might yet succeed if he could only get word to the people of Munich about what was going on. The overwhelming majority of the citizenry, he was sure, would come to his rescue if they could be effectively mobilized. He knew that the Nazi efforts in this direction so far had been inadequate: just a few posters around town announcing the national revolution. How might he better reach out to the Münchners and pull them behind his cause? This was the question he pondered as the milky light of dawn slowly spread over the city.

"Kahrfreitag"

It was Ludendorff who came up with the answer: "*Wir marschieren!* [We'll march!]" The Nazis and their allies, the general decided, must emerge from their beer hall bunker and advance upon the heart of the city. His experience as a military man told him that offensives were the best recourse in a tight situation, and furthermore, he believed that no Germans could resist the glorious sight of marching columns. Surely they would join in and the day would be won!

Hitler was dubious about the prospects for such a maneuver. He knew from reports filtering back to the beer hall that the bridges over the Isar were now guarded by state police; he knew too that police and Reichswehr units had blockaded Röhm in the District Military Headquarters, making any help from that quarter unlikely. Aside from threatening suicide, Hitler's instinctive response to these bitter realities was to try to overcome them through the power of the spoken word. He therefore sent Hermann Esser, Gottfried Feder, and other Nazi orators into the city center to talk up the revolution among the townspeople, most of whom were setting off to work as if nothing were happening. Hitler also sent an emissary to Crown Prince Rupprecht with orders to win him over. This move was entirely futile, showing once again the Nazi leader's penchant for wishful thinking.

Only as the morning wore on, with more bad news coming in by the minute, did Hitler finally allow himself to be convinced by Ludendorff's argument for a march. The more he came around to the idea, the more he adopted it as his own, refining it according to his personal vision. He personally would join Ludendorff at the head of the column; there would be flags and a brass band and marching songs. He could envisage crowds tagging along so that the column became one massive testimonial to Munich's enthusiasm for the Nazi cause. Hitler later described what he had in mind that day: "We would go to the city to win the people to our side, to see how public opinion would react, and then to see how Kahr, Lossow, and Seisser would react to public opinion. After all, those gentlemen would hardly be foolish enough to use machine guns against a general uprising of the people. That's how the march into the city was decided on."

Hitler's glowing vision aside, 9 November 1923 was not a good day for a demonstration. Dark clouds hung over the city and flurries of wet snow swept down from the Alps. Hitler succeeded in finding a brass band, but the players were surly because they had had no breakfast; they made a hash of the "Badenweiler March," Hitler's favorite, which they played as the column began to assemble outside the beer hall.

Nonetheless, most of the men who joined the column on that miserable November morning were happy enough to be leaving the Bürgerbräukeller, where by now all the beer and food had been exhausted. They were pleased too to be finally undertaking *some* action, even if they were not quite sure what that would entail. "No one can describe the

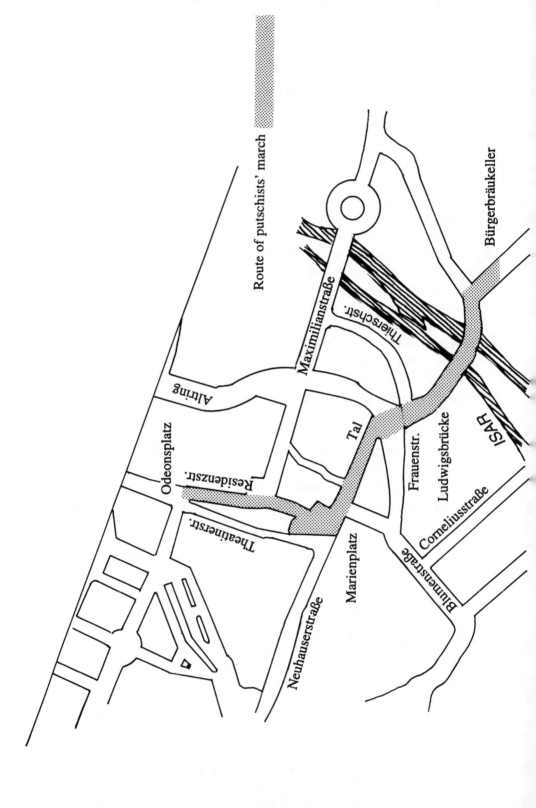

Route of putschists' march

Bürgerbräukeller

Maximilianstraße

Thierschstr.

Altring

Odeonsplatz

Residenzstr.

Tal

Frauenstr.

Ludwigsbrücke

ISAR

Theatinerstr.

Corneliusstraße

Marienplatz

Blumenstraße

Neuhauserstraße

sense of dedication we felt at that moment," wrote one participant later. "The deep joyful enthusiasm. The uniform, elevated, holy seriousness with which we set out. We: workers, students, officers, burghers, craftsmen, old and young. We sang 'Oh Germany, High in Honor.' The song of Germany's honor rose thunderously to the heavens."

The column that set out from the Bürgerbräukeller at about noon contained some two thousand men. There might have been more, but a contingent of the Bund Oberland stayed too long at lunch and got left behind. Most of the marchers wore improvised uniforms of surplus army gear combined with civilian odds and ends, such as feathered hats and mufflers. One of the marchers thought that the group looked like "a defeated army that hadn't fought anybody." Another worried that the column's unimposing appearance would not inspire much confidence among the citizenry. But what could people expect? The men had not known that they were going to be marching through town, and they had spent the previous night with no sleep and lots of beer; some were suffering from painful hangovers.

One marcher who stood out from the rest through his distinguished bearing was Theodor von der Pfordten. A high official of the Bavarian judiciary, he had joined the Nazis because he found Bavaria's traditional conservatives insufficiently nationalistic and racist. On instructions from Hitler, he had drawn up a constitution for the new order. It called, among other things, for the elimination of parliamentary government, the firing of all Jewish officials, and the incarceration of "subversive persons and superfluous consumers" in special camps. This too was a revealing document, one that was a harrowingly accurate harbinger of the Nazi future.

The column that presently wound its way westward down the Rosenheimerstrasse had eight rows. Hitler, Ludendorff, Scheubner-Richter, Göring, Hermann Kriebel (military head of the Kampfbund), Friedrich Weber (head of the Bund Oberland), Ulrich Graf (Hitler's bodyguard), and Wilhelm Brückner marched in front. Directly behind them came the Stosstrupp Hitler, a special unit of the SA. Unlike most of the marchers, these men looked convincingly military, with gray-green uniforms and steel helmets, carbines over their backs, and hand grenades hanging from their belts. The other marchers carried guns too, but many were nonfunctional for lack of firing pins. All the weapons were supposed to be unloaded, for Hitler wanted to avoid a shoot-out with the authorities. As if expecting that all might not go smoothly, however, he instructed Dr. Walter Schultze, the Munich SA's physician, to trail the column in his yellow Opel car, with a red cross painted on the side.

The putschists displayed ominously aggressive tactics early in the march when they encountered a small force of state police stationed at Ludwigsbrücke on the Isar. Under orders to prevent the column from crossing the bridge, the police ordered the marchers to turn back. The policemen, however, were heavily outnumbered and understandably frightened. The putschists pressed their advantage with a charge directly into the police ranks. No one was shot, but the rebels jabbed at the police with bayonets and beat them with rifle butts. The police line collapsed as officers scampered for safety. Those who did not get away were escorted to the Bürgerbräu, where they were spit upon and beaten by the contingent guarding the building. Later, as they built up a convenient mythology about the putsch, the Nazis claimed that they had "fraternized" with the police at Ludwigsbrücke. In reality, they had shown their true colors, the true extent of their respect for "law and order."

Cheered by their easy rout of the police, the marchers swarmed across the Ludwigsbrücke and proceeded up the broad Tal toward the Marienplatz in the city center. Now their crusade began to pick up some of the popular momentum Hitler had hoped for. Hundreds of spectators on both sides of the street shouted their support. Clots of onlookers—clerks, students, and even some workers—fell in behind the column, swelling its size. So large was the group that it easily pushed aside another small cordon of police arrayed across the Tal. It truly seemed as if, as Johann Aigner later claimed, "the mood of the city was thoroughly in favor of the putsch."

Ludendorff and Hitler were still in the lead. Although the former wore a wrinkled civilian suit rather than his military uniform, he commanded respect, even awe. The ubiquitous Professor von Müller, watching from a corner, considered the admiration for Ludendorff understandable; the man was, after all, "one of the greatest generals of the old German army, the architect and victor of glorious battles." But Müller found the men behind Ludendorff distinctly less impressive: They were "a motley gang with helmets and military caps, a bunch of civilians without order, all higgledy-piggledy."

From the Tal the swelling horde entered the Marienplatz, Munich's great central square, and swept past the Mariensäule, a seventeenth-century column topped by a bronze Madonna overlooking four cupids representing Hunger, War, Plague, and Heresy—evils very much still present. In anticipation of the marchers' arrival, an advance guard of SA men had stormed the Rathaus on the north side of the square and arrested a number of city councillors and the Socialist mayor, Eduard Schmid. A huge swastika flag now flew from a balcony of the building. The scene in front resembled more a street festival than a putsch. Buskers competed with food vendors for the attention of the huge crowd, which carpeted the square from end to end, totally enveloping some streetcars from the Sendlingen line. People sang patriotic songs until their voices gave out. Beneath the Mariensäule, gnomelike Julius Streicher, personification of Munich's new political plague, claimed that Hitler's Germany would hang Jewish profiteers from the lampposts, shut down the stock exchange, and nationalize the banks. Any who opposed the movement would be eliminated, whereas those who cooperated could look forward to a glorious German future, he declared.

As they entered the square, the putschists were swallowed up by the mass of celebrants. Understandably many of the marchers assumed that their cause was now triumphant and began to celebrate with the crowd. Munich was theirs, they believed, and Berlin would soon follow. Yet Hitler knew full well that most of Munich's military and governmental installations were still under the control of the police or army and that Röhm's contingent was surrounded by Reichswehr troops. Faced with the conundrum of how to translate the energy and enthusiasm of the Marienplatz crowd into an actual takeover of the city, Hitler wallowed once again in doubt and indecision, giving no orders at all.

Again it was Ludendorff who took control. The column must, he said, continue on to rescue Röhm and his men at the military headquarters. This prospect excited the former general, for now the march had a military goal, not just a propagandistic one. He therefore barked a command to move out, and the column slowly began to push on once again behind the Hero of Tannenberg and his somewhat reluctant ally, former Corporal Adolf Hitler.

To get to Röhm on the Schönfeldstrasse, the marchers had to proceed through another square, the Odeonsplatz, which was connected to the Marienplatz by a pair of small streets on either side of the vast Rathaus. Ludendorff at first selected the larger one, Theatinerstrasse, but when he saw a contingent of state police blocking its end, he swung the column to the right onto the Perusastrasse and then to the left up the Residenzstrasse, which ran like a narrow canyon between the hulking Residenz and some commercial buildings. At the left end of this architectural Thermopylae loomed the Feldherrnhalle, Ludwig I's Italianate monument to Bavaria's greatest generals. Beneath the hall, blocking the street, was another cordon of green-coated state police, small in number but supported by heavy machine guns and an armored car.

If they wished to reach Röhm, the marchers now had no option but to push past this cordon, as they had done at the Ludwigsbrücke. Yet this batch of police looked altogether more resolute, and they were quickly reinforced by men from the Theatinerstrasse contingent. As if to give themselves courage, the marchers started singing, and some of them shouted to the police to put down their weapons and join the crusade. In front of the column Ludendorff hardly slowed his pace, while Hitler, much less sure of himself, locked arms with Scheubner-Richter.

After only a few steps the marchers made contact with the first police guards, whom they successfully pushed aside. But then the police began to fight back, working, as their commander, Lieutenant Michael von Godin, put it, "with rifle-butt and night stick." Suddenly, according to Godin, a putschist fired his pistol and hit a police sergeant. This may or may not have been the first shot that was fired that day; postputsch investigations remained inconclusive. It is certain only that *someone* fired a shot and that immediately thereafter both sides began shooting in earnest (suggesting, of course, that Hitler's order regarding unloaded weapons had not been followed). The police, with their machine guns and superior position, had the advantage, and amid a hail of bullets putschists in the front rows began hitting the pavement or stampeding backward, hurling themselves against men farther back in the column.

Göring was among the first to be hit. He took a shot to the groin and crawled for protection beneath the central gateway of the Residenz. Eventually one of the putschists carried him into a nearby apartment building, where he was given first aid by the wife of a Jewish furniture dealer. Soon he managed to slip over the border to the Austrian Tyrol, where he convalesced from his wound with the help of morphine, to which he became hopelessly addicted. He did not return to Germany for four years.

Hitler also went down, but not because he was hit. As the first shots rang out, he instinctively threw himself toward the pavement. At that very moment Scheubner-Richter, still intertwined with him, dropped with a bullet through his lungs. Hitler hit the ground with such force that his shoulder was separated. Further injury was prevented by the self-sacrificing action of bodyguard Ulrich Graf, who covered Hitler with his bulk, absorbing in the process eleven bullets in his own body. Hitler lay under Graf for the duration of the firefight, which lasted about thirty seconds. Then, while confusion reigned and wounded men screamed in agony, he limped into a side street, where he was spotted by the SA physician Dr. Schultze. The doctor helped Hitler to his car, which was filled with medical supplies. On the way to the car the men picked up a young boy who had been wounded in the crossfire. Before speeding out of town, they delivered the boy to his home. Later Nazi spin doctors transformed this episode into the useful myth that "the Führer had left the scene of action in order to carry a little child to safety." According to Johann Aigner, this gesture also showed "the great love the Führer harbored for Germany's youth."

While Hitler clearly needed a cover story for his less-than-heroic behavior on that November afternoon. General Ludendorff had nothing, save his usual dim impetuosity, to be ashamed of. He too had instinctively thrown himself down when the shooting started but then had picked himself up and continued to march, seemingly oblivious of the chaos around him. Walking right through the main police line, he reached the Odeonsplatz, where an officer approached him and said sheepishly, "Excellency, I must take you into protective custody." Ludendorff chivalrously replied, as if he were back on the battlefield. "You have your orders, and I will follow you."

The scene behind on the Residenzstrasse really did resemble a battlefield, with bloody corpses sprawled here and there, discarded flags and clothing scattered over the pavement, wounded men calling for help. Among the corpses was the jurist Pfordten, in whose pocket the police found a bloodstained copy of the Nazis' intended constitution. Pfordten's obituary, published the next day in the *Bayerische Staatszeitung,* lamented the loss to Bavarian justice of "a genuine German man full of glowing love for his fatherland."

Including Pfordten, the putschists lost thirteen men at the foot of the Feldherrnhalle. Another body in the street belonged to one Karl Kuhn, a waiter who happened to be walking home along the south side of the Residenz when a stray bullet caught him in the head. Two more putschists fell in the less extensive fighting at the military headquarters, where Röhm was forced to surrender. A total of four policemen died at both battle scenes. Dozens of wounded received treatment at Munich University's teaching hospital by Professor Sauerbruch, who now saved the lives of Nazis as he had once saved Count Arco auf Valley, Kurt Eisner's assassin.

Even before the dead and wounded had been carted away, arrest warrants went out for the Nazi and Kampfbund leaders who had escaped the scene. The Nazi Party was outlawed, and its offices were occupied by the police. Gustav von Kahr and the other Bavarian leaders swore that Hitler's legions would never again be allowed to terrorize the streets of Munich; the Nazis were finished, they said. "The Munich Putsch definitely eliminates Hitler and his National Socialist followers," agreed the *New York Times.* Breathing a sigh of relief, some anti-Nazi Münchners began speaking of November 9 as "Kahrfreitag" (Kahr Friday), a pun on Kar-Freitag (Good Friday). The general commissar, they said, had nailed his enemies on a cross of gunfire at the Feldherrnhalle. The problem with this metaphor was that it implied a resurrection on the part of the chief victim, who in any event was always happy enough to compare himself with Christ.

The anti-Nazis in Munich who thought that they had seen the last of Hitler and his party had little reason to be satisfied with the behavior of their town during the chaotic events of 8–9 November 1923. Unlike the similarly abortive Kapp Putsch of March 1920, the Beer Hall Putsch (as it soon came to be known) had been suppressed not by an outraged populace but by the police and military. Indeed, a significant number of townspeople (one can never know exactly how many) had registered their support for the putschists as they sought to take control of Munich in preparation for their long-promised assault on Berlin.

The people's enthusiasm raises the question of what might have happened had the putsch attempt been better prepared and organized, if, more specifically, the rebels had had the time to mobilize all factions in the city that supported them. In that case mobs of citizens might have taken over key municipal and state institutions, as Eisner's supporters had done in November 1918. This would have forced the military and state police to decide if they wanted to engage in a full-scale civil war. Of course, a Nazi victory in Munich—if indeed, this was even possible—would have shifted the conflict to the national level, where the struggle would have been considerably more challenging.

Aftermath and Trial

Following the putsch failure, Munich was in a rebellious and angry mood. In the late afternoon of 9 November pro-Nazi groups ran through the streets vilifying Kahr, Lossow, and Seisser for not going along with Hitler. State police had to use force to clear demonstrators from the Odeonsplatz, Karlsplatz, and the Tal. Charged by the police, the crowds fought back with fists, clubs, and pieces of pavement. Sometimes they isolated an individual policeman and beat him bloody. According to one of the officers, the most violent assailants were members of the "so-called better classes."

The situation did not improve on subsequent days; indeed, the atmosphere remained so menacing that Kahr moved his office into the main military barracks. On the afternoon of 10 November a crowd gathered on the Odeonsplatz screaming, "Down with the traitor Kahr! Up with Hitler!" This time the police had to use live ammunition to clear the square. Meanwhile, at the university about two thousand nationalist students staged a violent demonstration against the government. When Professor Sauerbruch, fresh from the operating table, tried to calm the students, they assaulted him, sending him back to his clinic as a patient.

In their attacks on "the traitor Kahr," pro-Nazi elements in Munich were animated not just by frustration but also by hopes that the results of 9 November might be reversed. Rumors floating around Munich had it that Hitler was holed up somewhere in the mountains preparing for a new assault on the Bavarian government.

The reality was considerably less promising—at least from the pro-Nazi perspective. Hitler had found refuge at Putzi Hanfstaengl's home at Uffing on the Staffelsee, about thirty miles south of Munich. Putzi's wife took him in, for Putzi himself had fled to Austria as soon as the putsch collapsed. A story later circulated that Hitler had spent his brief time at the Hanfstaengl house having furious sex with Putzi's beautiful sister, Erna, but Putzi insisted that Erna was not present and that, in any event, Hitler was in too much pain from his injury to "behave like Tannhäuser in the Venusberg."

No matter how he deported himself at Hanfstaengl's, Hitler understood that this could only be a short-term refuge since the police were certain to come there in search of him. The Nazi leader therefore telephoned the Bechsteins to send a car to pick him up and take him to a safer hideout. In his choice of helpers in a crisis, Hitler showed once again how dependent he was on Munich high society.

On 11 November, before the Bechstein car could arrive, a detachment of state police appeared at the Hanfstaengl house. Apparently they had been tipped off by a gardener that Hitler was there. As the police surrounded the house, Hitler pulled out a pistol and shouted to Putzi's wife: "This is the end. I will never let these swine take me. I will shoot myself first." Frau Hanfstaengl, according to the account she later gave Putzi, used a jujitsu trick to wrestle the gun away from Hitler. If this account is true, the Nazi leader had survived his second close brush with death in the space of three days.

Hitler and his primary coconspirators appeared before a special tribunal in Munich on 26 February 1924, exactly four years after the Nazis' pioneering mass meeting in the Hofbräuhaus. The formal charge was *Hochverrat* (high treason). In the interval between his arrest and trial, Hitler was detained in cell number 7 at Landsberg Fortress, Arco auf Valley's room, while Eisner's assassin was moved to other quarters.

By all rights, Hitler and his colleagues should not have been tried in Munich at all. Since they were charged with high treason, they should have gone before the new National Court for the Protection of the

Republic in Leipzig. But the Knilling government refused to give the central court jurisdiction in this case. Partly this maneuver was another assertion of states' rights, but Munich was also acting out of fear that a trial under Reich auspices would reveal the extent to which the Bavarian triumvirate, especially Kahr, had collaborated with Hitler in the period leading up to the putsch.

Before the trial began, Hitler once again threatened suicide but settled instead for a brief hunger strike. He worried that the regime he had tried so hard to overthrow was now prepared to treat him as the dangerous political criminal he was.

In fact, however, he had little to fear from the Bavarian authorities who took charge of his case. Bavaria's minister of justice, Franz Gürtner, did not try to hide his sympathy for the Nazi cause. The chairman of the Munich court that tried the case, Georg Neithardt, was a rightist who in his earlier handling of the Arco trial had shown that abstract justice was not his highest priority (later he became a high judicial official under the Nazis). When Reich officials proposed that Hitler be deported under the Law for the Protection of the Republic, Neithardt declared that this law "should not apply to a man so German in his thinking as Adolf Hitler." Once the trial began, Neithardt made sure that the prosecution had little room for maneuver. By contrast, the defense was given every advantage, and as star defendant Hitler was allowed to turn his time in the dock into an extended explication of Nazi ideology. Hitler and his fellow putschists got more propagandistic exposure from the trial than from the putsch itself.

The Nazi leader's defense, in essence, was that he and his colleagues had not committed treason in the true sense because the Weimar Republic itself was a treasonous enterprise. But if he was to be branded a traitor, he declared, so too must the Bavarian leadership. "The fact was that for the whole time [before the putsch] Seisser and Kahr shared the same goal as we; namely, the removal of the Reich government . . . and its replacement by an absolute, nationalistic, antiparliamentary government—a dictatorship. . . . If in fact our undertaking was high treason, then Kahr, Lossow, and Seisser also must have committed high treason because for months on end they agitated for nothing other than that for which we sit in the dock."

Hitler's aggressive rhetoric threw his accusers on the defensive. Lossow responded by denouncing the Nazi leader as a harebrained adventurer with delusions of grandeur; he flew into a rage when Hitler called him a turncoat. Kahr seemed hapless in the witness box, refusing to answer questions and claiming he could not remember crucial facts about the period before the putsch. In the opinion of the British consul, a witness at the trial, Kahr "cut an extremely poor figure."

While Hitler attacked the Bavarian government, his coconspirator Ludendorff argued that he had participated in the undertaking only because Hitler convinced him that it had the backing of the army. He implied that he should have known better than to trust a foreign agitator like Hitler. Clearly the Hero of Tannenberg and the Austrian ex-corporal would no longer be marching side by side toward a glorious German future.

In smaller ancillary trials involving members of the Stosstrupp Hitler, defendants insisted that they had believed they were acting in collaboration with the Bavarian authorities and simply following orders. For example, Karl Fiehler, who became mayor of Munich in the Nazi era, noted that the Kampfbund forces had gotten most of their weapons and training from the Bavarian Reichswehr.

Throughout the entire judicial spectacle, members of the public stormed the courtroom to show their support for the defendants. Some of Hitler's female followers sought permission to take baths in his tub (presumably with him absent). There were frequent demonstrations in Munich on behalf of the men in the dock. The city's leading nationalist paper, the *Münchener Neueste Nachrichten,* editorialized: "We make no bones about the fact that our human sympathies lie on the side of the defendants and not with the November criminals of 1918." Down at the Hofbräuhaus, the folk singer Weiss Ferdl provided his own commentary on the trial to the cheers of his stein-thumping audience: "German men stand today at the bar of the court / Courageously they confess their deed; they've nothing to conceal / Tell me, what have they done wrong? / Can it really be a crime to try to save one's fatherland from disgrace and despair?"

The verdicts and sentences were handed down on 1 April 1923. Ludendorff, who had had more to do with the final shape of the putsch than any of the other conspirators, was acquitted. Hitler and the other putsch leaders were found guilty of treason with "extenuating circumstances." The court declared that the men had acted out of "pure patriotic motives and the most noble selfless ideals." They had "believed that they were rescuing the fatherland from its terrible plight." The judges also concluded that the defendants had honestly thought they were "acting in concert with the leading men of Bavaria." Hitler, Weber, Kriebel, and Pöhner got the lightest sentences the court could issue for their crime: "fortress arrest" for a period not to exceed five years. Five other putschists, including Röhm and Frick, each received a sentence of fifteen months but were allowed to spend their sentences on probation. As they left the court-room, the defendants were given a standing ovation. "Munich is chuckling over the verdict, which is regarded as an excellent joke for All Fools Day," commented the London *Times*.

But the mood in the city remained anything but lighthearted. Five days after the verdict, in new elections for the Bavarian Landtag, a party calling itself the National Socialist Freedom Movement, a front for the outlawed Nazis, won 17.1 percent of the vote statewide and more than 50 percent in Munich. Its total of twenty-three mandates equaled that of the SPD. Bavarian authorities interpreted this result as a reaction to the propagandistic effects of the Beer Hall Putsch trial. As a Munich police report observed, "The popularity of Hitler and the other leaders was only increased by their conviction and their quasi-martyrdom."

As Hitler returned to Landsberg Fortress to begin serving his sentence, he had time to contemplate the meaning of the Beer Hall Putsch. He concluded that it had failed because the army and police had not been drawn into the effort. Never again would he try to grab power by force, and he would make every attempt to win over the armed forces for his movement.

Later, after becoming chancellor, Hitler came to see the putsch not as a failure but as a useful stepping-stone on his path to power. "Before the march to the Feldherrnhalle," he said, "I had seventy or eighty thousand followers. After this march I had two million." As so often, Hitler was grossly bending the facts, but it is certainly true that the failed putsch had its uses for him, not the least of which was an even firmer bond with the city where the drama had taken place. Having fought and survived this battle in the streets of Munich, he was convinced more than ever that the Bavarian capital was his city of destiny. No wonder he later made the Feldherrnhalle the central shrine of the Nazi movement, the sacred place to which he and the other Old Fighters returned time and again in ritual reenactment of the historic march of 9 November 1923.

6

"The Dumbest City in Germany"

IN 1932 THOMAS Mann, who had by then shed his unpolitical conservatism to become a vocal defender of the republican order, proposed that the town in which he had chosen to live for the past thirty-eight years might serve as a "world-German" city combining the best German traditions with an openness to the world. As Mann himself well knew, however, Munich in the Weimar period harbored neither the healthiest German traditions nor much inclination toward cosmopolitanism. On the contrary, it combined extreme conservatism with a defensive parochialism. And far from being touted for its sophistication, the erstwhile Isar

Athens was being lampooned by many non-Bavarians (especially by liberals and leftists in Berlin) as "the dumbest city in Germany."

Hitler and the Nazis contributed their share to the dumbing of Munich, but they had plenty of help from the political and religious establishment, which waged a bitter crusade against what was left of the city's avant-garde culture. In matters of the intellect, Nazis and Bavarian conservatives found plenty of common ground. As their antiliberal campaign gathered momentum, modernist artists and progressive intellectuals who had weathered earlier storms of cultural backlash and nativist hostility left for friendlier climes, particularly for Berlin.

Despite being among the winners in this cultural war, the Nazis had their own troubles in the middle years of the Weimar era, which was a time of relative economic and political stability, inimical to a party that fed on chaos and despair. The Nazi movement, moreover, was racked with dissension in the wake of the Beer Hall Putsch. The sources of friction included a growing hostility among the northern branches of the party to domination by the Nazi bureaucracy in Munich. It took all of Hitler's leadership skills to pull the party back together and to keep it centered in the Bavarian capital.

Hitler's tenacity regarding his favorite city turned out to be a piece of sound political thinking, for Munich continued to provide a secure operational base even as the national organization suffered repeated internal crises, government restrictions, and a loss of momentum that led some observers to write the party off as a credible threat. Munich's "dumbness," in other words, was yet another godsend for Hitler.

The Landsberg Interregnum

True to their word, Hitler's followers did not forget their leader simply because he was sitting in Landsberg Fortress. At Christmas in 1923 a group of artists in Schwabing put on a tableau called "Adolf Hitler in Prison." Against a backdrop of falling snowflakes and a choral rendition of "Silent Night," a sallow-faced prisoner sat in a cell with his head in his hands. As an angel delivered a Christmas tree to the cell, the inmate—a spitting image of Hitler hired by Heinrich Hoffmann—slowly turned his face to the audience. According to Hoffmann, "a half-sob went through the hall." The following April, on Hitler's thirty-fifth birthday, some three thousand Münchners held a rousing demonstration in the Bürgerbräukeller, demanding their leader's immediate release and the rehabilitation of the Nazi Party.

Since Hitler could not come to Munich, Munich came to him. Sympathizers trooped down to Landsberg to spend a few hours with him in his cell, a spacious suite connected to a common room, which was festooned with Nazi insignia. Among the visitors were Carin Göring, who relayed good wishes from her fugitive husband; Winifred Wagner, who promised to "fight like a lioness" for the Nazi cause; and Helene Bechstein, who got extra time with her hero by claiming to be his adoptive mother. The pilgrims to Landsberg found a scene that, according to one witness, was "more like an officers' casino than a prison." When not entertaining visitors, the captive putschists "played cards, smoked, and ordered refined gourmet meals from the warden." They supplemented their prison fare with food shipments from their friends in Munich. Putzi Hanfstaengl, a frequent visitor, said that one "could have opened up a flower and fruit and wine shop with all the stuff" stacked in Hitler's quarters.

The Nazi leader was putting on so much weight as a result of his prison diet that Putzi advised him to take up some kind of sport. "No," replied Hitler emphatically, "I keep away from such things. It would be bad for discipline if I took part in physical training. A leader cannot afford to be beaten in games." Hitler claimed that he could lose weight just by talking, and that may have been true, since he did so much of it. He lectured his colleagues on political and cultural themes, illustrating his points with episodes from his own life.

Even these devoted disciples eventually tired of Hitler's harangues. According to Otto Strasser, they hit upon a "Machiavellian" means to divert the flood of words: They encouraged their chief to write his memoirs. Hitler did not need much persuading to embark on this project, for he was anxious to show the world that despite his minimal formal education, he was a serious thinker.

Accordingly, he began spending several hours a day dictating his life story and political ideas to the dutiful Rudolf Hess, who typed it up on an old Remington machine. (The reams of paper used for this purpose, incidentally, came from Winifred Wagner.) Hitler's working title was "Four and a Half Years of Struggle against Lies, Stupidity, and Cowardice," but Max Amann wisely convinced him to go with the pithier *Mein Kampf.* Virtually completed by the time Hitler left Landsberg, the manuscript was so badly written that several colleagues, notably Father Stempfle, had to rework it before sending it on to the Nazi-owned Eher Press in Munich for publication. A first volume appeared in July 1925, and a second volume about a year and a half later. In 1930 the volumes were combined in an inexpensive edition that soon became de rigueur on every good German bookshelf. (By the end of the Third Reich Hitler's memoir had been published in sixteen languages, as well as in braille, and had sold more than ten million copies. Yet within months of the end of World War II the book had become so rare in Germany that the American occupation government had difficulty finding copies for its Amerika Haus libraries. In 1949 the Bavarian government, which took over the copyright, prohibited further publication or dissemination of the book in Germany, making the remaining copies quite valuable on the black market.)

Hitler attracted new followers even as he sat in prison. One of them was a frustrated young literary intellectual from the Rhineland named Josef Goebbels. Dwarfish, clubfooted, and full of venom, Goebbels was like a personification of Thomas Hobbes's definition of life: "nasty, brutish, and short." But he was also an intelligent and complex figure: a rationalist who hungered for faith and overarching certainties; a skeptic who managed to convince himself that it mattered not so much what one believed as that one believed. He also possessed brilliant oratorical gifts and an oily charm that enchanted the ladies. Goebbels had not met Hitler at the time of the Beer Hall Putsch, though he, like most of the men who came to rule the Third Reich, had spent time in Munich in the immediate aftermath of the war. He had gone there from his native Rhineland to study literature at Munich University and was in residence at the time of the Eisner assassination, which he heartily applauded. Yet as a self-proclaimed "Socialist" Goebbels was not yet attracted to the fledgling Nazi movement, which struck him as hopelessly reactionary. He registered his contempt by doodling a cartoon depicting a child sitting on a chamber pot, saying "*Seh ich nur ein Hakenkreuz, kriege ich schon zum Kacken Reiz* [Just thinking of a swastika while I sit, gives me the urge to shit]."

Goebbels did not begin to see possibilities in Hitler until he read accounts of his testimony in the Beer Hall Putsch trial. Convinced that Germany needed a savior, he began to think that the Nazi chief might be the answer to his hopes. "If only [Hitler] were free," he wrote in his diary, he might "fill me with new courage and new self-confidence. Things can't go on this way." Two years later he wrote that Hitler had expressed at his trial not just his "own pain and struggle" but "the suffering of an entire generation who were yearning for real men, for meaningful tasks."

Yet Goebbels continued to worry that Hitler was too caught up in the provincial, petit bourgeois world of his Munich entourage. Like Göring, the Rhinelander believed that this "backward" element was preventing Hitler from reaching out beyond the geographic and class confines of the movement. The Bavarian cadres, in response, began patronizing Goebbels as "our little doctor" (he received a Ph.D. in German literature from Heidelberg University in 1922). Characteristically they also made fun of his physical deformity, belittling his pathetic claim to have acquired his affliction in the war.

The Goebbels-Munich antagonism reflected a North-South division in the *völkisch* movement. While Hitler was in prison, some of the Munich Old Guard, above all Gottfried Feder and Hermann Esser, complained that the remnants of the National Socialist Party were falling under the pernicious influence of "Prussians" like Ludendorff, on whom they blamed the failure of the Beer Hall Putsch. A contingent of northerners, meanwhile, countered that the Munich cadres had isolated Hitler. In August 1924 a faction of northerners connected to the German Nationalist Freedom Party (an offshoot of the outlawed Nazis) proclaimed Ludendorff their leader in Hitler's absence. Their spokesman, Adalbert Volck, heaped abuse on Esser, calling him a "destructive and disintegrative influence." Hitler, Volck declared, should move to the North and surround himself with "men of Nordic blood . . . who want and are able to do something." Volck later added a stock North German prejudice toward the Bavarian character: "The South is easy to inflame but has no staying power; that was seen in the war, when the Bavarian was brilliant in the attack but weak in holding a position; down there 'Rome' inhibits their striking force; only in the North can a real *völkisch* assault be generated." Kurt Ludecke, a playboy and international traveler who helped raise funds for the Nazis, proposed moving the party headquarters to Thuringia, which was more centrally located. But Hitler would not hear of abandoning Munich; the people there, he claimed, were "devoted to me, to me and to nobody else." Just because the movement was threatened in its home base, he added, was no reason to retreat. "The most sacred place is where one has suffered most."

With the exception of the Munich question, Hitler tried to stay out of internal feuds while he was in prison. He believed that it made no sense to back a particular faction when he could not personally enforce his decision. From his point of view, moreover, there was a hidden blessing in the squabbles: They kept his lieutenants occupied and prevented any one of them from grabbing total control in his absence. To maintain his Olympian distance, he informed his followers in the summer of 1924 that he had decided to "withdraw from active politics until my restored freedom offers me the possibility of being a real leader." In the meantime, he said, no one should presume to act on his behalf.

Hitler was scheduled to be released from Landsberg in late 1924, after having served a little more than a year behind bars (counting his pretrial detention). The decision to release him early came as no surprise, for the Munich court had never intended to hold him for the full five years of his sentence. Perhaps his cause was also helped by glowing reports from the Landsberg warden, who wrote that Hitler had shown himself to be "a man of strict discipline and order." The court could also justify its action on the ground that in the recent Reichstag elections (7 December 1924) the radical Right had slipped dramatically from its success of the previous May, garnering only 907,000 votes, or about 5 percent of the total. The *völkisch* fever seemed to have peaked right after the Beer Hall trial; now the rightist radicals were in retreat.

Nonetheless, the Munich police and the Bavarian government preferred to deport Hitler to Austria as soon as he got out of Landsberg. They worried that he would again become a menace to state security, as well as to the tourist industry, which had bitterly complained that Hitler was bad for business. In September 1924 an official of the Bavarian Ministry of Interior raised the issue with Austrian Chancellor Ignaz Seipel, but Seipel made clear that Austria did not want Hitler back. Indeed, the Austrians indicated that they would return him to Bavaria if Munich tried to dump him over the border. (Later, in August 1925, Hitler himself sought to make an expulsion to Austria impossible by formally asking Vienna to revoke his Austrian citizenship, as Vienna was happy to do. This meant that Hitler, who did not obtain German citizenship until 1932, was legally stateless for almost seven years.)

On 20 December 1924 Hitler became a free man. Looking almost like a real Bavarian, with a pair of let-out lederhosen hugging his prison paunch, he posed outside Landsberg's gates for a Hoffmann photograph before rushing back to Munich. A small group of disciples, led by Hermann Esser and Julius Streicher, awaited him in his apartment on Thierschstrasse. His shabby room was filled with flowers and food, but the mood was somber. Hitler immediately left for Putzi Hanfstaengl's residence, where he asked his friend to welcome him home with a rendition of Wagner's "Liebestod."

Stabilization

The political climate in Munich had changed substantially while Hitler was out of action. General Commissar Gustav von Kahr, whose ambiguous role in the Beer Hall Putsch had made him (in the words of the British consul) "the best-hated man in Bavaria," had resigned his position in early 1924. The nationalist Right could not forgive Kahr for "betraying Hitler," while the Left believed, with considerable justice, that he had actually egged Hitler on. The ineffectual Eugen von Knilling had also left office and was replaced by Heinrich Held. Although not a Bavarian by birth, Held had been one of the founders of the BVP and was a former president of the German Catholic Assembly. He was a strong federalist who did all he could to promote states' rights. Yet he ended the Kahr-Knilling regime's "state of emergency" and allowed the local Reichswehr to resume taking its oath of allegiance to the nation. Above all, he proved an adept and popular leader, bringing continuity to the political scene by remaining in office for nine years.

Held's counterpart in Munich municipal politics was Karl Scharnagl (BVP), who was elected lord mayor in the communal elections of 1924. A former baker and Center Party Landtag delegate, Scharnagl made palatable political pastry out of a mixture of Bavarian pride and traditional conservative nationalism. As a veteran of the annexationist Fatherland Party and a convinced federalist, he could never fully accept the Weimar Republic. Thus he refused to beflag municipal buildings when Paul von Hindenburg, who was elected Reich president in 1925 after Ebert's death, swore allegiance to the Weimar Constitution. On the other hand, Scharnagl saw to it that the president became an honorary citizen of Munich when he paid an official visit to the city in the same year. Like Held, Scharnagl was a figure of continuity, holding his office until the Nazi takeover in 1933 (and again after the collapse of the Third Reich).

Accompanying these political changes was a gradual and always precarious stabilization of the economic situation. In mid-November 1923 the central government introduced a new currency, the Rentenmark. Backed by mortgages on real estate, rolling stock, gold, and foreign exchange reserves, the new currency soon became widely accepted, bringing the terrible days of hyperinflation to an end. Germany's financial situation was also benefited by the introduction in spring 1924 of the Dawes Plan (named after the American banker Charles Dawes), which reduced the Reich's annual reparation payments and made foreign loans available to help the country meet its treaty obligations.

In early 1924 Munich's Chamber of Commerce noted that currency stabilization had brought "a calming tendency" and a "sense of relief" since businessmen now sensed "firm ground" beneath their feet. A year later the British consul, newly arrived from England, was surprised to find less poverty and economic insecurity in Munich than in London; he wished "the people of London looked as contented as those I encountered in and around Munich."

Yet if the consul had looked more closely, he would have found plenty of lingering malaise in the Bavarian capital. Many citizens had been so devastated during the Great Inflation that they could not recover their financial footing. Those who had held on to their savings accounts and government securities found that these assets were now virtually worthless.

Moreover, like many German cities, Munich suffered from a lack of available capital in the wake of the currency reform. In an effort to alleviate the situation, Mayor Scharnagl took the extraordinary step of leading a delegation of local politicians and businessmen to the international mecca of money, New York City, in 1926. There they arranged for a loan of $8.9 million. In the following year Scharnagl brokered another substantial loan from the British. There was something fitting about this: American and British visitors had long led the parade of foreign tourists to Munich; now the Anglo-Saxons were giving something back to their favorite German city. But, of course, the loans were not motivated by altruism, and the need to repay them accelerated the city's financial tailspin once the Great Depression hit in the early 1930s.

In the meantime the outside help allowed Scharnagl to undertake some needed socioeconomic projects. Describing Munich's chronic housing shortage as the "chief misery of our people," the mayor pushed the construction of approximately three thousand new apartment complexes. He also presided over the expansion of the public transportation network and the development of a commercial airport on the Oberwiesenfeld. In the late twenties Munich got its first skyscraper, the twelve-story Technical City Hall, as well as its first traffic light. Yet such innovations could not disguise the fact that in the realm of urban sophistication, Munich was falling ever farther behind Berlin, which was advertising itself as the "New York of Europe."

"The Moscow of Our Movement"

Upon his return to Munich following his enforced leave of absence, Hitler turned to the task of getting the Nazi Party relegalized. Fourteen days after his release he met with Prime Minister Held to discuss the terms under which the party's prohibition in Bavaria might be lifted. Warily the premier asked if the Nazis would henceforth eschew attacks on the church and the conservative establishment. Hitler replied that these institutions had never been his target: his "only enemy" was Marxism, and he would support any government that combated this plague. He also apologized for the Beer Hall Putsch, blaming it on Ludendorff, with whom he promised to have no more traffic. Held was skeptical but agreed to lift the ban on the party and its newspaper, the *Völkischer Beobachter*, as of 16

February 1925. "The wild beast is checked," he said; "we can afford to loosen the chain."

There was more to this move, however, than a grudging willingness to give Hitler the benefit of the doubt. Like other Bavarian leaders before him, Held apparently hoped that the Nazi beast, if properly domesticated, could actually become a wholesome influence in the state. Justifying the legalization of the party to the Landtag, Held explained that he had told Hitler he would "place no obstacles in the path of orderly action and agitation [by the Nazis], since I myself see the great need for the patriotic development of our people, especially the youth."

Almost immediately Held had reason to regret his decision to unfetter the Nazis. To mark the refounding of the NSDAP on 27 February 1925, Hitler delivered a vitriolic speech before three thousand followers at the Bürgerbräukeller. In his two-hour harangue, entitled "Germany's Future and Our Movement," he claimed that only the Nazis were capable of dealing with Marxism and "the intellectual carriers of this world plague, the Jews." The Nazis would take up the battle "with all means necessary," he declared. "Either we walk over the dead bodies of our enemies, or they will walk over ours." Hitler also ridiculed the Reichstag, likening it to a beer hall where people babbled on endlessly.

Obviously these remarks did not show much evidence of a domesticated Hitler, and the Bavarian authorities moved quickly to slap him down. Effective March 1925, Hitler was banned from addressing public meetings in Bavaria. Interior Minister Karl Stutzel, who orchestrated the ban, explained that it was necessary to protect the security of the state and (once again) the tourist industry. Bavaria's action inspired similar restrictions in many other German states, including Prussia, Saxony, and Baden. It is significant, however, that the punitive measures applied only to mass meetings addressed by Hitler. The authorities apparently saw Hitler, not his fragmented party, as the primary danger.

The speaking ban was a source of great frustration for Hitler, inasmuch as it came just as he was trying to rebuild the Nazi Party in the face of fractious internal disagreements over policy and direction. Among the internecine challenges was a new push by some of his followers to move the Nazi headquarters out of Munich. Unable to address this issue in mass meetings, Hitler used small gatherings of regional leaders to reinforce his determination to keep the Nazi base in the Bavarian capital. In Saxony in June 1925 he declared: "Rome—Mecca—Moscow! Each of these places embodies a world view. Let us remain with the city that witnessed the first blood martyrs of the movement; it must become the Moscow of our movement!" A little later, in Stuttgart, he repeated this theme: "Our movement is inseparably tied to Munich because it was born there and lost its first martyrs there. The city is . . . holy ground." In Rosenheim, east of Munich, where the first party branch after Munich had been founded, Hitler acknowledged that the Held government was making life difficult for the Nazis, but he argued that it was imperative to make a stand "where we are opposed most fiercely."

Hitler's decision to keep the party headquarters in Munich fueled other controversies, for many in the *völkisch* camp tended to see his Munich entourage as soft on Catholicism and all too inclined to make deals with the Bavarian federalists. Ludendorff argued that Hitler had become so corrupted by his Bavarian followers that he had "sold out" to Held in order to get the party rehabilitated. Captain Ehrhardt, now thoroughly estranged from Hitler, summed up the northerners' distrust when he acidly commented: "Don't forget, the man is an Austrian!"

Even Hitler's old colleague Ernst Röhm began denouncing the Nazi leader for abandoning the putsch as a means to power. Röhm had established a new paramilitary unit called the Frontbann, to which he wanted to subordinate the SA in preparation for another putsch attempt. Hitler would have none of this; in April 1925 he gave Rohm the choice of accepting the new policy or resigning his leadership of the SA. Choosing the latter, Röhm sulked in semiretirement for the next four years before accepting an offer to move to Bolivia as a military adviser.

Within the newly reconstituted Nazi Party there was little direct criticism of Hitler but plenty of carping at the Munich central bureaucracy. Goebbels, who had earlier grumbled about the "reactionaries" around Hitler, played a key role in the anti-Munich campaign from his new position as business manager of the North Rhineland Gau (district) in Elberfeld. He was joined by Gregor Strasser, a former pharmacist from Landshut, who was in charge of building up the party in northern and central Germany. Strasser, like Goebbels, was convinced that the Nazis must take their programatic socialism more seriously if they hoped to win over the industrial workers. He argued for the nationalization of banks and large firms. This policy could not be effectively pursued from Munich, he believed, for the city lacked a large manufacturing base and a militant work force. Furthermore, he said, the Münchners were lazy, small-minded, and intent upon imposing their petty bureaucratic regulations on the rest of the movement. When Strasser outlined his objections to Goebbels, the doctor fully agreed. He confided to his diary on 21 August 1925: "[Strasser] brought much sad news from Munich. About that abdominable and wretched management of the central office. Hitler is surrounded with the wrong people. I believe Hermann Esser is his undoing. With Strasser we shall now organize the entire west. . . . That will give us a weapon against those sclerotic bosses in Munich. I am sure we shall convince Hitler."

To coordinate their campaign to wean Hitler from Munich, Strasser and a number of other dissidents calling themselves the Working Group of Northern and Western Gauleiters met at the Hanover home of Gauleiter Bernhard Rust on 25 January 1925. Hitler was not present, but he was represented by Feder. During the meeting most of the conferees expressed support for a Communist proposal in the Reichstag to expropriate the property of the former royal houses of Germany, a move that Hitler was known to oppose. Blaming Hitler's position on his Munich entourage, Goebbels went so far as to suggest that "the petit bourgeois Hitler" be expelled from the party unless he broke free of the pernicious southern influence. When Feder objected to Strasser's "Socialist" program, Goebbels denounced him as a "servant of capital and interest."

Feder's report to Hitler on the Hanover meeting convinced the latter that he had to act quickly to pull the party together. In February 1926 he invited all the regional leaders to Bamberg, where the southern influence predominated. Goebbels hoped that he and his northern allies would be able to convince Hitler to take a more Socialist path. "In Bamberg we'll play the coy beauty and lure Hitler onto our turf. In all the cities I observe to my joy that our spirit, i.e., the Socialist spirit, is on the march. No one believes in Munich anymore. Elberfeld will become the Mecca of German socialism."

But Hitler quickly dispelled the doctor's illusions. Speaking in an authoritarian tone, he said he would brook no further disagreements about the location of party headquarters or the direction of Nazi policy. The National Socialist movement, he declared, must act as a disciplehood of true believers fighting together for a sacred cause. Just as Munich had to remain the center of Nazism because of the holy sacrifices that had transpired there, the original party dogma could not be revised, for it "was the foundation of our ideology."

The northern dissidents were disappointed with what they heard, but they were unwilling to stand up for their beliefs in the presence of Hitler and his strong southern contingent. Strasser concluded that his faction was too weak to overpower the Münchners or to start a separate party. Suffering in silence, Goebbels fumed in his diary over having to put up with the "swine from down under."

Aware that complete cooperation on the part of his northern lieutenants was by no means secured, Hitler traveled around the Reich, stroking the egos of regional potentates. He concentrated on Goebbels, for he understood how useful the little man might be. In a move reflecting a good appreciation of Goebbels's character, Hitler invited him to Munich for a speaking engagement in April 1926. The Nazi chief's red Mercedes picked up Goebbels at the train station and drove him past signs proclaiming that "Dr. Goebbels" would speak at the Bürgerbräukeller. As Hitler's personal guest Goebbels toured party headquarters and saw the place where the Beer Hall martyrs had fallen. He attended Hitler's thirty-seventh birthday party and had dinner with Geli Raubal, a pretty twenty-year-old who was the daughter of Hitler's half sister, Angela. Geli, disparaged by Putzi Hanfstaengl as "an empty-headed little slut," flirted with Goebbels, throwing him into transports of delight. After his two-and-a-half-hour speech at the Bürgerbräukeller, which was warmly applauded, Hitler tearfully embraced him, evoking the effusive admission "I am really happy." Goebbels's bliss continued when Hitler treated him to a lengthy explanation of his ideas on foreign policy. "We had a meeting of minds," wrote Goebbels in his diary. "He talked brilliantly. I love him thoroughly. . . . He has thought everything through. I am totally reassured. . . . I bow before the greater man, a political genius!" Leaving the Bavarian capital, Goebbels gushed: "Farewell, Munich, I love you very much!"

"No Madamoiselle, You Will Not Dance in Munich"

With economic stabilization and relative political stability prevailing in the land after 1923, the Nazis searched for controversial issues that they could exploit to keep themselves in the public eye. Cultural politics provided a key to this strategy, and the Nazis made Munich's ongoing cultural wars one of their primary battlegrounds in the "Golden Twenties." Aside from keeping their cause in the headlines, their zealotry helped lower the tone of intellectual debate. Yet they could not have polluted the waters so effectively without help from Munich's political and cultural leadership.

When the Nazis breached the Munich City Council and the Bavarian Landtag in 1925, they made attacks on Jews in Munich's cultural life central to their agenda. One of their Landtag delegates, for example, fulminated against "the seduction of the people by the Jewish operetta, with one hundred women turning their legs up in the air, and by the Jewish movie house." Nazi city councillors demanded the ouster of State Opera conductor Bruno Walter on the ground that as a Jew he was not fit to conduct German music. The Nazis' house organ, the *Völkischer Beobachter*, complained that Jews got all the best building contracts, while "good German architects" were going hungry.

The Nazis combined their demand for "racial purity" in cultural matters with a crusade for moral probity and patriotic virtue in the arts. Official censorship in Munich had softened after the collapse of the monarchy, but the Nazis took it upon themselves to be the city's unofficial guardians of family and national values. To promote their cultural vision, they relied not just upon speeches and publications but on violent demonstrations and physical intimidation. Favorite tactics included setting loose packs of rats in theaters and throwing stink bombs during performances. When they wished to run the Jewish author Lion Feuchtwanger out of town, they laid siege to his house, screaming anti-Semitic slogans and pelting him with stones whenever he ventured out. Their brutal tenaciousness paid off: Feuchtwanger fled to Berlin in 1925. (His novel *Erfolg*, published five years later, contained cutting caricatures of Hitler and his followers.)

The Nazis focused much of their wrath on Munich's theatrical scene, which in the early twenties still showed fitful signs of its old exuberance. Their prime target in the early twenties was the radical young playwright Bertolt Brecht, who had moved to Munich from his native Augsburg in 1918. As a political leftist and cultural rebel (Wedekind was his idol), Brecht believed that Munich would be an ideal place to work. For a time he felt at home there, but the Nazis soon put an end to his idyll. When his *In the Jungle of Cities* opened at the Residenztheater in May 1923, a group of SA men tried to drown out the performance with foot stomping and chants. The play went on only because Brecht's followers, who outnumbered the Nazis, shouted them down. During the third performance, however, the Nazis set off a stink bomb, which shut down the production for good. Calling the SA "the excrement of Adolf Hitler," Brecht left for Berlin in 1924.

On several occasions the Nazis received support from the Munich establishment in their drive to "cleanse" the city. For example, Frank Wedekind's play *Pandora's Box* was canceled because the Nazis were joined in their protest by the police, the church, and the BVP. A Nazi campaign against performances by Tilla Durieux, a Jewish actress from Berlin, was effective because, on the advice of the conservative *Bayerische Kurier*, some members of the audience emptied chamber pots in the hall. Sometimes the police summarily suspended performances that the SA disrupted. After closing Arthur Schnitzler's sexually evocative play *Der*

Reigen (*La Ronde*) in the wake of a Nazi riot, the police chief declared: "The police are not in the position, without neglecting more important tasks, to place a large contingent at the constant disposal of the business director [of the theater], in order to ensure the orderly performance of a play that mocks all healthy sensibilities of the people, and that therefore has rightly awakened heavy protests in wide circles."

Mayor Scharnagl, though condemning the Nazis' more violent tactics, shared their views on art and culture. In his inaugural address in 1925 he defined his cultural agenda as "the furthering of noble, elevated expressions of human life among all sectors of the population; the perpetuation of old customs and traditions; the suppression of modernist, un-German, and demoralizing practices and views through the cultivation of indigenous, fully native and rooted inheritances." In this spirit he chastised the Kammerspiele's talented director, Otto Falckenberg, for mounting plays that explored "the sexual and sensual side of human nature [without offering] any joy or nobility." He also saw to it that a prominent square in Schwabing was named after Max von Feilitzsch, the archconservative interior minister who had led the Catholics' charge against cultural modernism in the Prince Regency period.

Munich's city council did its best to keep the town free from what the mayor called "cheap fads, degrading extravagances, and works of questionable political import." Thus, when the African American dancer Josephine Baker, famous across Europe for appearing in a banana skirt and little else, sought to include Munich in one of her tours, the council replied: "No mademoiselle, you will not dance in Munich, a city that respects itself." (By contrast, Baker was a great hit in Berlin, despite Nazi demonstrations calling her "inhuman.") On grounds of "questionable political import," the council banned Alfred Eisenstein's great film on the Russian revolution of 1905, *Battleship Potemkin*. Later in the decade the council blocked the installation of a statue on the Sendlingerplatz because the work featured a naked fisherman figure. "Christian-thinking circles in Munich," said a vigilant councilman, "would consider it a provocation if we proceeded in this direction."

Important segments of the artistic community were just as anxious as the Nazis and conservative political leaders to keep Munich free from alien influences. Shortly after the war, at a Glaspalast demonstration against the Versailles Treaty, local artists urged their colleagues "not to lose their German face." There seemed little chance of this, for the artists who controlled the exhibition space generally kept out works that might have been considered "un-German" or aesthetically subversive. Paul Klee's iconoclastic abstractions were unwelcome in this environment, and the artist leaped at the chance to join the new Bauhaus school in Weimar in 1921. Even Expressionism, though eminently German in inspiration, was initially unacceptable in Munich. When Ludwig Gies's Expressionist crucifix found its way into the German Arts and Crafts Exhibition of 1922, a group of artists, backed by the Catholic press, ensured its quick removal.

The Bavarian capital's literary scene also showed tendencies toward parochialism. A popular anthology of contemporary Munich writers, published in 1926, asserted that the artists included therein were determined that their city "should not constitute one of those foreigner-ridden literary centers [i.e., Berlin], where business acumen and suspect progress determined the intellectual current of the day." Rather, they would engage in a "creative restoration" defined by the rediscovery of "nature and home, the holy world of childhood, Christian belief, and German history."

Literary upholders of these principles could take comfort in a growing exodus of socially critical writers: in addition to Feuchtwanger and Brecht, the old bohemians Ernst Toller and Erich Mühsam left for Berlin, as did Johannes Becher, Ricarda Huch, Ödön von Horváth, and Heinrich (but not Thomas) Mann. The city that had once attracted hundreds of writers and artists from the chilly German North was now actively repelling them.

Munich's famed institutions of higher education—the Ludwigs-Maximilians Universität and the Technische Hochschule—were also suffering a creative hemorrhage. The schools still boasted prestigious faculties, but some of the most respected professors were leaving because they could no longer stomach the atmosphere of extreme nationalism and anti-Semitism. Significant losses included the physician Sauerbruch, the historian Hermann Oncken, the art historian Heinrich Wöfflin, and the chemist Richard Willstätter. (After resigning his chair in 1924, Willstätter, a Jew, stayed on in Munich almost until it was too late, escaping only in 1939.) Like Max Weber, whose death in 1920 was a crucial loss for the university, these men were all German nationalists, but they were also humanistic and broad-minded, and as such they were forced to suffer repeated attacks from superpatriotic colleagues and students. In 1926, when the university celebrated the one-hundredth anniversary of its move from Landshut to Munich, Rector Karl Vossler warned of a "growing danger of provincialism and intellectual intolerance" at the institution. He was right to do so; in the following year Baldur von Schirach, future leader of the Hitler Youth, became head of the Student Association at the university.

Munich's embrace of traditionalist culture in the 1920s occasioned considerable derision outside the Bavarian capital. Writing in 1922, an observer from Berlin argued that Munich, previously "overestimated" as an art center, was now nothing but a "provincial town without an intellectual core." Another debunker declared that Munich's previous sophistication, "shallow and imported," had entirely evaporated in the wake of a "postwar revival of *Ur-Bajuwarentum* [Ur-Bavarianism]." Yet another insisted that Munich, having fallen into "ever-sharper antagonism with the rest of Germany and the world," could be revived only "in opposition to the spirit of Münchnertum." Lion Feuchtwanger agreed, insisting that art in his former hometown was "academic and philistine," maintained by "a stubborn, stunted, mentally-stale populace, mainly for reasons of tourism." Comparing Munich with Berlin, the *Manchester Guardian* proposed that whereas the national capital was "the city of today and tomorrow," Munich had become "the city of yesterday and the day before."

These were harsh words, but they paled in comparison with a 1924 article in the Berlin periodical *Das Tagebuch,* which identified Munich as indisputably "The Dumbest City in Germany." Munich earned this distinction, said the article, because it had the Reich's most backward leaders, cretinous population, reactionary press, xenophobic atmosphere, and brutal police. Tongue only partly in cheek, the article went on to attribute these qualities to the enormous amount of beer consumed yearly by the average Munich male, a figure it estimated at five hundred liters. "Naturally that does something to the brain," said the paper. "Hitlerism, von Kahr, hate-filled judges, the *Münchener Neueste Nachrichten*—all these are easily explained by 500 liters of beer."

Munich's officials and boosters were of course indignant over these insults and sought to disprove them with well-orchestrated displays of cultural prowess. The grand opening in 1925 of the German Museum for Technology and Industry, planned by Ludwig III but delayed by war and revolution, offered a good opportunity for self-congratulation. It was celebrated with a play by Gerhart Hauptmann and an opera by Hugo von Hofmannsthal and Richard Strauss. In his dedication Mayor Scharnagl reminded the world that Munich was a leader in industry as well as in art and learning. "To the realm of the arts, which we cultivate so lovingly, and to the domain of the sciences, which we hold in such high esteem, we now add technology, which for some time has provided a solid base for our cultural and intellectual life," he proclaimed.

Concerned to counter the view that their town was no longer the capital of German art, city officials acquired Franz von Lenbach's villa and turned it into a municipal gallery of art in 1925. An advisory board drawn from the art community was appointed to help shape the collection. Its mandate was to feature the works of important Munich-based painters and sculptors. As it turned out, however, most of the museum's budget went to the procurement of relatively conventional works by artists long dead. (Only after World War II did the gallery develop its impressive collection of the Blue Rider school.)

When it came to honoring Munich's literary achievements, there was also a strong tendency to look to the past. In 1928, on the occasion of the one-hundredth anniversary of Ibsen's birth, Mayor Scharnagl recalled the Norwegian dramatist's twenty-three-year association with the city, insisting that its easygoing atmosphere had been crucial to his artistic development. In the same year the municipality established a Literature Prize of the City of Munich. The selection of the earliest winners was revealing. Thomas Mann, who sat on the jury, proposed Karl Wolfskehl, the mercurial veteran of the Cosmic Circle, but Wolfskehl had no chance of winning because he was Jewish. Oskar Maria Graf, another candidate, could not be honored because he was a notorious leftist who had been highly critical of his native city. It stood to reason, then, that the first recipient of the prize should be Hans Carossa, and the second Hans Brandenburg. Neither writer could be faulted for modernistic tones or positive views of democracy.

The writer who brought the greatest glory, but also the greatest challenges, to the Isar city was Thomas Mann. His star burned all the brighter because so many of his colleagues had left. He too threatened to leave but could not bring himself to do so. Pleased to have such a celebrity in residence, the city council sent him a congratulatory telegram on his fiftieth birthday, in 1925, to which Mayor Scharnagl personally added ten bottles of excellent wine "so the greeting would not be too dry."

Yet throughout this period Thomas Mann was deeply disturbed by what was happening in Munich. He worried that the city was sinking into a swamp of provincialism and boorishness. His concerns on this score were embedded in a larger change of outlook that took him increasingly away from the "unpolitical" conservatism he had championed in the war and revolutionary era. As early as October 1922, in a speech entitled "On the German Republic," Mann urged his audience to defend Germany's beleaguered experiment in democracy. He proposed that if the Germans came to understand that the concepts of culture, republic, and humanism were interdependent, they would know that "they must become republicans."

Mann continued on this new tack in an article he wrote in spring 1923 for the *Dial,* an American publication that paid him welcome hard currency for his observations on the situation in Germany. Here the writer addressed forthrightly the alarming conditions in his adopted city. He lamented the absence of "the literary-critical spirit of European democracy"—a spirit that in Germany was "most prominently represented by Jews." Through its hostility toward this spirit, he said, Munich had become "the city of Hitler, of German fascism, and of the swastika. . . ."

Well aware that local university students were among the most fervent backers of Nazism, and hoping to encourage those who resisted this trend, Mann addressed a prorepublican group at the university on 22 June 1923. Because this was the anniversary of the murder of Walther Rathenau, Mann spoke out on the mentality behind the crime. Political hatred, he said, was not generated by the much-maligned values of individualism and liberalism, but by their opposite: "collectivism, iron social ties, unconditional obedience." These values admittedly had "seductive appeal," but they were "frightful" in the human sense, pushing confused young people into the deceptive consolations of obscurantism and absolutism. The only genuine "idea of the future," Mann concluded, was humanism.

At the time he was delivering this address, Mann was composing the crucial "Snow" chapter in his seminal novel *The Magic Mountain.* The novel is set in the pre–World War I era and concerns, among other things, Europe's plunge into the irrationalism of war, but it can also be understood as an indictment of the dark forces ravaging postwar Europe. This borne in mind, it is significant that the key sentence in the "Snow" chapter reads: "For the sake of goodness and love, man shall let death have no sovereignty over his thoughts."

In his campaign against the forces of darkness, Mann not only lectured widely on the importance of cultivating humanistic values but fought against the ongoing efforts in his hometown to curtail artistic and intellectual freedom. In 1926 he joined a small group of fellow writers in protesting a new Law for the Protection of Youth from Smut and Filth. The ordinance ordained a kind of secular "index" through which the authorities could remove from circulation any works that they considered obscene or immoral. Mann denounced the measure as an "inquisition" that could have currency only in an "atmosphere of repression."

In November of the same year Mann joined a group called Münchener Gesellschaft 1926, whose purpose was to help Munich recover its cultural and intellectual strength. Addressing the group, Mann noted sadly that Munich had been "poisoned" by anti-Semitism and extreme nationalism. Taking up the Munich-Berlin dichotomy (which he had raised to Berlin's disfavor in his wartime *Reflections of a Nonpolitical Man*), he suggested that whereas Munich had once stood for the free intellect and Berlin for political authoritarianism, now the relationship was reversed. True, Munich had a new "German Academy," but this was "an institution in which, alongside many professors, military officers, and businessmen, exactly two [of which he was one] German authors have the honor of being represented."

Yet for all his criticism of the Munich scene and for all his despair over its increasing provincialism, Mann continued to believe that the place retained powers of the intellect and spirit that, if aggressively reasserted, might alter the political climate for the better. Thus in November 1926, with five other Munich intellectuals and artists, he participated in a forum entitled "Struggle for Munich as a Cultural Center." The forum was sponsored by the Left-liberal German Democratic Party, but Mann insisted it involved everyone concerned with the fate of Munich, "this beautiful city whose honor and happiness is so close to our hearts. . . ." The gathering, he said, should be taken as a signal that there were still those who "stood at Munich's side" at a time when its "soul" hung in the balance. The challenge was great, for the Bavarian capital had degenerated into "a center of reaction, [a] hotbed of resistance against the [democratic] will of the age, an essentially stupid city." Yet he still saw reason to hope: "There is an intellectual revolution in the air. Munich is restless. It wants to throw off a yoke that has weighted it down and besmirched its name in Germany and abroad—a name that once stood for goodness, openness, freedom, and joyousness."

Heinrich Mann, whose republican politics had earlier helped estrange him from his brother, also appeared at the "Struggle for Munich" forum. He had become even more despairing over the city's postwar evolution than Thomas. In June 1923 he had written a friend: "You would not believe how desolate Munich has become in spiritual and artistic matters." At the forum in 1926 Heinrich focused on Munich's theatrical scene, lamenting recent disruptions of modernist plays and an alarming number of suicides among actors and dramatists. Yet he, like Thomas, chose to see a brighter side. Noting that the majority of Munich's population belonged to parties that were "neither nationalistic nor unconditionally reactionary," he proposed that the "once so hospitable city" might become so again. Heinrich may truly have believed this, but at the time he said it he was spending most of his time in Berlin, and two years later he established his residence there.

The Mann brothers' hope proved illusory that events like the "Struggle for Munich" forum would generate a broad movement for liberal cultural renewal. As the leader of the prorepublican forces and an apostate from his earlier conservatism, Thomas Mann now came in for special abuse. The *Münchener Neueste Nachrichten,* assessing his comments at the forum, condemned his "fatal error" of holding up artists and intellectuals as worthy judges of politicians and businessmen. Did Mann not realize that intellectual creativity could exist only "in an orderly and prosperous environment"? the paper asked. The nationalistic *Süddeutsche Monatshefte* accused Mann of seeking to blunt the conservative thrust of his wartime *Reflections* by excising some of the more aggressively patriotic passages from a recent edition of that book. Mann's effort to touch up his past, said the journal, was a genuine travesty, for the unadulterated *Reflections* had been a work of brilliance compared with his recent prodemocratic babblings. The most meanspirited and ugly attack, however, came from the Nazis, who had followed Mann's political odyssey in the Weimar era with derision. Now, in the wake of his "Struggle for Munich" speech, the *Völkischer Beobachter* combined mockery of his political stance with slurs against his family. Referring to him throughout as "Mann-Pringsheim" (a reference to his Jewish wife, Katia), the paper noted that he had a young son (Klaus) who "precociously worked his deep-seated sexual problem [homosexuality] into his adolescent dramas." Mann's familial ties, the paper proposed, were behind his hand-wringing about anti-Semitism and alleged cultural provincialism.

Stagnation

If Thomas Mann found himself under pressure on his home turf during the middle years of the "Golden Twenties," so did his nemesis, Adolf Hitler. The Nazi leader knew that he needed to rekindle his movement's momentum in its Bavarian base, where crucial ground had been lost since the abortive putsch of 1923. Once again he had to make people aware that there was a viable alternative to the current rulers. Banned from addressing mass audiences in Bavaria, he turned back to his old society friends in Munich for help in making his presence felt. Elsa Bruckmann hosted a series of dinners with influential figures from the local artistic, business, and academic communities. Here Hitler explained that the central government's policy of fulfillment toward the Western powers was a betrayal of legitimate German interests. In the judgment of one witness, the Nazi leader seemed tougher and more focused than ever: "He was much changed from the years before the putsch and prison. The small, pale, sickly, often almost empty-seeming face was more powerfully concentrated; his facial bones, from forehead to chin, stuck out more prominently;

where earlier there had been dreaminess, there was now an unmistakable strain of hardness."

For all of Hitler's efforts, however, the Nazi Party was having difficulty reestablishing itself as a political contender. In 1926 Hitler allowed Strasser and Goebbels to launch an "urban plan" designed to strengthen the party in the industrial regions and large cities of the North and center. The idea here was to win workers to the Nazi cause by emphasizing the anticapitalist dimensions of the party program. Goebbels, appointed Gauleiter of Berlin, took on the demanding job of turning the "Red" capital into a "brown" bastion. He employed so much violence in his crusade that the Nazi Party was banned in Berlin and Brandenburg between May 1927 and April 1928. Even before the ban, however, the party was having difficulty attracting industrial workers because Hitler was unwilling to countenance independent unions. In March 1927 the Reich commissioner for the protection of public order could report: "In general, the [Nazi] party has not made great progress. It has not been able to bring its membership anywhere near the level it had in 1923." The Nazis were having difficulties even in Munich, their would-be Moscow, where the combined effects of sociopolitical stabilization and a resurgence of the BVP were thwarting the movement's progress. In early 1927, two years after legalization, the Munich branch had only 1,600 members, of whom 150 were in danger of being expelled for nonpayment of dues.

The party was also having financial difficulties. Traditionally it had raised much of its revenue through admission charges to Hitler's speeches, an avenue now closed in much of the Reich. Expenses were piling up, for Hitler was never one to economize. In 1925 he moved the party's headquarters into new offices at 50 Schellingstrasse, in the heart of Schwabing. An innovative plan to finance renovation of the headquarters by "selling" bricks to individual donors did not get very far. In the year after the move party income exceeded expenditures by a mere 534 marks. In 1927 party headquarters registered an income of 254,000 marks and expenditures of 252,000; largely because of election campaign costs from previous years, the party carried a debt of 14,000 marks.

Against this backdrop of relative stagnation in Nazi Party fortunes, the Bavarian government (though not that of Prussia) thought it safe to lift the speaking ban on Hitler. As Interior Minister Stutzel explained to the Reich's envoy in Munich, "In Upper Bavaria and especially in Munich National Socialism is almost completely ruined and even Hitler has lost his old attraction for the Bavarian population."

While Stutzel and his colleagues may have had reason to believe that the Nazis were moribund, that condition was at least partly caused by the very factor they now elected to remove, the muzzling of Hitler. By unmuzzling the Nazi leader, they made it easier for the party to survive the "stable" years of the mid-twenties and to revive their fortunes once circumstances again turned in their favor.

Hitler staged his oratorical return on 9 February 1927 at Munich's massive Zirkus Krone, scene of so many earlier Nazi rallies. The streets were plastered with red posters announcing the event. SA men, now dressed in their characteristic brown shirts (they were leftovers from the defunct German colonial service, purchased on the cheap) paraded around the area, singing fight songs and intimidating passersby.

The Krone filled up fast despite a relatively high entrance fee of one mark (twenty pfennigs for the unemployed). The crowd was "excited and filled with high expectations," reported a police observer. There was a large contingent of women, who were "as always very enthusiastic about Hitler." On the whole the audience looked to be petty bourgeois, but there was also a sizable sampling of the "better classes," including "representatives of the intelligentsia." As people took their seats, SA men went down the aisles hawking tiny swastika flags, which sold briskly. A "deep longing for sensation hung in the hot sticky air," noted the police observer.

Eventually Hitler entered, dressed in his brown trench coat. He strode to the stage, right arm outstretched, surrounded by party luminaries and SA guards. He sat down to one side as Dr. Rudolf Buttmann, a recent convert from the German National People's Party, assured the faithful that Hitler had not submitted to any "conditions" in order to get the speaking ban lifted. Then Hitler began to speak. His performance, in the judgment of the police observer, was not terribly impressive. At times he spoke so fast that his words were jumbled. He "gestured wildly with his arms and hands and jumped around excitedly to get the crowd's attention." His central argument was that only the Nazis could deal effectively with Germany's socioeconomic problems, which he said were as severe as ever. He compared his own "oppression" by the Bavarian government with the trials of Christ, who had also been forced to spend time in the wilderness. To the disgust of the police observer, the crowd responded enthusiastically to this "stale evangelism." Toward the end of Hitler's speech, however, the applause was getting a little thinner, leaving the witness to wonder "what sort of echo" the event might have.

A tentative answer began to emerge at Hitler's second public appearance, also at the Krone, on 30 March 1927. This time there was no rush for admission and tickets were readily available at the door. Their price had been reduced to fifty pfennigs to promote a large turnout: Hitler was on sale! Yet the hall remained only two-thirds full, the rear benches totally unoccupied. SA men again peddled swastika flags, as well as subscriptions to the *Völkischer Beobachter* and autographed pictures of the Nazi leader. "The whole thing gave the impression of a need for money," reported the police observer.

This time almost all the spectators seemed to come from the less prosperous classes. When Hitler made his appearance, he seemed desperate to whip up enthusiasm. In addition to his wild gestures, he made "cheap jokes." The serious part of his performance was devoted to the strategies through which Germany could become a "world power like England." To achieve this end, he said, Germany must divide the constellation of powers arrayed against it and find new allies. Neither France nor Russia could serve this role; the former would always oppose Germany, and the latter was a "Jew state" bent on expanding to the West. Britain and Italy were the only possibilities: Britain was not determined to keep Germany weak, and Italy was ruled by a man who did "not bow to the Freemasons and the Jews." Germany would be "lucky," Hitler added, if it had a "statesman like Mussolini."

This last comment reaped applause from the audience, but lavish praise of Mussolini was not likely to sell very well in Munich as a whole. Too many Münchners recalled how the Fascist leader had been a fervent backer of Italian intervention against Germany in World War I and had pushed for annexation of the ethnic German South Tyrol. He was also infamous for his assertion that Rome had built a great empire while Germans were still baying at the moon. Hitler's effort to wrap himself in the Duce's toga was not one of his more inspired gambits.

Lack of inspiration was again a problem at Hitler's next appearance at the Krone a couple of weeks later. It happened to be raining, but that alone could not have explained the low turnout. "The earlier mass enthusiasm is definitely missing," reported the police observer. Hitler was not pleased by the poor turnout. Before beginning his prepared speech, he shouted that the people of Munich had better "take off their sleeping caps."

But the Nazi rallies in Munich over the next few months continued to attract relatively small crowds. Moreover, most of the meetings organized by the party's district branches were so sparsely attended that two of the twelve sections (Sendlingen and Thalkirchen) had to be merged, and the Neuhausen branch was incorporated into the Gern-Nymphenburg section.

In 1926 financial difficulties, combined with restrictions on activities imposed by the party leadership, plunged the Munich SA into crisis. SA activists complained bitterly that they lacked funds to carry on propaganda campaigns and that "cowardice" in the central bureaucracy was keeping them from engaging in their usual street demonstrations and head bashing. To calm them down, Hitler personally assured them that his "whole heart" was with them and that once he came to power, he would turn them loose. Even Hitler's promises, however, could not generate much sense of momentum, and the group had to be reorganized because of membership losses.

Elsewhere in Bavaria, the party seemed equally stagnant. Observing these developments, the Munich Police Headquarters concluded in January 1928: "Hitler's repeated claims that the National Socialists are making progress do not hold water, especially in Bavaria. In reality, interest in the movement is declining in the countryside as well as in Munich. Branch meetings that drew 300 to 400 people in 1926 now bring in 60 to 80 at the most."

National and state elections in May 1928 largely confirmed the Nazis' difficulties. In the Reichstag elections the party won only 10.7 percent of the votes in Munich, putting them in third place behind the SPD and BVP, which won 32.6 percent and 23.1 percent respectively. The Nazis' most successful candidate was General Ritter von Epp, who was really a Bavarian monarchist. In the Landtag elections the Nazis captured only 6.1 percent across the state and 10.3 percent in Munich, which gave them a total of nine seats. These showings were especially disappointing in view of the elaborate and expensive campaigns the party had run all across Bavaria. To make matters worse, high debts accrued during the elections forced Hitler to call off the 1928 party rally scheduled for Nuremberg.

These difficulties were real enough, but the relatively low turnout at rallies and the indifferent electoral results distorted the group's actual condition, at least in its birthplace. A recent statistical analysis of the Munich branch of the party in the period between 1925 and 1930 reveals that the organization retained a number of important strengths, even in this difficult time. The local contingent actually grew, albeit very slowly, over these years. Perhaps more important, its demographic base was more diverse than many thought. Audiences at rallies might have *looked* overwhelmingly lower middle class, but in reality only about one third of the Munich membership came from this socioeconomic group. One fourth was comprised of workers, and the rest belonged to the solid middle and upper classes. As for the party's gender breakdown, women were, as the rally audiences suggested, prominent in the movement; in 1925 almost half the Munich membership was female. Over the next few years, however, female membership fell off sharply, which may have been a relief to party propagandists, who had always touted the movement as a bastion of manliness. Throughout this period the age of the membership conformed fairly accurately to Nazi claims that theirs was a youth movement. The average age was only thirty-one, and that made the Nazis the youngest party on the Munich scene. It was also unusual in having footholds in virtually every part of the city, though it was strongest in the middle-class districts. The most solid bastion was Schwabing, the old bohemian quarter that Hitler had always favored, where disgruntled artists joined students, teachers, civil servants, and white-collar workers in placing their faith in the failed painter from Austria.

Taken together, these demographic and geographical factors helped the party weather the tough times in the postputsch era. Because the movement was not confined to one social group or urban district, it was harder to isolate or contain. As a party of youth it remained resilient despite setbacks and could aspire to represent the future. The Nazis had always claimed that they were not a traditional political party but a *Volksbewegung,* a popular movement representing broad crosscurrents of the people. Albeit still an exaggeration at this stage, the boast had a certain validity in Munich.

"Munich Must Again Become the Hope of Germany"

On 12 November 1929 the Swedish Academy announced that Thomas Mann had won the Nobel Prize for Literature. In December, after he had returned from the award ceremony in Stockholm, Munich honored him with a banquet in the Rathaus. The writer took this opportunity to declare that contrary to persistent rumors, he was not leaving his adopted city. Still, Mann could not have been heartened to notice that in his hometown, as in the rest of the Reich, Hitler's *Mein Kampf* was now outselling both *Buddenbrooks* and *The Magic Mountain.*

Also in Mann's Nobel year, Nazi ideologue Alfred Rosenberg founded a Munich-based cultural organization called the Combat League for German Culture. Its declared aim was "to arrest the disintegration of our cultural foundations." Although it recruited artists and scholars from around the country, its composition was strongly Bavarian.

The Combat League for German culture was formed just in time to help the Nazis contest Munich's municipal elections held in early December 1929. The Nazis campaigned intensely, adopting the slogan "Munich Must Again Become the Hope of Germany." Hitler brought in speakers from all over the Reich for mass rallies, one of which he claimed attracted thirty thousand people. On 1 December 1929 two thousand SA men marched for five hours through all parts of the city save "Red" Giesing. A couple of days later the party mounted twenty rallies in Munich beer halls. Hitler scurried from rally to rally, whipping up enthusiasm. According to a shocked Mayor Scharnagl, Munich had never witnessed a more hateful and unscrupulous campaign. But the hatefulness paid off. The Nazis won 51,226 votes, or 15.4 percent of the total. They were still behind the SPD and BVP, but they had more than doubled their seats in the city council, now holding eight (out of fifty).

Even as Münchners were going to the polls in late 1929, the precarious economic recovery that had so hindered the Nazis' progress during the mid-1920s was collapsing in a heap of layoffs and bankruptcies. The immediate cause was the American stock market crash of October 1929, which plunged much of the industrialized world into deep depression. Germany was especially hard hit by the crash because of its dependence on short-term American loans and because parts of its economy had remained semidepressed even in the "recovery" years between 1924 and 1929. Unemployment had remained relatively high (in 1926 reaching 10 percent), and the agricultural sector had long been struggling against intense foreign competition, high production costs, dwindling sources of credit, and falling prices. The worst off were small farmers specializing in meat and dairy production. The Great Depression was the final blow for many of these marginal operators, as it was for thousands of small businesses and craft shops in the towns. In 1930 bankruptcies occurred with twice the frequency of 1928. Unemployment rose accordingly: By January 1930, just two months after the American crash, the jobless count in Germany had increased to three million, 200 percent higher than in 1928.

Regionally the hardest-hit areas were the northern and central parts of the Reich, especially the industrial region of Saxony and the small farming sections of Schleswig-Holstein and Hesse. But the Depression quickly engulfed Bavaria as well, for this state too had many small companies, and a number of its larger manufacturing firms were now controlled by banks and holding companies in the North.

Not surprisingly the economic crisis quickly segued into a political crisis. The Müller cabinet in Berlin fell apart over disagreements regarding welfare and unemployment compensation payments. President Hindenburg called upon the Center Party politician Heinrich Bruning to form a new national government "above parties." Bruning attempted to deal with the worsening economic crisis by raising taxes and reducing government spending. When the Reichstag refused to accept his austerity budget (the Nazis and Communists joined to vote it down), Bruning dismissed the Reichstag and called for new elections, to be held in September 1930. In the meantime, he imposed his austerity measures through Article 48 of the Weimar Constitution, which allowed the government to take emergency actions without going through parliament.

Given the mood in the nation, Bruning's decision to call new elections was a terrible mistake. The Nazis had been gaining in regional elections in late 1929 and early 1930. Their gains had come largely at the expense of the liberal centrist and conservative parties. Undoubtedly they had benefited from growing economic insecurity and from a decision to tailor their propaganda to discontented rural voters. Pointing toward the usual scapegoats, they explained to angry farmers that their troubles were caused by unscrupulous Jewish middlemen and predatory international bankers. Now, with the September Reichstag elections impending, they mounted their most vitriolic campaign to date, all of it tightly controlled from Munich.

On the Nazis' home turf the Held government tried to hold them down with some new regulations, but these were pathetically petty. In the larger towns, including Munich, the beer halls that hosted most of the Nazi (and many of the Communist) meetings were prohibited from serving alcohol and food on the ground that few Bavarians would attend meetings where they could not eat and drink. The government also ordered the removal of ashtrays at political gatherings to prevent their being used as missiles. In June 1930 Held's regime imposed a ban on the public wearing of uniforms by political factions. This was aimed primarily at the SA, whose members were thought to be more inclined to cause trouble when dressed in their fighting colors. But such regulations were little more than irritants to the Nazis. They dealt with the beer and food ban by filling up before meetings, and in response to the uniform ban they paraded around in white shirts with black ties. Absence of their fighting brown did not discourage them from engaging in a bloody brawl with members of the German State Party in the Bürgerbräukeller on 23 August. A little later the entire Nazi delegation to the Landtag, claiming immunity from the new regulations, showed up in brown uniforms.

Although its efforts to curb the Nazis were ineffectual, the Bavarian government was justified to try to slow them down. In the September elections the NSDAP scored a stunning victory, winning 6.4 million votes nationwide and 104 (out of 577) seats in the Reichstag, up from 12 (out of 491) in 1928. They were now the second-largest party in the nation after the SPD. The only consolations for the Bavarian government were that the Nazi vote in that state (17.3 percent) fell a little below the national average of 18.3 percent, and the Catholic BVP also did well. The somewhat larger Nazi success in the center and North was primarily due to a breakthrough with rural voters in places like Schleswig-Holstein and Lower Saxony.

Aside from their economic troubles, these regions were heavily Protestant, and their swing to the Nazis suggested that German Protestantism, lacking a coherent political organization of its own, was more vulnerable to the appeal of National Socialism than was Catholicism. In fact, a similar tendency was evident in Bavaria itself, where the predominantly Protestant areas of Middle and Upper Franconia recorded the highest Nazi votes in the state. Heavily Catholic Upper Bavaria had the lowest Nazi support. But Catholicism was no infallible inoculation against the brown plague. Arch-Catholic Passau (the city later made infamous by the film *The Nasty Girl,* about a young woman who caused a furor by exposing her town's Nazi past) gave the Nazis a hefty 31 percent. Munich itself, still roughly 80 percent Catholic, polled 21.8 percent for the Nazis, significantly higher than the national average.

Anti-Nazis in Munich were legitimately alarmed. As Pastor Rupert Mayer, later a victim of Nazi persecution, warned, "It is incredible but nevertheless true that the Hitler swindle has laid hold of the widest, even Catholic, circles of the people; and not merely in the towns has the movement gained ground but to an enormous degree in the country." Thomas Mann was shaken enough by the election to give a rousing anti-Nazi speech in Berlin in mid-October. He compared the Hitler movement with orgiastic nature cults and the worship of pagan gods; the Nazis were bent on seducing Germany with "high-flown, wishy-washy cant, full of mystical euphoria with hyphenated prefixes like race- and folk- and fellowship-. . . ." His words were almost drowned out in a wave of heckling led by the novelist Arnold Bronnen, formerly a friend of Brecht's but now an avid Nazi.

The results of the September elections were made even more worrisome by the fact that the Great Depression, which had influenced them, was settling in ever more tenaciously across the land. Munich, which Hitler continued to regard as his springboard to power, was once again full of misery and fear. "Where once 3600 workers stood at machines," reported the Maffei factory in December 1930, "there are now only a couple of hundred, and every one of them waits daily for the fateful blue letter, which tells them that they are no longer needed." Hardly a worker in Munich did not have reason to fear the dreaded blue letter. According to a report of the Industrial and Trade Chamber of Munich in 1931, in the preceding year and a half the local construction industry had shrunk by one half, wood production by one quarter, optics by one third, while machine manufacturing had collapsed entirely.

Jobless workers roamed the streets and lined up outside unemployment centers, public shelters, and soup kitchens. By early 1933 the Employment Office in Munich listed 85,933 people out of work, almost a third of the entire work force. In November 1931 municipal soup kitchens fed 37,000 hungry persons daily. Since the shelters were jammed beyond capacity, people slept in the streets or erected makeshift settlements on the edges of town. Oskar Maria Graf noticed in summer 1931 that "all the park benches were occupied by hungry unemployed. Some tried to peddle shoestrings or combs or pencils that nobody wanted, but most threw dice or played tarok for a few pennies day after day. Occasionally they went on demonstrations against new cuts in public assistance." Many people simply gave up; the number of suicides rose from 182 in 1926 to 321 in 1932.

Because of dramatic declines in tax income—city revenues sank 22.2 percent between 1929 and 1932—Munich's government was in worse financial straits than ever. Following his reelection as mayor in December 1929, Karl Scharnagl was obliged to cut back severely on municipal programs. Deep cuts came not just in social services but also in cultural outlays. Most of the cultural expenditures were locked in to a few relatively expensive projects, like the symphony orchestra and the Lenbach Gallery. When the famous Glaspalast burned down in 1931, the city had no funds to replace it. In the following year the municipal government cut all spending in the plastic arts deemed not absolutely essential.

The consequence was a new pauperization of the art community and further grievous losses for *Kunststadt München*. In 1930, 350 professional musicians were on the dole. To help them out, the local Employment Office established a clearinghouse for musical jobs around the city, so that classically trained musicians could, on occasion, earn a few marks by playing weddings or birthday parties. Yet the musicians were better off than the performers at Munich's famous Puppet Theater, whose entire subsidy was canceled in 1932. The puppeteers appealed the decision by pointing out that their theater was widely recognized as "one of Munich's cultural jewels," whose closing would be "an irreparable loss for the city." The appeal was fruitless; henceforth the only puppets to perform on Munich's stage were political ones.

Keen to exploit the mounting crisis, the Nazis sent propaganda speakers to employment offices, mounted vigils outside failing factories, ran various charity functions for the destitute, and even set up their own Employment Office for the Protection of the National Work Force. On the basis of such opportune activism, the party grew substantially. In 1929 it had about 100,000 members nationwide; between 1930 and 1932 it added 720,000 new members. The Munich membership grew from 1,600 in 1927 to more than 20,000 in 1931.

The SA, now under the leadership of Ernst Röhm, who at Hitler's request had returned from Bolivia to reorganize the group, also made great headway. Largely self-financed through the sale of party newspapers, along with such consumer items as Stürmer razor blades, Kampf margarine, and Sturm cigarettes, it became a kind of paramilitary welfare operation, offering its members clothing, food, insurance policies, and occasional small stipends. Reich-wide, the SA counted 77,000 members in January 1931; by August 1932 the figure had risen to 471,000. In Munich alone the Brownshirts now totaled over 5,000 active members. The group grew despite attempts by the Bavarian government to restrict its activities, and despite some internal scandals, notably the revelation by the *Münchener Post* that Röhm was a practicing homosexual.

In January 1931 the party moved into a bombastic new national headquarters, the Brown House. Formerly the Barlow Palace, the building was located on the fashionable Brienerstrasse. Purchased in 1930 with a loan from the industrialist Fritz Thyssen and a tax of two marks on every party member, the building had been thoroughly renovated by the pro-Nazi architect Professor Paul Ludwig Troost. A tour de force of Nazi vulgarity, it boasted a grand entrance with swastikas on either side of a giant bronze door. On the first floor was a Flag Hall containing banners from the early years of the party, including the sacred Blood Flag from the shooting during the Beer Hall Putsch. On the second floor were the offices of the party leadership, the national SA chief, national treasurer, and—sanctum sanctorum—Hitler's private study.

Hitler, however, spent little time in his fancy new headquarters; instead, like the bohemian he was, he continued to hold court in his favorite Munich cafés, such as the Café Heck in the Hofgarten and the posh Carlton Tea Room on the Briennerstrasse. Klaus Mann chanced upon him at the Carlton in early 1932. Watching Hitler stuff himself with strawberry tarts, Mann found him "surprisingly ugly, much more vulgar than I had anticipated." He could not understand the "secret of his fascination" or how he managed to "make people lose their minds." Such a creature, he was sure, could never come to power in Germany. "You have no chance, silly little mustache," he mumbled in Hitler's direction. "Five years from now, nobody will know your name. . . ."

Among Hitler's frequent companions on his café crawls was his pretty niece Geli Raubal, now twenty-one and studying medicine at Munich

University. "Uncle Alf" installed her in one of the nine rooms of his new luxury apartment on Prinzregentenplatz, to which he had moved in late 1929 with the financial help of his wealthy Munich backers. According to Putzi Hanfstaengl, Hitler "hovered at [Geli's] elbow with a moon-calf look in his eyes in a very plausible imitation of adolescent infatuation." Most of Hitler's inner circle believed that his relationship with his niece was "not strictly avuncular," and Putzi claimed to have seen drawings of her made by Hitler that were "depraved, intimate . . . with every anatomical detail." Clearly he loved her deeply—as deeply as he could love anyone. With that love, however, went a need for total control and domination. Determined that she not go out with anyone but him, he kept her tightly cloistered in the Prinzregentenplatz apartment. This soon drove her to rebellion and a secret affair with her uncle's chauffeur, Emil Maurice. When Hitler learned of the affair, he fired Maurice and confined Geli even more strictly to her golden cage. She managed somehow to stike up a liaison with another young man, an artist from her native Austria, but Hitler squelched that relationship as well. At the same time, he made clear to Geli that he could never marry her, for that would reduce his attractiveness to his female supporters. "Women," he liked to say, "have a disastrous influence in politics. Look at Napoleon. And the dancer Lola Montez who was the ruin of King Ludwig I of Bavaria. Without her he would have made an excellent monarch." Hitler's treatment of his niece, one historian has noted aptly, "reveals, in miniature, what Germany, Hitler's future bride, could expect from a liaison with this man."

While keeping Geli cloistered, Hitler was beginning to pay court to another woman, the vivacious young Münchnerin Eva Braun. Eva worked for Hitler's photographer Heinrich Hoffmann. They met when Hitler came into Hoffmann's studio and noticed Eva standing in a short skirt on top of a ladder. Although Eva's aesthetic tastes ran toward "hot jazz" and romantic movies, she allowed Hitler to take her to the opera and to tea at the Carlton. On these occasions, according to one of her girl-friends, "Eva would stuff her brassiere with handkerchiefs in order to give her breasts the fullness they lacked and which seemed to appeal to Hitler. . . ." After one of their assignations she wrote Hitler a polite note thanking him for "a memorable evening." She could not have known that this note would be found by Geli Raubal, who made a point of going through her uncle's pockets.

The next day, 17 September 1931, Hitler left on a campaign trip to Hamburg. Refusing to take Geli along, he also forbade her to go to Vienna to visit friends. Shortly after his departure she locked herself in her room and shot herself above the heart with Hitler's Walther pistol. No one in the building heard the shot, and Geli slowly bled to death on the floor.

Upon hearing the news of Geli's death, which was relayed to him by Rudolf Hess, a devastated Hitler broke off his campaign trip and hurried back to Munich. There he and his aides arranged with Justice Minister Franz Gürtner to forgo an inquest so that Geli's body might be shipped immediately to Vienna for burial. Then Hitler went into seclusion for two days at a friend's house at Tegern Lake south of town. He threatened to withdraw from politics and (once again) to kill himself. His aides hid his gun to preclude the latter option. Eventually he bestirred himself to make a secret trip to Geli's grave in Vienna. Upon returning to Munich, he ordered Geli's room locked up and allowed no one to enter but his house-keeper, who was instructed to place fresh flowers each day next to a bust of Geli that Hitler had commissioned from a local artist. Thereafter, on anniversaries of the tragedy, Hitler would sit alone in the room for hours.

While Hitler grieved, his enemies in Munich tried to make the most of the incident. The *Münchener Post* reported that Hitler had violently quar-reled with Geli on the day before her suicide; it even suggested that he had broken her nose. Other loose tongues circulated stories that Hitler had ordered Geli killed because she had become impregnated by a Jew or because she was carrying his child. Presumably there was no truth to these rumors, and they quickly faded away. Hitler, however, remembered them, and they certainly inflamed his determination to get revenge on such calumniators once he came to power.

AS THE GREAT Depression continued to deepen, the streets of Munich once again became a stage for violent political confrontations. There were bloody fights between the SA and the paramilitary forces of the Communists and Socialists. Brazenly the Nazis even attacked gov-ernment officials. In June 1932 some 6,000 uniformed SA men marched through Munich and laid siege to the home of Prime Minister Held. The police intervened and arrested 470 Nazis, but they were released shortly thereafter. As one frustrated legal official complained, the state could hardly expect the Nazis to obey the law when the system proved unwill-ing "to harm a hair on their heads."

In the midst of ideological strife and economic misery, Munich, like the rest of Germany, tried to find refuge and hope in a much-ballyhooed national celebration, the one-hundredth anniversary, in 1932, of Goethe's death. By now Goethe had become a comfortable household icon, quoted by everyone and understood by few. In his centennial year, wrote the Berlin journalist Carl von Ossietzky, he was celebrated "not as a poet and prophet, but above all as opium." Goethe had never had much to do with Munich, but the city had no intention of being left out of this pious occasion. As Mayor Scharnagl explained, the "Goethe Year" could be a source of renewed cultural pride, not to mention tourist revenues. A city council report entitled *Munich's Place in the Goethe Year* agreed that Goethe's legacy should be honored not only in cities (like Frankfurt and Weimar) where he had spent considerable time but—since he was a great German artist—also in cities strongly identified with German genius. Goethe's last years, after all, had "coincided with the extraordinarily rich cultural and intellectual flowering in Munich under Ludwig I," an effervescence that had enlivened "all other cultural centers in Germany."

Breakthrough?

In spring 1932 new presidential elections were held because Hindenburg's seven-year term had expired. Pressured by Goebbels, Hitler decided to challenge the old field marshal's bid for reelection. To do so, he had to become a German citizen, which he finally managed to accomplish in February 1932. Interestingly he obtained his citizenship not via Bavaria, which as late as December 1929 had rejected his application (citing his treason conviction in 1924), but through Nazi-controlled Brunswick, where he got himself appointed a state councillor. (According to law, citizenship in any German state automatically conferred Reich citizenship.) Citizen Hitler campaigned hard for the presidency in hopes that he might be swept into office on a tide of popular emotion. Yet, when the results came in on 13 March, Hitler had lost by a considerable margin to Hindenburg (whose 49.6 percent, however, was just short of the absolute majority necessary to avoid a runoff contest among the leaders). The Nazi chief received 30.1 percent of the votes nationwide, 29.9 percent in Bavaria, and 24.4 percent in Upper Bavaria, the electoral district in which Munich was located. The seven electoral districts that he had won were all located in the Protestant North and center. His relative difficulty in Bavaria can be explained largely by the BVP's decision to back the Protestant Hindenburg over Hitler, whose devotion to the Catholic faith was rightly seen as questionable. Angered by this rebuff but encouraged by the fact that he had won almost one third of the votes, Hitler declared that he would campaign even harder for the runoff.

This he did, although he was distracted in the midst of the campaign by another revelation about Röhm from the *Münchener Post*. It published some letters between Röhm and a psychologist in which the two men discussed their mutual interests in homosexuality and astrology. Hitler was livid at both the *Post* and Röhm but decided not to repudiate his SA chief as long as he confined his sexual attention to grown men.

The runoff election for the presidency, held on 10 April, brought the necessary majority for Hindenburg, who received 53 percent of the tally. Hitler improved his showing to 36.8 percent nationwide but won only 32.3 percent in Bavaria and 24.9 percent in Upper Bavaria. Again, his strongest support was in the Protestant North, and the Upper Bavarian result was the second worst that the Nazi leader achieved in the entire Reich. Munich voted more heavily Nazi than the surrounding countryside, but its core of BVP voters was holding firm. Many of the city's conservative Catholics, it seemed, continued to see the Nazis as a threat to states' rights and the interests of the church.

Trends exposed in the national elections since 1930 were partly confirmed in the Bavarian Landtag elections held on 24 April 1932. Winning 32.5 percent across the state and 28.5 percent in Munich—impressive gains—the Nazis drew roughly even with the BVP. Yet they still could not banish the Catholic party to the historical dustbin, as Hitler had hoped to do. Bavaria's regionalist conservatism was proving to be a barrier to Nazism, just as it had earlier been to liberalism and socialism. As for Munich itself, Hitler might call it a brown city, but it still had strong components of black and red. The Nazi Party's apparent inability to break down these bastions of opposition despite the misery of the Great Depression suggested that Hitlerism might be exhausting its potential in the city of its birth.

In midsummer 1932 Hitler was obliged to turn his attention once again to the national arena because new Reichstag elections were scheduled for 31 July. The restless Nazis had helped make this test necessary by refusing to back the new government of Franz von Papen unless he dissolved parliament and called elections. Hitler was counting on the worsening Depression and increasing street violence to bring him yet another influx of voters. His hopes proved well founded. Nationwide the Nazis garnered 37.3 percent of the vote, enough to make them, for the first time, the largest party in the Reich. In most of Germany their success came at the expense of the middle and center-Right bourgeois parties, which were now in complete disintegration.

In Bavaria and Munich, however, the Catholic center-Right still held its own against the Nazis, who won 32 percent statewide, 28.9 percent in the capital. This was embarrassing for the Bavarian Nazis because the performance at home, though credible, was below the national average. Once again the North (though not Berlin, where the Nazis received only 28.6 percent of the vote) was showing more enthusiasm for Nazism than the South. The Nazi pope did not seem able to dominate his own Vatican.

Frustration over the showing in Munich and Bavaria prompted some local SA men to call for a new putsch. But Hitler, who had learned his lesson in 1923, told a rebellious audience at the Zirkus Krone on 15 September that since the Nazis had been struggling for power for fifteen years, it would not hurt to wait a little longer.

Yet in truth Hitler was also restless. While convinced he must come to power "legally," he believed that the breakthrough had to come soon, for he knew that followers quickly won could be just as quickly lost. Therefore, on the basis of controlling the largest party in the Reichstag, he demanded to be appointed chancellor of the republic. The current chancellor, Franz von Papen, rejected this bid, as did old President von Hindenburg, who gave the former corporal a stern lecture on his "duty" to support the existing government.

Deeply angered by this rebuff, Hitler got revenge on Papen by teaming up with the Communists to force yet another dissolution of the Reichstag and new national elections, set for November 1932. Again Hitler hit the campaign trail, or rather the campaign skies, flying from rally to rally in a lightplane.

Just as he was hitting his stride, however, he was called back to Munich by another personal crisis. Like the recently departed Geli Raubal, Eva Braun, his new mistress, had come to resent Hitler's Victorian strictures and his busy schedule, which kept him away from Munich for long periods. To show her frustration, she shot herself in the chest with a pistol, inflicting a serious but not fatal wound. This was becoming an ugly pattern, not to mention a nuisance.

Eva Braun's suicide attempt was a minor setback compared with the election of November 1932. The Nazis had campaigned hard across the Reich, but they dropped substantially from their performance in July. Losing a total of two million votes, the party had to give up thirty-four Reichstag seats, while their arch enemies the Communists gained eleven. The party declined even in some of its former strongholds, like Schleswig-Holstein. This was a significant reversal, suggesting that people were becoming weary of waiting for Hitler to take power and were drifting off to other alternatives.

In Bavaria and Munich the Nazis had put another major effort into the elections, which Upper Bavarian Gauleiter Adolf Wagner boasted would be contested with "brutality and force." Yet they managed to win only 30.5 percent statewide, 24.9 percent in Munich. Here too the party was in decline.

The November elections generated a new wave of frustration and bitterness among the party faithful in Munich. By contrast, the Nazis' opponents were quick to cite the election results as proof that the Nazis were not the wave of the future after all. Of course, Hitler did not share this verdict, though he now began to doubt the efficacy of the ballot box as the sole key to power. He would have to find some new tactic to reach his goal. And given the difficulties he was having in the city and state where his movement had originated, he had to wonder whether the last leg of his journey to Berlin would, after all, run through Munich.

7

Capital of the Movement

IN JULY 1935, two and a half years after becoming chancellor of Germany, Adolf Hitler officially designated Munich Capital of the Movement. In fact, the city had been using this title informally since Hitler took power, and the chancellor's action simply legitimized the practice. Now city officials commissioned a new municipal coat of arms, in which the Third Reich eagle and swastika replaced the Bavarian lion. At the same time, local leaders drew attention to Munich's prominent role in the early history of Nazism by installing a museum in the Sternecker beer hall, where the party had its first headquarters. They also put up plaques at sacred sites like the Hofbräuhaus, the Feldherrnhalle, and the buildings in which Hitler had lived. It was impossible after 1933 to walk around Munich without being reminded that this was the cradle of the Nazi movement.

Hitler bestowed upon his favorite city another honorary title: Capital of German Art. Like a latter-day Ludwig I, he was determined that Munich should again be the focal point of the German art world, the place to which people had to come to understand the aesthetic dimensions of the new order. This commitment to artistic rejuvenation may seem at odds with the Nazi movement's notorious anti-intellectualism and disdain for high culture, an aversion best summed up in Hermann Göring's famous boast: "When I hear the word 'culture,' I reach for my revolver." Yet top Nazi leaders (including Göring) saw themselves as defenders of genuine national culture. From the outset, they were as committed to reshaping Germany's cultural terrain as they were to transforming its political landscape. Their vaunted political revolution was based in part on a calculated refusal to acknowledge any clear boundaries between politics and art. The Nazis understood, better than most parties of the modern era, the advantages of embedding political issues in elaborate spectacle and self-dramatization. That this impulse would find its most characteristic expression in Munich should hardly surprise us; after all, the city had long been famous for its theatricality and love of pomp.

Ironically, Munich's cultural elevation came at a time when the city's actual power was diminishing. Munich remained the headquarters of the Nazi Party and the SA, but Berlin was the undisputed capital of the Nazi Reich, a Reich that was more centrally controlled than its Weimar and imperial predecessors had been. The emphasis on Munich's cultural prowess and importance to party history served partly as compensation for a lack of political influence in the Nazi system.

"You Have Triumphed After All!"

"We've made it. We're sitting in the Wilhelmstrasse. "It's like a dream." So wrote Josef Goebbels in his diary on 31 January 1933, the day after Hitler became chancellor of Germany. This moment is generally referred to as the seizure of power, but Hitler's assumption of the chancellorship was constitutionally legal. As we have seen, President von Hindenburg had firmly opposed the appointment despite the Nazis' status as the largest party. However, he was induced to change his mind by a coterie of prominent conservatives led by Franz von Papen, who had become convinced that there could be no viable government unless Hitler were allowed to take over. The men insisted as a precaution that the new cabinet be dominated by conservatives. "We have [Hitler] framed in," bragged one of Papen's friends.

Berlin, not Munich, provided the immediate backdrop for Hitler's assumption of power, and it was in the national capital that the grandest celebrations, orchestrated by Goebbels, took place. A torchlight parade passed through the Brandenburg Gate, symbol of German military prowess. Goebbels arranged for the spectacle to be broadcast over the radio, the first of hundreds of such propaganda spectaculars under the Third Reich.

The radio station in Munich, however, refused to carry Goebbels's broadcast. The rejoicing in the Bavarian capital was mainly on the part of local Nazis. A couple of thousand SA men gathered on the Königsplatz to hear Gauleiter Wagner jubilantly proclaim that "Adolf Hitler can now begin his work." Otherwise the city took relatively little notice of the momentous events in Berlin. As one Münchner observed, Weimar Germany had seen a parade of chancellors come and go, and there seemed little reason to imagine that Hitler would stay around for very long: "We all thought [his chancellorship] was simply a transition phase." Moreover, the governmental change occurred at the beginning of Carnival season; many Münchners were more interested in the selection of a new "Carnival Prince" than in the inauguration of yet another chancellor.

The Munich Nazis expected immediate and dramatic changes in the city on the Isar. More precisely, they expected the imminent establishment of pro-Nazi regimes at the municipal and state levels. Many local Nazis also believed that Hitler's triumph would elevate Munich to new prominence in the Reich. Was the Bavarian capital not the birthplace of National Socialism? Was it not the headquarters of the party? Did it not house the movement's most sacred shrines? Above all, was it not the residence and favorite city of Hitler, now Führer of Germany? As Hermann Esser declared, "For the first time in history a citizen of Munich has become chancellor of the Reich. I believe that we as Münchners have every reason to be proud and that the city administration must take cognizance of this great event."

Responding to this demand, Mayor Scharnagl said tepidly: "If indeed the interests of Munich are advanced by the Reich, we will all be pleased." In the meantime, the conservatives who ran the Bavarian government made it clear that they were not prepared to hand over power to the new regime in Berlin. Hearing that Hitler planned to replace the existing Bavarian regime with a Reich commissar, Prime Minister Held struck a note of particularist defiance: "If Hitler dares to send a commissioner from Prussia, we shall arrest him at the frontier for breach of the peace!"

Brave words, though many conservative Bavarians feared that Held would not be strong enough to hold out for long against the impatient Nazis. A delegation of monarchists urged him to call in Crown Prince Rupprecht to help run the government. A dam of Wittelsbach blue, the reasoning went, was the best hope for holding back the brown flood. Interestingly, the Bavarian Social Democrats expressed their willingness to back this step. But Rupprecht would accept the call only if he could become king and name his own government. Citing constitutional objections, Held rejected a full-scale restoration.

The Nazis were indignant over the Bavarian government's display of resistance. In Munich, Gauleiter Wagner warned darkly that Hitler was prepared to bring "a reluctant state to its senses." Determined to force Munich into compliance, the Führer flew to the Bavarian capital in early February. Before a cheering crowd at the Theresienwiese, he claimed Bavarian ancestry and crowed that he was the "first Bavarian" to hold the office of chancellor. (This was incorrect; a Bavarian prince, Chlodwig zu Hohenlohe-Schillingsfürst, had served as chancellor between 1894 and 1900.) Declaring his "boundless love for Munich," Hitler warned that he would not tolerate efforts to seal the city off from the changes engulfing Germany.

To strengthen his hand, Hitler decided to dissolve the Reichstag and hold new elections in early March 1933. He planned to exploit an expected landslide victory to get rid of elections for good. In the upcoming contest the Nazis could terrorize their opponents and browbeat the electorate with all the power of the state behind them. From their viewpoint this promised to be an enjoyable exercise.

Just as the campaign was getting under way, the Nazis got another break. On 27 February the Reichstag building in Berlin was extensively damaged by a fire that was clearly the result of arson. Hitler privately called the conflagration "a beacon from heaven," and some Germans at the time (along with many commentators since) assumed that the Nazis themselves had set the blaze. More recent scholarship has suggested that this was probably not the case. In the event, only one person, a demented Dutch Communist named Marinus van der Lubbe, was apprehended at the scene. Hitler and his lieutenants insisted that this poor half-wit was merely the fall guy for a vast Communist conspiracy, but no such plot was proved. Nonetheless, Hitler effectively exploited the incident for his own purposes. On the very next day he secured a decree from President von Hindenburg suspending civil liberties guaranteed by the Weimar

Constitution. Crucially for Bavaria and Munich, the new decree also allowed the central government to assume power in any state "to restore security."

In their electoral campaign following the Reichstag fire, the Nazis cast themselves as Germany's only effective defense against a threatened Red takeover. "Without Hitler we would have Communism," proclaimed one of their speakers. The Nazis pushed this theme with particular vigor in Bavaria, where they hoped to lure rural Catholic voters from the BVP, which they depicted as soft on the Reds. "Every Catholic vote for List 1 [the NSDAP], fight for us against the Red flood," appealed the *Völkischer Beobachter*. In Munich SA men ransacked the houses of prominent Communists in search of "subversive" material. In the course of their search they beat a young Communist to death.

Hitler himself was very active in this campaign. Running for a Reichstag seat from his new home district of Munich-Upper Bavaria, he asked voters to give him "four years" to bring order and economic prosperity to Germany. Once this was accomplished, he said, he would return to Munich, the city he "loved the most," and devote himself to literary pursuits.

In the elections of 5 March 1933 the Nazis won 43.9 percent of the vote nationwide. This was something of a disappointment given the party's advantages and high expectations. Lacking an absolute majority, the NSDAP had to form a coalition with the conservative German National People's Party. On the other hand, the Nazis could take comfort in the fact that they had reversed their electoral slide of November 1932. In Bavaria the Nazis' percentage (43.1) was marginally lower than the Reich average, but they managed to score substantial gains over their nearest rivals, the Socialists and Bavarian People's Party. This was true also in Munich, where the Nazis won 37.8 percent of the total. The Bavarian electorate, including that of the capital, was clearly becoming more enthusiastic about the Nazis once they had taken power and were in a position to dispense political largess. Goebbels could rejoice in his diary: "South Germany has especially taken the lead in the entire electoral success; that is all the more gratifying since it enables us to take radical measures against a policy of separatist federalism."

This development shocked local anti-Nazis, who had come to believe that their region was relatively resistant to the brown plague. One of the most alarmed was Thomas Mann. He was out of the country on a lecture tour at the time of the March elections. Upon learning the result, he dashed off a worried letter to Mayor Scharnagl, expressing his surprise that the Bavarians would "vote against themselves" and inquiring whether the mayor thought this presaged an imminent Nazi takeover in Bavaria. On a personal level, he wondered if it was safe for him to continue to live in Munich. He hoped he could do so because he was "too good a German and too tightly tied to the cultural heritage and language" of his native land to regard exile as anything other than "extremely painful."

In a revealing reply Scharnagl admitted that he was surprised by the March elections and conceded that there would probably have to be a "change in government" in Bavaria. But he added that he and his fellow conservatives would cooperate with moderate elements in the Nazi camp to ensure the continuation of responsible rule. Furthermore, he expected that "within one or two years the entire revolutionary wave of National Socialism would have petered out and conditions in Bavaria would have returned to their fruitful course." As for Mann personally, Scharnagl proposed that the writer's "elegant reserve" should keep him out of "conflicts with unpleasant consequences."

But Mann remained unconvinced. On the morning of 10 March he wrote his friend Ida Herz that he considered himself "physically threatened" by developments in Bavaria. The recent elections, he reasoned, meant that Hitlerism would soon have a "free hand" in Munich. Under these circumstances, he doubted whether it was safe "for me to return to my house at all."

On 8 March Hitler decided that the time had come to move in Munich. He ordered Ernst Röhm and Gauleiter Wagner to engineer a takeover there. The next day Röhm and Wagner informed Prime Minister Held that Ritter von Epp, the "liberator of Munich" in 1919, would take charge of the government as Reich commissioner. They warned that if Held did not step aside immediately, the SA would revolt and Hitler would have to send in the Reichswehr to "restore order."

Held continued to resist, however, and the Nazis were forced to proclaim the governmental change by fiat. At 7:00 P.M. on 9 March, Max Amann, Hitler's former sergeant, appeared on a balcony of the Rathaus to announce that Ritter von Epp had become Reich commissioner on orders from Berlin. He further stated that Heinrich Himmler was taking over the Bavarian police. Meanwhile, on the tower above, Christian Weber, former stableboy, unfurled a long swastika flag.

That night the Nazis held a victory celebration in front of the Feldherrnhalle. Speaking to the assembled faithful, Ritter von Epp reminded the crowd that "the cradle of the National Socialist movement" stood in Munich. Bavaria would now shape the future of the entire Reich, he promised. And he added: "You Münchners know me too well to believe that I would ever allow anything amiss to happen to our beloved city."

Three days later Hitler flew to Munich to help the city celebrate its awakening. In a speech he said it was highly gratifying that "this historic development has come as a result of Bavaria's own determination to integrate itself into the great front of the reawakening nation." At the Feldherrnhalle he laid a wreath in honor of the Nazi martyrs of 1923. "You have triumphed after all," said a banner attached to the wreath.

Having seized the reins of state government, the Nazis turned their attention to the municipality of Munich. The *Völkischer Beobachter* began running editorials demanding that Mayor Scharnagl resign forthwith. Gauleiter Wagner, who as Bavaria's new interior minister was the real power behind Ritter von Epp, supported this demand. Seeing that resistance was pointless, Scharnagl resigned on 20 March. On the same day Karl Fiehler, Nazi city councilman and Beer Hall Putsch veteran, became Munich's new governing mayor. In a speech before the city council Fiehler said: "It is especially here in Munich that we have the responsibility to see to it that the will of our Führer is implemented. . . . We must make Munich once again a truly German city—a city in which German art and German ideals, German customs and German style, German sensibility and German joyousness reign supreme. After all, we will be held accountable by history and by the people for our actions."

The city council was quick to embrace the new line. Fiehler ensured a majority for the NSDAP in the body by banning the Communists and reducing its size. Socialist councilmen were expelled after voting against awarding Hitler and Epp honorary citizenships. The Nazis now had their free hand in the city of the party's birth.

As elsewhere in Germany, Nazi officials in Munich used their new power to persecute and terrorize old enemies. In this operation Himmler and his aide Reinhard Heydrich (chief of Bavaria's political police) could rely on help from Munich police veterans like Heinrich Müller, who ran the department's anti-Communist division. A native Münchner, Müller was the perfect political cop: doctrinaire, obsessed, and ruthless—qualities that served him well in his later job as head of the Gestapo. On the night of 10 March Müller and his men rounded up several Socialist members of the city council and placed them in "protective custody." At the same time SA thugs, assisted by the Munich police, raided the headquarters of the local chapter of the General German Workers' Association. There they rousted some three hundred members of the Reichsbanner, the SPD's paramilitary group, and beat them to pulps. Yet another target that night was the *Münchener Post,* long a red thorn in brown flanks. As they had done during the Beer Hall Putsch, SA men trashed the place, destroying printing presses and furniture, throwing typewriters into the street. After making the newspaper's insurance company pay for the restoration work, the Brownshirts converted the *Post* building into a rest and recreation center.

Ordinary Münchners added their part to the persecution campaign by denouncing their neighbors for political offenses. For example, a shop-keeper fingered a rival store owner and his wife for laughing at him when he raised the swastika flag over his establishment. Some vigilant citizens turned in a group of teenagers for joking about Röhm's sexual prefer-ences. The police were shocked to note that many of the denouncers turned out to be "old friends" or even relatives of their victims. According to a Malicious Behavior Law of 21 March 1933, all cases involving report-ed disrespect for the regime had to be heard in a special court for political crimes. Within a few weeks this court was so overburdened that the judges complained of an "ugly denunciation fervor" and "purely person-al vendettas."

"Dachau Wasn't Built for Geese"

As a result of the huge number of political arrests in the early days of the Nazi regime, prisons and ad hoc detention centers in and around Munich were bursting at the seams. Hence the regime decided to experiment with a form of mass detention that the British had pioneered in the Boer War, the concentration camp. On 21 March 1933 Munich newspapers carried an announcement from Police Chief Himmler that a concentration camp was opening near the village of Dachau (about twelve miles north of Munich), capable of holding five thousand persons. Communists and members of the Reichsbanner were to be incarcerated there so they could "no longer endanger state security." Himmler added primly: "We have taken these measures without regard to any petty considerations [of human rights] and are convinced they will have a calming effect upon the nation in whose interest we have acted."

The site of the new camp was a former munitions factory that had closed down shortly after World War I. Most of the buildings were dilap-idated, and the grounds were overgrown with weeds. Only about a mile and a half from the village of Dachau, the camp seemed worlds away from that old town, which had been known heretofore as a center of gen-tle landscape painting. There was nothing gentle about the village's new claim to fame. As one old lady put it, "Dachau [camp] wasn't built to hold geese."

Dachau's first 60 inmates arrived by truck from Stadelheim, Neudeck, and Landsberg prisons on 22 March. Among them was a leftist lawyer from Munich named Claus Bastian. He is noteworthy because he bore the designation "Prisoner Number One." This made him the first of some 206,000 registered inmates of the camp during its twelve-year existence. According to camp statistics, 31,951 died in custody. (The precise number of inmates and fatalities can never be known because many were not registered, especially toward the end of the Third Reich.)

The initial contingent of guards at Dachau were all members of the Bavarian State Police. They were not unusually brutal, and some made an effort to ease the prisoners' lot by giving them blankets from their own supplies. On 11 April, however, Himmler put the camp under SS jurisdiction with the goal of turning it into a pilot project for an envisaged national camp system. Thereafter the facility became a place of systematic degradation, torture, and murder.

Dachau, it was said, "showed that if the Nazis didn't like you, being dead wasn't good enough." Apparently, however, being dead was a good start. Just one day after taking over the camp, SS guards marched four prisoners, all Jews with leftist backgrounds, into a nearby pine forest and mowed them down with automatic pistols. Three died immediately, but one, a businessman named Erwin Kahn, remained alive after being hit five times. Inexplicably the SS delivered him to a Munich hospital rather than simply finish him off. Camp officials then announced that there had been an "unsuccessful escape attempt from Dachau" in which three detainees had been killed and one wounded. State prosecutors made discreet inquiries into the case, only to be told that Dachau was "off limits."

Before dying from his wounds, Kahn told doctors what had actually happened to him and his comrades. His was the first of many such stories to filter out of Dachau, despite rules that former inmates must not talk about what went on in the camp on pain of being sent back. Ordinary citizens were also warned not to show undue interest in the place. Two people caught looking over the wall in May 1933 were detained overnight "to satisfy their curiosity," and citizens were informed that that anyone caught snooping around the facility would be "given the opportunity of studying the camp from inside."

Despite these precautions, rumors of atrocities at Dachau spread. At the end of May Himmler, a stickler for discipline, became concerned that his penal experiment was getting a reputation for arbitrary persecution. He therefore replaced the first camp commandant with a slightly more disciplined (but equally brutal) thug named Theodor Eicke. Under Eicke's dispensation, Dachau became a slave labor facility for the SS and for selected private companies like BMW, Dornier, and Messerschmitt. It also served as a training center for guards and commandants at other camps. Among its graduates was Rudolf Höss, later commandant at Auschwitz.

The Persecution Widens

Although the Nazis' campaign of persecution and political terror focused initially on Communists and Socialists, it soon swept up conservatives as well. Former Prime Minister Held was briefly detained after being forced from office; upon his release he fled to Switzerland, then returned to a reclusive existence in Bavaria for the rest of his days (he died in 1938). Former Interior Minister Karl Stutzel, who had imposed the gag order on Hitler in 1925, was pulled from his house, badly beaten, and delivered to an informal SA prison in the Brown House basement. Paul Nikolaus Cossmann and Erwin von Aretin, staunchly conservative editors of the *Süddeutsche Monatshefte* and the *Münchener Neueste Nachrichten,* shared a cell in Stadelheim. Fritz Gerlich, whose paper *Gerade Weg* had repeatedly attacked the Nazis from a conservative viewpoint, also found himself in a Munich jail cell, bloody and bruised from a Brownshirt thrashing. While being pummeled, he had called out indignantly: "You beat *me*? A founder of the patriotic movement?" Gerlich's shock that the Nazis could thrash a patriot encapsulated the delusions that many Bavarian conservatives harbored regarding the events of 1933.

Thomas Mann avoided a possible similar fate by continuing to stay clear of the Reich. In March 1933 Himmler's police issued a protective custody warrant for the absent writer, accusing him of harboring "un-German, Marxist, Jew-friendly, and antimovement views." (The order was issued despite the fact that Mann, still hoping to avoid a permanent break with Germany and a ban on his work, refused to denounce the Nazi regime publicly during the first years of his exile.) Learning of the arrest order from a Swiss newspaper, which speculated that if he had returned to Germany, he might "be sitting in the new concentration camp at Dachau," Mann remained for a time in Switzerland, then moved briefly to France before settling into a long-term exile in California. In his absence the Nazis confiscated his house, his cars, and most of his personal property. His house was eventually sold in auction to the SS, who used it for its *Lebensborn* program (a system of maternity wards for unmarried "Aryan" women made pregnant by SS or police officers). It was only through the hasty intervention of friends and relatives that Mann was able to recover part of his library, his manuscripts, and his highly revealing diaries. (Sadly, a lingering horror that his diaries might have fallen into the hands of his enemies helped convince him in 1945 to burn the volumes covering the period between January 1922 and March 1933.) In early April 1933 Mann's passport expired, and his efforts to renew it from abroad were rejected.

Painful as these measures were, Mann suffered more from a blow dealt him by his fellow artists and intellectuals in Munich. On 10 February 1933 the writer had delivered a speech at Munich University to commemorate the fiftieth anniversary of Richard Wagner's death. In subsequent weeks he repeated the lecture in Amsterdam, Brussels, and Paris. The speech (later published as "The Sorrows and Grandeur of Richard Wagner") involved a penetrating appraisal of Wagner's work as well as an appreciation of the Master's persistent appeal. The lecture was applauded by each of its audiences, including the one in Munich, but the *Völkischer Beobachter* found it "disgraceful" that "the half-Bolshevist Thomas Mann" had been allowed to sully the name of Wagner. Shortly thereafter, on 16 April 1933, the *Münchener Neueste Nachrichten* published an open letter entitled "Protest of Richard Wagner's Own City of Munich." The letter attacked Mann for, among other offenses, seeing Wagner's work as "a fertile field for Freudian psychoanalysis." It accused him of denigrating Wagner as a modernist dilettante and of failing to recognize the composer as "the embodiment of the deepest German sensibilities."

Instigated by Munich Philharmonic conductor Hans Knappertsbusch, the attack was endorsed by forty-five signators. Among them were not only Nazi bosses like Adolf Wagner, Max Amann, and Karl Fiehler but fellow artists whom Mann had considered his friends: musicians like Hans Pfitzner, Richard Strauss, and Siegfried von Hausegger; the painter Olaf Gulbransson; and the theater director Clemens von Frankenstein.

For the exiled Mann, this "currish document" came as a terrible shock. He felt horribly betrayed by the city that (despite recent events) remained closest to his heart. Only now did he fully realize how deeply corrupted this place had become. His disgust over the affair was so profound and lasting that he cited "the illiterate and murderous campaign against my Wagner essay" in refusing to take up residence again in Munich after World War II.

Had Mann miscalculated and ended up in Dachau in 1933, he would soon have had the company of all sorts of "asocial" types whom the Nazis believed had no place in the new German order. A number of beggars and homeless people were rounded up and shipped to the camp in fall 1933. Significantly, in arresting them, the Nazis could make use of a 1926 Bavarian law aimed at the *Arbeitsscheue* (people unwilling to work). This law applied explicitly to Gypsies, though there were relatively few of them in Munich and Bavaria in the 1920s and early 1930s. Nonetheless, citing a "Gypsy plague," the Nazi government ordered in July 1933 sharper measures against them, including incarceration in Dachau. Homosexuals suffered a similar fate. Following an order from Himmler to rid the Reich of this "sickness," Munich police began rounding up homosexuals and sending them to Dachau for "reeducation." Yet another group to suffer early persecution were Jehovah's Witnesses, whose faith was banned on 13 March 1933. Their transgression was to oppose military conscription, which Hitler planned to reintroduce as soon as possible. Finally, the camp included a few dozen Munich retailers accused of gouging their customers. Dachau's very mixed assortment of detainees (to whom soon were added thousands of Jews) shows that the Nazis, from the very outset, interpreted the notion of "enemies of the state" in the broadest possible terms.

"Coordination"

Linked to the Nazis' persecution of political opponents and social outsiders was a far-reaching campaign to "coordinate"—that is, to neutralize—all institutions, organizations, and agencies that might challenge the regime's claim to total power. While this campaign naturally applied to the entire Reich, it seemed particularly urgent in Munich, whose conservative leaders had shown such reluctance to swim with the brown tide.

Since rival political parties were obviously incompatible with the Nazis' totalitarian aspirations, the regime not only jailed opposition politicians but wiped the organizations themselves off the political map. The KPD was the first to go, though in Bavaria there was not much left to ban because the Held government had already outlawed most of its activities. Once the Nazis consolidated their power in Munich, most of the Communists who had evaded the first sweeps fled Germany or went underground. Some tried to keep the party alive through small cells, but Heinrich Müller's Gestapo proved very adept at penetrating them.

The Bavarian Social Democratic Party was formally outlawed on 22 June 1933. Oddly enough, this came as a shock to many Socialists. Before the Nazis took power in Munich, local Socialists, like many conservatives, had tended to think that their region could avoid falling under Nazi domination. Erhard Auer even proposed in early March that the Bavarian police would "slap the Nazis down" if they tried to take power there. Sharing this illusion, some northern Socialists hastily moved to Munich after 30 January 1933. The Nazi takeover there sobered the Socialists but did not eradicate their hope of surviving as a party. After all, they had survived other hostile regimes, such as Bismarck's in the 1880s and Kahr's in the early twenties. Thus, when the Nazis forced the SPD leaders into exile, the expellees did not make the transition easily. For the next twelve years they moved from one foreign haven to another, always wrestling with the reasons for their failure to stop Hitler before he had tightened his grip on power.

The leaders of the BVP were also prone to illusion. They believed that their party could function in the new order as a kind of loyal opposition, protecting regional and religious interests through gestures of goodwill toward the regime. Their willingness to compromise got them nowhere, however; the BVP was summarily banned in early July 1933. Shortly thereafter some BVP members of Munich's city council tried to attend a council meeting as if nothing had happened. They were told that they had no mandates because their party no longer existed. To make their status clearer, on 19 July 1933 Bavarian police rounded up 1,917 BVP functionaries and placed them in "protective custody." A week later the council swore in 17 new members, all Nazis, and proclaimed itself ideologically pure. So much for the conservative dream of cooperation with National Socialism.

Munich's 8,000-man civil service could not be purged so rigorously since the regime needed competent bureaucrats to function. A new Law for the Restoration of the German Civil Service (April 1933) allowed for the dismissal of obvious undesirables, such as Jews or known leftists. There were relatively few of these in Munich's bureaucracy, however, and only 333 officials were fired. In any event it soon became apparent that most of the bureaucrats needed no browbeating to toe the new line. As one student of the Nazi coordination in Munich has written, "The new regime encountered a tide of sympathy from the ranks of officialdom. . . . The ideal of an authoritarian state, which the Nazis promised to install, had a seductive ring in the ears of administrative officials of the old school."

Coordination of economic, commercial, and labor institutions posed a greater challenge, for these bodies harbored traditions of independence and self-administration. As they did across the Reich, the Nazis in Munich took control of the labor market by dissolving the free trade unions into the state-run Labor Front headed by Robert Ley. Like other cities, the Bavarian capital established an Economic Police Force to monitor key businesses and services. Party members were placed in leading positions to ensure "control over the economic lifeblood of the city." Revealingly, some enterprises objected to the control on the ground that it was unnecessary. For example, the Builders' Association claimed that its coordination was superfluous because the group consisted of "entirely reliable persons" standing "without reservations behind the new regime."

Munich's Economic Police also watched over the press, whose ideological conformity was an early priority. Having arrested a number of anti-Nazi editors immediately after taking power, the regime quickly moved to shut down opposition publications or to staff their editorial boards with reliable people. Bavaria's largest daily, the *Münchener Neueste Nachrichten,* suffered such a fate, though it had long been a model of patriotic sentiment. The *Süddeutsche Monatshefte,* which in January 1933 had urged a Wittelsbach restoration to avert a Nazi takeover in Bavaria, also became a dependable cheerleader for the new government.

Simplicissimus, Munich's once-feared satirical journal, posed a problem for the regime because the old red dog had begun to get some of its bite back in the early thirties and had even taken a few nibbles at the Nazis. Once Hitler was in power, the magazine found itself in the odd position of hoping for protection from Bavarian Catholic conservatives, who had long been one of *Simpl*'s chief targets. The editor Franz Schoenberner admitted in his memoirs: "Bavaria, we thought, with her stubborn particularist animosity against all that came from Berlin, would be the last bulwark of common sense against the rising flood of mass hysteria and mass terror engulfing the German states one after another." But Bavaria's beleaguered conservatives were in no position to protect *Simpl* even if they had wanted to. In March 1933 the SA raided and vandalized the magazine's offices. Terrified, Schoenberner and T. T. Heine, the gifted Jewish cartoonist, fled Germany. The remaining staff saw to it that the red dog barked faithfully for its new master. "Our patriotic duty," said an editorial, "is to defend in our way the great domestic and foreign policy goals of the new Germany."

Munich's main cultural and educational institutions—its museums, opera, orchestras, theaters, universities, and scientific associations—quickly fell under the control of Nazi Party members or of functionaries prepared to do the regime's bidding. This is hardly surprising since the heads of these institutions were civil servants beholden to the state for their jobs. Moreover, all civil servants were subject to the Professional Civil Service law of April 1933, which made it easy to fire officials on racial or political grounds. Under the new law, six Jewish professors at Munich University were immediately fired. Five more quickly emigrated, and one took his life. The Nazis refused to allow the university to replace the renowned Jewish physicist Arnold Sommerfeld with the Munich-born Werner Heisenberg because the young scientist was an advocate of quantum mechanics, a heresy in the world of Nazified "German physics." In the meantime, on 10 May 1933, Munich students joined colleagues across Germany in burning the books and plays of writers deemed *Reichsfeinde* (enemies of the Reich). Among the literary combustibles in the Munich University courtyard were works by Heinrich (but oddly not Thomas) Mann, Oskar Maria Graf, Erich Mühsam, Ernst Toller, Lion Feuchtwanger, Sigmund Freud, Helen Keller, and Ernest Hemingway. Heinrich Heine once said that when books burned, people were certain to follow. Rarely has a writer been so prescient.

Munich's Catholic and Protestant leaders were, like the civil servants, generally anxious to get along with the new regime. With some notable exceptions, the keepers of Christ's flame on the Isar proved as politically opportunistic and morally bankrupt as their coreligionists elsewhere in the Reich.

Munich's Protestants (numbering about one hundred thousand in 1933) had always played an important role in rightist politics and had provided substantial backing for the Nazis in the Weimar period. Now that Hitler had taken the helm, Protestant spokesmen in the city were quick to document their loyalty. Their community newsletter welcomed the advent of "Germany's first truly anti-Marxist regime" and reveled in the notion that Christianity and Nazism could now fight the Red evil together. "Against the pitiless Marxist teaching," declared the paper, "arises a belief in the eternal, indelible values of the human soul. This is a belief in which the Nazi freedom movement and the Christian faith can come together." On Easter Sunday, 16 April 1933, Protestant pastors across Bavaria delivered an official blessing of Nazism:

> A state that once again rules in God's name can count not only on our applause but also on enthusiastic and active cooperation from the church. With joy and thanks we see how this new state rejects blasphemy, attacks immorality, promotes discipline and order with a firm hand, demands awe before God, works to keep marriage sacred and our youth spiritually instructed, brings honor back to fathers of families, ensures that love of people and fatherland is no longer mocked, but burns in a thousand hearts. . . . We can only plead with our fellow worshipers to do all they can to help these new productive forces in our land reach a complete and unimpeded victory.

In their enthusiasm for the new regime, Munich's Protestant pastors passed the collection plate on Hitler's birthday, beflagged their churches on state holidays, and even marched in the 1933 May Day Parade for National Labor with swastikas stitched to their vestments. In August two

Munich pastors assessed the first six months of Nazi rule as follows: "Guilt for the November [1918] crimes, whose stain prevented God from blessing our people, is now atoned. Leadership of the state safely resides in the hands of those who wish to make Germany great and strong again. Many [in the church] must now feel ashamed that they held themselves cautiously aloof while others strove and struggled at great personal cost for the national awakening."

Munich's much larger Catholic community, in contrast with the Protestants, had shown considerable ambivalence toward National Socialism during the Weimar era. The community's leader, Cardinal Faulhaber, had combined condemnation of the Weimar system with attacks on Nazi vulgarity, radicalism, and violent anti-Semitism. In 1931, disturbed by what he perceived as anti-Christian tendencies among the Hitlerites, Faulhaber forbade priests from joining the movement. But once the Nazis took power in Bavaria, Faulhaber and other Catholic bishops began to change their tune. Much like the Protestants, though not with quite the same enthusiasm, they let Nazism's rabid anti-Marxism convince them that the Third Reich merited their toleration. As early as 10 March 1933, after an audience with Pope Pius XI, Faulhaber publicly proposed that it was time "to practice more tolerance vis-à-vis the new government." Soon he went further. In a pastoral letter of 5 April he urged local priests to show "civic obedience to the duly constituted state authority." Faulhaber made no effort to support the BVP when the Nazis forced it to disband; indeed, he suggested it dissolve itself. The "era of parties is over anyway," he declared.

Toward a "Jew-free" Munich

Some of the more radical Nazis, such as Goebbels, Heydrich, Himmler, Wagner, and Rosenberg, despised the traditional Christian churches, but the regime did not directly attack these institutions. The Nazis, after all, liked to say that they were God's defenders against atheistic Marxism. Besides, they needed the churches' cooperation as they consolidated their power.

With the Jews matters were different. The Nazis persecuted them from the outset, though levels and forms of oppression differed from time to time and place to place. Munich's new overlords made a point of being especially zealous in this domain, as they did in many other areas of Nazi policy. They rushed through a host of anti-Semitic measures, some of them in anticipation of national regulations imposed by Berlin.

We have already seen that Munich's initial roundup of Socialists and Communists included some Jews and that Jewish leftists constituted the first fatalities at Dachau. But the initial persecution of Jews in Munich was not aimed exclusively at leftists; on the contrary, it focused on prominent Jews regardless of party. In its first days of power the new regime in Bavaria placed 280 Munich Jews in "protective custody" on grounds that they were a threat to state security. The local SA and SS immediately began to attack Jews in the streets. On 10 March 1933, when a Jewish lawyer named Michael Siegel complained of such tactics to the police, he was made to walk through town barefoot, his pants cut off at the knees, carrying a sign saying I WILL NEVER COMPLAIN AGAIN TO THE POLICE.

Mayor Fiehler, who hoped to keep Munich in the anti-Semitic limelight as a way of proving the city's centrality in the Nazi system, announced his intention to free municipal agencies of Jewish influence. He ordered that all Jewish doctors working at municipal hospitals be summarily fired. When this proved impossible, without a law on the books to make it legal, Fiehler commanded that Jewish doctors be allowed to treat only Jewish patients. Grotesquely, he also ordered that Jewish pathologists deal exclusively with Jewish corpses.

The city council followed up Fiehler's directives with anti-Semitic measures of its own. All city offices were advised to conduct no business with Jewish lawyers, notaries, or consultants. As of 24 March, the municipality would award no contracts to Jewish firms. Municipal employees were instructed not to buy their uniforms or supplies at Jewish-owned stores. Jews could not take part in municipal auctions or trade fairs. That summer Munich became the first city in the Reich to close its public bathing facilities to Jews. And as if dead Jews were just as dangerous as live ones, the city ordered that all Jews, whether or not they practiced the Jewish faith, must henceforth be buried in Jewish cemeteries, where they could not contaminate the Christian dead. In some special cases this rule was applied retroactively. Thus the remains of Kurt Eisner and Gustav Landauer were removed from the Ostfriedhof and turned over to Jewish authorities for reburial.

On 1 April 1933 Propaganda Minister Goebbels ordered a boycott of Jewish stores, cafés, restaurants, banks, and services. In cities and towns across the Reich, SA men painted "Jude" and "Germans Don't Shop Here!" on the windows of Jewish shops.

In Munich, as in some other towns, the anti-Jewish boycott was not as successful as the Nazis had hoped. While some patrons studiously avoided the targeted stores and services, many others did not. However, most of those who resisted the boycott probably did so not out of solidarity with the Jews. Rather, their behavior seems to have reflected a disinclination to let Berlin dictate shopping habits. If Jewish shops offered the best values, and often they did, many Münchners would ignore official edicts and perhaps even their own anti-Semitic inclinations to patronize them. The continuing success of the annual sales at a popular Jewish clothing store prompted the Munich police to complain that many women still "had not understood the lines laid down by the Führer for solving the Jewish Question."

On the other hand, when economic advantage and racial prejudice coincided, as they generally did with Gentile retailers and craftsmen, there was strong pressure for a hard line against Jewish competitors. On 28 March Munich's Association of Small Businessmen and Artisans urged Mayor Fiehler to compile and publicize a list of all Jewish-owned shops so that they might be closed down. "The rebirth of Munich's German middle classes," they said, "demands the exclusion of all non-German businesses."

The Nazi authorities themselves sometimes put economics before politics when these two imperatives collided. Thus the government in Munich allowed a Jewish-owned department store to expand because it brought in more tax revenue than the small "German" shops it displaced. The regime was also careful in the early years to forgo harsh anti-Semitic policies in the tourist trade, for these might have frightened away foreign visitors. Like their conservative predecessors, the Nazis continued to market Munich as the world capital of *Gemütlichkeit*.

The leaders of Munich's Christian churches, pursuing their efforts at a modus vivendi with the Nazi regime, did not leap to the defense of Jewish citizens. On the contrary, some Protestant pastors encouraged their flocks to join the party's campaign to "curb Jewish influence" in public life. On the Catholic side, Cardinal Faulhaber delivered a series of Advent sermons in 1934 urging that "love of one's own race" should not be turned into "hatred for another people," an admonition that prompted local Nazis to brand him the "Jewish cardinal." Yet he also endorsed Nazi efforts to keep the "national blood" pure through racial separation. Even when the regime began including Jewish converts to Catholicism among its victims, Faulhaber was reluctant to object. In a letter to Papal Nuncio Pacelli, Faulhaber justified his inaction as follows: "At the present time it is inadvisable [to protest], because the war against the Jews would then turn into a war against the Catholics, and because the Jews can take care of themselves, as was seen in the rapid disintegration of the [April] boycott."

Attitudes like Faulhaber's facilitated the Nazis' policies of coordination, and not only in Munich. There could be no broad opposition to

Hitler's consolidation of power when people thought only in terms of narrow sectarian interest. Some citizens might stand up for their own kind, but few would defend groups generally perceived as alien or outside the sociocultural mainstream. Citizenship counted for less than blood or belief in this atmosphere of neotribalism. In short, the Nazis could create their racial and political *Volksgemeinschaft* (people's community) only because a genuine civil community did not exist in the first place.

Even Nazi Germany's much-celebrated racial community, however, was by no means free of internal divisions and mutual backstabbing. Munich became a hotbed of discontent because people there harbored high expectations for the new regime while remaining distrustful of authority handed down from Berlin. Ordinary citizens quickly became irritated when Nazi Old Fighters got preference in municipal hiring, whether or not they were competent. Münchners resented new rules that forced employees to join the Nazi Labor Front or be fired. They bristled when city council chairman Christian Weber moved into the Wittelsbach Residenz and Gauleiter Wagner took over the old Kaulbach villa. This did not look like the austere dedication to duty that Hitler had advertised as the hallmark of Nazism. Popular anger, however, was generally not directed at Hitler himself but at his rapacious aides. As a Munich hairdresser put it in 1934, "Yes, yes, our Adolf is all right, but that lot around him, they're nothing but rogues."

Many of the Nazi transgressions against Bavarian and Münchner traditions were largely symbolic, but symbols can be extremely important, as the Nazis well knew. The regime generated considerable antagonism by removing the blue and white Bavarian colors from popular festivities like the Oktoberfest and the annual May Pole rites, substituting the national black, white, and red. In their desire to celebrate Munich's place in the new order, city officials renamed a host of streets and squares for Nazi heroes. In so doing, they obliterated not only designations with a republican taint (such as Friedrich-Ebert-Strasse and Stresemann-Platz) but names with great Bavarian pedigrees. Thus they changed Schyrenplatz to Georg-Hirschmann-Platz (Schyren was the family that became the Wittelsbachs, and Georg Hirschmann was an SA man who had been murdered by the Communists in 1927). A local paper, though itself firmly Nazi, futilely protested that Nazi martyrs should not be honored at the expense of important figures in Bavarian history. Interestingly, Hitler himself saw the danger in this policy and therefore rejected an effort to rename the Odeonsplatz Adolf-Hitler-Platz or Platz der deutschen Freiheit.

It is important to emphasize that none of this discontent or malaise focused on matters of fundamental policy or ideology. While irritating to some zealots, it did not threaten any Nazi programs, much less the regime itself. Muttering about the colors on the May Pole was not resistance. Moreover, complaining about various abuses or excesses on the part of local officials was often compatible with faith in the regime and its Führer. After giving vent to this or that private complaint, people often added that the problem would soon be cleared up "if only the Führer knew."

The Night of the Long Knives

By mid-1934 the Nazis had seemingly killed, imprisoned, exiled, or intimidated all those who were tempted to practice active opposition, along with a few others who had never harbored such intentions at all. Hitler, whom many pundits had expected to be a passing phenomenon, was apparently firmly in control.

Nevertheless, at this juncture Hitler's regime faced an internal challenge that it had to sweep aside if the Führer was to obtain the total power he craved. His grisly liquidation of this problem—a mass-murder spree known as the Night of the Long Knives—played itself out in many different locales in Germany, but the central stage was Munich and its environs. Once again the Bavarian capital became Hitler's city of destiny.

In the early-morning hours of 30 June 1934 Adolf Hitler boarded a plane in Bonn and flew to Munich. He did so in order to confront what many of his top lieutenants—especially Himmler, Goebbels, and Göring—claimed was an insidious plot to overthrow the Nazi government by the party's own paramilitary army, the SA. Much of the evidence for the alleged putsch plot was fabricated, but that hardly mattered, for the SA had indeed become a genuine liability for the Hitler regime.

Some of the SA leaders, especially Ernst Röhm, were boisterously complaining that the Nazis' vaunted national revolution had not gone nearly far enough and that Hitler had made unhappy accommodations with what Röhm called "the gentlemen with uniforms and monocles." The ex-captain and his cohorts demanded a "second revolution" that would "submerge the gray rock in the brown flood"—that is, wash away the vestiges of the old regime and absorb the army into the SA. At a ceremony in Munich on 19 March 1934, celebrating the first year of Nazi power in Bavaria, Röhm declared that he would "rather be making a revolution than celebrating one." It was impossible, he added, to "renew" a whole people in a year or two; much remained to be done, and only if the Nazis remained "revolutionaries" could they realize the goals they had set for themselves. Himmler, on the other hand, spoke of the need for order and discipline, insisting that the Nazis must not "break out" unless commanded to do so by the Führer. Hitler himself put the Nazi revolution in historical context as an accomplished fact. "The revolution of the year 1933 was in truth the springtime revolution of the German people," he said. "It ushered in a beautiful spring in which we now happily live. We see that the German people have thrown aside the burdens that have weighted them down for centuries."

While SA leaders blustered about the need for a second revolution, SA units, including some stationed in Munich, carried out their own brand of radical politics. They extorted protection money from businesses, blockaded entrances to banks and the stock exchange, shook down passersby for contributions to SA charities. On 29 June thousands of them paraded through Munich, shouting revolutionary slogans, breaking windows, and demanding free drinks in the beer halls. Obviously these beggars in brown were no inspiring advertisement for the new order, any more than Röhm himself was an ideal poster boy for Nazi probity.

While Röhm's rivals like Himmler and Goebbels complained to Hitler of the SA's many vices (Himmler whispered of "homosexual orgies"), the regular army leaders were indignant over the SA's challenge to their traditional monopolization of armed force. The generals approved of much of what Hitler stood for, but their loathing for the SA impeded a full-scale commitment to the new regime. The military men had considerable leverage because Hitler, though at heart closer to the plebeian SA than to the aristocratic officer corps, needed the gray-coated "monocles" more than the brown-shirted beer bellies if he was ever to realize his dream of a Greater German Reich. Thus, at a secret meeting in mid-April on the battleship *Deutschland,* he promised the generals and admirals that he would soon take care of the SA problem.

Not surprisingly, Germany's "gentlemen"—the frock-coated conservatives who had helped Hitler to power in hopes of using him for their own purposes—were equally appalled by the socially radical SA. In Munich and elsewhere conservative interests bombarded party officials with complaints about the Brownshirts' rough tactics. But the old Right's frustration went much deeper than this. Ultimately the conservatives recoiled at the Nazis' pursuit of total power, their destruction of all forms of political expression other than their own. On 17 June 1934, in a provocative speech at Marburg University, Vice Chancellor Franz von Papen spoke for many of his colleagues when he insisted that no nation could tolerate a "permanent revolution from below." He hinted boldly that the best way to stem the radical tide was to restore the Hohenzollern monarchy. His hope, clearly, was that President Von Hindenburg and the army generals would join him in a restorative crusade.

Hitler was acutely mindful of this when he arrived at the Munich airfield before that fateful dawn on 30 June. Met by Gauleiter Wagner, he drove immediately to the Interior Ministry, where he ordered the arrest of two high SA officials. Protesting vigorously, the men were hauled off to Stadelheim Prison.

Accompanied by Goebbels, who felt honored to be allowed to participate in such an important mission, and by some SS guards (the main bodyguard had not yet arrived from Berlin), Hitler drove to Bad Wiessee on Tegern Lake, now dubbed Lago di Bonzi (Lake of the Bosses) because so many Nazi bigwigs had bought villas there. Hitler's destination was a resort hotel called Pension Hanselbauer, where SA chief Röhm, along with dozens of his cronies, had been ordered to gather in anticipation of a "conference" with the Nazi leadership. As the Führer's car pulled up to the hotel, the SA guests, having put in a strenuous night drinking and playing manly games, were still asleep.

Riding crop in hand, Hitler burst into Röhm's room and ordered him to dress. "You are under arrest for treason," he screamed. Before the drowsy captain could respond, Hitler stomped down the hall, pulling other Brownshirts from their drunken slumbers. Some, like Silesian SA chief Edmund Heines, were found abed with young boys. "A disgusting scene, which made me feel like vomiting," wrote Goebbels in his diary. (Later Goebbels planted the rumor that Röhm had also been found with a boy in his bed.)

As Röhm and the other SA leaders were herded into the Hanselbauer's cellar, a truck filled with Röhm's followers arrived from Munich. Having learned of their two leaders' arrests in Munich and guessing Hitler's plans at Bad Wiessee, the Brownshirts had rushed down with hopes of rescuing the captain and his entourage. This was a precarious moment for Hitler. The angry SA men far outnumbered his own small guard and presumably could have pushed the Führer aside had they wanted to. But Hitler, asserting his harshest commanding manner, convinced the men to return to Munich.

Once the Munich Brownshirts had departed, Hitler ordered his prisoners dispatched by bus to Stadelheim. He and his party then headed back for Munich, occasionally stopping to arrest SA men en route to the supposed conference in Bad Wiessee. The Führer and his men arrived at the Brown House just as the town was waking up. There Hitler's lieutenants regaled him with horror stories about SA abuses. Martin Bormann, always looking to promote his own cause by denouncing rival satraps, told him that Brownshirt leaders regularly skipped mandatory Wagner operas to go whoring. Another aide showed him menus from SA feasts featuring frogs' legs and fine French wines—just the fare to disgust the vegetarian, teetotaling Führer.

Finally, at about 5:00 P.M., Hitler had heard enough. He drew up a list of names and handed it to Sepp Dietrich, head of his personal bodyguard, the Leibstandarte Adolf Hitler. He ordered Dietrich to go to Stadelheim and to execute the men on the list. Intriguingly, Röhm was not among them; Hitler could not for the moment bring himself to kill his old friend.

Upon arrival at Stadelheim, Dietrich ordered the men on his list marched into a courtyard and gunned down without ceremony. One of the victims, Munich SA chief August Schneidhuber, could not understand how his old friend Dietrich could be ordering his execution. "Sepp, Sepp, what on earth is happening?" he shouted. "You have been condemned to death by the Führer," answered Dietrich crisply. "*Sieg Heil!*"

The executions in Stadelheim were just the beginning. From the Brown House, Goebbels called Göring in Berlin and whispered "Colibri"—code word for the liquidation of enemies in the Reich capital. These included the former chancellor General Kurt von Schleicher and his aide General Kurt von Bredow. Gregor Strasser, Hitler's old Nazi Party rival, was quickly dispatched, as was Erich Klausener, head of the Conservative Catholic Action. Papen's aide Herbert von Bose was shot "trying to escape," and Edgar Jung, a young conservative intellectual who had ghostwritten the vice-chancellor's Marburg speech, met a similar fate. Papen himself was placed for a time under house arrest but escaped any harsher treatment because of his many friends in the diplomatic world. Moreover, Hitler well understood that this self-promoting fop, now thoroughly cowed, was too spineless to cause him any further trouble and might indeed be valuable. Papen soon became Hitler's emissary to Vienna (1934–1939) and then to Ankara (1939–1944). Throughout his service to the Third Reich, Papen tried to maintain the self-deception—typical of conservative collaborators—that by helping Hitler, he was preventing the Nazi regime from becoming even worse than it was.

Former Premier Gustav von Kahr, living quietly in a Munich villa since his retirement from the Bavarian Administrative Court in 1930, was no longer in a position to give Hitler difficulty. As we know, however, he had done so in November 1923, which was enough to seal his fate now. As part of a wholesale retribution accompanying the Night of the Long Knives, the seventy-one-year-old Kahr was dragged from his home, driven to Dachau, and tortured to death.

Hitler's henchmen settled another old score in Munich when they did away with *Gerade Weg* editor Fritz Gerlich, who had been languishing in prison since his arrest in March 1933. Gerlich was taken from his prison cell on 30 June, driven out to Dachau, and promptly shot. Another prominent Munich victim was Father Bernhard Stempfle, who had advised Hitler on church affairs but then developed second thoughts about the Nazi leader, which he made the mistake of uttering.

Prominence, it turned out, was not a prerequisite for death in the Nazis' rush to get even. Lowly victims included a clerk whose testimony had helped get Hitler three months in jail in 1922, a barman at the Bratwurstglockl tavern beside the Frauenkirche who had overheard too many Nazi conversations, and a lawyer who had tried to sue the *Völkischer Beobachter* for libel.

While these men were killed because they had somehow crossed the Nazis, another victim, the *Münchener Neueste Nachrichten* music critic Dr. Willi Schmid, died merely because he had the wrong name. It seems that his killers mistook him for a Munich SA leader named Wilhelm Schmidt, who had already been executed by another death squad.

Ernst Röhm, meanwhile, sat in his cell in Stadelheim, still confused regarding the reasons for his arrest. He did not have long to wait for clarification. Hitler, having returned to Berlin on the night of 30 June, came under great pressure from Himmler, Göring, and the army leadership to get rid of Röhm. Was he not the chief culprit in the whole affair? they asked. How could they justify the other killings if Röhm were left alive? Reluctantly Hitler gave in to this logic. On the afternoon of 1 July he telephoned Theodor Eicke, the Dachau commandant, with orders to go to Stadelheim and take care of Röhm. As a final gesture of friendship Hitler ordered that the captain be given the opportunity to shoot himself.

A few hours later Eicke and two SS guards entered Röhm's cell and explained Hitler's decision. They placed a loaded revolver on his table, telling him to make honorable use of it. When, after about ten minutes, Röhm had not done so, the men returned and gunned him down. "*Mein Führer! Mein Führer!*" he reportedly gasped as he fell to the floor.

A week and a half later Hitler went on the radio to justify his resort to killings during the "Röhm putsch." He insisted that the actions were a necessary response to a planned mutiny of the SA. Taking a line from his conservative critics, he said that the state could not tolerate efforts to perpetuate revolution for the sake of revolution. While not divulging the full scope of the action, he boldly declared that his government had complete authority to identify enemies of the state and to take whatever measures it saw fit to deal with them.

As far as most ordinary Münchners were concerned, Hitler did not have to do much justifying. They had become thoroughly fed up with the excesses of the SA and were not displeased to see these roughnecks taken to task.

A few Bavarian officials who knew more about the extent of the butchery were appalled by what had happened, but none openly protested. Ritter von Epp, who had vainly fought to save Röhm's life, blamed the whole affair on "Prussians in Berlin," thereby falling back on the standard Münchner explanation for all that was evil in the world.

In Munich as elsewhere, the SA was allowed to continue to function, but it was henceforth a shadow of its former self. By contrast, the SS, having humbled its brown-shirted rivals, went on to become the dominant instrument of terror in the Third Reich. Eventually its influence surpassed even that of the Nazi Party. It also built its own military branch, the Waffen-SS, which challenged the regular army more effectively than the Brownshirts had ever done.

The city of Munich also came out on the short end of this affair because it remained the headquarters of the discredited SA and the party bureaucracy, while the SS moved to Berlin to be at the center of power. Moreover, Munich was closely associated with the Old Fighters around Röhm, men whose future was largely in their past. The irony, then, is that while Munich had once again served as the main stage for Hitler's bloody pursuit of power, the drama enacted on the Night of the Long Knives helped confirm the transfer of real power to Berlin.

It also helped ensure Hitler's own domination. The military leaders, whose absolute loyalty Hitler had wanted to secure, were so pleased with his intervention against the SA that they made no protest against the brutal murder of two of their own. Once the dust had settled, they offered Hitler the military's unconditional allegiance, sealed by the inauguration of a personal oath to the Führer. Eighty-seven-year-old President von Hindenburg, who many conservatives had hoped would act as a brake on Hitler, was too senile to appreciate what had actually happened during these fateful events; he addressed Hitler as His Majesty when the latter patiently related how he had just saved Germany. Shortly thereafter, on 2 August 1934, he obligingly died. This allowed Hitler to absorb the office of president into that of chancellor. Now it could be said that the campaign Hitler had begun in Munich fifteen years before was at last realized: The Führer was uncontested dictator of Germany.

The Brown Cult

It is appropriate that the Night of the Long Knives was centered in Munich and its environs because this grisly spectacle was a kind of Nazi morality play, a tour de force of Grand Guignol. It harmonized well with the region's rich tradition of political theater and religious drama, such as the anti-Semitic Passion Play at Oberammergau, which was drenched in ancient fears and hatred of the Other.

Another, less bloody but equally revealing form of political theater in the Third Reich involved a series of rituals that celebrated "sacred" moments in party history. As the birthplace of Nazism and Capital of the Movement, Munich naturally took the lead in this enterprise. The Isar city hosted theatrical observances of Hitler's birthday, the date of his army enlistment, the foundation of the Nazi Party, the Battle of the Hofbräuhaus, National Youth Day, and Reich Labor Day. But the center of the brown cult was a ceremonial reenactment of the Beer Hall Putsch march, preceded by a speech from the Führer. This occurred every 8–9 November from 1933 to 1939, after which the march (but not the speech) was discontinued for security reasons.

Of the seven putsch observances, the one in 1935 was by far the most noteworthy, for on this occasion the "martyrs" of 1923 were ceremoniously transported to a new resting place. A closer look at this bizarre rite affords a good sense of Nazi cultish theater in the Capital of the Movement.

On the afternoon of 8 November 1935 the Nazi elite gathered in the Hotel Bayerischer Hof on the newly renamed Ritter von Epp Platz (formerly Promenadeplatz). The dignitaries drove to the Bürgerbräukeller, where Hitler delivered a speech on the "days of struggle." Following the speech, at midnight, the Nazi brass motored to the Feldherrnhalle, which had since been transformed into a major Nazi shrine. On the east side of the building, next to the place where the putsch had met its bloody end, loomed a bronze plaque inscribed with the names of the martyrs. An eagle encircled by a wreath stood atop the plaque. In front of the shrine two armed SS men maintained a permanent honor guard. On the occasion of the 1935 commemoration there was an additional piece of pomp: sixteen flag-bedecked sarcophagi with the martyrs' remains, which had been exhumed from cemeteries around Munich. Having arrived at the shrine, Hitler stood for a minute in silence with his head bowed. Then he sped off in his Mercedes.

At noon the next day Hitler, Göring, Himmler, and about one hundred Old Fighters set out from the Bürgerbräukeller along the route of the

1923 march. Behind Hitler walked three men carrying the movement's most precious relic, the Blood Flag, stained by the fluids of the fallen. Along the way the marchers passed squat black pylons, each bearing the name of a departed hero. Upon their arrival at the Feldherrnhalle, an honor guard fired sixteen shots and a band struck up "I Had a Comrade." Then all was quiet as Hitler laid yet another wreath at what the *Völkischer Beobachter* called "Our Altar."

After a few moments of reverence the marchers set off again, accompanying the horse-drawn sarcophagi down the Brienner Strasse to the Königsplatz, where two Grecian-style "honor temples" had been erected to house the coffins. Along the way a band played the German anthem over and over, each time a little louder, so that it reached a thunderous crescendo as the parade reached the "Square of Resurrection." Then the caskets were slowly carried into the temples. As they disappeared inside, Gauleiter Wagner called out each martyr's name, which was repeated by the assembled multitude. Finally, Hitler walked alone into each temple and laid wreaths "to decorate his colleagues with the garlands of immortality."

In this ceremony, as in most other Nazi rites, the regime borrowed helter-skelter from a variety of sources: ancient Greece and Rome, medieval Christianity, Germanic myth, and Wagnerian opera (Siegfried's "Funeral March"). The Nazis were clearly trying to create the trappings of an ersatz religion in hopes of generating the deep loyalties associated with passionate belief. Witnessing or participating in such rituals would, the brown cultists hoped, produce a stronger sense of common purpose and lend an air of sanctity to their enterprise. The trick was to bend the religious sensibility to new purposes without seeming too blasphemous in the process.

This was by no means easy, especially in Munich. Commenting on the popular response to the 1935 putsch commemoration, the Nazi press spoke of "universal enthusiasm." Other assessments of the Nazi cult, however, conveyed a more nuanced picture. One observer called the ritual a "bombastic travesty of the Passion Play." The Nazis' march, he said, was "an evocation of the Stations of the Cross—with one signal difference: the Savior marched upright, grim-visaged and jack-booted, in the front rank of his disciples; Calvary and Resurrection blended into one sombre, soul-stirring event." A report compiled by Munich's small and demoralized Socialist underground admitted that the putsch ceremony seemed to have a "powerful effect" and generated "many admiring comments." Another report by the same group, however, claimed that the Münchners' "natural piety" was offended by the "massive mumbo-jumbo with the fallen." Still another report cited objections to the "high cost" of the production and to the fact that "poor people" always had to pay for such "wasteful pomposity."

Even the reports that emphasized disgruntlement, however, were careful to add that there was no open protest and that the irritations were too "unpolitical" to yield genuine resistance. "The people just stand, stare, and swear," wrote one Socialist observer, resignedly.

Mixed emotions regarding the Nazi ritual carried over to the Feldherrnhalle shrine itself. Visiting the site in December 1933, the now-famed British travel writer Patrick Leigh Fermor noted that "the right arms of all passers-by shot up as though in reflex to an electric beam." This is hardly surprising, for such practice was ordained by the regime, and those caught walking by without saluting were subject to arrest. There was, however, a way out for walkers who wanted to reach Odeonsplatz from Marienplatz without performing the obligatory salute. They could cut through a narrow passage behind the Feldherrnhalle onto the Theatinerstrasse. This route became known as *Drückeberger-Gassl* (Dodger's Alley), and one might say that it was a characteristic Münchner way of dealing with the daily demands of the brown cult.

"Capital of German Art"

If Munich—along with Nuremberg, which hosted the annual party rallies—became the center of Nazi ritual, it was also the focal point of Nazi aesthetics, the stage on which the regime displayed its artistic side to the world. This was a very important role for the Isar city. After all, for Hitler, art and politics were inseparably mixed, and by "rejuvenating" German art, the Führer believed he was simultaneously rejuvenating German politics. It was natural that having found his political vocation in Germany's erstwhile "art capital," he would want to revive the city's reputation as *the* font of German creativity in the plastic arts. This would allow Munich fully to live up to its other assignment as Capital of the Movement.

Hitler's decision to turn his hometown into the Reich's primary exhibition space for Nazi aesthetic principles had the secondary advantage of inflating Munich's municipal ego, which had taken something of a beating since the Führer's move to Berlin. This policy, contrary to the regime's recent trampling on local traditions and sensitivities, exploited entrenched values and attitudes. By declaring Munich to be Germany's capital of visual arts, Hitler reinforced an image of the city that many Münchners continued to harbor despite all the talk of cultural decline. The Führer thus allowed the citizens of his favorite city to feel that they were again where they rightfully belonged: at the center of the artistic universe.

The Nazis accompanied their cultural enthronement of Munich with a chorus of praise for the city's "easygoing, love-of-life atmosphere" and "classless society"—clichés that were all the more welcome for distorting real conditions. Tapping into a rich vein of local patriotism, Nazi spokesmen argued that Munich's traditional preference for "healthy feeling" over "arid rationalism" perfectly harmonized with the Nazi sensibility. Munich's rejuvenation under Hitler also meant, declared the *Völkischer Beobachter* in 1936, that the old rivalry between the Isar city and Berlin was now past. The seat of the Reich's government was Berlin; the seat of its spirit was Munich.

But Munich's cultural consecration in the Third Reich was not all talk; in its effort to turn the town into a showcase of Germanic genius, the regime made significant investments in artistic and entertainment infrastructure. Here too it was careful to tie into earlier traditions of cultural patronage, particularly those of the hallowed Wittelsbachs.

As often in the past, the majority of Munich's artists welcomed the official patronage as a godsend in times of economic hardship and rampant competition. Moreover, there was a widespread ideological consensus between artists and the regime that belies the usual picture of a cowed cultural establishment simply bowing to coercion and terror.

THE CENTERPIECE OF the National Socialist cultural campaign in Munich was the Haus der deutschen Kunst (House of German Art), the only new art museum to be built during the Third Reich. Hitler had long dreamed of building a grandiose museum that he might fill with the kind of art he admired: sensible, solid, "German" art. In 1929 he promised that National Socialism would create a "home for German art" in Munich, "the most German of all German cities." The destruction of the Glaspalast in 1931 added urgency to this ambition because it left a cultural void waiting to be filled. Even before coming to power, Hitler settled on an architect for the project: Paul Ludwig Troost, the renovator of the Brown House. In June 1933 Gauleiter Wagner established a museum fund so that "the Führer might be granted his favorite wish." Most of the twelve million Reichmarks needed for the building came in the form of large, tax-deductible contributions from industry and the banks.

Hitler personally presided over an elaborate cornerstone-laying ceremony on 15 October 1933. Bunting-covered bleachers circled the site, which lay on Prinzregentenstrasse flanking the Englischer Garten. Units from the SA, SS, and Hitler Youth stood in formation. When the Führer arrived, he was welcomed by a mason dressed like Hans Sachs, who handed him a silver hammer. An orchestra struck up the prelude to *Die Meistersinger*. Hitler stepped to the podium and declared that "young Germany" was building "its own house for its own art." That this should transpire in Munich reflected the Third Reich's judicious division of municipal labor. "If Berlin is the capital of the German Reich, Hamburg and Bremen the capitals of German shipping, Leipzig and Cologne the capitals of German commerce, Essen and Chemnitz the capitals of German industry, then Munich shall once again be the capital of German art," intoned the Führer.

Upon finishing his remarks, Hitler vigorously rapped the cornerstone with his silver hammer. The tool broke in half. A hush fell over the crowd, for this seemed a singularly inauspicious sign. Goebbels tried to ease the tension by joking: "When the Führer strikes, he strikes mightily." But Hitler was too superstitious to pass this episode off lightly. He rushed shaken from the scene and hid in his apartment for the rest of the day. Not long thereafter Paul Troost, who had designed the hammer as well as the museum, died of pneumonia. "When that hammer shattered I knew at once it was an evil omen," Hitler told the young architect Albert Speer. "Something is going to happen, I thought. Now we know why the hammer broke. The architect was destined to die." As if to make amends to Troost, Hitler visited his widow every time he came to Munich. As for the metalsmith who had made the fragile hammer, he was questioned by the Gestapo to determine if sabotage was involved. Fortunately for him, no evidence of skulduggery was found.

Munich's Nazified press reported nothing about broken hammers but plenty about "realized dreams"—about the Führer as a neo-Ludwig I, patron of glorious transformations. Munich had been "sleeping," recalled *Das Bayernland,* until Ludwig I appeared and awakened its artistic potential. Hitler too understood Munich's "destiny," the "promise of its blue sky." He was making Munich once again "a city of art and artists," laying the foundation of an enterprise that would "make Munich famous and unique in the entire world." But Munich's fame, the magazine added, resided also in its spirit, in its "earthy culture full of health and good humor." And since creativity was ultimately a function of "heart," of which Munich was known to have a robust and Germanic specimen, great art could "grow and prosper [in Munich] as nowhere else in the German land."

The House of German Art formally opened in mid-July 1937 against a backdrop of elaborate festivities that recalled the art carnivals of prewar Schwabing. Labeled the "Days of German Art," the seventy-two-hour spectacle featured gala concerts by three orchestras, command performances in the state theaters, a marathon folk dance in the Englischer Garten, and a three-kilometer-long parade celebrating "2000 Years of German Culture." The festival's official program gushed, in perfect Nazi-speak:

> And now, a newly risen Reich, still echoing from the marching of political battalions, suddenly convoked a Reichstag of the Arts in the Capital of its Movement, at the cradle of its birth, over the coffins of its first victims! And through the mouth of its Führer, it bound the artists in oath and duty, as if they had been lords of provinces! And assembled the people to be witnesses on the streets and squares! And embroidered the earnest hour with a garland of merriment, the ringing of songs, the bobbing of dances, and the nocturnal glare of shooting rockets!

The "2000 Years of German Culture" parade broke new ground in the field of Nazi kitsch, and that was no small feat. As its name suggests, it celebrated the high points of German creativity through the ages. Famous buildings, historical figures, and aesthetic ideals were represented via costumed marchers and giant models mounted on carts pulled by horses or grunting storm troopers. There were, for example, floats depicting the Nuremberg Cathedral, Goethe's head, and the Cosmic Oak Tree wrapped in green foil. A buxom Amazon sitting on a clamshell topped by an eagle represented "The Germanic Ages." The "Modern Era of National Socialism" was symbolized by three massive warrior statues bearing the designations "Sacrifice," "Belief," and "Loyalty." Another float carried a replica of the House of German Art, only slightly smaller than the real thing. Behind it marched men dressed as Charlemagne, Henry the Lion, and Frederick Barbarossa. There were also troops of Hitler Youth in period costumes and strapping Valkyries wearing iron bras. Ominously, the final entries were units of the Wehrmacht and the SS. The parade's ideal of establishing continuity with the Germanic past was pushed home by the *Völkischer Beobachter*:

> Germanic warriors, Germanic women, Germanic priests and seers pass before us. . . . Even these mere imitations of mighty symbols drawn from the mythical world of our ancestors have the power to overwhelm our modern sensibility. The sun, the symbol of the day, the moon, the goddess of the night, are

convincing and impressive in their brilliant colors. Figures from our forefathers' sagas are suddenly among us. . . . The stirring tones of trumpeters and drummers on horseback rouse us from our ecstatic meditation.

On 18 July, the last day of the festival, Hitler dedicated his new art temple and opened the "Great German Art Exhibition" contained within its cavernous precincts. Like the surrounding festival, the exhibition tied in to well-established traditions, in this case the yearly shows in the Glaspalast sponsored since 1888 by the Münchener Künstler-genossenschaft. The new home for the Nazi exhibitions (held annually until 1944) was less modernistic than its predecessor. Designed to resemble a Greek temple, the building was a long, low, multicolumned affair constructed of light gray limestone. It earned the nicknames White Sausage Palace, Greek Railway Station, and House of German Tarts (because of all the nudes inside). But there could be no mistaking its solemnity or ideological thrust. Engraved over its central entry was a slogan coined by Hitler himself: "Art is a noble mission, demanding fantastic devotion."

For museum patrons, many of whom were expected to come from abroad, the regime put out a promotional brochure in several languages. A paragraph from the English version, entitled *The Temple of German Art,* reads: "Vital powers will stream from the great temple of art, the enchanting breath from the mountain ranges in the south will course through its colonnades and around its cornices of lime-stone, and the blue sky of Munich will captivate the German and foreign visitors and will persuade them to tarry at the Bavarian city, the birthplace of national rejuvenation."

In his speech opening the exhibition, Hitler set out the principles of German art as he understood them. Germany's greatest art was rooted in the *Volk* soul and native landscape, he said; it had nothing to do with the "optical delusions" of those modern "internationalist" artists who made "meadows blue and skies green and every person look like a cretin." Works of art that "cannot be understood but need a swollen set of instructions to prove their right to exist" would no longer be tolerated. If artists painted in this manner because they really saw things in this way, "then these unhappy persons should be dealt with in the department of the Ministry of the Interior where sterilization of the insane is conducted. . . ." He concluded by restating the fundamental nexus between culture and politics that was so central to the Nazi self-image: "I will now clear away the empty phrase making in Germany's artistic life just as I did the confusion in our political existence. . . . With the opening of this exhibition we end the moronization of German art and the related cultural destruction of our people."

Hitler's guidelines notwithstanding, squabbles over the selection of paintings and sculptures for the inaugural exhibition suggested that it was not so easy to know what constituted Great German Art. The lineup of works approved by an eight-person jury (including, incidentally, Troost's widow) so appalled Hitler and Goebbels that they stalked out of a private preview mumbling about "un-German monstrosities." To avoid such transgressions in the future. Hitler delegated the selection of displays to his friend Heinrich Hoffmann, who supposedly had a trustworthy eye in such matters. Whatever his aesthetic judgment, Hoffmann was efficient: He could complete the whole selection process in a matter of hours by whizzing through galleries on a motorized wheelchair shouting "Accepted!" or "Rejected!" as he passed each prospective entry.

Hitler's irritation over the works in the first Great German Art Exhibition is hard to understand; virtually all of them were eminently safe and predictable: homey still-lifes; lush landscapes; portraits of noble peasants bending to the plow; nudes advertising in no uncertain terms the glories of German womanhood. One critic aptly noted that most of the paintings showed close ties to the academic Munich school at the turn of the century; the large number of landscapes constituted a continuation of "the old traditions." Some of the pictures were little more than propaganda posters in oil: German soldiers on the advance, SA men marching stoutly behind swastika banners, and, as the pièce de résistance, the Führer himself in shining armor, backlit by a rising swastika sun. The local press, of course, heralded these works as "clear, clean, serious, and full of character"—all "testaments to the national renewal of the arts under National Socialism."

According to official statistics, some four hundred thousand people visited the exhibition in 1937, but this was no doubt an exaggeration, for the long halls were often nearly empty. Some of the visitors were undoubtedly inspired by what they saw. Others, however, could not resist making jokes about the collection. One of the jokes pertained to a constellation of four naked women called *The Four Elements*. The ensemble, wits said, should be renamed *The Five Elements* to signal that there was one element missing: taste. Sales of works at the exhibition were disappointingly slack; most of the major purchases were made by the municipality of Munich or by Hitler himself, who was building a private collection. One of the pictures Hitler bought in 1937 was called *Terpsichore,* a full-length, photographic female nude. *Time* magazine's man in Munich called it "the kind of thing to be put on a beer calendar."

On 19 June 1937, one day after the Great German Art Exhibit opened in Hitler's new temple, another exhibition began not far away in a dilapidated building formerly used to store plaster casts of classical statuary. This was the infamous *Ausstellung Entarteter Kunst* (Exhibition of Degenerate Art), a display of some 650 works by German artists identified with the avant-garde. A deeply bizarre and quintessentially Nazi affair, the event was designed to engender horror and contempt, not pleasure or admiration. People were encouraged to compare the works in this show with those in the nearby House of German Art so that they might better understand the urgency of Hitler's "renewal" of German art.

The Degenerate Art Exhibition had antecedents in the often bitter battles over modern art that had raged across Germany (indeed, across the Western world) since the late nineteenth century. As we have seen, the battle was taken up by the Nazis in the 1920s as part of their populist crusade. Since 1933 they had already put on a number of small "antiart" shows in cities like Mannheim, Karlsruhe, and Stuttgart. Nor were the Nazis alone in this practice; in 1937 the Tretiakov Gallery in Moscow mounted an exhibition of "degenerate" Russian art. (As is well known, the Communists and Nazis had many qualties in common, including similar tastes in art and architecture; this had been graphically evident in their monumental pavilions at the 1937 Paris World's Fair.)

The Munich Degenerate Art Exhibition was special, however, in terms of its size and symbolic weight. Never had so many images been assembled with the specific purpose of horrifying the public, never had the political message been so explicit, and never had so many heavyweight propagandists been on hand to drive the message home. Goebbels himself was the chief sponsor, though he was miffed because he had wanted the show to open in Berlin. Most of the organizational work was done by a blue-ribbon committee under the chairmanship of Adolf Ziegler, president of the Reich Chamber for the Visual Arts. Ziegler had ingratiated himself with Hitler by painting a portrait of the Führer's beloved niece, Geli Raubal. His favorite genre, however, was recumbent nudes of startling verisimilitude, a specialty that won him the sobriquet *Reichsschamhaarpinsler* (official pubic hair painter of the Reich). Ziegler and his staff combed thirty-two public collections, including those in Munich, for the works they wanted. These they simply confiscated. The collection they assembled contained works by Max Ernst, Paul Klee, Wassily Kandinsky, Oskar Kokoschka, Georg Grosz, Max Beckmann, Ernst Barlach, Otto Dix, and Emil Nolde—to name just a few. Interestingly, Barlach and Nolde protested against their inclusion in the show on the ground that they sympathized with National Socialism.

Apparently, however, it was not enough to think like a Nazi; one also had to paint like one.

Ziegler opened the exhibit with a tirade against "offsprings of delusion, impertinence, incompetence, and degeneration." He closed with the appeal "German people, come and see for yourselves."

What people saw was a deliberately chaotic assemblage of unframed, crookedly hung paintings crammed together on makeshift partitions. Grouped according to categories like "Anarchist-Bolshevist Art," "Negro-Inspired Art," "Jewish Art," and "Total Madness," the works carried identifying labels listing not only the artist's name and the lending museum but how much the item had cost. Some also bore helpful explanatory notes like "Thus do sick minds view nature!"; "German peasants perceived in the Yiddish manner"; "The Nigger as racial ideal"; "Degeneration of the German woman as cretin and whore." Another stratagem involved pairing avant-garde works with drawings by certified idiots (the idiots were identified, so as to avoid confusion).

Unlike the Great German Art Exhibition, the Degenerate Art show attracted mobs of people; lines formed around the block, and admission had to be temporarily suspended. By the time it closed in November, some two million visitors had seen it.

Their recorded reactions echoed the organizers' intentions. "These artists ought to be tied to their pictures so that every German can spit in their faces," wrote one man in the guest book. A fellow with a heavy Bavarian accent was heard to say: "My four-year-old Sepp can make this kind of shit!" It would have been risky, of course, to express contrary views in this place, and no one seems to have done so. Taking the comments and large attendance at face value, Goebbels declared the show a "huge success." Yet one can never know how many people came dutifully to jeer or how many simply wanted to pay their respects to admired works that they were not likely to see again.

After the Degenerate Art exhibit closed in Munich, it moved on to other German cities, starting with Berlin. There too it attracted the masses. When it finally finished its tour in 1939, a question arose of what to do with the paintings. Göring, later to become the Reich's master art looter, realized that this collection had significant monetary value and insisted it not be dispersed or discarded. So did Goebbels, who confided in his diary that he hoped "to make some money from this garbage."

And make money the Nazis did. A Commission for the Exploitation of Degenerate Art, bristling with Nazi bigwigs, sold some of the most valuable paintings to foreign museums and placed another 125 works with a Lucerne auction house. On 30 June 1939 collectors from around the world flocked to the Lucerne sale, which netted the commission a handsome sum. As for the works not deemed "exploitable," they were taken to the main Berlin fire station and burned.

While the Degenerate Art Exhibition illustrated the cultural dangers from which the Führer had supposedly saved Germany, another large Munich exhibition. "Bolshevism: The Great Anti-Bolshevist Show," focused on the insidious political enemy that (along with the Jews) Hitler believed the Reich must vanquish to survive. The show opened on 7 November 1936 in the library wing of the massive German Museum of Technology on the Isar. Visitors entered a "consecration room" dedicated to the Nazis who had died fighting communism. Rooms devoted to the Bolshevist enemy were made to resemble prison cells, with low ceilings, bare concrete floors, and poor lighting. Display cases contained photographs of Communist atrocities, along with items like rubber truncheons and brass knuckles (as if these were a leftist monopoly). Much was made of the "Red Terror" in Munich in 1919 and its connections to the existing Soviet regime. Another room, where atonal music blared, featured examples of "cultural Bolshevism" in painting, sculpture, and literature. Significantly, there was also an Italian section illustrating Mussolini's victory over Latin communism. The point here was to help justify Germany's recent rapprochement with Italy and the fascist powers' joint intervention against the Soviet-backed government in the Spanish Civil War. Since Nazi Germany was also about to formalize an Anti-Comintern Pact with Italy and Japan, the exhibition represented these nations as bulwarks against the international Communist threat. According to the *Völkischer Beobachter,* more than three hundred thousand people visited the show. The demand to see it was so great that it was extended to 31 January 1937, when it moved on to Berlin.

Some nine months after the Anti-Bolshevist Exhibition left the city, another huge propaganda display was mounted in the German Museum: "Der ewige Jude" (The Eternal Jew). Likewise a transparently didactic enterprise, its purpose was to provide visual justification for the Reich's anti-Semitic policies, notably the Nuremberg Race Laws of 1935, which stripped Jews of many of their citizenship rights. Josef Goebbels, whose Propaganda Ministry helped organize the show, opened the gates on 8 November 1937 with a predictable harangue about the "poisonous" Jewish influence in German life.

Like the Degenerate Art and Anti-Bolshevist exhibits, everything about the Eternal Jew show was designed to disgust visitors. Next to the entrance stood a thirty-foot cardboard Shylock, looking as if he wanted to pick the pockets of all who passed by. Inside, a chamber of horrors displayed "Jewish ritual knives used for circumcisions," "Talmud torture instruments for the killing of Gentiles," and pictures of "kosher butchers massacring defenseless cattle." Another room contained bloodstained ceremonial robes, skeletons, kosher food, and menorahs, as if these were all insidiously connected. There were hundreds of photographs of dwarfish, hook-nosed, hirsute, bow-legged *Ostjuden*—illustrations of "racial degeneration." Special attention was given to politically influential Jews, domestic and foreign, who had "worked to undermine Germany." These included Marx, Trotsky, Eisner, Rathenau, Disraeli, Henry Morgenthau, and Franklin Roosevelt (!). To illustrate Jewish cultural perversity, the exhibit featured examples of "degenerate" painting, scratchy phonograph recordings of Richard Tauber's songs, and old film clips of Jewish comedians. An entire section was devoted to "that evil American Jew, Charles Chaplin." (Three years later Chaplin got his revenge with the brilliant send-up of Hitler, *The Great Dictator*.)

The Eternal Jew exposition attracted 412,300 visitors during the period between 8 November 1937 and 31 January 1938, when it closed in Munich and went on tour to other German cities. Among the visitors in Munich were entire school classes, enjoying a racist field trip on an island in the Isar. According to the local press, many foreigners were in attendance too, adding this new attraction to old tourist standbys like the Hofbräuhaus and the Alte Pinakothek.

As with the other Nazi exhibitions, it is impossible to know what these visitors actually thought. As usual the guest book registered only politically correct observations. There are no grounds to assume, however, that the majority did not respond in the manner intended by the regime. After all, the show tied into established stereotypes, and (unlike the Degenerate Art affair) there was little reason to visit it save to have those prejudices graphically confirmed. The show could have opened in any German city, but Munich, as cradle of a virulently anti-Semitic movement, was undoubtedly an appropriate site. Moreover, given the still-lively hatreds left over from the revolutionary era, the organizers did not have to worry that the show would be poorly attended.

8

Babylon on the Isar

THE ABILITY TO enjoy life's sensual pleasures, like the capacity to appreciate fine art, had long served Münchners as compensation for secondary political status in the German nation. This continued to be so in the Nazi era. Indeed, during the 1930s Munich reasserted its claim to being Germany's capital of good times, a distinction it had ceded to Berlin in the Weimar period. This development was due largely to the efforts of Munich's brown bosses, who believed that if their city could not be the most powerful, it could be the most lively. Even Hitler, consolidating his dictatorship in Berlin, tended to loosen up and show his "bohemian" side when he returned to his old hometown.

In addition to providing diversion for party bosses, Munich's amusement culture served useful social and propagandistic functions. To the majority of Münchners, as well as to the thousands of Germans from other parts of the Reich who visited during the Nazi era, the frolicsome scene suggested that Nazism could mean glamour, culture, and fun—not just sacrifice and hard work. Because Nazi play often involved carefully choreographed mass spectacles, participants gained a greater sense of *Volk* unity. Employment of historical motifs in the public festivals reinforced the Nazis' claims to be the rightful heirs of past Germanic conquerors. Festival-Munich even worked its charms on foreign guests. Many came away impressed by what they took to be an easygoing and cheerful side to the Hitler regime. Nazi Germany might not be such a cruel and menacing place after all, some reasoned.

Of course, this impression was deeply illusory. Munich's fun-loving bosses were the same ones who administered the policies of coordination and repression, and the amusement was available only to the politically and racially approved. Nonetheless, ritualized play, drawing upon Munich's traditions of street carnival and art festivals, proved an important source of seductive appeal for the Hitler regime.

While most ordinary Münchners seem to have enjoyed the Nazi festivals, and some profited from them, a sizable number of citizens continued to find fault with the new order. The Capital of Carnival also became the Capital of Complaint. But even as the complaints grew in volume, they rarely translated into sustained or fundamental opposition to the regime. In the end, as a matter of fact, Munich's carnivalesque culture may have had a bread-and-circus effect on the local population, helping to drown dissent in diversion.

Nazi Playground

Nazi Germany's leaders hurried to Munich and its alpine environs when they wanted to get away from the stress of running the Thousand-Year Reich. Hitler himself spent as much time as he could in Munich. He retained his apartment on Prinzregentenplatz, which he furnished to his taste. The walls were decorated with landscapes by Spitzweg, a portrait of Bismarck by Lenbach, and one of the many versions of Franz von Stuck's *Die Sünde* (Sin).

The wonderful thing about Munich, in Hitler's eyes, was that there he could return to his bohemian roots, carouse in his favorite restaurants, and talk endlessly about art and architecture. Whereas in Berlin he had to entertain diplomats, in Munich he could court artists and actors.

This was a role that most of his top lieutenants had no trouble emulating. According to the Reuters correspondent Ernest R. Pope, who followed Hitler and his cronies around Munich in the mid-to-late 1930s, the Führer became an intrepid man-about-town whenever he visited the Isar city. Following operetta performances at the Gärtnerplatz Theater—Hitler's favorite piece was *The Merry Widow,* starring erotic "beauty dancer" Dorothy van Bruck, whose every move he studied with the aid of powerful military binoculars—the Führer liked to host all-night parties at the newly renovated Künstlerhaus. This establishment, claimed Pope, was a "hotbed of Nazi intrigue, orgies, and artistic turpitude." Guests always included the prettiest actresses and dancers from the theatrical cast. Dorothy herself might perform a "blitz-tease" so close to Hitler that he had no need of his binoculars. Members of his entourage, when not gorging on foie gras and champagne, disappeared with a partner into one of the convenient *chambres séparées.* At about 3:00 or 4:00 A.M. Hitler would leave for his apartment, followed shortly thereafter by Dorothy or one of her colleagues. The lady in question would be driven by a lackey to the Prinzregentenplatz, shown into Hitler's building, and, "after less than an hour," driven away again. "Adolf Hitler is a great protagonist of the blitz technique," insisted Pope.

Maybe he was. Other sources suggest that Hitler, despite his claims to have no time for a love life, managed several passing affairs (aside from his ongoing relationship with Eva Braun) while he was chancellor. A German film director testified after the war that he had supplied Hitler with film starlets, and U.S. military intelligence found evidence of at least two intimate affairs. But apparently even the Führer could not get sex whenever he wanted. The beautiful filmmaker Leni Riefenstahl claims that Hitler made an awkward pass at her, which she successfully rebuffed. Putzi Hanfstaengl insisted that Hitler went down on his knees to his wife, Helene, in a vain effort to get her to sleep with him. There is evidence, on the other hand, that Hitler feared physical contact with women; he once compared sexual intercourse with the trauma a soldier faces in battle. But whatever the exact nature and scope of his sex life, Hitler clearly enjoyed the company of beautiful women, which he said stimulated "the artist" in him. The fact that Munich afforded him ample opportunities to indulge this passion enhanced his affection for the place.

In perhaps his most bizarre relationship Hitler was more the pursued than the pursuer. In 1934 Unity Valkyrie Mitford, daughter of the right-wing British peer Lord Redesdale, arrived in Munich to study art—and to be close to Hitler. A follower of the British fascist Oswald Mosley (who married her sister Diana), Unity had become delirious over Hitler after watching him at the 1933 Nuremberg party rally, which she attended as a guest of Putzi Hanfstaengl. On that occasion Putzi had warned her to wipe off her violent makeup so she would not offend "the newly proclaimed Nazi ideal of German womanhood." Now, having moved to Munich, Unity spent her days in eager anticipation of Hitler's visits, when she would tarry at his favorite haunts in hopes of catching his attention. She need not have been pessimistic on this score, for she was an attractive young woman, with pale white skin, wavy blond hair, and deep blue eyes, lacking only the opulent breasts the Führer favored. Hermann Göring, who had an eye for female pulchritude, said that (next to his wife, Carin) Unity was the "most beautiful Nordic woman" he had ever seen.

Unity frequently stalked her prey in a rustic Italian restaurant in Schwabing called the Osteria Bavaria. Hitler had been going there since his early days in Munich. He loved to consume generous helpings of ravioli even while complaining that as Führer he had to watch his waistline. He felt so at ease in the Osteria that he went there without bodyguards, making him a sitting duck for potential assassins. In fact the anti-Nazi Friedrich Reck-Malleczewen encountered Hitler at the Osteria in 1932 when he, Reck, was carrying a loaded pistol. "In the almost deserted restaurant, I could have shot him," he later claimed. "If I had known the role this piece of filth was to play and of the years of suffering he was to make us endure, I would have done it without a second thought. But I took him for a character out of a comic strip and did not shoot." Jessica Mitford, Unity's radical leftist sister, also failed to shoot the Führer, though she later claimed to have made his acquaintance through Unity just for this purpose. If retrospective claims were bullets, Hitler would have been dead a dozen times.

As for Unity herself, she sat at a table near the Osteria's entrance and stared at Hitler whenever he came in. No doubt her upper-class British background gave her the courage to do this; most of the women who swooned over Hitler were content to gaze upon him from afar. The Munich ambiance also helped Unity's cause. As one of her biographers put it, "In Munich Hitler was still the hopeful bohemian who would not drag himself off to bed, nor attend to business in the morning. In Munich he was the coffee-house maestro, out to harvest his due applause in person. His vanity, his fitfulness, created a vacuum around him, and Unity rushed into it, one might-have-been-artist to another. Personality and place combined to give her a unique opening, and she seized it: that was her coup."

In February 1935 Hitler responded to Unity's none-too-subtle signals by inviting her to his table at the Osteria for a chat. During their conversation (she now had enough German to follow him), he told her that the "international Jews must never again be allowed to make the two Nordic races [Britain and Germany] fight against one another." Afterward she wrote her father that she was so happy that she "wouldn't mind a bit dying." She guessed she was "the luckiest girl in the world to deserve such an honour."

Over the next four years Hitler saw Unity periodically at the Osteria and at other favorite haunts, such as Café Heck and the Carlton Tea Room. As far as we know, however, he never invited her to spend time alone with him in his apartment. No doubt he found her eccentric and a little off-putting; even he could not have approved of her packing a pistol in her purse "with which to shoot Jews." Hitler preferred his women submissive and demure, and that Unity was not.

Hitler's lack of ardor, however, did not cool Unity's. She stayed on in Munich, careering about town in a convertible emblazoned with swastikas, shouting, "Heil Hitler," to all she encountered, including the startled British ambassador. This behavior was an irritant to Hitler's entourage, which seems to have had little use for the flamboyant British fascist.

Unity may also have done some genuine harm. It was widely believed that she listened for anti-Nazi comments at parties and denounced their authors to Hitler. One would think that the natives would have been aware enough of her sentiments to watch their tongues in her presence, but not all did so. She wrote her sister Diana after attending a dress show in Munich: "The entire Munich *Adel* [nobility] was there, and it felt *exactly* like an underground Gunpowder Treason and Plot meeting. I sighed with relief when we left." One of Unity's biographers suggests that she turned in a Prince Lippe-Biesterfeld for criticizing Hitler at a dinner party, and the ubiquitous Mr. Pope insists that Unity denounced so many people that she became known as "the most dangerous woman in Munich." Yet, as another commentator has pointed out, there is no concrete evidence that she ever denounced anyone at all.

On one occasion Unity's mouth certainly did get someone in trouble, though her motives were probably innocent enough. It seems that in February 1937 her friend Putzi Hanfstaengl bragged to her that he envied the men fighting for Franco in the Spanish Civil War. Unity relayed this bravado to Hitler. The Führer, long exasperated with Putzi's posturing, decided to play a little practical joke on him. He sent him up in a plane with sealed orders that he was to open only in flight; they instructed him to parachute behind enemy lines in Spain and to gather data on the Reds.

In fact, the plane never went anywhere near Spain and, after flying around for a while, landed in Leipzig. The excitable publicist, however, was now convinced that Hitler wanted to get rid of him and fled Germany for Switzerland.

Unity ultimately paid a high price for her obsession with Hitler. When war broke out in 1939, the Führer instructed her to return to her native land. But unable to bear leaving Munich and the man she loved, she walked into the Englischer Garten and shot herself in the head. Her wound was not fatal, and Hitler sent her via Switzerland to England, where she died in 1948.

If Hitler found Unity trying, he also began to tire of the endless importunities of the Nazi Old Fighters, who always wanted to monopolize his time in Munich. As Albert Speer recalled, he resented their "air of unseemly familiarity" as well as their extraordinary boorishness and stupidity. Even Gauleiter Wagner, while still very useful to Hitler, was a trial to be around, for he smoked one hundred cigarettes a day, drank to excess (even by Bavarian standards), and chased everything in skirts (despite his pegleg and sagging paunch). Hitler began to dread the Beer Hall Putsch reunions because there was no way to avoid the old boys on these occasions.

The public's intrusiveness also began to fray his nerves. In Munich he had little privacy, part of the price he paid for being the hometown hero back in his old neighborhood. People were constantly asking him for autographs and to kiss their babies. Crowds assembled outside his apartment building to watch him come and go. Exasperated, he ordered a barricade constructed to keep the masses at a respectful distance. He even began curtailing his theater visits to avoid the mobs.

Ultimately, however, there was no escaping the Munich masses without leaving town. So—shades of King Ludwig II—during his Bavarian visits he began to spend less time in the city than in the nearby mountains. He enlarged his cottage at the Obersalzberg into a sizable alpine retreat. The three-story Berghof was done up in faux-Bavarian peasant style, though it lacked the customary crucifix in the kitchen corner. To be close to their Führer, other top Nazis—Göring, Bormann, and Speer—built houses nearby. Soon the entire mountaintop was blighted by a 2.7-acre compound, replete with paved paths, a huge garage, and a guest hotel. Protected by a barbed-wire fence and SS patrols, it was a strange mirror image of the concentration camps below. The scenery was breathtaking, but the daily social routine was stifling. Mostly Hitler's satraps sat around with their bored wives listening to the Führer pontificate. In the evening they joined him in eating rich pastries and watching movies sent up by Goebbels. Hitler's favorite was Mickey Mouse. No doubt his guests often thought longingly about what was going on down in Munich.

Munich's Nazi bosses, it turned out, did not need their Führer or his top aides by their side to keep the party going in town. The subaltern who contributed most to the carnival atmosphere there was Christian Weber, erstwhile stableboy and chairman of the city council. As the Nazis' power expanded, so did Christian. Never slim, he became so fat that his custom-made lederhosen required the skin of an entire calf. This was impressive even in Munich, and the townspeople began to joke about his porcine features, saying he lacked only for trotters and a snout. It was also reported that he had become incensed at a local gallery after examining a portrait of himself that he said made him "look like a pig"; the "portrait" turned out to be a mirror. Aside from gluttony, Weber's passions included horseracing, hunting, wenching, graft, and neopagan pageantry. He was, in short, the perfect Falstaff for Hitler's Munich.

In 1934 Weber organized the Brown Ribbon of Germany, an international horserace with a grand prize of a hundred thousand Reichsmarks. The race was held annually in the suburb of Riem on land that Weber had owned and sold to the city. Despite its unhappy name, which called to mind a strip of used toilet paper, the event became a great success, attracting horse people from all over Europe. Weber bragged that he had made Riem as sophisticated as Ascot, and a lot more fun.

To make his race even more attractive, Weber added to it a nocturnal pageant called the "Night of the Amazons." Held in the Nymphenburg Palace Park, the event was a cross between the "2000 Years of German Culture" parade and a girlie show. Mythological theme floats crowded with seminude young women rolled down paths lit by torchlight. "Amazons" galloped around bareback, waving spears and showing off their armor, which consisted of a light dusting of gold paint. Meanwhile, spotlights picked out "Chinese Temple Goddesses" performing dances rarely seen in Chinese temples. The show was open to the general public, but ordinary patrons could not enter a secluded VIP area where Weber introduced special guests to the performers.

Weber's Amazon Night and Brown Derby were by no means his only contributions to Munich's amusement culture. For the Carnival season he organized a new festivity called the *Aufgalopp*. Installed in Munich's largest vaudeville hall, the event combined all of Weber's passions. Ernest Pope, on hand for one of these extravaganzas, provided the following account:

> Imagine the Metropolitan Opera House in New York with the orchestra seats removed to make way for a dance floor. Picture to yourself the cellar of the

Metropolitan as a maze of beer halls, *chambres-séparées* and necking laboratories, where beer, champagne, kisses, hot dogs, re- and pro-creation mingle in gay abandon, according to the individual's need and tastes. Imagine further a succession of horses and nude women parading across the stage of this theater, while bottles pop and curtains are drawn in the box seats and balconies. Visualize an inebriated, radiant 350-pound ex-stable boy in billowing starched shirt and tails as the patron saint of the nights's festivities. Add a buxom contralto from the legitimate Munich State Opera, a nude ballet of clumsy former milkmaids and shopgirls (unshaven), a Turkish striptease artiste that Christian himself salvaged specially for the occasion from Paris, rococo waltzes danced to the music of an SS Black Guard orchestra, a poor, naked girl trying very hard to look like Diana as she straddles a rather ripe deer shot in the Bavarian forests last week, and hundreds of "Strength through Joy" workers, Riem stable fans, local Nazi brass hats, reckless Munich students, and all kinds of women from Christian's mistresses to blond Hitler Girl Leaders—and this may give you an approximate description of the *Aufgalopp*, Christian Weber's artistic triumph, the crowning glory of countless decades in the history of Munich carnivals.

Also during Carnival, the city's new Office for Festivals and Leisure Time, which Weber headed, introduced yet another gala procession, the Carnival Parade. The one in 1935 was nearly five miles long and contained 156 floats, marching groups, and bands. Once again the idea was to snatch a bit of Munich's fabled *Gemütlichkeit* for the Nazi cause and to show the world that the regime had its lighter side. But even the Munich Nazis did not laugh when a foreign guest turned up for the Carnival Parade in a tuxedo dyed brown. This was regarded as a deliberate "profanation" of the movement.

Weber and his cronies also turned their hand to the city's Oktoberfest, which was only natural for a movement that had grown up in beer halls. It was the Nazis' good fortune that the 125th anniversary of the festival rolled around in 1935. For this occasion they laid on a massive torchlight parade with hundreds of marchers dressed in traditional Bavarian outfits. As chairman of the Oktoberfest board Weber revived the horseraces that had once been part of the festival. Yet he and his lieutenants also made efforts to infuse the event with Germany's most recent ideological obsession: Oktoberfest kitsch now bore Nazi themes. A decal featured the municipal trademark *Münchner Kindl* bereft of his monk's robe, hoisting a beer stein and a radish above a swastika; a festival poster proclaimed: "Proud City—Happy Land." The official program promised that the centennial festival would display "the joyful but disciplined affirmation of life characteristic of the revived fatherland." In 1936 organizers ordered that swastika flags fly in place of the traditional blue and white banners. In 1938 they changed the name to Greater German Folk Festival to mark the recent annexation of Austria.

One other contribution of Weber's deserves mention: his creation of a German Hunting Museum. Hunting had always been a favorite pastime of the German aristocracy, especially in the heavily forested South. Among the Nazi bosses, Weber and Göring were particularly keen on this sport. (Hitler, on the other hand, despised hunting and called the hunting fraternity a "green Freemasonry.") While Göring, "Master of the German Hunt," was a relatively responsible hunter who sought to protect as well as to kill game animals, Weber simply slaughtered as many beasts as he could. He established the Hunting Museum partly to show off his trophies. He also saw to it that the museum's opening was accompanied by a gaudy spectacle: "1000 Years of Hunting—1000 Years of Native Costume." Weber's parade was at once a reach for historical legitimacy and another excuse for a drunken party.

With Weber's help, Nazi Munich took advantage of its role as the Reich's festival capital to reassert itself as a major tourist destination. Thousands of visitors came from other parts of the country courtesy of cut-rate package tours sponsored by *Kraft durch Freude* (Strength through Joy), the regime's leisure-time program for the common man. For many Germans, this was their first trip to Munich, and they were doubtless grateful to the government for making it possible.

Munich's hospitality industry was also eager to attract foreign tourists, who aside from bringing in welcome revenue would by their very presence help undercut recent charges of parochialism and cultural backwardness. Even the Nazis liked to think of Munich as "cosmopolitan," though by this they meant primarily the rustle of foreign currency. Foreign ideas and values were less welcome than ever.

The year 1936 was a banner one for German tourism because of the Winter Olympic Games in Garmisch-Partenkirchen and the Summer Games in Berlin. Munich managed to profit handsomely from both.

This was natural for the Winter Games, since the site was close to Munich but lacked adequate housing for guests or any facilities for the extracurriculars that were part of the Olympic experience. Thus Munich's Hofbräuhaus, not Garmisch, hosted Reichssportführer Hans von Tschammer und Osten's gala *Bierabend* for visiting Olympic officials. Throughout the games guests were shuttled to Munich by train for various festivities, including a special Olympic ballet with music by Richard Strauss. Entitled *The Olympic Rings,* the piece featured five ballerinas dressed in flimsy costumes of red, yellow, black, blue, and green. At the end of the games all the competitors were invited to an Olympic Ball in Munich for two thousand people. It lasted all night and featured a skit entitled "The Master Singers from Gudiberg," a "Snow Flake" ballet, and a "Can-Can for Twelve."

For Munich, the Summer Games in Berlin had the disadvantage of being much farther away, but they attracted far more people. To lure some of them down to Bavaria, the city sponsored, at the conclusion of the games, an International Congress on Leisure and Recreation. This helped make the Olympic summer a boom tourist season in the Bavarian capital. "Never has our city seen so many foreign visitors," crowed the *Neues Münchener Tagblatt*. The paper claimed that most of the visitors headed straight for the Nazi shrines at the Feldherrnhalle and Königsplatz. "Truly, Munich is once again a world city." For the *Völkischer Beobachter*, Munich's tourism success was an answer to charges spread in "the Jewish press" that Nazi Germany's cultural capital was "hostile to foreigners or devoid of international flavor." In the streets, the paper insisted, one heard nothing but praise from the visitors for the glories of Munich and the "obviously peaceful intentions of the German people."

The strange thing about this commentary is that it contained a measure of truth. Many foreign visitors to Munich seem to have been impressed by the discipline, cleanliness, and cultural vitality they found there. Influential guests like the Duke of Windsor and Charles Lindbergh spoke glowingly of the good beer and boisterous fun. So did the American novelist Thomas Wolfe, who loved it that he could stay drunk all the time without feeling out of place. Spending a month in Munich in 1935 between his junior and senior years at Princeton, the future distinguished historian of Germany Gordon Craig was struck by how seriously Hitler was working "to make München the cultural center of Germany." The Nazis, he noted in his diary, were "making much of Wagner and his search for a new European culture centered in Germany." Seeing "no evidence of Jew-baiting," and finding the Münchners on the whole "happy and prosperous," young Craig got the impression that "the government here is more liberal than people at home believe." (Admittedly this was an initial impression; after a couple of weeks Craig, a shrewd observer, began to perceive behind the glittering facade a "fear in the air" that made some citizens reluctant to talk candidly to foreigners.) All in all, foreign visitors tended to reason that if Munich was so peaceful and contented, this must also be true for the rest of Germany. The city's indefatigable festival culture and apparent joie de vivre were therefore an effective cover for the ugly realities of Nazi policy. Put in another way, Munich still meant Oktoberfest, not Dachau, to most of the world.

But this mood was not to last much longer. Munich's tourism industry reached its peak in 1936–1937, then fell off sharply as Germany became increasingly bellicose and preoccupied with building up its armed forces. In the wake of the Czech crisis of 1938, as we shall see, it became harder and harder to view Nazi Germany's "cultural capital" as a center of innocuous gaiety.

"Capital of the Earth Movement"

Because Munich performed such important symbolic and representational functions in the Nazi system, the regime was determined to give it a physical facade commensurate with its showy role. Like Berlin, which Hitler intended to transform into a monumental capital called Germania, Munich would showcase the Nazis' grandiose political visions in mortar and marble. Municipal architecture and urban design would capture the Nazi ideology and overwhelm Germans and foreigners alike with the majesty of the Third Reich. As Hitler put it, "Our buildings are our word in stone." In the event, only a tiny fraction of the regime's architectural and urban renewal plans were realized. Nonetheless, both the completed projects and the unrealized plans can tell us a great deal about the Nazi urban aesthetic and Munich's place within it.

We have already mentioned some of the Nazis' early contributions to Munich's architectural topography: Troost's renovated Brown House, the House of German Art, the Honor Temples for the Beer Hall martyrs. In addition, the regime built a House of German Medicine on Brienner Strasse and a House of German Law on the Ludwigstrasse. These were important constructions but only the beginning. Hitler was determined to step forth as a latter-day King Ludwig I in his favorite city. Accordingly, after launching the House of German Art, he turned his attention to Ludwig's great legacy, the Königsplatz. He instructed Paul Troost to transform the square into a fitting administrative and representational center of the Nazi movement. What was to emerge, said the Nazi press, was an "Acropolis Germaniae" or a "Forum of the Party."

When Troost received this commission, he did not have long to live, but before his death in 1934 he drew up an ambitious blueprint that, with some modifications, became reality over the next three years. On the east side of the square flanking the Honor Temples rose two imposing buildings that still stand as monuments to Nazi taste. Their identical three-story neoclassical exteriors featured two "Doric" porticoes and long rows of rounded-arch windows. On the third level, overlooking each entryway, perched massive iron eagles clutching swastikas in their talons. The building on the left (looking away from the square down Brienner Strasse, called by the Nazis the Via Triumphalis) was the Führerbau. As its name suggests, it contained living quarters and an office for Hitler, which was larger and grander than his room in the Brown House. Here was also a suite for his deputy, Rudolf Hess. But the building's most important feature was a cavernous central hall, sixty-five feet high and a hundred feet wide, with two stone staircases leading to a large conference room on the second floor. The interior walls, made of red Saalburg and yellow Jura marble, were hung with rich tapestries and enormous history paintings. The other building, somewhat less opulently appointed, was the Verwaltungsbau, an administrative center housing offices for the Nazi Party's financial and legal departments. Many top Nazis based in Berlin kept second offices in this building. The two structures were connected by an underground tunnel that could serve as a bomb shelter should Hitler and his aides ever be caught in Munich during an air raid. These buildings might take their inspiration from the past, but the builders were clearly thinking ahead.

To make the Königsplatz more functional as a parade ground, the Nazis covered its grassy expanse with granite blocks. This gave it a look of empty monumentality that perfectly suited the Nazi ideology. However, since it rained frequently in Munich, the square was often covered with water. Irreverently, Münchners called it the Plattensee (Block Lake—also a reference to shallow Lake Balaton in Hungary).

Like the House of German Art, the new Königlichen Platz (as the Nazis officially renamed it) was meant to show an inspirational tie between King Ludwig I and Hitler. A Nazi architectural historian gushed in 1938: "The greatest German chancellor has now taken up the inheritance of the greatest Bavarian king. . . . Thus the Royal Square has found its rightful completion. A hundred years ago a noble mind and admirer of classical culture created his testament to the elevated spirit. On the stone square today the [Nazi] dead hold watch. These martyrs laid down their lives for the same elevated spirit: for a new united Germany and its great culture."

On 1 May 1938 a Special Commission for the Development of the Capital of the Movement, which had been established under Mayor Fiehler's auspices a few months earlier, unveiled its plans for Munich's architectural future in the Thousand-Year Reich. Among other innovations the blueprint called for the relocation of the main train station about a mile and a half to the west. The idea here was to clear the central parts of town of automobile congestion and the unsightly railroad tracks. In place of the tracks there would be a majestic new avenue on the model of the Champs-Élysées. Along the projected avenue would rise a host of new constructions, most of them fittingly grandiose: a new opera house (three times larger than the Vienna or Paris opera); a slightly smaller operetta theater; conference centers, sports complexes, film theaters, and cafés. This being Munich, massive beer halls and beer gardens were also planned. Around the expansive square in front of the new train station would stand majestic skyscrapers housing a Strength through Joy hotel and the Nazi Party Press. In place of the old train station at the other end of the avenue would spread an even larger square, dedicated to the Nazi movement and providing a suitable space for contemplation of the movement's achievements. A second grand avenue was to connect the new train station with the Theresienwiese, whose Exhibition Hall was to be enlarged to make it the largest facility of its kind in the world.

Another, rather more practical part of the plan was devoted to public transportation. Munich's narrow streets were congested with private cars, honking and belching clouds of smoke. Their noisy presence clashed with the Nazis' ideal of municipal grandeur. Thus the Capital of the Movement was to have an extensive subway system, a model of its kind in Europe. The first line would connect the new train station to the town center, whisking people to the Square of the Movement in a matter of minutes. As Nazi ideas went, this was by no means stupid; perhaps for this reason little headway was made on it during the Third Reich. The authorities made more progress with the surface trolley system, which Mayor Fiehler identified as Munich's most important form of public transportation. A new line was installed along Arnulfstrasse, and a new terminal built in West End. Nonetheless, the trolleys, with their exasperating rules and regulations, served as a metaphor for life under National Socialism. "What do the Munich trolleys have in common with the Party?" asked a popular joke. The answer was a tour de force of puns: "*Es ist verboten, mit dem Führer zu sprechen. Wer nicht hinter dem Führer steht, sitzt. Das Kleingeld ist bereitzuhalten. Bei besonderen Anlässen werden die alten Anhänger hervorgeholt* [It is forbidden to speak with the driver (leader). Those not standing behind the driver must sit (go to jail). Have small change ready at all times (for party collections). On special occasions, vintage cars (the Old Fighters) will be brought out of storage].

Of course, Munich could not ban automobiles entirely, and to facilitate their passage in and around the city, a number of streets were widened and new bridges (such as the Donnersbergerbrücke and a redesigned Ludwigsbrücke) were constructed. Broad access routes were also necessary to tie the existing road network to the new autobahn connecting

Munich and Salzburg. These magnificent highways, like the subway scheme and street-widening projects, illustrated the functionalist and "modernist" side of the Nazi system. Yet ideology was always present, even in roads, bridges, and smaller urban improvements. Hitler personally intervened in the construction of the Ludwigsbrücke to ensure that its Nazi iconography was sufficiently grandiose. He threw a fit when a "garden island" surrounding the Peace Angel monument on the Isar was not designed to his specifications. Aside from illustrating the ideological thrust in everything the Nazis did, these examples show how intimately Hitler was involved in the reconstruction of his favorite city.

To clear space for all the construction projects, a host of existing streets, squares, buildings, and bridges had to disappear. Like many modern dictators, Hitler could be ruthless in giving voice to his word in stone. To provide a better parade route to the House of German Art, a row of handsome houses on the south side of the Von-der-Tann-Strasse was torn down in 1937. Then, just after the plans for Munich's "renewal" were unveiled, Gauleiter Wagner ordered the demolition of an apparent impediment to progress, the beautiful St. Matthäus-Kirche, which had served Munich's Protestant community since 1837. In just a few days, in June 1938, the church was reduced to a pile of rubble. Wagner and Fiehler claimed that they had cleared this action with the resident pastor, but in fact, the church officials had been ordered to abandon the building on a day's notice.

At about the same time, another prominent ecclesiastical structure went down: Munich's central synagogue on Herzog-Max-Strasse. This too was justified as an "urban renewal measure," though the synagogue was far from any of the planned construction sites. It was, however, next door to the Künstlerhaus, where Hitler liked to hold his après-theater parties, and he is reported to have been profoundly irritated by the proximity. Apprised of the problem, Gauleiter Wagner informed the head of the Munich Jewish community that the synagogue must go and that demolition work had to be completed by the Day of German Art festivities on 8 July 1938. After consulting his community, the Jewish leader reported to Wagner that he was "prepared to abandon" the synagogue. This was akin to telling the Grim Reaper that one was prepared to abandon life.

Ruthless as such action seems, Hitler was not satisfied with the pace of redevelopment in Munich. In December 1938 he named a new architect, Hermann Giesler, as general building master of the Capital of the Movement. Giesler was a fanatical Nazi who shared Hitler's conviction that "Every great era finds its most lasting expression of values in its works of architecture." Initially intimidated by his assignment, Giesler took heart when Hitler promised to give him all the money and support he needed.

Determined to do for Munich what Albert Speer was planning for Berlin, Giesler redrew the initial redevelopment blueprint to make it even more grandiose. Under his pen, the projected train station would house the largest waiting room in the world; the avenue leading up to it would be continued on the other side, making it—with a length of 22,000 feet and a width of 394 feet—the longest and widest in the Reich. At the eastern end of this "Axis," a "Pillar of the Movement," capped by eagle and swastika, would majestically commemorate the birth of National Socialism in the Isar city. Hitler himself reworked the pillar's design, ensuring that it would dwarf the twin towers of the Frauenkirche. Had this staff actually gone up, one can only imagine what the Münchners might have nicknamed it.

Giesler also turned his attention to Troost's Party Forum. He drew up plans for a massive Hall of the Party to complement the existing complex. A bridge over the Gabelsbergerstrasse would connect the hall with another new structure, Hitler's mausoleum. Hitler drew a sketch of his mausoleum, telling Giesler that he intended to rest forever in the Capital of the Movement. (Speer is wrong in his memoirs when he says that Hitler planned to be buried in Linz.)

Contemplating the plans for Munich's new party district, the *Völkischer Beobachter* enthused that Hitler would fashion a district combining a "generosity of spirit and strict discipline never known before." The Führer was planning for the "next decades and centuries." But the paper warned: "We Münchners will have to get used to thinking and feeling in greater dimensions, which will allow us to elevate our entire existence." Describing an enormous architectural model of the New Munich, which was put on public display, the *Münchener Neueste Nachrichten* echoed: "It is difficult in the face of such greatness to bring clarity to the storm of impressions and feelings that descend upon one. But what seems to emanate most powerfully from this model is a flow of ideas, a great harmony of line, a wonderful ceremony of confirmation. Here diversity becomes unity; the thrust of the new gives way to a comforting sense of peace. . . . This is a gesture of love from the Führer to his adopted city. All our love goes back to him in return."

Well, not quite. Many Münchners wondered if their city really needed glorious new avenues and massive new public buildings. They worried about the high costs, destruction of existing structures, and disruption to their routines that the construction would entail. It was not long before people were muttering that the Capital of the Movement might better be called the Capital of the Earth Movement.

However, as usual, most Münchners were careful not to carry their criticism too far. There were no demonstrations against the destruction of St. Matthäus-Kirche, let alone against that of the central synagogue. Instead of protesting, Münchners repaired to a cabaret on the Platzl to watch actors in Biedermeier-era costumes take veiled shots at Hitler by making fun of King Ludwig I's monumental architectural visions. "Have you heard?" hissed a player. "He wants to build a grand avenue. A grand avenue! What do we need a grand avenue for? And he's going to destroy a lot of good buildings!" As the actor spoke, a figure flitted by in the background: King Ludwig I. The performers leaped up, raised their right arms, and yelled, "*Heil, heil,* the king!"

"Capital of the Anti-Movement"?

As the Third Reich settled in, Münchners increasingly had more pressing matters to worry about than their Führer's architectural fantasies. The honeymoon phase in the marriage between Bavarian Christians and Nazis gave way to considerable distrust and acrimony, though not—at least as far as the official institutions were concerned—to an open break. On the economic front many Münchners soon found that the Third Reich brought more burdens than rewards, and once again they thought that they were carrying more than their fair share of the weight.

In late 1934 Bavaria's Protestant Church faced an internal crisis when the newly appointed "Reich Bishop," Ludwig Müller, attempted to end the traditional institutional independence of the provincial churches by amalgamating them with the Reich Church. He also demanded that all Protestants accept a Nazified "German Christian" doctrine that rejected the Old Testament and embraced elements of Germanic paganism. In response a number of Munich pastors joined Martin Niemöller's Confessing Church, which split off from the main Evangelical Church. But the mainstream Bavarian Protestants protested as well. Bishop Hans Meiser, headquartered in Munich, put up such resistance to the decrees from Berlin that Müller summarily deposed him on 11 October 1934. Meiser's deposition, however, ignited a storm of protest so fierce that Hitler himself stepped in and ordered the reinstatement of the Bavarian bishop. For the time being the Bavarian Protestants preserved a nominal independence.

This episode showed that the Nazi regime, for all its claims to totalitarian control, was vulnerable to concentrated explosions of popular protest. Yet it also illustrated the limits of acceptable opposition in the Third Reich. First of all, this protest was effective because the protesters belonged to the political and social mainstream, not to some despised minority like the Jews, Gypsies, or Communists. Secondly, the confrontation could be reduced to organizational issues that might be resolved without sacrificing serious ideological ground.

A narrowness of scope also characterized the Bavarian Protestants' protest—joined by the Catholics—against a Nazi campaign to eliminate confessional schools and to restrict religious instruction in the remaining institutions. This was a major issue in Munich, where most of the schools were denominational and virtually all offered religious instruction. While opposed to the new policy, Bishop Meiser pointed out that his protest was circumscribed: "Our Church is not carrying out a political struggle against National Socialism. In truth we fight only against the disparagement and undermining of our biblical faith. We reject the substitution of political motives."

Meiser's protest failed to alter Nazi policy in this domain. Through coercion and intimidation, the Nazis induced parents in Munich and other Bavarian cities to vote in special referenda to replace the denominational schools with so-called Community Schools. By 1937 Munich's secondary educational system was out of clerical hands and in those of proparty administrators and teachers. It was clear that in an area so important to their mission—indoctrination of the youth—the Nazis were unprepared to tolerate much dissent.

The Protestant Church's failure on the school issue did not prevent the hierarchy from supporting the regime in most of its other policies. As before, Protestant officials endorsed Hitler's campaign to throw off the shackles of Versailles. Bavarian Protestantism also maintained an official silence on the increasing persecution of Jews and other minorities.

Munich's Catholic community, despite its much more imposing size and historical clout, also found itself increasingly on the defensive in the Third Reich. The 1933 Concordat with the Vatican notwithstanding, the Nazis began a systematic campaign to weaken the clergy's influence. This campaign, and the church's dogged opposition to it, resembled the bitter Kulturkampf of the Bismarckian era, though this time the stakes were even higher and this time the church lost.

The ink on the Concordat was hardly dry in 1934 when the Munich police prohibited Catholic youth groups from wearing uniforms or insignia. This was done to keep them from competing effectively with the Hitler Youth. Since the Catholic groups hung on tenaciously, the regime

Vom Hitlerputsch 9. Nov. 1923 in München
Säuberung der Strassen.

Laienrichter   Ob-Landesgen-R. Simmerding   Vorsitzender Landger.-Dir. Neidhardt   Ob-Landesgen-R. Leyendecker   Laienrichter   Protokoll-Führer

Stenographen

Hitler hält seine Verteidigungsrede

Stenographen

TOP: *Clearing the streets after the Beer Hall Putsch.* (Library of Congress)
BOTTOM: *Hitler defending himself at his Beer Hall Putsch trial, 1924.*
(Library of Congress)

TOP: *"A Raw and Brutal Bunch": Members of the Munich SA, circa 1925.*
(Library of Congress)
BOTTOM: *Hitler at the speaker's table at Munich's Zirkus Krone after the*
Bavarian government lifted its speaking ban against him, March 1927.
(Library of Congress)

Heinrich Hoffmann protrait of Hitler (1928), later used as propaganda postcard. (Library of Congress)

RIGHT: *SA men mark Jewish shop for boycott, 1 April 1933.* (Stadtarchiv München)
BELOW: *Karl Fiehler, mayor of Munich during the Nazi era, inspects reconstruction of the Ludwigsbrücke, 1935.* (Stadtarchiv München)

TOP: *Marchers arrive at the Feldherrnhalle during the reenactment of the Beer Hall Putsch march, 9 November 1936.* (Stadtarchiv München)
BOTTOM: *House of German Art.* (Library of Congress)

TOP: *Interior of the House of German Art.* (Library of Congress)
BOTTOM: *Hitler inspecting an architectural model of Munich renovations in the House of German Art.* (Library of Congress)

TOP: *Bronze coffins of the Beer Hall Putsch "martyrs" in one of the Honor Temples on the Königsplatz.* (Library of Congress)
BOTTOM: *Hitler and Mussolini during the Duce's state visit to Munich, September 1937.* (Library of Congress)

The Kaufingerstrasse decorated for the Munich Conference, September 1938.
(Stadtarchiv München)

RIGHT: *Night of the Broken Glass: A vandalized Jewish-owned shop in Munich, November 1938.* (Stadtarchiv München)

BELOW: *A narrow miss: the Bürgerbräukeller after the explosion of Johann Georg Elser's bomb, November 1939.* (Library of Congress)

ABOVE: *Unemployed workers make a "snow mobile" in the Marienplatz during the Great Depression.* (Library of Congress)
RIGHT: *Adolf Wagner, Gauleiter of Munich-Upper Bavaria.* (Library of Congress)

banned them outright in 1937. In the mid-1930s the Bavarian capital witnessed a number of highly publicized trials against priests and nuns, who were charged with sexual abuses and various financial transgressions. Not content with slander, Nazi hooligans vandalized Catholic shrines and daubed swastikas on churches. In 1938 a group of Brownshirts attacked the offices of the Munich archbishopric, smashing its windows. To reduce the church's presence in everyday life, the regime imposed restrictions on the traditional Corpus Christi parade and curtailed the number of religious holidays.

Along with attacks on Catholic institutions, the Nazis promoted various forms of paganism as alternatives to traditional religiosity. The Munich SA transformed its annual Christmas celebration into a Nordic Winter Solstice festival, replete with storm troopers and their Valkyries dancing around a swastika-covered "Sun Tree." Not to be outdone, the SS cooked up an ideological stew containing bits of old Nordic legend, Greek mythology, Roman soldiers' cults, and Knights of the Round Table. In place of traditional christenings they held pagan name-giving ceremonies. On one such occasion, at Himmler's villa on the Tegern Lake, the ritual was conducted by an Austrian seer calling himself Weisthor (White Thor), who claimed to be in supernatural contact with the Germanic heroes of old. In his priestly role Weisthor spoke of *Got* rather than *Gott*, on the ground that the Ur-German deity spelled his name with one *T*. In the hills south of Munich, the SS celebrated the two solstices as the ancients supposedly had, with sporting contests, feasting, and lots of fornication (all with racially approved partners). While such pagan rites never entirely supplanted traditional Christian customs, not even among the SA and SS, they succeeded in horrifying the Munich clergy, which viewed them as a terrible new manifestation of the old Schwabing heathenism.

In response to the Nazi onslaught, the Catholic Church launched some counteroffensives of its own. Priests not only exposed the injudiciousness of the clerical "immorality" trials but called attention to the many examples of official corruption in the Nazis' Brown Babylon. Priests and nuns encouraged their flocks to retain the traditional *Grüss Gott* greeting, instead of the politically correct *Heil Hitler,* and to display church flags rather than swastika banners on days of national celebration. Local clerics made traditional Catholic festivals occasions for demonstrations of Catholic solidarity.

Most active in this regard was Father Rupert Mayer, a charismatic Jesuit with a huge popular following from his charity work with the Munich poor. A staunch nationalist who had received congratulations from Hitler on his twenty-fifth anniversary as a priest in 1924, Mayer had turned sharply against the Nazis because of their violations of the Concordat and advocacy of neopaganism. He often preached against the regime, on one occasion even asking his parishioners to take a sacred oath to defend their religious faith to the death against Nazi violations. Exasperated, the Gestapo jailed him repeatedly in 1937 and 1938. On the day of his first arrest 400 people protested outside the Munich police station and another 150 engaged in what the police called an "ideological scuffle" with Nazi partisans at the Gestapo headquarters on Brienner Strasse. In 1939, accused of maintaining contacts with "monarchist conspirators," Mayer was sent for seven months to Sachsenhausen concentration camp near Berlin. Upon his release he was banned to the Bavarian monastery of Ettal, where, isolated and sick, he spent the war years. He suffered this fate despite the energetic intercession of Cardinal Faulhaber, who branded Mayer's persecution "a sign that the Kulturkampf against the Catholic Church in Germany has entered a new phase."

Another anti-Nazi activist among the Munich clergy was Pastor Emil Muhler, who, like Mayer, catered primarily to the poorer citizens in the city. Unlike his conservative colleague, Muhler had ties to the underground Left, which kept him informed about what was going on in Dachau. He began as early as 1934 to speak to fellow priests about murders at the camp, which brought an investigation from the Gestapo. Claiming to uncover Socialist literature in his apartment, the authorities placed him under arrest, while the *Völkischer Beobachter* howled about a "Red-Black conspiracy." Later, in the wake of the 20 July 1944 assassination attempt against Hitler (with which Muhler had nothing to do), the pastor himself was delivered to Dachau, where he died in April 1945.

Cardinal Faulhaber made no protest against Muhler's persecution, presumably because of the priest's leftist connections. Moreover, the hierarchy remained wary of open conflict with the Hitler regime. A pastoral letter of the Bavarian bishops stated on 13 December 1936:

> Nothing could be further from our intentions than to adopt a hostile attitude toward, or a renunciation of, the present form taken by our government. For us, respect for authority, love of Fatherland, and the fulfilment of our duty to the State are matters not only of conscience, but of divine ordinance. This command we will always require our faithful to follow. But we will never regard as an infringement of this duty our defence of God's laws and of His Church, or of ourselves against attacks on the faith and the Church. The Führer can be certain that we bishops are prepared to give all moral support to his historical struggle against Bolshevism. We will not criticize things which are purely political. What we do ask is that our holy Church be permitted to enjoy her God-given rights and her freedom.

In general, Faulhaber was careful to combine his criticism of the regime with calls for strict legality on the part of irate Catholics. He ordered his priests to read a declaration from the pulpit urging Catholics not to demonstrate against the Mayer arrest, despite his belief that it represented a new stage in the Kulturkampf. In a sermon, he warned against giving the Nazis any excuse for cracking down even more severely on the church: "No greater service could we do the police than to furnish them with means to bring action with cudgels and arrests, with lockouts and dismissals against the odious Catholics, nowadays more hated and persecuted than the Bolsheviks. You have obeyed Father Mayer's wishes in keeping order and refraining from thoughtless words and deeds. There is a time to be silent."

Not all Munich's lay Catholics were prepared to abide by this meek policy. In 1938 a Catholic anti-Nazi group calling itself Bayernwacht (Bavarian Watch) began holding secret meetings at the home of one of its leaders. Their goal was nothing less than to reverse the verdict of 1866: to create a new Catholic state combining southern and western Germany with Austria, minus Prussia and the Protestant North. Munich would be the capital of this new southern state, gloriously free of tutelage from Berlin. Alas, the Gestapo soon penetrated the Bayernwacht and imprisoned or executed its members. The church hierarchy maintained a discreet silence on this entire affair, which had been conducted without its blessing.

As it had during the "coordination" phase of the Third Reich, the Catholic Church, like the Protestant hierarchy, also remained reticent about the Nazi regime's escalating persecution of Jews and other targeted minorities. Faulhaber may have been labeled "the Jewish Cardinal" by Nazi zealots, but Munich's Jews could not regard him as their advocate when the regime began robbing them of their rights in the name of "Aryanization." He and other top church leaders said nothing about these policies, primarily because they feared more than ever that any objections would bring down Nazi wrath on Catholic heads.

But there was more behind the reticence than fear. While most clergy, both Catholic and Protestant, certainly disapproved of radical anti-Semitism, the church in Munich was not above preaching milder forms of racism. Thus the Jesuit Hermann Muckermann delivered a series of well-attended sermons in the Frauenkirche in December 1936 that argued that Christ was not a Jew at all but an opponent of Jewry. Like Faulhaber, Muckermann embraced the theory of racial eugenics and insisted that the church stood behind the government's efforts to keep the races apart.

■ ■ ■

IF THE NAZIS' religious policies generated a measure of popular discontent but little genuine resistance from the Münchners, this was also true of the regime's economic and trade policies. Nazi rule was supposed to bring an economic boom to Munich, as to the rest of the Reich. In fact, it did so to a degree, but the primary beneficiaries were party bosses and the firms they favored, not the average man on the beer hall bench. Like brown mafiosi, Munich's new leaders grabbed lucrative business opportunities for themselves and their friends. Weber, for example, secured a corner on Munich's garbage collection, bus service, and much of its retail fuel trade. As Bavarian minister of education, Gauleiter Wagner took control of textbook selection to his immense financial advantage. When lucrative military business started to flow toward Munich in the mid-1930s, the local bosses saw to it that companies in which they had an interest received large contracts.

Other economic beneficiaries—aside from the hundreds of clerks employed by the bloated party bureaucracy and the small army of artisans making floats and costumes for the 2000 Years of German Culture festivities—were the factories and shops that produced Nazi-related gear and knickknacks, from uniforms to tin soldiers. This was an area in which Munich, with its rich tradition of high craftsmanship and low kitsch, could excel. The venerable firm Loden-Frey, famous for its upscale alpine wear, produced custom-made uniforms for Nazi officers. The tin foundry Babette Schweizer made painted models of all the figures in the 2000 Years of German Culture parade. Deschler und Sohn, metalsmiths, turned out most of the party's service medals, lapel pins, tie clasps, cuff links, and collar studs. Of particular importance was the Porzellanmanufaktur Allach (Porcelain Manufactory Allach, or PMA), which became part of the SS's sprawling economic empire. It employed local artists to design tableware with Nazi motifs, a sort of brown Meissen. It also produced beer steins and candleholders with the SS insignia, Bund Deutscher Mädel girls in traditional Bavarian dress, SS man statuettes, and German shepherd figurines for the mantel. Demand for such items was so high that the company set up a branch factory at Dachau, where labor costs were attractively low.

Numerous as they were, companies capable of exploiting new business opportunities in the Third Reich constituted only a tiny part of Munich's economy in the 1930s. The vast majority of small and middle-scale producers—still the backbone of the local commercial scene—had relatively little to show for their faith in the Führer. Nazi policies had much to do with this. Taxes were onerous and became even more so as the regime geared up for war. Berlin imposed trade and currency restrictions that hindered economic growth. The government's anti-Semitic and militarist policies alienated some foreign investors and trading partners. As we have seen, foreign policy also hurt tourism, a key part of the Munich economy. Even the companies that managed to land fat government contracts often found that Berlin was slow to pay, and that generated cash-flow problems. After the reintroduction of military conscription in 1935, companies had to contend with the loss of valuable workers. Such problems were not limited to Munich and Bavaria; as so often before, however, the southerners believed that they were being discriminated against by the policy makers in Berlin.

Disappointment over economic realities in the prewar 1930s engendered a steady undercurrent of complaint in the Capital of the Movement. The Socialist underground reported that Münchners were worried about a new *Zwangswirtschaft* (centrally directed economy) and that morale was "miserable" even among the Old Fighters, who felt that they were being passed over. The cabaret comedian Weiss Ferdl told audiences that while he knew for a fact that 98 percent of the people stood solidly behind the regime, he somehow had the bad luck only to encounter the other 2 percent in the streets. Criticism was so widespread that some malcontented Münchners began to claim that their city should actually be rechristened "Capital of the Anti-Movement."

This would hardly have been justified. Like the religiously motivated discontent, the economic grumbling lacked political direction, organizational coherence, and decisive leadership. While it certainly belied Nazi claims of unadulterated popular enthusiasm, it did not threaten the regime in its fundamentals. In fact, the authorities seem to have allowed a surprising measure of open complaint because this acted as a safety valve, bleeding off popular anger. As the Third Reich wore on, most Münchners who had become disenchanted with the regime chose, as did their counterparts elsewhere in Germany, simply to muddle through as best they could, hoping that their volatile Führer would not do anything to bring on a genuine crisis.

"A Hugger-Mugger Affair"

Münchners had ample reason to worry about their Führer's intentions in the late 1930s. It was one matter to throw off the shackles of Versailles through adroit diplomacy and the bullying of minor nations. But it was quite another to risk a second major war in pursuit of world power status. Hitler had won great popularity at home through his string of impressive foreign policy victories culminating in the Anschluss with Austria in March 1938. This last achievement was especially welcome in Bavaria because many thought (wrongly) that it would give the Catholic South more clout in the Reich.

Yet even as Münchners took pride in Hitler's foreign policy successes, they fretted over certain ominous signs of the times. One was the introduction of ration cards for lard in early 1937. A police report of 1 February 1937 stated that the population feared that this step was "just the beginning of an enforced regulation of all food products. . . ." Equally ominous were the conversion of many factories to arms production and the requirement that workers in these plants sign pledges not to talk about their products.

Even more sobering were the various officially sponsored campaigns to make the public more mindful of the dangers of aerial bombardment, for which the First World War, with its minimal and ineffective bombing, had hardly prepared the populace. As far as Munich was concerned, these efforts began as early as spring 1933, with an exhibition on the subject at the Old Botanical Garden. Visitors saw posters, maps, casualty graphs, photographs of destroyed buildings, and technical drawings on how to make structures more resistant to high explosives. The local press reported that interest in the exhibit "grew from day to day." One paper summarized the display's message as follows: "10,000 [enemy aircraft] stand poised on Germany's borders. . . . Therefore, Michl, look to the skies!"

On 5 August 1933 Munich's chapter of the Reich Civil Defense League staged a macabre spectacle, a simulated air raid on the city. At noon some sixty vehicles raced through town with sirens screaming. Overhead a number of low-flying planes dropped paper "bombs" weighted with small sacks of sand. Notices attached to the missiles described the various kinds of bombs and their effects. Shortly after the drop SA men in gas masks swarmed through the streets, clearing "rubble" and tending to the "wounded." The mock raid, according to published reports, had demolished most of the central city and caused huge loss of life.

As tensions escalated in the late 1930s, Münchners, like the residents of other German cities and towns, were made to participate in frequent air-raid drills. Prizes were given to the apartment block dwellers who could most quickly reach basement shelters. In periodic blackout exercises Münchners were required to turn out their lamps and to drive around without headlights. Everyone was encouraged to buy the "People's Gas

Mask," which came in various sizes for men, women, and children. Renters and homeowners, meanwhile, were instructed to clear attic spaces of flammable junk and to keep pails of sand at the ready. These measures were supervised by block wardens, mini-Hitlers who reveled in the task of ordering other people around. Finally, as if all this were not enough to make people keep their eyes to the skies, the authorities suspended dummy bombs from streetlamps, like air age swords of Damocles.

Yet despite all the training and preparations, the Nazis seem to have had little confidence in the country's ability to withstand prolonged aerial bombardment. Their planned strategy of blitzkrieg was designed to keep a future war as short and as far away from German cities as possible. Thus, even while promoting civil defense, Nazi leaders like Air Marshal Göring reassured Germans that the Luftwaffe would keep enemy planes out of home skies. Moreover, as if they believed such promises themselves, the Nazis did not actually invest much hard cash in the infrastructure of civil defense. Even Munich, which as Nazi Germany's symbolic capital was expected to be high among the enemy's targets, was neglected. Authorities there proceeded so slowly with bomb shelter construction that only about one quarter of the planned structures were completed by the time the war broke out.

In the meantime, anxieties over the international situation grew apace. An army report in fall 1938 warned that despite high employment and record patronage at amusement centers, the mood in Munich was "depressed about the future." Much of the population, said the report, harbored "the deep fear that, sooner or later, a war will break out and . . . bring devastation to Germany."

War certainly seemed a distinct possibility in September 1938, since Hitler, even while still digesting Austria, was clamoring for another territorial meal, the Sudeten region of Czechoslovakia. The problem was not that the people of this region, who were predominantly ethnic German, wished to remain with Czechoslovakia or that the Western powers were terribly anxious to uphold the territorial integrity of the new Czech state, which British Prime Minister Neville Chamberlain referred to as "a far-away country [of which] we know nothing." The problem was that Hitler was threatening to invade Czechoslovakia immediately if his demands were not met, and an invasion might force the powers to come to Prague's aid.

Desperate to save the peace, Chamberlain made a daring flight (it was his first time in an airplane) from London to Germany to meet with Hitler. Because the meeting was to be held in Hitler's mountain retreat on the Obersalzberg, Chamberlain landed in Munich and took a train from there to Berchtesgaden. On his way from the Munich airport to the train station, crowds turned out to cheer him. According to Hitler's personal interpreter, Paul Schmidt, Chamberlain's reception was much "friendlier" than the one accorded Mussolini on his state visit the year before.

At the Berghof the two leaders agreed in principle that the Sudetenland might be annexed to Germany (Prague was not consulted on the matter) and agreed also to meet again in Bad Godesberg two weeks later to work out the details of the transfer. When Chamberlain came to Godesberg, however, he learned that Hitler now demanded an *immediate* military occupation of the Sudetenland, which the prime minister feared that his own Parliament, as well as the French, would not accept. In any event he had no authority to agree to this course, and he flew back to Britain filled with fear that a war was inevitable.

Learning of the Godesberg stalemate, Europeans on both sides of the sharpening diplomatic conflict began grimly preparing for war. In London civil defense crews handed out gas masks, dug trenches in Green Park, and lined the Thames Embankment with antiaircraft guns. In Paris the authorities placed sandbags around public buildings to help protect against air raids. In Berlin motorized divisions rolled through the streets headed for the Czech border. But here as elsewhere there was little excitement about the preparations; spectators stood silently as the tanks rumbled by. Witnessing this scene, American foreign correspondent William Shirer judged it "the most striking demonstration against war" he had ever seen.

Matters came to a head on 28 September, when Hitler's ultimatum for a surrender of the Sudetenland was scheduled to run out. The Wehrmacht was poised on the border, ready to invade. But equally poised for action was a cabal of anti-Hitler military officers, led by Army Chief of Staff Ludwig Beck, who planned to stage a coup against the Führer if his grab for the Sudetenland resulted in war with the West, which the officers believed Germany could not win. Beck and company were also prepared to act if the West forced Hitler to back down in this confrontation. They expected that such a humiliation would render him vulnerable to a military coup.

Everything was put on hold, however, when word came through that the leaders of Britain, France, and Italy would meet with Hitler in an eleventh-hour attempt at a peaceful resolution of the conflict. At the request of the British government, Mussolini had interceded with the Führer, who agreed to the Duce's proposal for a four-power conference in Munich on the very next day, September 29. Hitler's willingness to meet suggests that for all his bluster he did not want a major war at this point (though he did fancy a minor conflict with Prague). By agreeing to a conference, Hitler was more or less acquiescing in a peaceful solution, for he had just learned through the British and French ambassadors that London and Paris would accommodate his latest demands. It remained only to work out the details and seal the agreement.

It seems that Hitler accepted Mussolini's proposal of Munich as the site for the meeting partly because this event was to be more ceremonial than substantial. The conference was to be another piece of political theater, this time with an all-star cast. The Isar city seemed the perfect place for such a grand gesture: It offered a magnificent stage in the new Nazi "Acropolis" on the Königsplatz and a public that Hitler was sure would cheer him on.

However, because the Munich Conference, which opened in the morning of 29 September, took place on such short notice, it could not be as meticulously choreographed as the Nazis might have wanted. It turned out to be a "hugger-mugger affair," in the words of one participant. Sessions were held in the second-floor conference room of the Führerbau, which was aflutter with "flocks of spruce young SS subalterns in their black uniforms, haughty and punctilious," heel clicking and *sieg Heil*ing "as though life were a drill." For much of the morning session, the four leaders and their aides all tried to talk at once, and little progress was made. Finally, Mussolini put forward a draft agreement that he claimed was his own but that in fact, Hitler had given him during their joint train ride from the Italian border to Munich. The meeting adjourned to allow the British and French to study the draft over lunch.

Mussolini's proposals must have tasted as flat as their hastily eaten meal, but Chamberlain and Daladier were so committed to an agreement that in the afternoon session they merely haggled over some details before accepting the "Italian" draft. It allowed for the immediate military occupation of the Sudetenland by the Wehrmacht, exactly what Hitler had demanded in Godesberg. France and Britain would guarantee the new Czech borders, but Germany and Italy could defer their own acceptance of them until various irredentist claims by the Poles and Hungarians in Czechoslovakia were satisfied. Although the fascist leaders cared not a whit for the Hungarian and Polish claims, they knew they could use them to destabilize and eventually pry apart what remained of the Czech state. The Munich Conference was thus "hugger-mugger" not only in its haphazard organization but also in its content.

While the European leaders were meeting on the Königsplatz, Münchners continued to worry that the discussions might all be for naught. A rumor spread through town that the meeting was deadlocked and the leaders were about to declare war. Workers at one of the large munitions plants demanded to know from management what was going on at the talks and refused to work until the rumor of war was dispelled.

The relief was therefore all the greater when the results of the Munich Conference were announced on 30 September. A Bavarian official accurately summed up the popular attitude in Germany when he reported: "The peaceful solution of the Sudeten-German question found a happy response everywhere and released the population from its severe anxieties over the preservation of peace. The return of Sudeten Germans into the Reich is greeted everywhere with tremendous joy and the Führer receives heartfelt gratitude for achieving this success without warlike entanglements."

Nowhere was the jubilation greater than in Munich itself. Cardinal Faulhaber, despite his ongoing feud with the Führer, ordered church bells rung and sent Hitler a telegram of gratitude on behalf of the Bavarian bishops. Münchners of all classes jammed the streets and beer halls, toasting their apparent escape from war. Some gathered outside Daladier's hotel and awoke the exhausted Frenchmen with a raucous serenade. But the greatest enthusiasm—even more than for Hitler himself—was reserved for Chamberlain, whose dapper personage had become synonymous with peace. Interpreter Schmidt, riding with Chamberlain through the streets after the conference, thought he detected in the spontaneous outpouring of gratitude to the British prime minister a certain "undertone of criticism" directed toward Hitler. So, perhaps, did Hitler himself, for he was not pleased that "his Münchners" were showing themselves so unbellicose in the presence of foreign leaders. This was no way to intimidate potential foes.

Yet there can be no doubt that Hitler's diplomatic triumph, even if it tasted bitter in his mouth, added substantially to his cult at home. It now seemed as if the Führer could do no wrong, that he was indeed the genius of political maneuvering he claimed to be. Moreover, his avoidance of both war and a diplomatic humiliation convinced the anti-Nazi officers around Beck that now was not the time to try to overthrow him; they put their coup plans aside.

Those who rejoiced at what Chamberlain called "peace for our time" following the Munich Conference could not have known how brief their respite from tension would be. The Sudetenland was simply another course in Hitler's extended European banquet. His next dish was rump Czechoslovakia, which he swallowed in March 1939 despite the guarantee promised by London and Paris. This success only whetted his appetite further, leading to his fateful invasion of Poland in September 1939.

The Munich Agreement has therefore gone down in history as a milestone in the history of appeasement. Indeed, in diplomacy the very name Munich has become a byword for ill-advised submission to insatiable bullies. Perhaps it is unfair that the city of Munich should be saddled with this historical legacy, for there were plenty of other critical acts of appeasement between the wars, and the meeting itself essentially formalized earlier secret understandings. Yet history needs symbols, and it may be fitting that Nazism's symbolic center should be associated with Hitler's most famous diplomatic triumph. Perhaps it is also appropriate that the city that gave birth to Nazism should have hosted an occasion that greased the slide toward war, thereby hastening the ultimate collapse of the Thousand-Year Reich.

Night of the Broken Glass

On 7 November 1938, a week after the Munich Conference concluded, word reached Berlin that a young Polish Jew had shot and seriously wounded a German Foreign Ministry official, Ernst von Rath, in Paris. The German press declared that the shooting was part of an international Jewish conspiracy designed to intimidate the Reich. Acting as if Rath were already dead, the *Münchener Neueste Nachrichten* warned the following morning: "If international Jewry thinks that it can solve the Jewish problem in Germany with assassinations, then Germany accepts this challenge and will answer it in the ways one must to convince people who are prepared to use murder as a political weapon."

On the afternoon of 9 November, as party leaders assembled in Munich for their annual commemoration of the Beer Hall Putsch, Rath died of his wounds. After consulting briefly with Hitler, Goebbels delivered an anti-Semitic tirade in Munich's Old Town Hall. He said that if Rath's murder inspired "spontaneous anti-Jewish riots," this was only to be expected. "The Jews must feel the people's wrath!" he added.

Munich's Nazi bosses were highly pleased with this turn of events. As we have seen, they had been especially zealous in their anti-Semitic policy since the beginning of the Third Reich. Nevertheless, their relentless persecution had not done much to rid the city of its Jewish presence. Some 3,574 Munich Jews had emigrated between January 1933 and November 1938, but almost as many Jews had moved into the city from the Bavarian countryside, where the persecution was often even worse. While some Jewish businesses had closed as a result of boycotts, bank foreclosures, and official intimidation, a number of firms hung on, their owners hoping to wait out the storm. In 1938 there were still twelve Jewish-owned banks in

Munich. To the leaders of the Capital of the Movement, this was an affront.

Thus, no sooner had Goebbels signaled an impending pogrom than the Munich bosses decided to provide a model for the action. Gauleiter Wagner sent SA men in civilian clothes into the streets to smash Jewish shops, burn places of worship, and terrorize any Jews they could find. Only after splinters of shopwindow glass littered many Munich streets and a pall of smoke choked the city did the police receive orders to control the damage. Nonetheless, the attacks continued through the small hours of 10 November. In addition to smashing forty-six Jewish shops and beating to death one elderly Jewish shopowner, the roving SA bands set fire to Munich's Orthodox synagogue in the Herzog-Rudolf-Strasse. The fire department rushed to the scene, but only to prevent the flames from spreading to neighboring buildings.

The SA thugs who did the vandalizing and burning could not resist wholesale looting, though this was not part of their instructions. They stole everything from furs and watches to typewriters and paper. In their greed they cut themselves on broken windows; their blood mingled with the glass shards on the sidewalks. At the luxurious Bernheimer home-furnishing store, which provided Himmler and Göring with beautiful antiques and oriental rugs, the SS stepped in to prevent extensive looting. Clearly it would not do to allow such valuable items to fall into the hands of the plebeian SA. The storm troopers' thievery notwithstanding, Wagner reported to Martin Bormann that "everything has proceeded with perfect discipline."

While the SA was vandalizing shops, the Gestapo rounded up hundreds of Jews and trucked them out to the Dachau camp, where they were held for a few days. Mayor Fiehler wanted to prohibit the Jews from returning to Munich, but the Gestapo allowed them to come back in the expectation that their stint in Dachau would convince them to emigrate, leaving behind their property and personal goods. The terrifying experience persuaded hundreds that is was indeed time to get out for good. Jewish emigration from Munich (as from the rest of the Reich) accelerated dramatically following the Night of the Broken Glass.

This infamous pogrom, Germany's largest since the Middle Ages, was not confined to Munich. It spread across the entire Reich in a wave of destruction, looting, killing, and arrests. All in all, some 7,500 stores were destroyed, 171 synagogues burned, 100 Jews murdered, and an estimated 20,000 deported to concentration camps. The pogrom was especially destructive in Berlin, where 9 of the city's 12 synagogues were torched. In comparison to the Reich capital, and even to Julius Streicher's

Nuremberg, the physical damage in Munich was light. Nonetheless, Munich's Nazi bosses could take pride in the fact that the huge pogrom had been orchestrated from their city and that they had again set the tone in the war against the Jews.

On the other hand, despite all the government's talk of "spontaneous popular fury," it must be said that the vast majority of Munich's population had nothing to do with the pogrom. When they discovered what had happened, many Münchners reacted in a manner unbecoming of citizens of Nazi Germany's first city. As they walked through the streets littered with broken glass and debris, some became so angry that they openly expressed shame and outrage. A Munich Jew who had managed to evade arrest reported later that an "Aryan lady of the best social class" told him that she was ashamed to be German, while a banker assured him that "90 percent of the German people" opposed such practices. "Only a small clique," the banker added, had caused "this disaster." Else Behrend-Rosenfeld, a social worker who had recently moved to Munich from the countryside, heard many expressions of "horror" mixed in with sentiments of *Schadenfreude*. She was one of a number of Jews who found shelter with Gentile neighbors during the wave of arrests. Moreover, some shopowners brought food and other necessary items to Jews who, in the wake of the pogrom, were forbidden to shop in the central city. Taking note of the popular response, the government of Upper Bavaria was obliged to admit that the pogrom had engendered "much criticism."

Most of the criticism, however, was directed at the *methods* employed in the pogrom, rather than at the principles and policies that lay behind it. Many Münchners (like other Germans) seem to have been genuinely disgusted by the hooliganism and destruction of property carried out by a regime that advertised itself as orderly. No doubt some also felt sympathy for the victims of such loutish brutality. Yet there was no outcry against anti-Semitism itself or even against continuing efforts to isolate and segregate the Jews. Once again Munich's spiritual leaders proved no exception: While some individual priests and pastors spoke out against the inhumanity of the pogrom, both church hierarchies remained officially silent.

The Nazi leadership in Berlin, for its part, was not uniformly pleased with the pogrom, and not only because of the unenthusiastic public response. Göring complained that the smashed shopwindows contained fine Belgian glass that would be very difficult to replace. Himmler, who had not been consulted before the campaign was launched, was appalled by the disorderliness of the affair, which he knew would give Germany a black eye abroad. He believed that Jews should be persecuted in private, not in front of the world. Moreover, he hated to see the rowdy SA unleashed after its recent demotion. Unwilling to hold Hitler responsible for the fiasco, he blamed everything on "that airhead Goebbels," whom he despised as a Berlin city slicker with loose morals and an unruly temperament.

The lesson the Reich government thus took from the Night of the Broken Glass was that it was better for the time being to stick to lawful measures of anti-Jewish persecution. Hoping to deflect further criticism of the action, especially from abroad, the regime argued that the Jews had brought it on themselves by inciting the "people's fury." Following this logic, the Nazi Council of Ministers, presided over by Göring, levied a billion-mark fine on Germany's Jews to pay for the damages. In Munich as elsewhere the Jewish community also had to pay for police and fire department overtime and for the cleanup following the pogrom. Moreover, most of the stores that had been closed because of looting were not allowed to reopen under their previous owners.

These last measures constituted the beginning of a new wave of economic and social persecution designed to rob the Jews of their remaining vestiges of wealth and dignity. While this persecution, like that preceding it, was Reich-wide, Munich's Nazi bosses again took the lead and distinguished themselves through their rapaciousness. In accordance with a postpogrom decision by the regime to "Aryanize" all remaining Jewish businesses, Gauleiter Wagner established on 22 November 1938 the Wealth Administration Corporation of Munich, which amounted to an officially sanctioned den of thieves. The corporation liquidated Jewish businesses for a small percentage of their value, then sold them to third parties for handsome profits.

And what of the Jews who lost their businesses? Some emigrated, though this was becoming much harder to do as countries around the world closed their doors to potential Jewish immigrants. Jews remaining in Germany, now bereft of the opportunity to conduct most kinds of business, began desperately selling off personal items of value. In Munich, as in some other towns, the Nazi leaders took advantage of this by setting up a municipal Buying Office that became the only legal market for the disposition of Jewish personal property. Jews were forced to sell their belongings at 20 to 30 percent below the prices commanded by the Buying Office when it resold the goods. In March 1939 the office could report that it had disposed of thousands of items, ranging from furs to postage stamp collections.

Another part of the Aryanization program involved the expulsion of Jews from their lodgings and the transfer of these quarters to others.

Hitler proposed that non-Jewish Münchners who had lost their residences as the result of his reconstruction of the city be given first claim on confiscated Jewish real estate. Some properties were transferred to victims of the earth movement, but most went to the highest bidder. The chief profiteers were local party bosses, since Wagner and Weber had been quick to establish another "corporation" for the liquidation of Jewish real property.

"A Wonderful Day"

The fate of the Jews was undoubtedly not uppermost in most Münchners' minds in midsummer 1939, for the city was once again busy with preparations for the annual Great German Art Exhibit and culture parade. As usual, the atmosphere was electric with excitement. Before Hitler's arrival, Goebbels, speaking in the House of German Art, expounded "the reunion of art with the mass of the people." Hitler himself, opening the exhibition, was more critical of recent German painting, complaining that no contemporary artist had managed to capture the momentous events of National Socialism with the same skill that great artists of the past had applied to their own epochs. The 1939 exhibition's most discussed works, in fact, celebrated female flesh rather than Nazi accomplishments. Munich artist Sepp Hilz, known as the Master of the Rustic Venus, contributed a life-size portrait of a voluptuous young blonde dressed in nothing but woolen stockings—a folksy pinup. Paul Mathias Padua submitted a piece of mythoporn, *Leda and the Swan,* which showed the naked demigoddess opening her legs to Zeus, disguised as an enormous gander. Hitler may not have regarded Padua's work as Nazism's best answer to Michelangelo, but he snapped it up for his personal collection.

The pageantry surrounding the exhibition was no less elaborate or festive for the recent war scares and open persecution of the Jews. There exists a particularly vivid record of this occasion in the form of a sixteen-millimeter film commissioned by Gauleiter Wagner. The movie shows a city basking under blue skies (except for a short downpour during the 2000 Years of German Culture parade). Munich's historic buildings are festooned with colorful bunting and flags. Folkloric dance troupes trot their steps on the Marienplatz; girls in Grecian robes lounge in the Englischer Garten; contented burghers take afternoon tea on the terrace attached to the House of German Art. Nazi leaders, including Hitler, seem at ease and almost innocuous as they stroll the streets or view the gala proceedings from their VIP seats.

The parade that year offered the usual lineup of lavish tableaux glorifying episodes and heroes of the Germanic past: An ox-drawn wagon represented reverence for "Blood and Soil," a bust of Pallas Athena celebrated Germany's "classical heritage," and a golden image of "Father Rhine" commemorated Hitler's 1936 remilitarization of the Rhineland. But there was at least one float that looked to the future: a tableau with two Bohemian lions holding open the "Gates to the East," behind which stood Slavic-looking buildings. Moreover, in addition to the historically costumed marchers in their Viking furs and Crusader armor, there was an unusually high number of men in Wehrmacht gray.

Roughly fifty years later some Münchners who had witnessed or participated in the 1939 festival could still speak of it as if it had been nothing more than a happy street fair. Interviewers recorded the following comments from survivors: "It was a wonderful day. If you give Bavarians something like that, all that glitter and gold, they love it." "I was a rococo lady and belonged to the float with an organ on it. . . . It was really a beautiful day, a sunny day with a blue Bavarian sky, which later ended with a rainstorm. But that didn't really matter to any of us. As a young person you ignore all this. Anyway, it was very nice. A lot of fun really, one can say." "It was a wonderful day. It was a lovely experience that I haven't forgotten to this day at the age of seventy. And officially, for us, it didn't have anything to do with politics. For us it was just a lovely day, where you met other people and also where we could show ourselves off with different sorts of clothes and really show something—and then we were really quite happy."

Most people in Munich were probably too preoccupied with having a good time to notice that their Führer's guest of honor at the 1939 parade was one Georgi Astakhov, Soviet Russia's chargé d'affaires in Germany. Because the USSR was known to be Nazi Germany's sworn enemy, however, *Time* magazine's correspondent in Munich found this choice of guests "surprising." Only in retrospect do we know that it made a great deal of sense. German and Russian diplomats were at that moment secretly negotiating the nonaggression pact that was to astound the world a month later. For Hitler, this pact was the key to unlocking those Gates of the East through which his armies would soon launch their most devastating crusade.

9

Götterdämmerung

IN THE INTERWAR period Munich had distinguished itself from other cities of the Reich by giving birth to the Nazi Party and becoming the Capital of the Movement. But in World War II Munich's lot was hardly different from that of other large cities in Germany: It sent its sons to the front, celebrated early victories, hoped for a quick peace, deported its Jews to death camps, grudgingly tolerated food rationing and endless collections for the war effort, imported thousands of foreign workers and slave laborers, and eventually suffered air raids that reduced much of it to ruins. Surveying the destruction in spring 1945, most Münchners, like the occupants of other wrecked cities, wondered what they had done to deserve such a fate.

In Munich's case widespread wondering about the wisdom of the war had begun early and assumed an intensity that led some Nazi leaders to question the staying power of the Capital of the Movement. Münchners became convinced that they suffered disproportionately from the demands of the war. Nazism, a homegrown product, was increasingly decried as an alien imposition. Yet even now complaints about the Nazi leadership did not translate into serious campaigns to bring the regime down.

The Curtain Falls

World War II started on a beautiful day, as if Mother Nature wanted to show that she knew something about irony. On the morning of 1 September 1939 Münchners took advantage of the prevailing "Hitler weather" to lounge in their favorite beer gardens. But on this particular morning few could enjoy the sunshine and beer; every few minutes loud-speakers announced that, as of 5:45 A.M. German troops were "returning the fire of Polish aggressors." Reports from Berlin said that Wehrmacht units were already pouring into Poland.

On the heels of the Nazi invasion of Poland, Britain and France, honoring their treaties with Warsaw, demanded that Germany cease its attack or face war with the Western powers. Hitler refused to pull back, and Paris and London declared war on 3 September.

Unlike August 1914, there was little public rejoicing over the news that Germany was at war. In Munich, as in other cities, there were no mass rallies or parades. A newspaper reporter was struck by the stillness of the streets and the serious looks on people's faces as they clustered around radios and loudspeakers. The city council tried to put a positive spin on the public mood by describing it as "grimly resolute." This attitude was preferable, said a councilman, to the "Hurrah Patriotism of 1914." Meanwhile, some citizens may have found significance in the title of a film running at the time: *The Curtain Falls*.

The mood in Munich was further dampened by news that the upcoming Oktoberfest would be canceled and preparations for the 1940 Winter Olympics in Garmisch suspended. Employees in several factories protested the Reich government's announcement on 4 September that most workers' vacations would be shortened and bonuses for overtime eliminated. The central authorities also imposed food rationing, which they were careful to describe as a "measure to ensure equality of distribution" rather than as a precaution against shortages.

The sense of foreboding that gripped Munich in the opening days of hostilities faded as local cinemas began showing newsreels of German troops racing across the plains of Poland, cutting mercilessly through Polish cavalry units. Behind the German invaders came special SS units that systematically murdered Polish Jews and intellectuals. Poland's western front had all but collapsed when the Red Army fell upon the country from the rear, completing the rout.

On 29 September, Germany's traditional autumn celebration, Bishop Meiser, Bavaria's Protestant leader, gave thanks for the "rich harvest" gleaned on the battlefields of Poland. His Catholic counterpart, Cardinal Faulhaber, ordered church bells rung when German troops entered Warsaw. Faulhaber's celebratory sermon, however, was somewhat restrained because the victim nation was Catholic, whereas Germany's partner in conquest was the world headquarters of atheistic communism.

Münchners were excited not only because the war was going well but also because they believed that it might soon be over. On the Western Front nothing much was happening; instead of blitzkrieg there was *Sitzkrieg* (sitting war). With no great losses of their own to give cause for additional sacrifices and with Poland lost, Britain and France, it seemed reasonable to assume, might want out of the war. Thus, when Munich-based Wehrmacht units rolled back into town in early October, many citizens believed that the boys were home to stay.

Hitler also assumed that the Western powers would now seek some way out of their confrontation with Germany. On 6 October he issued an appeal for peace from the Kroll Opera House in Berlin. However, he was so confident of his position that he did not offer any significant concessions. If France and Britain chose to stay at war, he warned, they would face an enemy determined to fight to the bitter end. Unlike the German leaders in World War I, he would never surrender. The Western powers, for their part, would discuss peace only if Hitler withdrew from Poland.

In Munich the public mood turned sullen as the government announced an array of new taxes, including a ten-pfennig surcharge on beer. On orders from Berlin the city's restaurants were required to serve vegetarian meals two days of the week. The standard meatless dish, a low-fat potato and carrot casserole, was seen as an abomination in this land of sausage and sauerbraten connoisseurs.

While many Münchners complained about the direction their Führer was taking them, one citizen decided to do something about it. Josef Müller, a prominent lawyer and former BVP politician, had long since given up on the Nazis as possible allies against communism. Known as *Ochsensepp* (Joe the Ox), Müller was in close contact with a cabal of military and military intelligence figures who sought to revive the army's earlier effort to bring Hitler down. Once again Ludwig Beck was a central player, but Müller's main contact was Colonel Hans Oster of the Military Intelligence Service. Oster decided to enlist Müller in a secret effort to make peace with Britain through the good offices of the Vatican. In exchange for a favorable peace, one that left Germany with its recent Austrian and Sudeten acquisitions intact, the conspirators promised to get rid of Hitler and to install a new government.

Müller was sent to Rome in late September to deliver this message to representatives of Pope Pius XII, who in turn agreed to pass it on to the British. The Bavarian lawyer was chosen because he knew the pontiff from the latter's days as papal nuncio in Munich. Accounts of Müller's meetings are sketchy, but it seems probable that he had begun to make some headway in his negotiations when they were interrupted by a much more dramatic attempt to rid Germany of its bellicose Führer.

Bomb in the Bürgerbräu

For more than a month in autumn 1939 a slight, unprepossessing young man came every evening to the Bürgerbräukeller and spent a few hours chatting in a heavy Swabian accent with one of the waitresses. His name was Johann Georg Elser, and he was an unemployed carpenter from neighboring Württemberg. A former Communist, Elser had long been an opponent of Nazism, but it was the outbreak of war that had convinced him that he must act personally to prevent a continuation of Hitler's aggression.

Each night, just before closing time at the beer hall, Elser slipped into a storeroom carrying a small suitcase. There he hid until everyone but the night watchman had left. Then he crept behind a wooden pillar next to the speaker's dais and, with tools from his case, carved out a cavity in the pillar. After each night's work he covered the hole with a small door and swept the sawdust into his suitcase. He always left just before sunrise.

It may seem odd that Elser could have operated undetected night after night in such a sensitive site; everyone knew that the Führer would soon come there to participate in the annual Beer Hall Putsch commemoration. The Munich police chief, in fact, had proposed mounting patrols in the building during the weeks preceding Hitler's appearance. Christian Weber, however, had opposed this measure, insisting that security for the event should rest solely with a handpicked brigade of Old Fighters. Told of the jurisdictional quarrel, Hitler had come down squarely for Weber. "For this meeting," he declared, "I will be protected by my Old Fighters under the direction of Christian Weber."

By early November Elser had created a chamber about eighty square centimeters in volume. Into this space, on 1 November, he carefully fitted a metal shell and a timing device. On 6 November he filled the shell with explosive powder and set the timer to go off at nine-twenty on the evening of 8 November. At that moment Adolf Hitler was expected to be standing at the Bürgerbräu podium, haranguing his followers. If the bomb did its work, the Führer, and perhaps some of his lieutenants, would be blown away.

Hitler arrived in Munich on the morning of 8 November and attended to some personal business before settling into the commemoration ritual. As always, he visited Frau Troost, who asked him why he remained so lax about security. He replied that an "inner voice" told him he was destined to stay alive until he could lead the German people to victory. When he was no longer needed, he said, he would be "called away," like Christ.

Having spent the rest of the day preparing his speech, Hitler entered the Bürgerbräukeller precisely at eight. The hall was decorated in colorful bunting and filled to capacity. The audience cheered so wildly upon his entrance that he had to wait ten minutes before starting his remarks. His address focused on the war, which he vowed again to fight to the bitter end. After a little less than an hour he suddenly stopped and stepped away from the podium. Then, instead of chatting with members of the audience, as was his usual practice, he abruptly left for the railroad station to board a special night train for Berlin.

Why did he speak so briefly and leave the hall so soon? His reasons—pious mythmakers notwithstanding—had nothing to do with some "inner intimation" that his life might be in danger. He wanted to get back to Berlin as soon as possible to expedite preparations for the war in the West. This was no time to be socializing with the Old Fighters in Munich, an ordeal he had come to hate anyway. He could have flown back to Berlin on the following morning, but persistent fogs in the region made a timely takeoff uncertain. He had therefore ordered his special train to be ready for departure at nine-thirty.

Eight minutes after Hitler and his party left the Bürgerbräukeller, Elser's bomb went off. The explosion obliterated the speaker's dais and brought down the gallery and roof overhead. Seven members of the audience (six Nazis and a waitress) were instantly killed; another victim died a few days later. Sixty-three people were wounded, sixteen of them severely.

The Führer and his entourage heard a distant boom as they neared the railroad station. Thinking nothing of it, they boarded their train and departed as scheduled. Many Münchners, on the other hand, mistook the blast and sirens for a signal that the war was over, and they let out a collective cheer.

Hitler did not learn about his narrow escape until his train reached Nuremberg, where Goebbels got out to run some errands. He returned with a telegram from Munich, which he tremblingly handed to the Führer. Hitler first thought that the bomb report was a joke, but he verified its accuracy with a telephone call to Gauleiter Wagner. "Now I am completely content," he cried. "The fact that I left the Bürgerbräukeller earlier than usual is a corroboration of Providence's intention to let me reach my goal." Goebbels agreed. "He stands after all under the protection of the Almighty." he jotted in his diary. "He will not die until his mission is completed."

The smoke had hardly cleared at the Bürgerbräukeller when the police began combing through the pile of rubble, looking for remnants of the device that had nearly done in the Führer. Finding bits of metal casing and clock fragments, the authorities immediately launched an investigation into their origins. Little did they know, as they started this potentially laborious process, that they already had their man.

As his bomb was ticking away its final minutes, Elser tried to slip illegally over the German-Swiss border at Constance. He was caught by German border guards and subjected to a cursory search, which yielded a Red Fighter pin, bomb fuse material, and a picture postcard of the Bürgerbräukeller. Suspecting that the nervous young man was a courier for Red terrorists, the border guards delivered him to the Gestapo, which took him to Munich for questioning.

Elser quickly confessed to the deed. His interrogators, however, feared that he might be a decoy whose role was to deflect them from the real culprit. The items found in his pockets, after all, seemed almost too good to be true. The authorities did not change their mind on this score until questioning of Bürgerbräukeller personnel established that Elser had indeed been frequenting the hall before the bombing.

In his confession Elser insisted that he had acted entirely alone. The authorities doubted that an unemployed carpenter could have built such a sophisticated device and hidden it next to Hitler's podium all by himself. Early speculation regarding possible accomplices ranged from the Communists to the Bavarian legitimists. But on further reflection these forces seemed too puny for such a bold and complex plot, and the Nazi leadership, from Hitler on down, saw the hand of the British Secret

Service at work. They concluded that the British had contacted Otto Strasser, Hitler's old rival (now living in Switzerland) and enlisted his support in their effort to kill the Führer. Strasser in turn was believed to have used Elser as a stooge.

To corroborate this conclusion, Berlin decided to kidnap two British agents and subject them to interrogation. On the day after the Munich bombing, Germany's counterintelligence agency lured British agents Major Richard H. Stevens and Captain Sigismund Payne Best to the Dutch-German border by promising them a meeting with some dissident German generals. Arriving at the Dutch town of Venlo, Stevens and Best were overwhelmed and spirited across the German border. Under prolonged interrogation, they denied that the British had had any role in the assassination attempt. Nonetheless, Goebbels's propaganda machine blamed Britain for the attack.

While the Nazi regime sought to pin blame for the bombing on the British, a host of observers, German and foreign alike, assumed that the Nazis themselves had staged the incident in order to win sympathy for the Führer. "Most of us think it smells of another Reichstag fire," wrote William Shirer in his diary. "My own opinion is that the Bürgerbräu explosion was a job inspired by Goebbels and executed by Himmler in order to make the Germans hate the British," wrote the Reuters correspondent Ernest Pope. Friedrich Reck-Malleczewen, the embittered Bavarian conservative, observed in his journal: "No one doubts that the whole display is a bit of pyrotechnics set off by the Nazis themselves. The fireworks cost nearly a dozen lives, but they serve to whip up hatred against the English and to provide Herr Hitler with the halo of a martyr." According to a popular joke, the Bürgerbräu bomb had actually claimed "sixty million *Verkohlte*" (carbonized ones, but also slang for "bamboozled").

The Nazified press in Munich was quick to join in the chorus of outrage and to express its gratitude that the Führer had not been carbonized. The *Münchener Neueste Nachrichten* editorialized: "The capacity of the human heart is inadequate to fathom this most base and revolting crime. Fortunately, our heartfelt relief descends like a curtain before the pile of ruins. We give thanks to Providence for sparing our Führer and saving Germany from an inconceivable national tragedy." Not to be outdone, Cardinal Faulhaber sent Hitler a congratulatory telegram and ordered a Te Deum sung in the Frauenkirche "to thank Divine Providence in the name of the archdiocese for the Führer's fortunate escape."

Reck-Malleczewen, on the other hand, wrote in his diary: "There are, I think, probably no more than a thousand native Münchners who are not dejected because the [assassination] attempt has failed." Shortly after the bombing a secretary in a Munich legal office informed the Gestapo about a conversation she had had with a local salesman: "He spoke with me about the incident in the Bürgerbräukeller. I expressed my serious regret that such a thing could have happened. Laughing, he replied that many businesspeople in town regretted that the bomb had not gone off earlier. He insisted that one could hear this view expressed openly in all kinds of shops." This seems doubtful, for Munich was not so tolerant of political heresy that its citizens could go around openly wishing their Führer dead.

Whatever the majority of Münchners may have thought about their Führer's escape, the Nazi leadership understood that security needed to be improved. Weber and his Old Fighters would no longer be in charge of protecting Hitler at the Beer Hall Putsch reunions; that task now devolved to the SS. Hitler stopped moving around Munich with only a pair of bodyguards; reluctantly, he also curtailed his visits to known haunts like the Osteria Bavaria. At his apartment building residents could no longer gain entrance with their own keys; now they had to be admitted by guards. Regulations governing the production and issuance of explosives were also tightened.

Heightened vigilance on the part of the authorities undermined ongoing plans by anti-Nazi conspirators in the Military Intelligence Service to kill Hitler. Hans Oster was no longer able to get explosives for his colleague Erich Kordt, who hoped to blow up the Führer. Thus Elser's bold stroke in Munich, heroic as it was, reduced the likelihood that Hitler could be eliminated before he was able to do more damage.

And what of the lonely carpenter who had come so close to achieving his mission? After a long interrogation in Munich, Elser was moved to Sachsenhausen, where he was subjected to more questioning. Later he was sent to Dachau and housed in a section of the camp reserved for special prisoners. There he was allowed to set up a carpentry shop and to build a replica of his Bürgerbräu bomb, just to show that he could do it.

Why the regime kept him locked up, rather than execute him, remains something of a mystery. It has been suggested that Hitler, thinking that documents from a vanquished England might prove Elser's partnership with Britain, wanted to stage a show trial after the war. It has also been argued that the Führer, ever superstitious, came to believe that as long as his would-be assassin stayed alive, he too would cheat death. Whatever the explanation, Elser ceased to be useful to Hitler and the Nazis once their own days were numbered. On 9 April 1945, twenty days before the liberation of the Dachau camp, Elser was murdered.

"Munich Has Joined the Front"

Johann Georg Elser's bomb was the only high explosive to do significant damage in Munich in the early phase of World War II. The first enemy bombers to appear over Germany did not penetrate as far as Munich, and they dropped not bombs but leaflets accusing the Nazi government of leading the German people into an unnecessary conflict.

Of course, Hitler had always considered war necessary to his mission. He accompanied his invasion of the Low Countries with air attacks on selected cities, most notably Rotterdam, which the Luftwaffe pulverized in order to terrorize the Dutch into surrender.

The first Allied attacks against German targets came in response to the smashing of Rotterdam. Winston Churchill, Britain's new prime minister, ordered British planes to strike industrial targets in the Ruhr. Shortly thereafter, on 4 June 1940, the British extended their campaign to the South, including Munich. However, because the Isar city lay at the outer edge of the bombers' range, they had to drop their loads immediately and hurry home. Most of the bombs landed outside the city limits. One carved a crater near the BMW factory in the suburb of Allach; another damaged a farmhouse near the new airport at Riem.

Münchners had timely warning of the attack via air-raid sirens, which went off at 12:45 A.M. However, many did not bother to go to the shelters; others failed to abide by the blackout regulations. It seems that the government's earlier civil defense preparations, which had mixed dire warnings with promises of adequate protection, left many citizens confused or blasé about the threat that faced them.

The first raid's ineffectiveness confirmed such feelings of false security. The next evening many stayed in their beer gardens as a French bomber appeared over the city and dropped about thirty bombs before going down in the outskirts of town. The bombs damaged a few buildings and injured one person.

The skies over Munich remained clear throughout the rest of the summer and early autumn, as the Royal Air Force, following the fall of France in June, concentrated on defending British air bases against Luftwaffe attacks designed to clear the way for a planned invasion of Britain. On 18 June Hitler received his new ally, Mussolini, in Munich. The two dictators drove through streets filled with swastika flags and cheering citizens. Münchners were proud of the Wehrmacht's successes yet hopeful that the defeat of France would convince the British to reach a settlement with Germany. Even Churchill's insistence that Britain would continue fighting for as long as it took to defeat Germany did not generate much consternation, for there was confidence that the Luftwaffe would soon force a surrender.

In the meantime, the Reich's leaders promoted culture to boost morale. As Robert Ley, who ran the Strength through Joy program, put it in the summer of 1940, "We all know the old saying: 'When the cannons speak the muses are silent.' [But] in the new Germany lyre and sword belong together."

This was especially true in the Capital of German Art, whose mission now was to sharpen the German sword with inspirational works of the lyre, pen, and brush. As in World War I, Munich's opera and philharmonic orchestra mounted patriotic performances by German composers. The city's famous theaters, recognized by the regime as "a weapon of the intellectual struggle," performed works "worthy of the proud tradition of the Capital of the Movement." The Great German Art Exhibition, which opened as usual in the House of German Art in late July, featured in 1940 a portrait of the Führer standing on the "Westwall" in the pose of a conquering warrior. This and other cultural contributions caused the *Völkischer Beobachter* to gush that Munich was now more than ever "the heart of the Reich."

In addition to works of high culture, Münchners could enjoy a small circus, replete with a Ferris wheel, shooting gallery, and bratwurst stand. It was not exactly an Oktoberfest, but one could almost believe that there was no war in progress.

This changed abruptly on 8 November 1940, when, as usual, Hitler came to town for the annual Beer Hall Putsch commemoration. Just as he was finishing his speech in the Löwenbräukeller (the Bürgerbräu had been too damaged by Elser's bomb to use), twenty British bombers attacked the city. They managed to destroy twenty structures, kill one person, and injure ten. Compared with recent raids in the West and North, this was not very impressive, but it certainly embarrassed the regime's air defense forces. Hitler was livid over the damage, ordering as revenge the terror bombing of Coventry.

Rattled by the attack, many Münchners directed their anger more at their own government than at the British. Often they expressed their anxiety in jokes with Air Marshal Göring as their butt. Göring should adopt the name Tenglemann (a grocery store chain), it was said, because in every large German city he had a *Niederlage,* a term meaning both "branch" and "defeat." Another joke had Labor Front leader Robert Ley admonishing Göring to speak to the Münchners to lift their spirits. "I can't do that," says Göring, "because I haven't been able to prevent enemy planes from breaching our defenses. Your lot is much easier, Ley, for you've promised the people sunny and open dwellings, and that's what they're getting."

With only a few of their buildings as yet ventilated, most Münchners were still more concerned about economic and social pressures than bombs. In winter 1941 the regime lowered the daily meat ration from five hundred grams to four hundred. At the same time it raised penalties for hoarding and black-marketeering. The local SD (SS Security Police) reported a decline in morale among workers as the result of lower food, clothing, and coal allotments. Meanwhile, factory owners complained that the increasingly voracious draft was swallowing up all their skilled labor.

Despite its ideological commitment to keeping women at home, the regime sought to fill vacancies in the workplace with female labor. In Munich the percentage of women in the work force rose from 45.7 in 1938 to 52.7 in 1940—the first year in the city's history in which more women were employed than men.

It quickly became apparent, however, that the infusion of women into the work force could not meet the demand for labor. In Munich, as in other large cities of the Reich, POWs, Jews, Gypsies, and foreign civilians were pressed into service to keep the factories running. By August 1940 19,711 foreign workers, 3,190 of them female, were employed in Munich alone. Housed in primitive barracks, they were paid subsistence wages and denied access to virtually all public facilities. Many Münchners complained about the growing number of foreigners in their midst, whom they blamed for every petty crime.

The groundswell of discontent over wartime pressures and privations, though still muted, belied the image of total commitment and social harmony that the regime so diligently cultivated. This image became even more frayed when Nazi zealots, acting on their own, decided in spring 1941 to revive the regime's anticlerical campaign, which Hitler had suspended in 1939 in the interest of national solidarity.

The new campaign was prefaced by a small but telling move on the part of Nazi Party secretary Martin Bormann. In April 1941 Bormann sponsored a new edition of Oskar Panizza's anti-Catholic tract *Der deutsche Michel und der römische Papst.* Bormann sent a copy of the book to Mayor Fiehler, telling him that it had "the greatest meaning for the present era." Fiehler heartily agreed. Damned as a blasphemer and pornographer a half century earlier, Panizza had finally found favor with Munich's rulers.

While Panizza's lurid tale of the papacy's crimes against Germany was making the rounds in Munich, Gauleiter Adolf Wagner struck the major blow in Nazism's new Kulturkampf. On 23 April 1941 he issued a decree ordering that crucifixes on school walls be replaced by "pictures suited to the present time."

A cry of protest rang out across Bavaria, strongest in the countryside but audible also in Munich. Cardinal Faulhaber issued a pastoral letter condemning the decree, which he said clashed with Germany's Christian traditions. Ritter von Epp, still the titular head of Bavaria, protested to Hans Heinrich Lammers, chief of the Reich Chancellory, that Wagner's action was provoking demonstrations, strikes, and "unrest in the entire province."

Hitler, kept abreast of the situation by Lammers, ordered the crucifix decree rescinded on 28 August. The Führer was so angry at Wagner that he threatened to send him to Dachau if he did anything so "stupid" again. It should be emphasized, however, that Hitler was upset not because he had any sympathy for the Catholics but because he considered this the wrong time to alienate them.

The crucifix affair is one of the more revealing moments in the history of National Socialism in Bavaria. It raises the question of what might have happened had people protested so strongly against other dimensions of Nazi policy. But this upheaval, like earlier, less serious expressions of noncompliance, was resolved with only minor changes in direction. The people who protested Wagner's decree were for the most part prepared to back the regime in more crucial areas of policy. It also seems clear that the protest was successful largely because it attacked a measure that many leading Nazis, including Hitler, found inadvisable under existing circumstances.

Existing circumstances now included war against the Soviet Union, for Hitler had launched Operation Barbarossa, his invasion of Russia, on 22 June 1941. Unlike the Ribbentrop-Molotov pact, this move was ideologically consistent with Nazism, which had always claimed to be the archenemy of Bolshevism. As an anti-Communist crusade Operation Barbarossa could count on considerable support across Germany, including Munich. Cardinal Faulhaber embraced the enterprise, though he could not resist pointing out the contradiction between the regime's anti-Christian policies and its call for God's assistance in the new campaign.

Even resolutely anti-Communist Münchners, however, feared that Hitler had now taken on too much. A bank teller recalled that upon hearing the news of Barbarossa, he got "cold chills despite the summer heat." Reports of spectacular progress in the early phase of the campaign could not assuage fears that Hitler's armies might eventually suffer the same fate as Napoleon's in 1812 (the French emperor's army, most Münchners knew, had contained a large contingent of Bavarians).

In addition to anxieties regarding the fate of the Wehrmacht on the plains of Russia, Münchners, like their counterparts elsewhere in the Reich, faced much greater challenges at home because of this dramatic expansion of the conflict. Increasing demands for fresh troops generated tensions between recruiting authorities and civilian officials seeking to keep skilled workers in their jobs. Wehrmacht recruiters complained that potentates in Munich, including Wagner and Fiehler, often intervened to protect civilian jobs that were not crucial to the war effort. They cited in particular Wagner's refusal to allow drafting of employees from a ladies' glove factory that the Gauleiter maintained was a bulwark of the local economy.

A struggle also developed over the apportionment of POWs and foreign workers. Mayor Fiehler complained bitterly that Munich was not getting its share of forced labor because the Berlin authorities were directing most of the workers to the North. Fiehler also fought to gain control over the housing of foreign workers, hoping thereby to expand the availability of valuable slave labor to Munich producers. These internecine battles were reminiscent of the Munich-Berlin disputes during the First World War, with the Bavarian Nazis now playing the role of the aggrieved states' righters.

In addition to huge numbers of men, the Russian campaign consumed vast quantities of matériel. To meet this challenge, Berlin stepped up its collections on the home front of supplies and raw materials. In another echo of World War I the regime commandeered church bells for ammunition; all but the most valuable bells were to be turned over to the Reich Office for Metals by April 1942. As the Wehrmacht became bogged down in the Russian winter, a call went out for skis and boots. The collection focused on Munich, capital of German winter sports. Retailers were required to hand over their entire stocks, while private owners were requested to give up their ski equipment in exchange for a pledge from Reichssportführer Tschammer und Osten to return it after the war. Münchners contributed a total of 43,250 pairs of skis and 6,940 pairs of boots.

The skis, however, did not prove very useful on the Eastern Front, and the fancy boards often wound up as fuel in makeshift ovens. Meanwhile, many of the books sent from home met an even less dignified fate; as one soldier put it, they "performed the most necessary of services" in field latrines.

Although no one in Munich was going hungry yet as a result of the war, people once again had to put up with a proliferation of ersatz foods. Reck-Malleczewen complained in September 1941:

> Sugar is now made out of fir-wood pulp, sausage out of beechwood pulp, and the beer is a stinking brew made of whey. Yeast is made out of a chemical, and marmalade is colored to fool people into thinking it is the real thing. The same for butter, except that the coloring matter here also contains a vile and indigestible substance poisonous to the liver and doubtless responsible for the biliousness so common today. Everyone's eyes are yellow, and if I am to believe friends of mine who are doctors, the incidence of cancer has doubled in the last four years.

Reck was convinced that bad food and material shortages were causing a precipitous decline in personal hygiene and standards of decorum. Because of "fermentation from pulpy bread," he claimed, no one was bothering "to hold back his wind," and the air in the cafés was "pestilential." Meanwhile, the "daily hunt for immediate necessities" was producing "a slackness in behavior, such as would have been impossible even a short time ago." On the other hand, he fumed, Munich's Nazi masters were living high off the hog. Gauleiter Wagner, wherever he went, ordered animals slaughtered "to meet the needs of his entourage of drunkards and felons."

Although the Reich's massive expenditure of resources in the Russian campaign left the home territory more vulnerable than ever to air attacks, Munich managed, even three years into the war, to escape the large-scale raids that were smashing the great cities of the West and North. Some folks thought the city's beauty had something to do with this. As a popular rhyme of the day had it, *"Bomben auf Berlin, Rosen auf Wien, München wollen wir schonen, da wollen wir später wohnen* [Bombs on Berlin, roses on Vienna, Munich we'll spare, for later we want to live there]." No wonder Goebbels was worried about morale in Munich, convinced that its population could not withstand bombing with the same fortitude that people in the North were showing.

In any event, Munich's days of relative tranquillity were numbered. On 2 February 1942 the RAF appointed an aggressive new commander, Arthur ("Bomber") Harris, who pushed the rapid development of new bombers with longer ranges and higher payloads. The Wellington III and Halifax III planes that began rolling off British assembly lines were capable of doing vast damage to any city in the Reich, including Munich. Harris immediately added that city to a list of fifty priority targets for the next phase of the war. At about the same time Britain's powerful new ally, the United States, established a bomber command in England. It would be some time before the Americans could mount extensive air operations against the Reich, but the handwriting was now on Munich walls.

On the night of 29 August Harris sent his bombers on an ambitious raid against the Capital of the Movement. The planes dropped high explosive and incendiary bombs in the very heart of the city, causing many fires. The human casualties were surprisingly low—one death and four injuries—but Munich's fire department had difficulty contending with the blazes. Excited crowds gathered around the conflagrations. Some people mocked the government for its promises of protection. "Everyone expects now that there will be heavier raids in the future," wrote a woman in her diary.

And heavier raids came. On 20 September 1942 the British mounted their largest and deadliest sortie yet against Munich. Sixty-eight bombers participated in the raid, which killed 140 people, injured 404, and rendered 6,069 people homeless. While still not as devastating as the attacks on the North, this was horrible enough for all who had to live through it. Ludwig Rosenberger, whose *Münchner Kriegstagebuch* (Munich War Diary) provides a good eyewitness account of the bombing, wrote of the September raid: "The air pressure was terrible, our ears were half deaf. The British planes buzzed above our roofs like giant hornets. One of them fired its machine guns against the firefighters. It was utter hell for an entire hour." A lady who had been out of town during the attack returned the next day to find her entire street "a sea of destruction." Visiting the city a couple of weeks later, the art historian Wilhelm Hausenstein found it to resemble "a strange grisaille [gray-toned painting]—the houses dark gray masses before an indistinct pearl gray sky."

Upon learning of the big September raid against his former hometown, Thomas Mann, Munich's most famous literary exile, was not in the least sympathetic. He observed bitterly in his diary: "The idiotic place has historically deserved it." To a friend he wrote: "[Munich] is a citadel of stupidity."

On 23 September the Nazi authorities sought to make propagandistic capital out of Munich's misery by staging a mass funeral for the air-raid victims at the North Cemetery. One hundred and eight coffins draped in Reich flags stood in somber rows; above them loomed a giant wreath sent by Hitler, along with a message that these casualties were as much martyrs for the cause as the soldiers who had died at the front. The featured speaker was Munich's new gauleiter, Paul Giesler, who had replaced Adolf Wagner following the latter's incapacitating stroke in June 1942. The brother of architect Hermann Giesler, Gauleiter Giesler was not as corrupt as Wagner but even more fanatical. A would-be Pericles, he tried to transmute grief into glory by telling relatives that they should be proud of their loved ones since their sacrifice meant that Munich had now "joined the front."

Some Münchners may have been proud of this accomplishment, but there was growing bitterness over the fact that the war had finally come to them in all its fury. They saw themselves as victims not just of British bombers but of an "alien" regime, a new "Prussian occupation." In letters to Ritter von Epp, citizens complained of having been delivered to a "pack of hangmen." However, the authors of these complaints rarely gave any indication of being prepared to act against the regime; apparently they were content to wait for rescue by outside forces. According to Reck, the Anglo-American landings in North Africa in November 1942 were welcomed as "the first warm wind blowing over the ice."

White Rose in a Brown City

While some Münchners were looking to the Allies for delivery, one tiny group of dedicated anti-Nazis was convinced that Germany could be saved from total destruction only if the natives took matters into their own hands. In the summer of 1942 this group set about secretly printing and distributing incendiary anti-Nazi leaflets. The manifestos, calling for the forceful overthrow of Nazism, were laced with quotations from Ecclesiastes, Novalis, Goethe, Lao Tzu, and Aristotle. They were signed "The White Rose."

For all their erudite allusions, the White Rose leaflets were direct in their message. The first to appear (June 1942) spoke of the shame that "every honest German" must feel at being ruled by "an irresponsible clique that has yielded to base instincts." It demanded that every person "conscious of his responsibility as a member of Christian and Western civilization offer *resistance* [to] forestall the spread of this atheistic war machine before it is too late. . . ." The second leaflet condemned Nazism as a cancer that had spread through Germany because the nation's intellectuals had "fled to their cellars" rather than confront this malignant assault on human intelligence. Citing the "known facts" that "300,000 Jews had been murdered in Poland since the invasion" and "the entire Polish aristocratic youth" sent into slave labor or SS bordellos, it demanded that ordinary Germans recognize that their own apathy in the face of such monstrous crimes represented "a *complicity* in guilt." The third leaflet called for sabotage of war industry and Nazi communications, while the fourth admonished its readers that God had given ordinary people the strength to smite the "Anti-Christ" that was Hitler. "We are your bad conscience. The White Rose will not leave you in peace."

Just who were these pamphleteers who were so determined to poke their righteous thorns in the flabby flesh of the Bavarian body politic?

Hans Scholl, the central figure in the group, hailed from the town of Ulm in Württemberg. He had joined the Hitler Youth as a teenager and served as flag bearer of his unit when it attended the Nuremberg party rally in 1934. However, he soon grew disgusted with the group's rigid conformity and was appalled when one of his favorite teachers was sent off to a concentration camp. Soon he was briefly incarcerated for joining Die Jüngerschaft, a youth group whose passions for romantic poetry and Expressionist painting struck the Nazis as dangerous. By the time Hans arrived in Munich to study medicine in 1939, he was open to anti-Nazi impulses, which he found in the teachings of Karl Muth, editor of the conservative Catholic magazine *Hochland*, and in the writings of Theodor Haecker, a Catholic philosopher banned by the Nazis in 1935. Under the influence of these men, Hans's thinking took on a sharper religious cast as well as a distinct anti-Prussian tone. Like many South Germans, he came to associate Nazism with "militaristic Prussia," and he tended to overlook its Bavarian origins.

At the university Scholl was drafted into a company of medical students who performed occasional corpsman duties at the front. Here he encountered Alexander Schmorell, an elegant young man whose father was a prominent Munich physician, his mother the daughter of a Russian Orthodox priest. Born in Russia, Alexander maintained contact with that country through a nanny (his mother died when he was an infant) and the works of Dostoevsky, Gogol, and Pushkin. He attended a Russian Orthodox church in Munich and played the balalaika. As a Christian he had no use for Stalin's regime, but Hitler's brutal invasion of the USSR greatly pained him, helping to drive him into opposition. Like Hans, he harbored a profound ethical disgust for National Socialism, which was sharpened by discussions with Muth and Haecker.

Alexander introduced Hans to Christoph Probst, another dissident in the Munich medical student company. Born in Murnau (Kandinsky's adopted town), Probst was the son of an independently wealthy art connoisseur who regarded the Nazis as a pack of vulgarians. Young Probst attended various progressive schools, where he cultivated a love of literature, music, and philosophy, all passions he shared with the other White Rose students. Unlike them, however, he married young and started a family while still a student. An easygoing fellow, he was nonetheless grimly determined to ensure that his children did not come of age under Adolf Hitler.

A relative latecomer to the White Rose group was Willi Graf, who arrived in Munich in 1942 to continue his medical studies. Born in the Saar, Graf was a devout Catholic and former member of one of the religious youth groups dissolved by the Nazis. Participation in Hitler's invasion of France hardened Graf's antagonism toward the Nazi regime, but what pushed him into active opposition was his service in the Munich medical company on the genocidal Eastern Front. There, along with Scholl and Schmorell, he witnessed many German atrocities. He wrote his sister that he had seen things that he could not repress. "Every individual," he said, bore "responsibility" for what was transpiring in the East; everyone had "the duty to overcome inner doubts and take decisive steps." Though some of his later letters showed that he too had occasional doubts about the efficacy of resistance, he did not allow them to deter him from the path he had chosen.

Schmorell, Probst, and Hans Scholl were already writing their first anti-Nazi leaflets when Hans's twenty-one-year-old sister, Sophie, arrived in Munich to study biology and philosophy. She was an attractive young woman, earnestly high-minded but also full of fun. When she discovered what her brother and his friends were up to, she was horrified because she understood how dangerous this enterprise was. Nonetheless, after overcoming her qualms, Sophie became part of the conspiracy, furthering the cause by stealing precious paper supplies from university offices and smuggling them out under her blouse. She also joined the others in the even more dangerous business of carrying leaflets by train to other German cities. Her motivation was similar to her brother's: She could not stand by while the Nazis committed barbarous crimes in the name of her country.

Whenever they could, Sophie and the other White Rose students attended the lectures of Professor Kurt Huber on the history of philosophy. Rare among his faculty colleagues, Huber hazarded criticism of the Nazis through barbed asides and pointed quotations from out-of-favor humanists like Spinoza. The professor, however, had come rather late to his critical stance. Trained as a folklorist, he had initially been attracted to the Nazis' *völkisch* critique of industrial modernity, urbanization, and "cultural Bolshevism." But as the Nazis began attacking the churches, repressing regional idiosyncrasies, and industrializing the nation for war, Huber concluded that they were little better than brown Bolsheviks. As a native Württemberger, moreover, Huber became convinced that the Nazis embodied a peculiarly northern decadence, one whose destructive designs could best be thwarted by a revolt of the healthy South. Like many disgruntled conservatives, in other words, Huber hated the Nazis at least partly because they had proved to be false friends, betrayers of the old elites and their preindustrial dreams. What separated him from most of his academic colleagues was his willingness to vent his dim view of the regime, though he hoped that Germany's hallowed tradition of academic freedom would protect him from retribution. In any event, his lectures so impressed the White Rose students that they invited him to participate in their informal discussion evenings. After accepting their invitation, Huber soon began helping them write their leaflets, thus crossing the line from mentor to fellow conspirator.

The conspiracy took on added urgency as the Allied forces, in late 1942 and early 1943, seemed to be turning the tide against the Wehrmacht. The Anglo-Americans were advancing in North Africa while the Soviets encircled an entire German army at Stalingrad. To the White Rose students, it was now imperative for the Germans to free themselves before the Allies did it for them. Thus in January 1943, after a hiatus of several months, the White Rose prepared a new leaflet and began slipping it under doors and into mailboxes. It again urged its recipients to "cast off the cloak of indifference you have wrapped around you. Make the decision *before* it is too late!" Otherwise Germany would be "forever the nation which is hated and rejected by all mankind." Once freed of Hitler, Germany could rebuild itself as a "sound federal state." "A one-sided Prussian militarism must never again be allowed to assume power."

A few days later an event occurred in Munich that led the conspirators to believe that somebody (aside from the Gestapo) was paying attention to their message. On 13 January, in the auditorium of the German Museum, Gauleiter Paul Giesler delivered a lengthy address marking the 470th anniversary of the university. His audience consisted of professors, distinguished graduates, and hundreds of students. Many of the latter were off-duty soldiers who were allowed to attend classes while convalescing from wounds; present also were young women who (like Sophie Scholl) could study as long as they worked part-time in armaments factories. Displaying an insensitivity notable even by Nazi standards, Giesler took this opportunity to remind the students that they should be happy to be studying while their peers were bleeding for them on the front. Turning to the female students, he proposed that they would be better employed by making babies for the Führer than by taking up precious university space. If they were not pretty enough to find partners on their own, he added, he would be glad to assign one of his adjutants to this patriotic service, and he could promise the girls that they would have a "fulfilling experience." When he paused to allow appreciation for his wit, the students began to boo and hiss. The women in the gallery, Sophie among them, took off their shoes and beat them against the railings. The din was so loud that Giesler had difficulty resuming his speech. As soon as he was finished, the students sprang from their seats and rushed for the exits. SS guards tried to hold them back, but most escaped, rushing into the streets giddy with delight at having shouted down the Gauleiter.

Sophie brought a riveting account of the "uprising" to her fellow conspirators, who took it as a sign that Munich was finally stirring. Shortly thereafter, in early February, the town was rocked by news that General Friedrich Paulus had surrendered his entire army at Stalingrad. The White Rose believed that this disaster must turn even the most apathetic burgher into a rebel. To help push the people over the brink, Hans Scholl and his friends went into the streets at night and painted anti-Nazi slogans on the walls of public buildings. "Freedom!" and "Down with Hitler!" proclaimed the graffiti. This was the students' most brazen and reckless act yet; it suggested a kind of drunkenness, fueled by the drug of revolution. At the same time, the students (helped by Professor Huber) drafted another leaflet. Directed primarily to the university youth of Munich, it read in part:

> Fellow Fighters in the Resistance!
> Shaken and broken, our people behold the loss of the men of Stalingrad. Three hundred and thirty thousand German men have been senselessly and irresponsibly driven to death and destruction by the inspired strategy of our World War I Private First Class. Führer, we thank you!
> The German people are in ferment. Will we continue to entrust the fate of our armies to a dilettante? Do we want to sacrifice the rest of German youth to the base ambitions of a party clique? No, never! The day of reckoning has come—the reckoning of German youth with the most abominable tyrant our people have ever been forced to endure. In the name of German youth we demand restitution by Adolf Hitler's state of our personal freedom, the most precious treasure that we have, out of which he has swindled us in the most miserable way. . . .
> Our people stand ready to rebel against the National Socialist enslavement of Europe in a fervent new breakthrough of freedom and honor.

The White Rose ran off more than three thousand copies of this leaflet, too many to distribute in the usual way. Thus on 18 February 1943 Hans and Sophie Scholl took a batch of the flyers to the university and spread them on the stairs, window ledges, and railings of the main building's central hall. The area was empty of students at that moment, since all were in class. But just as the Scholls were finishing their work, a custodian picked up one of the leaflets and read it with horror. Then he looked up to see other flyers drifting down from the second story, a veritable rain of treason. A young man and woman were leaning over the railing above. The custodian, a loyal SA man, shouted for them to stay where they were, as they obediently did. He ran up the stairs, collared Hans and Sophie, and led them to the office of the rector, who belonged to the SS.

Questioned by hastily summoned Gestapo officers, Hans and Sophie claimed to know nothing of the leaflets. The fact that they had not tried to run away seemed to speak in their favor. But in searching through Hans's pockets, the Gestapo found a different anti-Nazi leaflet (written by Christoph Probst). A subsequent search of Hans's apartment revealed more incriminating material. Tragically, this led to the apprehension of the rest of the White Rose inner circle, as well as to the arrest of local supporters and some contacts in other cities.

The Gestapo was relieved by this turn of events, for it had been extremely frustrated by its inability to track down the conspirators. Especially embarrassing was the fact that the treachery was centered in the Capital of the Movement, the symbolic heart of Nazism. The Gestapo worried that if it did not squelch the outbreak there, other cities might become infected. There were already reports of White Rose leaflets turning up at universities in Freiburg and Hamburg.

Hoping to learn everything it could about the conspiracy, the Gestapo took the Scholls, and later Christoph Probst, to its headquarters in the former Wittelsbach Palace for interrogation. Trying to save his or her friends, each of the young people took full responsibility for the action.

Four days after their arrest the Scholls and Christoph Probst were tried in Munich before Judge Roland Freisler, the dreaded president of the People's Court, who had hurried down from Berlin to take personal charge of the case. Infamous for his fanaticism and brutality, Freisler could barely contain his rage when Sophie Scholl calmly told him that "Many people are thinking as we have spoken and written, only they don't dare do so openly." She added: "You know as well as we do that the war is lost. You are just too cowardly to admit it." Unwilling to stand for such impertinence and unable to extract incriminating information about other White Rose activists, Freisler and his Munich colleagues found the defendants guilty of high treason. They were stripped of their German citizenship and sentenced to die at the guillotine, the most dishonorable form of execution.

On that very afternoon, 22 February 1943, Hans and Sophie Scholl and Christoph Probst were transferred to the execution cell at Stadelheim

Prison. Contrary to the rules, the Scholls were allowed a brief visit from their parents, but Probst was forbidden to see his wife or children. Hans's father told him that he and his sister would "go down in history" and that there was "such a thing as justice in spite of all this." Probst, having been raised outside the church, was baptized. He told his friends that in a few minutes they would "meet in eternity." Sophie was the first to be led to the block. Before going, she accepted a piece of candy from a guard; "I've forgotten lunch," she said. Hans called out, "Long live freedom," as the knife came down. The executioner, who was later employed by Bavaria's American occupiers to hang leading Nazis, commented that he had never seen people meet their end so bravely.

The following day a brief notice of the trial and executions appeared in the Munich newspapers. Having "sought to undermine the fighting will of the German people," said the notice, the condemned had fully deserved "a quick and dishonorable death."

A few days later pro-Nazi students at the University of Munich held a rally on the campus to express their agreement with the sentences. They also praised the custodian who had cornered the culprits in their act of treachery. Otherwise there was no popular response to the execution of these young prophets of humanistic and Christian resistance. Munich's church officials maintained a discreet silence.

Other trials and executions of White Rose figures followed in subsequent months, also without much fanfare or echo. Professor Huber, Alexander Schmorell, and Willi Graf were tried in April 1943 and sentenced to death. At the same trial an additional eleven defendants—people who had helped out with the conspiracy in various ways—were sentenced to prison terms ranging from one year to life. Huber and Schmorell were executed on 13 July 1943. Graf followed on 12 October. In a last note to his sister and mother, Graf wrote, "For us death is not the end, but the beginning of true life, and I die with faith in God's will and mercy."

With respect to the immediate environment in which the White Rose figures met their untimely death, one must conclude that though these courageous resisters drew some of their inspiration from the Munich scene, they were in a more fundamental sense estranged from it. They overestimated both the degree of anti-Nazi sentiment there and the willingness of their academic peers, not to mention the rest of the townsfolk, to act against the regime. Ultimately their decision to put their lives on the line for their convictions was an individual one, not reducible to sociological determinants. Like Johann Georg Elser, they were lonely resisters who suffered a lonely martyrdom.

Yet news of their deeds and executions was soon spread around the world by opponents of Hitler. Helmut James von Moltke, an international lawyer who hosted a discussion group of anti-Nazis on his East Prussian estate at Kreisau, smuggled a copy of the White Rose's last leaflet to the bishop of Norway, who sent it on to London. That summer (1943) the RAF dropped a batch of the leaflets over the Ruhr. On 23 June 1943 Thomas Mann took up the White Rose story during his regular BBC broadcast to Germany. The students' courageous act gave him hope that Germany's educated youth might someday lead "a revolution of a thoroughly purifying nature that will enable the country to find its reunion with the future world commonwealth of nations."

The "Final Solution" in Munich

One of the early White Rose leaflets, as mentioned, made reference to three hundred thousand Jews killed by the Nazis in Poland. The murder of the Jews, in Poland and elsewhere, was the last stage of a barbaric process that took on ever more brutal forms once Germany began to expand to the East. As in the earlier phases of Jewish persecution, Munich provided a key scene to the concluding act of this genocidal tragedy.

With the outbreak of war Jews from the Bavarian countryside had begun flocking into the larger cities. In many cases they were forced to do so since their home villages expelled them. In Munich, which in 1939 had a Jewish population of about four thousand, the incoming Jews hoped to find relative anonymity. This intent quickly proved a cruel illusion, as local Nazi officials rushed to show that there was no security for Jews in the Capital of the Movement. Starting as early as November 1939, Jews whose houses or apartments had been "Aryanized" were forced to move into *Judenhäuser*. Also in 1939, Jews were subjected to a rationing regimen that was considerably more restrictive than that applied to the general population. Moreover, city officials limited shopping hours for Jews and banned them from the streetcars.

The problem with these regulations, from the Nazi point of view, was that they kept the Jews too much in evidence. To segregate them further and to open up more housing to non-Jews, Munich's government broke up the *Judenhäuser* in early 1941 and began forcing their occupants into primitive barracks in the suburbs. The first such ghetto took shape at Milbertshofen, about four miles from the city center. In August 1941 another Jewish settlement was opened within the confines of a Sisters of Charity convent in the suburb of Berg-am-Laim. Designed to house "privileged Jews"—half Jews and Jews married to Christians—it was considerably more comfortable than Milbertshofen. One of its residents, Dr. Else Behrend-Rosenfeld, praised the facility's linoleum-covered corridors and "wonderful terraces with expansive views of the Bavarian Alps." On the other hand, the occupants' lives were strictly regulated and they were allowed no contact with the nuns who still occupied part of the complex. The few comforts that Berg afforded could not disguise the fact that this was a jail, one from which eventual release was uncertain at best. (Of course, the occupants could not have known that they would soon face deportation to the concentration camps in the East.)

A month after the opening of Milbertshofen all Jews, the "privileged" included, were required to display yellow Stars of David on their clothing whenever they went out in public. This was a Reich-wide regulation, not a local ordinance, but Munich's officials made a point of being especially rigorous in its enforcement. Jews caught without their stars were beaten and sometimes sent to Dachau. Those dutifully wearing their insignia in the streets encountered widely differing reactions from the townsfolk. Some Gentiles acted as if they did not see the stars at all; others expressed gratification that the "Jew pack" was now instantly recognizable; still others showed a measure of sympathy for the victims of this latest inhumanity. One young Jewish girl managed to free her aged aunt from the obligation to wear the star by informing the authorities that the woman was the widow of an "Aryan" and the mother of a soldier at the front. The girl rightly recalled her achievement as "a small success in a dark time."

As the war progressed, Munich's Jews had fewer and fewer occasions to venture out from their quarantine. They were denied access to public facilities like parks, cinemas, and museums, could not use public telephones and toilets, and were barred from municipal air-raid shelters.

The point of these measures was not only to cut the Jews off from Gentile society but also to facilitate their transformation into forced laborers for the municipality and industry. Forbidden their traditional social and cultural outlets, Munich's Jews were reduced to beasts of burden, allowed to do little but shovel snow, clear rubble, cart away unexploded bombs, and perform manual labor in arms factories.

But even this exploitation, while useful to the German economy, conflicted with the Nazis' goal of making the Reich "Jew-free." Because the expanding war made it impossible to achieve this objective through coerced emigration, which Himmler officially terminated in October 1941, the regime embarked on a strategy of mass deportation to new concentration camps in the East. Here Jews and other targeted groups could be worked to death or anonymously exterminated in gas chambers.

The first transport left Munich on 20 November 1941. It included elderly Jews from Milbertshofen and a number of children from a *Kinderheim* (children's home) on the Antonienstrasse. Their destination was Theresienstadt in Bohemia. Technically not an extermination camp, Theresienstadt was for many a way station to the killing centers farther east. Else Behrend-Rosenfeld was forced to help organize the deportations. She wrote in her diary: "My life has become pure hell. Each Friday, week after week, comes the list of those to be deported. They are not just going to Theresienstadt but on to Poland." Because little or no news filtered back from those sent to Poland, Jews still in Munich had good reason to fear the worst. Some elected to commit suicide rather than wait for deportation. Because this was a crime, each suicide had to be investigated by a police officer. "You Jews are my best customers," joked one of the officers to Behrend-Rosenfeld.

Munich's non-Jewish population was certainly aware of the deportations, which took place in broad daylight, but Münchners seem not to have paid much attention. The local SD recorded neither cheers nor protests. There was no equivalent act in Munich of the now-famous demonstration on Berlin's Rosenstrasse, in which hundreds of "Aryan" wives of Jews being held for deportation protested so fervently that their men were released. The Müchners' behavior did not stem from a resigned acceptance of every Nazi policy, for as we have seen, outraged Catholics had been prepared to protest the regime's crucifix degree. But taking away venerated icons was one thing, expelling unloved people quite another. And by the time Munich's Jews were deported, they had gone from being marginalized to being totally isolated.

To the degree that Münchners *did* think about the Jews during the war, it was often to associate their persecution with their own tribulations. Some came to see the Allied bombings as revenge for the Nazis' anti-Semitic crusade. A Munich waiter was denounced to the Gestapo for saying, "If they had left the Jews here and not chucked them out this bloody war would not have happened." Another citizen was imprisoned for declaring that if Hitler had left the Jews and the Catholic church alone, "things would not have come to this pitch." While hostile to the regime, such reasoning embraced the Nazi vision of the Jews as part of a world conspiracy anxious to get revenge on Germany.

If Münchners were doubtless aware that the city's Jews were being deported, they did not necessarily know, or know very much, about what was happening to them in the East. The Nazi regime went to considerable lengths to keep these horrors secret. Party officials were ordered not to discuss such matters in public, and citizens could be jailed for passing on information about the camps. Yet the secrecy was by no means absolute. Soldiers returning from the front sometimes told of the atrocities they had witnessed. It was in this fashion that Reck-Malleczewen learned of a massacre in Poland in late 1942. Foreign broadcasts also spoke of atrocities, including, on rare occasions, gassings. A Munich woman was sentenced to a three-year jail term in 1943 for asking her neighbor's mother, "Do you think then that nobody listens to the foreign broadcasts? They have loaded Jewish women and children into a wagon, driven them out of town, and exterminated them with gas." But such reports, originating with the enemy, could be written off as hostile propaganda. Getting reliable information was dangerous, and few people seem to have tried. Moreover, even had there been a plenitude of accurate information about the Holocaust, many people would have refused to believe it, for the horrors of such mechanized mass murder defied most imaginations.

"Storm Break Loose"

On 18 February 1943, the same day that Hans and Sophie Scholl were arrested in Munich, Josef Goebbels delivered a speech at Berlin's Sportpalast in which he sought to terrify his audience into a radical frame of mind. He acknowledged that the Soviets were putting up a tenacious defense, which he attributed to the "stupid toughness of the Russian race." The Battle of Stalingrad, a "toxin of fate," had illustrated the terrible danger represented by the "hordes from the steppe." The Russians could be defeated only by a "total war" that eschewed "bourgeois squeamishness" (as if that had been a Nazi weakness!). Were the Germans ready to accept a war "more radical than we can even imagine today"? As a thousand mouths howled their affirmation, Goebbels shrieked: "Now, people, arise, and storm break loose!"

Using Berlin as an example of the kind of sacrifice he envisaged, Goebbels began closing down businesses that he thought were not important to the war effort. Gourmet restaurants were first on the list, for they catered exclusively to the wealthy. Horcher's, Berlin's most famous eatery, presented a particular problem: As Göring's *Stammlokal* it enjoyed the *Reichmarschall's* protection. Goebbels put it out of business by sending SA squads to smash its windows.

With Goebbels's Berlin breaking loose into total war, Giesler's Munich would not lag far behind. In early 1943 local authorities began closing down fancy restaurants and bars, including those in the great hotels.

Closed too were shops specializing in such items as perfumes, jewels, oriental carpets, furs, and pianos.

Luxury establishments were not the only victims of total war. Hundreds of small businesses, factories, and artisanal shops were forced to close because of shortages of raw materials, capital, and workers. The city's department stores, starved of inventory and customers, also went under. These establishments catered to the middle classes, the very people the Nazis had promised to save from the predations of Big Capital.

By contrast, Munich's larger industries, as in World War I, prospered with government contracts and priority allocations of materials and labor. With the transfer of arms factories from the more exposed North and West, the Capital of the Movement became the capital of the German arms industry. In addition to BMW and Krauss-Maffei, Munich boasted new outposts of Dornier, Rathgeber, Siemens, and I. G. Farben, which together employed thousands of workers to meet the voracious demands of the Wehrmacht.

Munich's working population was now a far cry from the city's traditional labor force. The greater reliance on foreign labor meant that by 1944 every fourth employee was non-German. BMW alone employed some seventeen thousand slave laborers, Krauss-Maffei three thousand. Like the Jews, the foreign workers were segregated from the natives in barracks, of which the city maintained more than four hundred. The workers were marched between their squalid quarters and places of work by armed guards, who had their hands full preventing fights between the foreign laborers and xenophobic natives. Münchners were horrified that a war launched to expand German Lebensraum was instead filling the homeland with "aliens."

If demands from the front were dramatically altering Munich's socioeconomic structure, the Allied bombing campaign, buttressed by the addition of American planes in spring 1944, was totally transforming the city's topography and the daily lives of its citizens. On the night of 9–10 March 1943 the British commemorated the tenth anniversary of the Nazis' seizure of power in Munich by hitting the city with an enormous raid that killed 205 people, injured 435, and rendered 8,975 homeless. Among the buildings seriously damaged were the Staatsbibliothek, the Alte and Neue Pinakotheks, the Glyptothek, and the Brown House. A huge tent camp of homeless people sprouted up in the mire of the Maximilianplatz. Unable to feed all its dislocated citizens, the city appealed for help from the commandant at Dachau, who put inmate cooks to work supplying emergency rations.

Munich's public and private shelters were also overwhelmed. Competition for access to these havens became a Darwinian struggle in which the weakest often fell by the wayside. At the giant Salvator brewery shelter a number of old people and children were crushed to death when a mob stormed the entrance. Much to the disgust of ordinary citizens, people with political clout demanded the most comfortable quarters in the shelters. One warden recalled being threatened with denunciation if she did not reserve a place for a zealous party member. The highest-ranking Nazis did not have to fight for places because they had special shelters reserved for them. Hitler's bunker in the tunnel complex under the Führerbau had carpets on the floors, a private bath, and a movie projection room. Eva Braun's house too had its own bomb shelter, "completely furnished with all the necessities of life."

Starting in spring 1944, American planes began hitting Munich by day, while the British continued to bomb by night; now the Münchners' hell functioned around the clock. The first U.S. raid, on 18 March 1944, killed 172 people, injured 296, and blasted another 4,085 out of their homes. The Americans were theoretically committed to sparing buildings of historical or artistic importance, but technical limitations made this impossible. In their initial raid they damaged or destroyed a number of cultural jewels, including the Residenztheater, Prinzregententheater, Allerheiligen-Hofkirche, Michaelskirche, and the Karmelitenkirche. Surveying the damage, the *Münchener Neueste Nachrichten* fumed that such an attack could only have come from the "Jewish brains" that ran Washington's war effort. After another American raid a little later the *Nachrichten* claimed that the Americans deliberately employed "nigger" pilots who were encouraged to unleash "their congenital hatred for the white race and its cultural achievements" against a great city. This policy betrayed "a level of moral degeneration that must fill every true European with disgust. . . ." (Like many Nazi claims, this was a fabrication: America sent no black pilots over Germany in World War II.)

The Nazified press was well advised to cultivate popular hatred of the enemy bombers, for resentment toward the Nazi regime, simmering in many quarters since the beginning of the war, was now coming openly to the surface. The police and SD reported that some party members were no longer wearing their party badges in public for fear of being cursed in the streets. On the other hand, the party was now more active in municipal life than ever, taking over almost all the city's emergency services and casting itself as "helper in the hour of need." The closing years of the war therefore represented a revival of the *Kampfzeit* (period of struggle in the early twenties) marked by party activism and social engagement.

Munich's Nazi rulers also did their best, amid the chaos and devastation, to keep their city alive as the Capital of German Art. As usual they promoted cultural strength to compensate for political weakness. Thus in early 1944 Mayor Fiehler proposed that a medal honoring the late Paul Troost be awarded annually to an outstanding German architect. This would, he suggested, "renew Munich's cultural influence across the entire Reich," which was especially necessary given "the well-known tendency of certain elements in Berlin" to keep the Isar city in its shadow. Alas, Hitler vetoed the idea on the ground that he would be unable to prevent unworthy recipients from winning the prize after he was gone. Goethe, he reasoned, would have been horrified by some of the morons who had received the Goethe Prize after his death. "Unfortunately, the dead are powerless," observed the Führer.

In general Munich's rulers and cultural bureaucrats were able, with a little improvisation, to keep the city's art and entertainment institutions functioning until the last few months of the war. When the National Theater complex fell victim to an air raid in October 1943, city authorities moved the opera to the German Museum, the State Theater to the Goethesaal, and the Munich Philharmonic to the university. The Great German Art Exhibitions continued to be held in the House of German Art, swathed in camouflage netting. Even Christian Weber's "Brown Ribbon" horserace ran through the summer of 1944. Most of Munich's cinemas also remained open, offering patrons a steady diet of escapist comedies and adventure films.

The quality of Munich's cultural life, spotty at best since the Nazis' takeover, suffered as the war progressed. Munich's great museums were emptied of their best works, which were shipped to safer locations in the countryside. Many of the works ended up in Neuschwanstein, where they were warehoused along with thousands of pieces looted from France. Theatrical and musical ensembles suffered from a loss of performers and support-personnel to military conscription. Despite a personal appeal from Mayor Fiehler, Richard Strauss refused to conduct the Munich Philharmonic on its fiftieth anniversary in June 1943. The great musician explained that he had given up conducting in public, but one suspects that his real reason was a desire to distance himself from the sinking Nazi regime.

On 8 November 1943, against this backdrop of growing malaise in the Capital of the Movement, Hitler returned to commemorate the twentieth anniversary of the Beer Hall Putsch. On his orders, the ceremony honored not just the Nazi dead of 1923 but all the German victims of the war. Speaking before his Old Fighters in the Löwenbräukeller, Hitler promised that Germany would lay down its arms only "five minutes after midnight." According to the SD, the Führer's speech calmed everyone's nerves. One witness insisted that the address "pumped up" the crowd so much that no one would be afraid to wear his party button again.

Defeat and Liberation

On 17 April 1944 Hitler returned to Munich to take part in a state funeral at the Feldherrnhalle for Adolf Wagner, who had died of a heart attack a few days before. This was the last time Münchners were to see their Führer, who had no desire to view the awful destruction his war had produced. As if holding Wagner responsible for the devastation of his favorite town, Hitler left the eulogy to Goebbels. As Wagner's coffin was carried to the Königsplatz for burial, the State Opera orchestra played the "Funeral March" from Richard Wagner's *Götterdämmerung*. It was an appropriate choice, for twilight was surely settling on the Third Reich.

Less than two months later the Allies landed at Normandy. This not only opened a new land front in the West but signaled an escalation of the air campaign against the wounded Reich. True to their determination to make Munich a priority target, the Americans hit the city with their second major daylight raid on 9 June 1944. This time the bombers belonged to the Fifteenth Air Force flying out of newly conquered southern Italy. Among the 147 victims of the raid, 23 were slave laborers, who were particularly vulnerable to the air attacks because they had no shelters in their makeshift compounds. Five days later, on 13 June, the Americans and British delivered a one-two punch that devastated huge sections of Schwabing as well as the SS barracks at Dachau. The bombers managed to avoid hitting the camp itself, but they killed 25 inmates working in the SS quarters. In mid-July the Americans staged six huge raids back to back. Their combined toll was more than 3,000 dead, more than 200,000 homeless, and another collection of important buildings, including the Siegestor, Propylaen, Staatsgalerie, National Museum, Maximilianeum, Army Museum, University, and Academy of Applied Arts. The zoo at Hellabrun was also hit; hundreds of animals were killed, while hundreds more lay maimed and bleeding in their wrecked cages. When the human victims finally emerged from their shelters, they found their city, as one witness put it, bathed "in a huge yellow-black fog, pierced weakly by a dirty wedge of July sun."

Münchners were still reeling from their midsummer nightmare when news came that a bomb had gone off inside Hitler's bunker at his eastern headquarters near Rastenburg (Poland) on 20 July 1944. Hitler survived the blast with only mild injuries—yet another miraculous escape that the Führer attributed to the workings of divine Providence.

It was soon revealed that the bomb had been smuggled into Hitler's compound by a dissident Wehrmacht officer, Count Claus von Stauffenberg. The count was a Swabian Catholic and an avid disciple of the poet Stefan George. Among the factors that had motivated him was his conviction that Hitler, whom he had originally admired, had backed away from the idealist tenets championed by the George Circle. Instead of a revival of nobility and purity, Hitler and his followers had plunged the Reich into thuggish bestiality. It was thus not accidental that the term Stauffenberg sometimes used for his group of anti-Hitler plotters—*Secret Germany*—derived from a George poem. Nor is it surprising that the count reread George's work "The Anti-Christ" before carrying his bomb to Hitler's bunker.

Like many cities around the Reich, Munich hastily organized an open-air rally to register its joy over Hitler's escape from the plotters of Secret Germany. Speaking on behalf of the citizens of "the hard-fighting Capital of the Movement," Gauleiter Giesler expressed "heart-felt relief that our Führer has been spared."

Giesler's representation of Munich's sentiments in this instance may not have been entirely inaccurate. There are no reliable reports on popular responses in the city to the 20 July assassination attempt, but we know that in most parts of the country the attack was widely condemned as a stab in the back in time of war. Munich, with its strong connections to Hitler, undoubtedly shared in this sentiment. Even Cardinal Faulhaber, long disillusioned with the Nazis, branded the assassination attempt a "sin" in a pastoral letter to priests in the Wehrmacht. On the other hand, there must have been keen disappointment on the part of those who were hoping for a miracle to end the war. Reck-Malleczewen was so disappointed that he condemned the plotters along with their quarry:

> Ah, now, really, gentlemen, this is a little late. You made this monster, and as long as things were going well you gave him whatever he wanted. You turned Germany over to this archcriminal, you swore allegiance to him by every incredible oath he chose to put before you—you, officers of the Crown, all of you. . . . And now you are betraying him, as yesterday you betrayed the Republic, and as the day before yesterday you betrayed the Monarchy. Oh, I don't doubt that if this coup had succeeded, we, and what remains of the material substance of this country, would have been saved. I am sorry, the whole of this nation is sorry, that you failed.

But then to think that you, who are the embodiment of the Prussian heresy, that sower of evil, that stench in the nostrils of humanity—that you may be Germany's future leaders? No.

Reck was too hysterical to be historically accurate. Aside from the dubiousness of blaming Prussia for Hitler, his dismissal of the plotters as a group of frustrated Prussian militarists (a viewpoint, incidentally, shared by the Left) overlooked the heterogeneous backgrounds of the conspirators. Some of them were indeed military officers of aristocratic Prussian ancestry, but others held civilian positions and hailed from other parts of the Reich. Stauffenberg himself, as we have seen, was not a Prussian. The tragedy of the 20 July affair was not that it was too Prussian, or even too military, but that it was belated and badly organized. Tragic too was the fact that it did not signal further insurrection across the Reich.

Although Munich itself did not figure significantly in the 20 July plot, there were loose connections between the conspirators in Berlin and a group of Munich-based Wehrmacht officers. Most of the Bavarian resisters favored a restoration of the monarchical system in Germany, with ex-Crown Prince Rupprecht as national regent. Rupprecht, who was hiding out in Florence, managed to escape the brutal Nazi vendetta that followed the abortive coup, but other Munich anti-Hitlerites were not so lucky. Among those executed were Wehrmacht officers Karl Friedrich Klausing, Ludwig von Leonrod, and Chaplain Hermann Wehrle (Leonrod's confessor). Also among the victims was Albrecht Haushofer, a professor (like his late father) of geopolitics at the University of Munich and a former tutor of Rudolf Hess's.

Visiting Munich from the countryside in late August 1944, Wilhelm Hausenstein noted despairingly in his diary: "The city is more or less destroyed. . . . The impression is horrible. I cannot imagine that Munich will ever again achieve the representative status it once enjoyed. The cleanup alone will be too much. Will the ruined core be left standing and new buildings be put up outside? And if so, when? Will generation after generation live amid the ruins?"

In fact, as devastated as Munich was in late summer 1944, more devastation was to come. The period between September 1944 and April 1945 saw the heaviest concentration of raids in the war. The attacks reduced partial ruins to total ruins, while hitting some notable buildings that had thus far escaped significant damage. These included the Frauenkirche, Theatinerkirche, Löwenbräukeller, and Feldherrnhalle. Still untouched, however, was Hitler's apartment building at Prinzregentenplatz 16.

Munich's Nazi press no longer tried to play down the physical damage, but it claimed that the inhabitants' spirit was unbowed. "They can never make us bend, never rob us of the certainty that our hour will toll," declared the *Münchener Neueste Nachrichten,* with unintended irony. Another paper spoke of the "solidarity" between the people and their intrepid Gauleiter, insisting that Munich's "common will to master the difficulties of the moment" was greater now than ever. On 24 February 1945 the Nazi Old Guard gathered in the partially wrecked Hofbräuhaus for the twenty-fifth anniversary of the proclamation of the party program. Hitler was not present, but he sent a greeting: "Twenty-five years ago I prophesied the victory of the movement; today I prophesy the victory of the German Reich!" In that same month Mayor Fiehler wrote candidly to a worried Munich soldier at the front: "Munich was especially hard hit by terror attacks on 17 December 1944 and 7 January 1945, and must now be regarded as one of the most devastated cities in the Reich. Many unique sites much loved by Münchners and visitors have been destroyed." Yet he dutifully added that "only the outer covering has been torn; the Munich spirit remains undamaged. . . . You can be sure that after our victory Munich will be rebuilt according to the great plans of the Führer, while retaining historical features and idiosyncrasies."

In the meantime, battered Munich made final preparations for Hitler's promised *Endsieg.* Cultural and intellectual distractions no longer played much of a role in this ultimate struggle. As of September 1944, all theaters and cabarets were closed, orchestras and conservatories shut down. Newspapers appeared with only four pages, perhaps a relief from more bad news. In January 1945 the regime launched a new series of collections. Among the items solicited were raincoats, shoes, hats, and tuxedos ("since people will be able to celebrate our victory even without fancy dress").

There was also a new collection of humans: In Munich, as elsewhere, all able-bodied men between the ages of sixteen and sixty were enrolled in the Volkssturm (Home Guard). Organized by Bormann and Himmler, this was supposed to be a Nazi *levée en masse* animated by a fantatical will to fight to the end. Reminiscent of the militia fantasies of Ernst Röhm, it can be seen as a desperate revenge by party radicals against the elites in the military, or what was left of them. But it quickly turned out that many of the members were too old or too young to fight effectively, and all were poorly equipped and badly trained. Rather than significantly impede the Allied advance, the Volkssturm merely showed the lengths to which the regime was prepared to go to stave off defeat.

In early spring 1945, as the Allied noose tightened around Germany, word went out that the Capital of the Movement and its mountainous environs would become an "alpine fortress" defended by loyal Nazis from all over the Reich. The Nazi regime would fall back on its place of origin, protected by Bavaria's mountains and Munich's spirit. Gauleiter Giesler was honored and excited by this prospect. He had visions of himself, Blood Flag in hand, surrounded by Old Fighters, making a last stand at the Feldherrnhalle. Alas, when he floated this plan among the Old Fighters, there were no takers. In general, not much came of the alpine fortress idea, though many Nazi leaders did stream to the South in hopes of saving themselves.

Giesler, however, was determined to hold Munich for as long as possible. To thwart the American advance, he put out an order to dynamite all of Munich's major bridges. This senseless act of destruction would have deprived the city of crucial supplies from the outside, and Hitler himself vetoed the plan. Giesler had to content himself with ordering the execution of citizens making defeatist comments and the shelling of apartment buildings bearing white flags in their windows.

On 28 April, with the Americans nearing the outskirts of Munich, a small band of Wehrmacht officers and dissident citizens, calling themselves Freiheitsaktion Bayern, decided that the time had finally come to liberate Munich from within. The rebels, about 450 strong, were led by Dr. Rupprecht Gerngross, captain of an army translators' unit. Wearing traditional Bavarian blue-white armbands, the group was staunchly conservative and particularist. Their immediate goal was to effect a peaceful surrender to the Americans, but their long-term ideal was to restore the Wittelsbachs to the throne of Bavaria.

Adopting the code name *Fasanenjagd* (Pheasant Hunt—Nazi leaders were popularly called golden pheasants), the rebels managed briefly to take over two radio stations and to broadcast calls for a mass rising against the Nazi "blood tyranny." They also urged the Volkssturm not to resist the Americans. Captain Gerngross contacted Ritter von Epp and pleaded with him to join in the rebellion. Ritter von Epp demurred, protesting that he could not betray his friends in the party. (At the same time, however, he secretly contacted American intelligence operatives with an offer to "take action against Himmler and the SS.") More grievously, the people as a whole ignored this final call for mass resistance, preferring to sit tight and wait for the Americans. Wehrmacht and SS forces loyal to the regime quickly overran the rebel enclaves, putting an end to the Bavarian Pheasant Hunt. Gerngross himself escaped, but many of his colleagues were caught and executed.

On their way to conquering Munich, elements of two American regiments paused to liberate the Dachau concentration camp north of town.

Unbeknownst to them, on 26 April a group of inmates had tried to take over the camp. The prisoners feared that the Nazis would make an effort to liquidate them before the Americans arrived. They were right. The SS Death's-Head unit guarding the camp managed to put down the desperate rebellion and to execute its leaders. That evening, on Himmler's orders, almost seven thousand prisoners were evacuated from the camp on a forced march in the direction of the Alps, where they were to be held as hostages. On the next day a train loaded with inmates from Buchenwald, many of them already dead, arrived at Dachau. With no room in the camp, which was still horribly overcrowded with some thirty thousand inmates, the Buchenwald prisoners were left in their boxcar prisons to die.

The first American soldiers reached the camp on the morning of 28 April. They opened the Buchenwald train and were horrified to find about two thousand corpses in tangled heaps. Battle-hardened though they were, they had never seen such a sight. Some wept; others vomited. One soldier was shocked to see "people whose eyes were still blinking maybe three or four feet deep inside the stack." Entering the Dachau compound itself, the GIs encountered hundreds of bodies littering the grounds, along with thousands of living skeletons in tattered rags, some able to cheer or smile, others able only to sit motionlessly in their own excrement. Driven to a frenzy of hatred by such sights, the GIs lined up more than a hundred German guards and mowed them down point-blank with their machine guns. They shot other guards in the legs to hobble them while prisoners hacked at them with bayonets. "The violence of Dachau," one commentator noted aptly, "had a way of implicating all, even the liberators."

The Americans then descended on Munich itself. Although never a center of anti-Nazi resistance, the city also proved in the end to be no hotbed of Nazi defense. On 29 April, after giving one last order to his cohorts to go down fighting to the last man, Gauleiter Giesler fled to Berchtesgaden, where a few days later he shot himself. Mayor Fiehler also fled but eventually gave himself up. American troops entered the city on 30 April, the very day Hitler and his new wife, Eva Braun, killed themselves in the Führerbunker in Berlin. As they rolled through the smashed streets, American soldiers encountered virtually no opposition; instead, amid the rubble, they found people busy trying to clear away signs and symbols of Nazi control. A crowd was beating with hammers on the bronze monument at the Feldherrnhalle. Castoff Nazi medals, party membership booklets, and pictures of the Führer littered the streets. Thousands of blue-white flags fluttered from windows, as if to say, "This is *Bavaria,* not Germany." To complete the image, Münchners cursed the few remaining Wehrmacht soldiers as "Prussians."

One advance group of GIs drove immediately to Hitler's apartment on Prinzregentenplatz, hoping to find Nazi treasure there. Instead in Hitler's safe they discovered twelve autographed copies of *Mein Kampf.* Another group rushed to Eva Braun's house, finding it, as one GI remarked, "as though she had just walked out and expected to return sometime soon." There were pictures on the walls, mementos on the shelves, and bedsheets monogrammed "AH." A captain announced that he would stay in the house to guard it against looters. The next day, when his colleagues returned, they found the place completely stripped save for one huge painting that was "too large for one G.I. to carry."

A few days after the Americans had taken over Munich, a military correspondent attached to General Clark's Fifth Army in Italy drove up to take a look around. He was Klaus Mann, Thomas's son. He wrote in his memoirs: "What a strange, nightmarish experience!—to walk through those once familiar streets, now reduced to masses of ruins and rubble. . . . With most of the characteristic landmarks missing, I could hardly find my way from the city center to the suburban district on the Isar River where our former home is situated." He eventually found the house, but it was now an empty shell, with its inside burned out and its roof partially collapsed. Poking around, he encountered a young girl sitting on a balcony on the second floor. He asked her if she knew whose house this had been. "I suppose it belonged to some writer," she replied. "One of those who didn't get along with the Nazis—so of course, he couldn't keep the house. Then the SS took it over; they had a *Lebensborn* established here. . . . Many fine babies were begotten and born in this house. . . . "

Munich could use all the babies it could get. Some 6,632 Münchners had been killed and another 15,000 wounded in the bombing of World War II. About 20,000 Munich residents died on the battlefields. More than 200,000 Münchners were living elsewhere in Germany as evacuees. The city's population had shrunk from 824,000 in 1939 to about 470,000 at war's end. Much of the remaining population lived in ruins, as about half the housing was severely damaged and almost 90 percent of the historic core of the city was destroyed. With some twelve million tons of debris piled up higher than most surviving buildings, many residents must have wondered, with Wilhelm Hausenstein, if the ruins would ever be cleared away.

Reckoning with(out) the Past in the "World City with Heart"

IN SEPTEMBER 1964 the German newsmagazine *Der Spiegel* wrote of Munich that it was "the only city in Germany that Hitler promised to make great—and that became great nonetheless." By the mid-1960s the former Capital of the Movement had become Germany's secret capital, the richest, fastest-growing, most culturally ambitious city in the Federal Republic. Its growth rate was twice that of any other major German city, it had passed Essen and Düsseldorf in industrial output, and it had more symphony orchestras, museums, theaters, and publishing houses than any other West German metropolis (including West Berlin, then a beleaguered island in the middle of the Communist German Democratic Republic). But most of all, Munich had recovered its reputation for cosmopolitan flair, boisterous good times, and decadent chic. The Oktoberfest was again in full swing, and so was Germany's first topless bar, the George-Club, housed in a *Jugendstil* building in Schwabing. No wonder Munich was West Germany's tourism king, drawing some 1.7 million foreigners every year.

Munich became "great" not only in spite of Hitler but also because it proved adept at repressing its central role in the Third Reich. Strategic amnesia was no rarity in postwar Germany, but the city of Alzheimer (the pioneering student of senility had practiced psychiatry in Munich before World War I) showed that the onset of memory loss could be a source of regained dynamism. At the same time, Munich was skillful in establishing lines of continuity with its pre-Nazi past. Once the city had been rebuilt—and that happened sooner than anyone had expected—one could easily get the impression while walking its cheerful streets that there had never been a Third Reich at all. Such an illusion was possible elsewhere in Germany too, but nowhere was it stronger than in Munich. Nowhere did the ghosts of the recent past seem more thoroughly banished.

Meteoric as it was, however, Munich's rise from the ashes ignited new fires of controversy and resentment. Moreover, it might be argued that despite the revival of its reputation for cosmopolitanism, tolerance, and warmth, Munich's exorcism of the spirits that had once nourished Nazism was less thorough than its sanitization of the outward signs of the brown terror.

IN THE IMMEDIATE aftermath of the Third Reich's collapse, Munich's new masters, the American military occupation, set up native administrative offices and appointed well-known conservatives with anti-Nazi credentials to run them. Karl Scharnagl, Munich's last pre-Nazi mayor and a survivor of Dachau, became governing mayor on 4 May 1945. Hans Ritter von Seisser, the former state police chief who had helped put down the Beer Hall Putsch, became head of Munich's police, while Michael Freiherr von Godin, leader of the police detachment that had stopped Hitler's march at the Feldherrnhalle, became chief of the Bavarian State Police. Fritz Schäfer, an archconservative Catholic whom the Nazis had thrown out as Bavarian finance minister in 1933, was appointed minister-president of Bavaria. (Schäfer did not last long; in September 1945 he was removed for being uncooperative with the occupiers.) These officials had two major duties, both difficult: They were to help the Americans maintain order in a time of severe economic dislocation and social turmoil, and they were to assist in the denazification of their homeland.

In pursuit of denazification, the Americans sent out questionnaires to the citizens of their occupation zone, requiring them to answer queries about their recent political activities. Those deemed tainted had to face *Spruchkammer* (hearing committees), composed of native non-Nazis, which assessed culpability and imposed sentences. Of course, most of the biggest offenders never went through this process either because (like Hitler, Himmler, and Goebbels) they had committed suicide, or because they faced the International Military Tribunal at Nuremberg or Allied military courts in the four occupation zones. It remained for the *Spruchkammer* to deal with secondary figures and fellow travelers, the so-called lesser fry of the Nazi regime. In the case of Munich this meant that the local denazification committees tried men like Heinrich Hoffmann, Karl Fiehler, Max Amann, Hermann Esser, Weiss Ferdl, Richard Strauss, Putzi Hanfstaengl, and Jakob Schmid (the custodian who had apprehended Hans and Sophie Scholl). Franz Ritter von Epp escaped a hearing because he died in American internment in 1947. Christian Weber was killed in a traffic accident while being transported to prison.

This approach to denazification proved highly problematical. The *Spruchkammer* lacked resources to determine whether the accused, who understandably minimized their involvement in the Nazi system, were telling the truth. Moreover, aware that the more serious cases were being handled by other courts, committee members were inclined to give defendants the benefit of the doubt. The result was a plethora of light sentences or acquittals, which the citizenry mockingly called Persil Certificates, Persil being a popular detergent.

Munich was no exception to the whitewashing. On the contrary, it soon gained a reputation for unusual softness, a development that recalled its reknown in the early 1920s as a haven for right-wing criminals. To take just the cases mentioned above, Amann, Hoffmann, Esser, and Fiehler each received only ten years in prison plus fines (none served out his full sentence). Jakob Schmid got five years, Weiss Ferdl a two-thousand-mark fine, and Richard Strauss, the careerist collaborator who had "signed what had to be signed," was given a slap on the wrist by the committee and an honorary doctorate by the University of Munich. Putzi Hanfstaengl, who had returned to Munich in 1946 following wartime internment in Britain and America, was acquitted.

An equally problematical dimension of the denazification process involved the purging of government bureacracies and public services of employees with brown pasts. At first the American Military Government ordered the wholesale dismissal of all personnel who had been members of the Nazi Party. By the beginning of August 1945 some hundred thousand former Nazi officials had been fired in Bavaria; about three thousand of these had belonged to the municipal bureaucracy of Munich (whose total membership of fourteen thousand had been assessed at 87 percent National Socialist on the basis of the American questionnaires). Because of the firings, many offices had difficulty functioning. Mayor Scharnagl, alarmed by the chaos in his administration and horrified by the suicide of a fired official whom he considered "no more Nazi than I," warned the Americans that their policy was radicalizing "thousands of people who otherwise could be useful citizens."

Such criticism found a sympathetic ear in America's new military governor for Bavaria, General George S. Patton, who assumed his position in July 1945. Patton became convinced that denazification was ill advised under the circumstances. Like Scharnagl, he believed that ex-Nazis no longer presented a danger in comparison with the Communists. Postwar Allied policy, he declared, was persecuting "a pretty good race" and opening German lands to "Mongolian savages." He therefore did his best to slow the purge of former Nazi officials in Bavaria and even employed some of them on his own civilian staff.

But soon Patton, always impulsive and impolitic, overstepped himself. At an informal press conference in September 1945 he made the fateful error of saying that "this Nazi question is very much like a Democratic and Republican election fight." That remark sealed his fate with his boss, Dwight Eisenhower, who had become impatient with the general's coddling of Nazis. With the support of President Truman, Ike relieved Patton of his post.

Yet Patton's policy of relative leniency toward former Nazis continued after his dismissal. In Munich an arrangement was worked out in late 1945 that allowed ex-Nazis deemed indispensable to keep their jobs on probation. Within months many who had been fired were being reemployed in their old positions or in similar posts. The reason for this development, of course, was not merely efficiency; with the onset of the Cold War, Washington began downplaying denazification in order to cultivate German support against the Soviets.

Denazification, such as it was, took place against a backdrop of socioeconomic chaos even worse than in the last days of the war. Munich, like many other West zone cities, was overrun by former concentration camp inmates, slave laborers, prisoners of war, and refugees from the East.

They competed for precious food and shelter with bombed-out natives, bunkered down in their smoldering ruins. There ensued a wave of plunder, robbery, rape, and murder. Münchners could not even find solace in their traditional liquid escape, for the great beer halls had been taken over by the Americans and brewing was forbidden to conserve grain for bread.

Such conditions generated a new surge of xenophobic anxiety. Rumors circulated around town in November 1945 that an army of foreigners and concentration camp survivors was about to sack the city in revenge for the Night of the Broken Glass seven years earlier. As often in the past, some Münchners demanded a purge of "alien" influences. There were calls for the expulsion of Sudeten and East Prussian refugees. Members of the archparticularist Bayern Partei protested the opening of a Chinese restaurant as yet another piece of "foreignism." Mayor Scharnagl wanted to reserve all viable housing for native Münchners and to confine refugees and displaced persons to suburban barracks. Such people, he said, "are not suited to live together with our population." Only pressure from the local military government kept him from implementing this policy.

City officials also sought to deny municipal employment to outsiders via the 1926 Law to Combat Gypsies, Vagrants, and the Work-shy. When a Jewish physician who had survived Dachau applied for a job in a Schwabing hospital, a city councilman opposed the hiring: "Can't we find someone other than this eastern Jew? I am no anti-Semite, but I'll be happy when we are rid of all [the Jews]." Previously marginalized types often found similar treatment when they tried to gain posts at the newly reopened university. The distinguished archaeologist Heinz Mode was rejected because, as he noted, he was cursed four times over: as a returning émigré, a Communist, a Jew, and a Berliner.

When they assumed control in Munich, the Americans directly confronted the Nazi legacy in the form of numerous Hitlerian buildings and monuments that had survived the bombing. Given the shortage of viable office and housing space, the military government decided to keep many of the Nazi buildings for their own use. The Führerbau, where the Munich Conference of 1938 had been held, housed Munich's Amerikahaus, one of a series of cultural centers that advertised the American way of life in the new Germany. (Today the Amerikahaus has moved to a new building on the Karolinienplatz, and the Führerbau has become part of the Hochschule für Musik.) The Nazi Verwaltungsbau became one of the Allied centers for art looted by the Nazis. Here American experts sorted and cataloged piles of precious plunder pending the works' return to their rightful owners. The House of German Art, site of the Nazi art exhibitions, became an American recreation center (the lines for a basketball court remained visible on the floor long after the building was reconverted to a museum). After extensive repairs the Bürgerbräukeller, from which Hitler had launched his ill-fated putsch in 1923, became an American canteen. Later it was demolished by the Bavarian authorities; they wanted no more marches from this particular shrine. The Nazi-built airport at Riem continued to operate until replaced by the more distant Franz Josef Strauss Airport in 1992. The Nazis' Honor Temples on the Königsplatz were originally scheduled to become Sites of Peace, replete with bells made from the melted-down bronze caskets of the Beer Hall Putsch martyrs (who were reburied in local cemeteries). Out of fear, however, that the temples might instead become pilgrimage sites for unreconstructed Nazis, the Americans demolished them. Today all that remains of them are their foundations, sprouting bushes and trees like giant planters.

According to the Munich architectural historian Winfried Nerdinger, most present-day Münchners are blissfully ignorant of the dark history of the surviving Nazi structures. Pleas by some historians to place informative signs on the former Nazi buildings have been repeatedly rejected on the grounds that this would "cost too much" or focus undue attention on an unfortunate moment in the past. City officials employed this excuse to reject the establishment of a proposed Documentary Center on Munich's National Socialist Past in the tunnels under the Königsplatz. Yet money was found in 1988 to tear up the Nazis' granite blocks covering the square and to replant it with grass.

The Feldherrnhalle, a treasured historical building that had become Nazi Munich's central shrine, was quickly cleansed of its Nazi iconography. Instead of the bronze plaque honoring the Beer Hall Putsch martyrs, the walls in late 1945 were covered with hand-painted sentiments like "Dachau—Velden—Buchenwald; I'm ashamed to be a German!" and "Diesel, Hayden, Robert Koch. I'm proud to be a German." The renovated structure later became the backdrop for all manner of demonstrations, from protests against watered beer to campaigns against nuclear power plants. In 1961 West Germany's new army, the Bundeswehr, paraded before the building, just as the Bavarian Army and Nazi storm troopers had once done. Starting in the 1970s, neo-Nazis placed wreaths there every 9 November; just as regularly, leftist groups removed the memorials, sometimes after scuffles with the rightists. In 1994 the city council installed a new monument in the building to commemorate the four policemen killed by the Nazis in 1923. Shortly thereafter a self-described "former East Front fighter" burned himself to death in front of the hall to protest Germany's "defamation of its honorable past."

The sanitization of the Feldherrnhalle was only a small part of a hastily launched campaign to rid Munich of its network of Nazi symbols. Municipal officials removed swastikas and Nazi slogans from public buildings and took down plaques proclaiming "The Führer lived here" from Hitler's residences. (Hitler's last habitation, his apartment on Prinzregentenplatz, passed through a number of owners before assuming its present function as a municipal fine-collecting office.) Ritter-von-Epp-Platz reverted to Promenadeplatz, Hermann-Göring-Strasse became Azaleenstrasse, and Adolf-Hitler-Allee was christened Diefenbachstrasse, after a little-known Munich painter. Yet it took time to eliminate all the signs of the recent times; in early 1946 one could still see advertisements for *Stürmer* magazine and the *Sparkasse der Hauptstadt der Bewegung* on some walls, while a few streetcars still carried signs warning, "Be careful what you say! The enemy is listening in!"

The temptation to forget the millions of victims of Nazism was as strong in Munich as elsewhere in postwar Germany, but in the immediate aftermath of defeat local officials did make some formal gestures of atonement. On 5 August 1945 Mayor Scharnagl spoke at a memorial service for victims of the Dachau camp at the Ostfriedhof, and on 10 November 1946 the city unveiled a monument to "Victims of Persecution 1933–1945" at the Jewish cemetery on Ungererstrasse. On this occasion the mayor honored the contributions of Munich's Jewish citizens, of whom only 250 had returned from the camps to join the 89 who had survived the war hiding in the city. As of 20 November 1945 the local Jewish Cultural Association counted 300 members; before the Nazi period it had boasted 12,000. Official Munich even took notice of the Third Reich's persecution of Communists: In September 1947 Scharnagl and other worthies spoke at a belated funeral for 3 murdered KPD resistance fighters at the Feldherrnhalle.

Such public gestures of atonement, however, masked abiding popular resentment of the persecuted groups, which were now accused of exploiting their suffering under the Nazis to win favored treatment in the new era. As one indignant citizen put it in a letter to the Bavarian minister-president:

My friends and I, ourselves victims of bombing and evacuation, have naturally followed closely the provisioning of foreign elements in the American zone. We accept that these people, to the degree that they suffered in camps or elsewhere, should be decently fed and clothed, and this has certainly happened. Today they are so bursting with health that one never sees a sick Jew, except for those who would have been sick anyway. . . . But how pitiful our own people are in contrast! At the very least this privileged treatment of foreigners [sic] must be suspended until the bombed-out German population is taken care of to an equal degree.

Privileges for victims of Nazism were in reality minimal and entirely the work of the occupation authorities. Munich Jews returning from camps or emigration found it very difficult to regain rights to their property or (until passage of a federal compensation law in 1953) any repayment for their material losses. This was true even for once-influential Jewish families like the Bernheimers, who had to fight long and hard to regain title to their famous art and antiquities gallery. Gypsies received no compensation at all, nor did foreign slave laborers.

THE MUNICH REGION'S most notorious relic of Nazi barbarism, the Dachau concentration camp, went through a series of postwar metamorphoses that reflected the changing political times as well as the widespread repression of inconvenient memories. Shortly after the liberation, General Eisenhower forced officials and some citizens of Dachau to walk through the camp and view piles of decomposing bodies, excrement-covered barracks, and the crematorium (the gas chamber there had never been put to use). GI guards ordered, "Hands down," when townspeople tried to cover their eyes. A delegation of U.S. congressmen and a group of influential American editors also toured Dachau in early May and did much to focus international attention on the horrors of the camps.

Once Dachau was cleared of its dead and dying, the American Army turned it into an internment center for former camp guards, SS men, and other Nazi functionaries. Some saw in this a certain revanchist symbolism, but the Nazis incarcerated there experienced nothing like the brutality they had meted out to inmates during their twelve-year reign in the watchtowers. Moreover, in the late 1940s, as the American occupiers began to transfer their animosity from the Germans to the Soviet Communists, they disbanded the internment center and turned it over to the Bavarian authorities.

In 1948–1949, with a wave of East German and Eastern European refugees streaming into the West, Dachau became a suburban housing complex (called Dachau-Ost), complete with a church, school, kindergarten, and small shops. Few of the refugee families living there had any sense of their new home's former life, which suited the Bavarian authorities. Indeed, local officials allowed a sand-mining company to churn up a mass grave near the camp in which thousands of internees were buried.

News of this desecration horrified some of the former inmates, who had gradually come to believe that Dachau and other camps must be preserved to memorialize the dead and to warn against future relapses into barbarism. In the early 1950s an association of camp survivors managed to install an informal exhibition about the Holocaust in the crematorium. In response to considerable international pressure, Bavarian officials supported this initiative, yet they allowed Dachau police to remove the exhibition two years later. In 1955 town officials announced plans to bulldoze the crematorium. Dachau's mayor, who been assistant mayor during the Third Reich, led this campaign. He argued that many of those who had been incarcerated in Dachau were ordinary criminals or political subversives who had "illegally opposed the government of the day."

This effort to scrape away an unwanted piece of the past ignited a new storm of international protest orchestrated by camp survivors and backed by a younger generation of Germans who were beginning to challenge their parents' historical amnesia. The pressure was great enough to induce the Bavarian government to forbid the bulldozing and to allow the survivors' group to submit plans for turning the facility into a permanent memorial. A decade later, twenty years after the camp was liberated, Dachau opened as a public memorial of the Holocaust.

Ever since, for many Dachauers, the presence of the installation has been a source of nagging irritation, despite the site's capacity—like a Neuschwanstein of genocide—to draw tourists from all over the world. Townspeople resented it bitterly that for the rest of the world Dachau had come to mean only the camp, not the nearby village with its hilltop palace and illustrious artistic traditions. But efforts to promote the "other Dachau" via colorful brochures dispensed in the camp museum had little success.

Especially galling was fact that other Germans sometimes shared in the defamation of Dachau. Thus, in 1988, when the national headquarters of the Goethe Institute (the cultural arm of the German Foreign Ministry) moved to a new building on Munich's Dachauerstrasse, Klaus von Bismarck, the institute's president, demanded that the entrance be situated on a different street so as to avoid having the dreaded D word on the agency's letterhead. Convinced that Munich officials had colluded in this effort, the mayor of Dachau fumed in an open letter that it was highly hypocritical for the former Capital of the Movement to act so fastidiously regarding the Nazi past.

In truth, the citizenry of Munich had never been terribly displeased to see places like Dachau, Berlin, and Nuremberg absorb much of the opprobrium for the Nazi crimes. Beginning immediately with the so-called Zero Hour in May 1945, Münchners began focusing on more positive associations for their city. For example, local officials touted Munich as a hotbed of anti-Nazi resistance, picking up on earlier claims that the city had become Capital of the Anti-Movement in the waning years of the Third Reich. They held up the eleventh-hour Freiheitsaktion Bayern as the only example of a municipal uprising against the Nazi system in the history of the Third Reich. To honor this enterprise, they rechristened Schwabing's central square Münchener Freiheit (in the Nazi period it had been called Danziger Freiheit). Munich Catholics celebrated the "resistance" of Cardinal Faulhaber, after whom a street was named. Munich's best-known resistance circle, the White Rose, came in for massive monumentalization in the postwar era. The plazas facing the university buildings on the Ludwigstrasse were named Geschwister-Scholl-Platz and Professor-Huber-Platz. (In September 1945 the city council posthumously restored Huber's Munich citizenship, and the university rescinded its 1943 annulment of his doctorate.) Speakers at annual commemorations of the White Rose invariably offered it as a powerful symbol of the "other Germany" that had supposedly always been alive and well in Munich. But while emphasizing the White Rose's importance, commentators were careful to argue that its failure showed how futile it had been to try to rise up against the Nazis.

If the official celebration of the resistance legacy promoted a more positive interpretation of Munich's place in the Third Reich, the city's physical reconstruction in the postwar era aimed at establishing continuity with the pre-Nazi past, especially with the architectural heritage of the Wittelsbachs. It was thus no accident that the first public building to be rebuilt was the Residenz, the former palace of the Bavarian kings. Many similar projects followed, for city officials, urged on by public opinion, made the decision to reconstruct the historic *Altstadt* as closely as possible to its original form. Modern designs, to the extent that they were attempted, were confined to the outer districts. One of the officials involved in this effort, Karl Meitinger, chief of the city building office (he had held a similar position in the Nazi era), explained that historic reconstruction would both facilitate continuity with an illustrious past and help promote economic revival by stimulating tourism. "If everyone pitches in," he wrote in 1946, "we can re-create that unique city of old Bavarian charm, with its *Gemütlichkeit,* its festivals and customs and love of life. . . . But we must understand that only what is uniquely Münchnerisch can provide the drawing card that will once again make Munich a center of international tourism."

This ideal was actively supported by Mayor Scharnagl, who, of course, was also a symbol of continuity. He had often condemned modernist architecture and art in the 1920s, and he continued to do so after the war. He too argued that restoration of the city's historic buildings was an effective way to recover healthy traditions and economic vitality. "Munich must hold strongly to its old look and its old coziness." he declared. The image of Munich that his office cultivated—and that was simultaneously promoted in a wave of *Alt-München* nostalgia in literature and memoirs—drew upon a wealth of clichés to depict the true Munich as easygoing, tolerant, instinctively democratic, socially harmonious, traditional yet forward-looking, rustic yet cosmopolitan. In short, Munich was sold as a *Weltstadt mit Herz* (world city with heart).

Munich's campaign to remake itself in a traditional image also required a revival of its status as Athens on the Isar, Mecca of the Muses. Just as in the nineteenth century, cultural prowess seemed especially important because most city officials (wrongly, as it turned out) believed that their town would never become an industrial or political powerhouse. As a theater director expressed it in a letter to Scharnagl, "As you well know, we are unlikely to be able to able to bring much industry back to life. In order for Munich to return to its place under the world sun, it must be *die Kunststadt* it once was. This can only be achieved by securing the very best in literature, theater, music, and the plastic arts."

With this goal in mind, Munich made a strenuous effort to lure back Thomas Mann, going so far as to offer him a new house. Word of the invitation sparked a new anti-Mann outcry among resident writers, who complained that the author had made himself unworthy of his former homeland by criticizing it from the safety of exile. Only if he began to write "correctly" about Germany might he eventually "win back his former good reputation among the Germans."

Mann, in any event, was not inclined to return; the most he would do was make brief visits in 1949, 1951, and 1952. On the occasion of his first visit he wrote to a friend: "There was something ghostly about finding this whole chunk of an outlived past in a smashed and tattered state and seeing human faces emerging that had aged, and I often found myself looking the other way." Instead of Munich, Mann chose to live his last years near Zürich, where he died in 1955.

In addition to Mann, Munich sought, albeit less aggressively, to woo back Karl Wolfskehl, erstwhile prince of Schwabing and lone survivor of the Cosmic Circle. Yet Wolfskehl could not forget that the city that had once called him its favorite son had rejected him; he would not return from exile.

Munich did not try to retrieve Lion Feuchtwanger and Oskar Maria Graf—their criticism of the city had been too harsh, and they were not famous enough—but civic leaders sought halfheartedly to make amends with prizes and invitations to ceremonial occasions. Over the bitter protests of some city councillors, the municipal cultural office awarded Feuchtwanger the Literature Prize of the City of Munich in 1957. A year later officials invited Graf to attend the festivities marking the eight-hundredth anniversary of the city. Yet Graf felt he was treated "swinishly" by his hosts, who provided him no place to stay and drove him around in a municipal delivery wagon. Nor was he impressed by the local literary crowd that attended his readings. "I got to know the authors there quite well," he wrote later. "[They are] a bunch of creeping collaborators and former Nazis, who claim to know nothing about the past." Thereafter Graf made no more visits to Munich; only his ashes returned in 1968.

Graf's observations notwithstanding, Munich did manage to attract some lively and socially engaged artists in the immediate postwar era, though their stay was often brief and rarely without controversy. Erich Kästner, a brilliant novelist and dramatist who managed to convince the Americans that he was politically reliable, made the Bavarian capital his base. Alfred Andersch and Hans Werner Richter, cofounders of a leftist-oriented literary paper called *Der Ruf,* were less fortunate: The Americans banned the paper after only seventeen numbers had appeared. The military government also ensured that Bertolt Brecht, who toyed with idea of making Munich the home of his postwar avant-garde theater, found no welcome on the Isar; instead he repaired to the Spree—its eastern side. But it was not just the Americans who held the line against "subversive" or unorthodox culture. In a move reminiscent of Catholic vigilance at the turn of the century, Bavaria's new cultural minister, Alois Hundhammer, suspended performances in 1948 of a ballet called *Abraxis* on grounds that it venerated human sexuality and black magic.

Despite such contretemps, Munich soon reclaimed its artistic prominence, especially in the realms of music and theater. The Philharmonic and State Opera, which both had reopened within months of the end of the war, were among the finest in the land, and the theatrical scene was as lively as ever. With the rapid renovation of the Alte Pinakothek, Munich could once again boast a first-class museum.

On the other hand, the old artistic center of late-nineteenth-century Munich, bohemian Schwabing, never really recovered its fabled vibrancy. Although painters and sculptors once again flocked there—by the late 1950s more than two thousand of them were in the district—the more experimental figures, as sometimes in the past, chose to move on. The noted avant-garde art collective ZEN 49, for example, soon abandoned the city. If Schwabing came to glitter once again, the light derived more from the district's plethora of bars and discos than from the creative brilliance of its artists.

In 1958, by which time many of the key restoration projects had been completed and the city exceeded a million inhabitants, Munich celebrated with great fanfare its eight hundredth anniversary. The theme of the occasion was "Munich is Munich again." An official anniversary catalog proclaimed the wonders of Germany's once and future cultural capital, newly risen from devastation and despair: "It is timely and correct to praise Munich . . . its ideal location in the heart of Europe and at the base of the Bavarian Alps, its diversity of architecture, plenitude of museums and libraries, rich offerings of theater, music, and exhibitions, its sense of measure and beauty, its tranquillity of spirit and unobtrusive supremacy of feeling—yes, all this stands to Munich's credit as it shows the world its credentials." In a keynote address Nobel Laureate Werner Heisenberg, who in 1955 had assumed the chair in physics at Munich University that had been denied him during the Third Reich, declared that on its eight-hundredth birthday Munich had no need to fear for its future. "The conservative and pious city will continue to remain open to all that is new, will continue to harvest the fruits of tolerance, which has always been one of its main virtues; and though perspectives will change, and new science and technology will alter patterns of life, Munich in other ways will always remain the same." While no one said so explicitly, the subtext of this celebration was that Munich's recent misfortune was now safely "overcome" and need not burden the city's ongoing revival.

Munich selectively celebrated its illustrious history in other anniversaries as well. In 1986 the House of Bavarian History commemorated the 200th anniversary of King Ludwig I's birth with a giant exhibition and scholarly symposium dedicated to the monarch's cultural and political contributions. Nine years later, in 1995, Munich marked "mad" King Ludwig II's 150th birthday with an even greater celebration. The city swam in a brackish tide of Ludwig kitsch, including busts made from butter, toilet seats with the royal coat of arms, and beer steins with the king's visage (showing him, of course, before he had become jowly and virtually toothless). At the city's White-Blue Gay Shop the king was touted as an icon of gay liberation.

Another historical legacy was rather more troublesome: the seventy-fifth anniversary of the Revolution of 1918, which occurred in 1993. Postwar Munich had repressed its revolutionary heritage as assiduously as its Nazi past, but after seventy-five years the Bavarian SPD decided it was time to commemorate the revolution and its chief political figure, Kurt Eisner. The state's conservative leaders, however, refused to attend the Socialists' ceremony. CSU chief Theo Waigel declared that Bavaria's current democracy had nothing in common with "Eisner's soviet." Minister-President Edmund Stoiber, by contrast, sponsored a counterceremony at the same time as the Socialist demonstration, claiming a tie between the original "Free State of Bavaria" and the present CSU-ruled bastion of "democracy, human rights, and federalism." As for the much-maligned father of the first free state, Munich never saw fit to name a street after Eisner, but the place where he was assassinated in February 1919 is now marked by an outline of his body on the sidewalk, which is often stepped upon by unknowing pedestrians.

IN THE EARLY 1990s, overcoming more than a generation of resistance, Munich finally began a concerted effort to reckon with the most difficult dimension of its recent past, its role as birthplace of Nazism and symbolic capital of the Third Reich. The municipality, in league with local museums and scholarly institutions, sponsored a number of exhibitions and conferences on various aspects of Munich's experience under Hitler. The process culminated in an ambitious exhibition in 1993 entitled "München—Hauptstadt der Bewegung [Capital of the Movement]. The exhibit was widely praised in the German and foreign press, though it did not escape notice that the former Capital of the Movement had needed a half century to undertake what many other German cities had started years before.

Better late than never. The official efforts to deal with Munich's dark past were especially salutary because the city had harbored for some time more than its share of extreme rightist organizations. Since the late 1950s it had housed the Gerhard Frey Press, West Germany's largest neonationalist publishing concern. Munich was also headquarters of Frey's Deutsche Volksunion, a nativistic, hypernationalist group that cooperated with neo-Nazis in a futile effort to gain representation in the Bundestag. As the Deutsche Volksunion faded into insignificance, another Munich-based extremist party, the Republikaner, rose to prominence. Its leader was a former Waffen-SS officer and talk show journalist named Franz Schönhuber. Careful to avoid falling afoul of West Germany's laws against blatant neo-Nazism, Schönhuber won a considerable following by exploiting well-entrenched currents of xenophobia. One of the ugliest fruits of the antiforeigner agitation was a bombing attack at the 1980

Oktoberfest, in which 13 people were killed and 219 injured. According to the journalist Michael Schmidt, who wrote a penetrating account of Germany's "new Right" in 1989, Munich has remained the Capital of the Movement for Germany's neo-Nazi scene.

Yet there were also many—and arguably more persuasive—signs pointing in a different direction. Since the early 1960s, when the SPD gained control of the mayor's office and city council, Munich's municipal government has become known for its progressive and innovative policies. The "Munich Line," a system for dealing with street demonstrations (of which Munich had plenty) with flexibility and restraint, became a model for Germany. Munich's 1972 Summer Olympic festival, the first in Germany since the Nazi games of 1936, was of course blighted by the deaths of eleven Israeli athletes at the hands of Palestinian terrorists. Nonetheless, the games showcased a city determined to demonstrate its modernity, from a new subway system to the spectacular tented Olympic Stadium, which became as much a symbol of the new Munich as the Frauenkirche was of the old. New Munich was also evident—in a much more important way—in various grass-roots campaigns to promote a spirit of tolerance that had often been honored more in slogans than in practice. The city took the lead in opposing the wave of antiforeigner violence that swept across Germany in the wake of national reunification in 1990. On 6 December 1992, under the motto "Munich: A City Says No," four hundred thousand citizens created a candlelit human chain that was the largest demonstration in Germany against ethnic prejudice. In the following year, on the sixtieth anniversary of Hitler's seizure of power, thousands of citizens again said no, this time to a legacy with which their city was closely linked but which now, at long last, they were determined to repudiate.

NOTES

N O T E S

ABBREVIATIONS

BAK	Bundesarchiv Koblenz
BA/MA	Bundesarchiv/Militärarchiv
BHSA	Bayerisches Hauptstaatsarchiv
BK	*Bayerische Kurier*
B.u.R.	Bürgermeister und Rat
HI	Hoover Institution
LC	Library of Congress
MInn	Ministerium des Innern
MNN	*Münchener Neueste Nachrichten*
MP	*Münchener Post*
NA	National Archives (Washington, D.C.)
NYT	*New York Times*
PRO	Public Record Office (London)
SOPADE	Sozialdemokratische Partei Deutschlands (in exile)
SA	Staatsarchiv München
SAM	Stadtarchiv München
SZ	*Süddeutsche Zeitung*
VB	*Völkischer Beobachter*
VfZG	*Vierteljahrshefte für Zeitgeschichte*

INTRODUCTION

xi. "within its walls": Adolf Hitler, *Mein Kampf* (Boston, 1943), 126.
xii. "the rough benches": G. H. Horstmann, *Consular Reminiscences* (Philadelphia, 1886), 322.

xiii. "and coach drivers": Max Halbe, *Jahrhundertwende* (Danzig, 1935), 33.

xiii. "sense of constraint": Robert Schauffler, "Munich—A City of Good Nature," *Century,* LVI (1909), 72.

xiii. "soul life in Germany": Katherine Mansfield, *In a German Pension* (Harmondsworth, 1964), 12.

xiii. "not know Munich": Eugen Franz, *München als deutsche Kulturstadt im 19. Jahrhundert* (Berlin, 1936), 68.

xiv. "nature's work alone": David Clay Large, "Life, Liberty, and the Happiness of Pursuit: Lola Montez in Bavaria," in *For Want of a Horse: Choice and Chance in History,* ed. John Merriman (New York, 1985), 34–39.

xiv. discounts this story: Bruce Seymour, *Lola Montez* (New Haven, 1996), 103.

xv. "*Ring* slowly fulfilled": Ludwig Hüttl, *Ludwig II* (Munich, 1986), 50.

xv. "at his table": Wilfred Blunt, *The Dream King: Ludwig II of Bavaria* (New York, 1970), 40.

xvi. "by arrogant foreigners": Rosalie Braun-Artaria, *Von berühmten Zeitgenossen* (Munich, 1918), 97–98.

xvi. he had rejected: Friedrich Prinz, *Ludwig II: Ein königliches Doppelleben* (Berlin, 1993), 77–78.

xvi. "general in the army": Maria Makela, *The Munich Secession* (Princeton, 1990), 15. See also Robin Lenman, "A Community in Transition: Painters in Munich, 1886–1924," *Central European History* 15 (1982), 3–33.

xvii. "dozen auspicious exhibitions": Makela, 8.

xvii. conducting "German music": Peter Gay, "Hermann Levi: A Study in Self-Hatred," in Peter Gay, *Freud, Jews and Other Germans* (New York, 1978), 189–230.

xvii. "genius among cities": On Ibsen in Munich, see Michael Meyer, *Ibsen* (Harmondsworth, 1985), 417–41; and Peter Jelavich, *Munich and Theatrical Modernism* (Cambridge, Mass., 1985), 23–24, 44–46.

xvii. "that cataclysmic force": Georg Franz, "Munich: Birthplace and Center of the National Socialist German Workers' Party," *Journal of Modern History* 29 (1957), 319.

xviii. "of the Nazi party": ibid., 320.

xviii. life of the city: "Die Hauptstadt der Bewegung," *Münchener Zeitung,* 10–11 Aug. 1935.

xix. "bathrooms in their houses": Carlamara Heim, *Josefa Halbinger: Jahrgang 1900* (Munich, 1980), 8.

xix. "down the walls": Karl Valentin, *Gesammelte Schriften in einem Bande,* ed. Michael Schulte (Munich, 1990), 536.

xix. "other cities in Germany": Consul to Assistant Secretary of State, 10 November 1883, American Consulate, Munich, C8-12, NA.

xix. "hearts are always open": Bettler in München, RA 57918, SA.

xx. "by the sleeve": Sybille Leitner, " 'Vermessene Frauen': Das Sozialprofil der Münchner Prostituierten," in *München—Musenstadt mit Hinterhöfen:*

Die Prinzregentenzeit 1886–1912, ed. Friedrich Prinz and Marita Krauss (Munich, 1988), 158.

xx. "can walk there": *MNN,* 9 Feb. 1911.

xx. "scientific respectability": *Das Bayerische Vaterland,* 8 Jan. 1911.

xx. "pretty Isar bank": Ludwig M. Schneider, *Die populäre Kritik am Staat und Gesellschaft in München 1886–1914* (Munich, 1975), 153.

xx. "in the greatest secrecy": *MNN,* 28 July 1911.

xxi. "workers in solidarity": Schneider, 35. On labor strife in Munich, see also Carl Fritz, *München als Industriestadt* (Berlin, 1913) and Richard Bauer, ed., *Prinzregentenzeit* (Munich, 1988), 225–28.

xxi. early twentieth century: On Patriots, see Jelavich, 13–14.

xxii. eight in 1907: On SPD's gains, see Merith Niehuss, "Parteien, Wahlen, Arbeiterbewegung," in Prinz and Krauss, eds., *Musenstadt,* 44–54.

xxii. had reached 8, 739: Peter Hanke, *Zur Geschichte der Juden in München 1933–1945* (Munich, 1967), 16.

xxii. "and thoroughly hated": Schneider, 187.

xxii. "secularized Talmud high school": Hanke, 18.

xxii. leading art patrons: *Die Prinzregentenzeit: Ausstellung im Münchener Stadtmuseum* (Munich, 1989), 296–97.

xxiii. "Munich middle class": Jürgen Kolbe, *Heller Zauber: Thomas Mann in München* (Berlin, 1987), 239.

xxiii. "call it home": Schneider, 189.

xxiii. "in your eye": ibid.

xxiii. "a hundred times": ibid., 196.

xxiii. " 'Schmulius Jew' ": ibid. On the Munich folk singers, see also Robert Eban Sackett, *Popular Entertainment, Class, and Politics in Munich, 1900–1923* (Cambridge, Mass., 1982).

xxiv. "and commercial mobility": Eva-Maria Tiedemann, "Die Frühe politische Formierung des Antisemitismus," in Prinz and Krauss, eds., *Musenstadt,* 304.

xxiv. "curse of the Jews": ibid., 305.

xxiv. for German culture: *Alldeutsche Blätter,* 18 Sept. 1898.

xxv. "throughout the world": Gary D. Stark, *Entrepreneurs of Ideology: Neoconservative Publishers in Germany, 1890–1933* (Chapel Hill, 1981), 114.

xxv. "and cultural life": ibid., 121.

xxv. "of our time": ibid., 124.

CHAPTER 1: GERMANY'S BOHEMIA

3. "in Munich itself": Peg Weiss, ed., *Kandinsky in Munich, 1896–1914* (New York, 1982), 27.

3. "synonymous with culture": Erich Mühsam, *Unpolitische Erinnerungen* (Berlin, 1961), 150.

4. "spirit of tolerance": Werner Heisenberg, *Across the Frontiers* (New York, 1974), 58.

4. "place to live": Viktor Mann, *Wir waren Fünf* (Frankfurt, 1976), 54.

4. "and fat hips": Theodor Lessing, *Einmal und nie wieder* (Gütersloh, 1969), 288.

4. "Sioux in North America": Friedrich Prinz, "Annäherung an München," in Prinz and Kraus, eds., *Musenstadt,* 9.

4. "the word 'healthy' ": Ronald Hayman, *Thomas Mann: A Biography* (New York, 1995), 118.

4. "some back alley": Richard Seewald, *Der Mann von Gegenüber* (Munich, 1963), 138.

5. "like sword blades": René Prevot, *Seliger Zweiklang: Schwabing/Montmartre* (Munich, 1946), 12.

5. local Socialist publisher: On Lenin in Munich, see Ernst Bäumler, *Verschwörung in Schwabing: Lenins Begegnung mit Deutschland* (Munich, 1991).

5. "working out of fate": Martin Green, *The von Richthofen Sisters* (New York, 1974), 92.

5. "name of Schwabing": M. J. Bonn, *Wandering Scholar* (London, 1949), 165–66.

5. "the modern spirit": "Münchener Flugschriften," in *Die Moderne* (Munich, 1891), 3–6.

6. "in the crush": Jelavich, 34.

6. "escalation of passions": Hanns von Gumppenberg, *Lebenserinnerungen* (Berlin, 1929), 158–59.

6. "way for them": "Gesellschaft für modernes Leben," RA 57851, SA.

6. "socially dispossessed": Jelavich, 41.

6. "two rival camps": Gumppenberg, 160.

7. "state his second": *Fremdenblatt,* 2 March 1891.

7. "who are atheists": Gumppenberg, 163.

7. "laughable fool": Jelavich, 36.

7. "example of me": Gumppenberg, 174–78.

8. "ground of atheism": Jelavich, 42.

8. "in this domain": ibid., 43.

8. "arm in arm with Socialists": *Fremdenblatt,* 17 Feb. 1891.

8. "of the national spirit": Jelavich, 42.

10. "Genius and Madness": Peter D. G. Brown, *Oskar Panizza: His Life and Works* (Las Vegas/Bern/Frankfurt, 1983), 2–23.

10. "chain of sexuality": Oskar Panizza, "Die Unsittlichkeits-Entrüstung der Pietisten und die freie Literatur," *Gegen Prüderie und Lüge* (Munich, 1892), 7–22.

10. humanity with syphilis: Brown, 24–32.

10. "heroes and martyrs": ibid., 41.

11. "out alive": ibid., 45.

11. "only forum"; "bourgeois courts": Jelavich, 60.

11. "sluttishness" and seduction: Oskar Panizza, "Prostitution," *Die Gesellschaft* (July 1982), 1159–83.

11. priests and Jews: Oskar Panizza, "Bayreuth und die Homosexualität," *Die Gesellschaft* (January 1895), 88–92.

12. "rather than slaughterhouses": Oskar Panizza, "Abschied von München," in *Die kriminelle Psychose, genannt Psichopatic criminalis* (Munich, 1978), 201–05.

12. especially satirical humor: Peter Gay, *The Cultivation of Hatred* (New York, 1993), 368.

13. "male strength pills": On *Simplicissimus,* see Ann Taylor Allen, *Satire and Society: Kladderadatsch and Simplicissimus 1890–1914* (Lexington, Ky., 1984); *Simplicissimus: Eine Satirische Zeitschrift, München 1896–1944. Ausstellung im Haus der Kunst* (Munich, 1978). Quotations are from Allen.

14. "broke even financially": Korfiz Holm, *Farbiger Abglanz* (Munich, 1940), 75.

14. "the whole show": Allen, 62–63.

15. "in the stockade": ibid., 115.

15. "a foreign power": *MNN,* 5 June 1903.

15. "I'd be delighted": Allen, 131.

16. "nary a care": *Simplicissimus: Ausstellung,* 240.

16. "has to scratch": ibid., 241.

16. "eat it all": ibid., 191.

16. "marriage for money": *Simplicissimus* 9 (1900), 69.

17. "intimate and exclusive": Harold B. Segal, *Turn-of-the-Century Cabaret* (New York, 1987), 145.

18. "reaction and obscurantism": Jelavich, 170.

18. "puppets' strings": ibid., 171.

18. "of greedy passion": Segal, 151.

18. "Asia and Africa": Jelavich, 173.

19. "most immoral manner"; "art and science": ibid., 172.

20. Schwabing's ideological legacy: On Fanny, see Richard Faber, *Franziska zu Reventlow und die Schwabinger Gegenkultur* (Cologne, 1993); Helmut Fritz, *Die erotische Rebellion: Das Leben der Gräfin zu Reventlow* (Frankfurt, 1980); J. Szekely, *Franziska Gräfin zu Reventlow: Leben und Werk* (Bonn, 1979).

20. "ridiculous prejudices": Franziska zu Reventlow, *Gesammelte Werke in einem Band,* ed. Else Reventlow (Munich, 1925), 11.

21. "come from Lübeck": Fritz, 44.

21. "sacred source": Szekely, 17.

21. "Venus from Schleswig-Holstein": Fritz, 29.

21. "to be elegant": Korfiz Holm, *ich—Kleingeschrieben* (Munich, 1932), 152.

21. "became its priestess": Fritz, 50.

22. studio modeling: Robin Lenman, "A Community in Transition: Painters in Munich, 1886–1924," *Central European History* 15 (1982), 3–33.

22. "person cannot work" (and following quotations): Franziska zu Reventlow, *Tagebücher 1895–1910* (Frankfurt, 1984), 41, 53, 72, 85–86.

23. "without deeper feeling": Fritz, 78–85.

24. "yeast . . . from good houses": Faber, 104–21.

24. "stand being alone": Reventlow, *Ellen Olestjerne, Gesammelte Werke,* 698.

24. "time in jail": Fritz, 29.

24. "their own bodies": ibid., 86–96.

25. "quietly like Nature": Claudia Koonz, *Mothers in the Fatherland* (New York, 1987), 108.

25. "of ancient rituals": Reventlow, *Herrn Dames Aufzeichnungen, Gesammelte Werke,* 128. On the Cosmic Circle, see Green, 73–100; Fritz, 59–70; Faber, passim; Roderich Huch, *Alfred Schuler, Ludwig Klages und Stefan George: Erinnerungen an Kreis- und Krisen der Jahrhundertwende in München-Schwabing* (Amsterdam, 1973); Hermann Wilhelm, *Dichter, Denker, Fememörder: Rechtsradikalismus in München von der Jahrhundertwende bis 1921* (Berlin, 1989), 9–35; Frederic V. Grunfeld, *Prophets without Honor* (New York, 1980), 67–95.

26. "will be decided": Green, 92.

26. and swan maidens: ibid., 89; Faber, 153–70.

26. "urn of paganism": Green, 354; Wilhelm, 19–21.

26. what nature was: Raymond H. Dominick III, *The Environmental Movement in Germany* (Bloomington, 1992), 19–20.

27. " 'progress and civilization' ": Fritz, 144.

27. "would be rejuvenated": Hans Eggert Schröder, *Ludwig Klages: Die Geschichte seines Lebens* (Bonn, 1966), 274.

27. "as a man"; "us all in": Fritz, 63.

28. "from a vault": Wilhelm, 15.

28. the modern world: Green, 76.

28. "wheel of fire": Huch, 8–9; Wilhelm, 19–20; Grunfeld, 71–72.

29. "a person is"; "flies on flypaper": Grunfeld, 71–72.

29. copper bracelets: Huch, 29–30. On Nietzsche and the Cosmic Circle, see Steven E. Aschheim, *The Nietzsche Legacy in Germany* (Berkeley, 1992), 71–84.

29. "beautiful Assyrian Prince"; "full of yearning": Fritz, 75.

30. "glory of everything"; "books of all epochs": Grunfeld, 68.

30. "most amazing things": Erich Kahler, *Die Verantwortung des Geistes* (Frankfurt, 1952), 166.

30. "and symbolic power": Wilheim, 14.

30. "be your Peter": Wayne Andrews, *Siegfried's Curse: The German Journey from Nietzsche to Hesse* (New York, 1972), 180.

30. "to what end": Grunfeld, 73.

31. "bloodless, very expressive": *The Journals of André Gide,* ed. Justin O'Brien (New York, 1956), I:114.

31. "Jews, and whores": Kolbe, 178.

31. "Miracle, Action, Life": Green, 92.

31. "evil and nefarious": Gerhard Masur, *Prophets of Yesterday* (New York, 1961), 120.

32. "their spiritual lord": Thomas Mann, "At the Prophet's," *Stories of Three Decades* (New York, 1966), 288.

33. "his pagan cool": Szekely, 112.

33. his real mother: Fritz, 68.

33. "negative-molochistic forces": ibid., 144–49.

34. "stood before me": Lessing, 309.

34. "do with politics": Wilhelm, 19.

34. "as we do": Grunfeld, 71.

34. lose their vitality: Wilhelm, 20.

34. "you to Juda": Grunfeld, 72

34. "Klages is a Jew": Wilhelm, 23–24.

36. light a purging fire: Thomas Mann, "Gladius Dei," *Stories of Three Decades,* 181–93.

36. the avant-garde: *Der Tag,* 13–14 April 1901.

36. oneself serious harm: Lenman, "Community," 27.

36. "Munich any longer": Robin Lenman, "Politics and Culture: The State and the Avant-Garde in Munich 1886–1914," *Society and Politics in Wilhelmine Germany,* ed. Richard J. Evans (New York, 1978), 92.

36. "only reaction": Makela, 136.

37. "even get tired": Kandinsky, "Correspondence from Munich," in Kandinsky, *Complete Writings on Art*, ed. Kenneth Lindsey and Peter Vergo (Boston, 1982), I:46.

37. "find enough support": Makela, 140.

37. "Semitic tendencies"; "of solid achievement": ibid., 138–40.

39. "a feeling soul": Hitler, 26–27.

40. "since that time"; "to this state": ibid., 264, 576.

40. "for political activity": ibid., 154–56. See also A. Joachimsthaler, *Korrektur einer Biographie: Adolf Hitler 1908–1920* (Munich, 1989), 77–98.

41. "roars of laughter": Thomas Mann, "A Brother," *Order of the Day* (New York, 1942), 153–61.

CHAPTER 2: THE GREAT SWINDLE

44. "the Isar city": Thomas Mann, *Doctor Faustus* (New York, 1948), 285.

44. than a ruler: Alfons Beckenbauer, *Ludwig III von Bayern 1845–1921* (Regensburg, 1987), 122–30.

45. "accession will bring": Ludwig Hummert, *Bayern von Königsreich zur Diktatur 1900–1933* (Munich, 1979), 35.

46. pan-Slav radicals: Polizeidirektion München an das Staatsministerium des königlichen Hauses, 15 July 1914, MInn 71523, BHSA.

46. "country manage it": Hummert, 43.

47. "king and fatherland": Ludwig Hollweck, ed., *Unser München* (Munich, 1967), 125.

47. "do your duty": Beckenbauer, 152.
47. "people of brothers": Wilfried Rudloff, "Notjahre. Stadtpolitik in Krieg, Inflation und Weltwirtschaftskrise 1914 bis 1933." in *Geschichte der Stadt München,* ed. Richard Bauer (Munich, 1992), 336.
47. over and over again: Karl Alexander von Müller, *Mars und Venus: Erinnerungen 1914–1918* (Munich, 1954), 14–15.
47. "was the uncertainty": Modris Eksteins, *Rites of Spring: The Great War and the Birth of the Modern Age* (Boston, 1989), 91–92.
48. "sense of hope": Kolbe, 252.
48. "brotherhood of arms": Sackett, 70.
48. "station to volunteer": Kolbe, 247.
48. "second-class citizens": *MP*, 1 Aug. 1914.
48. "my overflowing heart": Hitler, 161.
49. "six years later": ibid., 163.
49. "A Serbian": Bruno Walter, *Themes and Variations: An Autobiography* (New York, 1946), 220.
49. German passport: *I Was a German: The Autobiography of Ernst Toller* (New York, 1991), 63.
49. "the English spirit": Klaus Mann, *Kind dieser Zeit* (Munich, 1965), 68.
50. "have a say": Lenman, "Politics and Culture," 92.
50. "of the hour": ibid., 103–4.
50. "secure their existences": Hermann Sinsheimer, *Gelebt in Paradies* (Munich, 1953), 229–30.
51. "we will succeed": *Simplicissimus: Ausstellung,* 254–65.
51. "holy war begins": Eksteins, 93.
51. "a white nation": *Aufrufe und Reden deutscher Professoren im Ersten Weltkrieg* (Stuttgart, 1975), 48.
51. "in couplet form"; "his German name": Sackett, 74.
51. "press is unanimous": Hans Rudolf Vaget, "Musik in München," *Thomas Mann Jahrbuch* 7 (1994), 56.
52. "the Hitler movement": *VB,* 6 May 1934.
52. "person of the Kaiser": Nigel Hamilton, *The Brothers Mann* (New Haven, 1979), 159.
52. "aestheticism and Europeanism": ibid., 168.
52. "public order": Sackett, 76.
53. "with furloughed soldiers"; "Kabarett im Kriege": *Der Zwiebelfisch* 7 (1916).
53. "weapon of thought": Hamilton, 161. On Thomas Mann in World War I, see also Vaget, "The Steadfast Tin Soldier: Thomas Mann in World Wars I and II," in *1914–1945: German Reflections on the Two World Wars,* ed. Reinhold Grimm and Jost Hermand (Madison, 1992), 3–12.
53. "again and to win": Vaget, "Tin Soldier," 7.
54. *"might and mind"*: Hamilton, 166, 170.
54. path of decency; "condition each other": Kolbe, 263.

54. "slander and deception": Hamilton, 169.
55. "produce nothing else": Thomas Mann, *Reflections of a Nonpolitical Man* (New York, 1983), 3.
55. "unrestricted submarine warfare": Klaus Mann, *The Turning Point* (New York, 1984), 40.
55. "has no basis": Thomas Mann, *Reflections,* 100.
56. "thoroughly related": Kolbe, 333.
56. bohemian rebellion: Anton M. Koktanek, *Oswald Spengler in seiner Zeit* (Munich, 1968), 60–69.
56. "Germany means Berlin": ibid., 122.
56. "centuries—not years": Oswald Spengler, *The Decline of the West,* vol. I, *Form and Actuality* (New York, 1926), 46–47.
57. "been the tradition": H. Stuart Hughes, *Oswald Spengler* (New York, 1952), 66.
57. "to the surface": Kolbe, 333.
58. than the Prussians: Karl-Ludwig Ay, *Die Entstehung einer Revolution* (Berlin, 1968), 134–88.
58. in a factory: Rudloff, 337–38.
58. "present political situation"; "in another way": Sackett, 78.
59. "the [manual] workers": Gerald D. Feldman, *Army, Industry and Labor in Germany 1914–1918* (Princeton, 1966), 467.
60. "for their misfortune": ibid., 422.
60. "building out back": Sackett, 81.
60. to the list: Rudloff, 339.
61. "for philosophical contemplation": Koktanek, 192–93.
61. "and infinitely sad": Klaus Mann, *Turning Point,* 36.
61. "the winter months": ibid., 39.
62. "gelatin—vile": Eva Maria Volland and Reinhard Bauer, eds., *München— Stadt der Frauen* (Munich, 1991), 114.
62. "grew desperate": Toller, 130–31.
62. "egg-ham-and-butter hunters": Klaus Mann, *Turning Point,* 36.
63. "mice and rats": Sackett, 82.
63. "food per se"; "frustration and bitterness": Rudloff, 342.
63. "us like this": Erich Mühsam, *Tagebücher 1910–1924,* ed. Chris Hirte (Munich, 1994), 174–77.
64. "in the countryside": Ay., 141.
64. "to swallow dishwater": Toller, 144.
64. 13,725 soldiers; bells into shells: Rudloff, 344, 343.
65. "sharply curtailed": ibid., 343.
65. "their entire lives": ibid.
65. in military hospitals: Volland and Bauer, 112–13, 117–19.
65. "spineless cowards"; "at the front"; "into the abyss": Hitler, 192–94.
67. "Social Democratic newspaper": Sterling Fishman, "Prophets, Poets and Priests: A Study of the Men and Ideas That Made the Munich Revolution

of 1918/19" (Ph.D. Dissertation, University of Wisconsin, Mad., 1960), 15–16.

67. "no looking back": Allan Mitchell, *The Revolution in Bavaria 1918–1919: The Eisner Regime and the Soviet Republic* (Princeton, 1965), 60.

67. "a new humanity"; "be carried over": Fishman, 39.

68. "believers in Munich": Ernst Müller-Meiningen, *Aus Bayerns Schwersten Tagen* (Berlin, 1923), 106–7.

68. "has dominated Germany": Polizeidirektion München, 27 Jan. 1918, MInn 66283, BHSA.

69. "from foreign influence": Stark, 128.

69. "against the vile"; "deepened and transformed": ibid., 129, 130.

69. "of national mourning": Thoma quoted in Constance Hallgarten, *Als Pazifistin in Deutschland* (Stuttgart, 1956), 29.

70. only business papers: Rudolf Sebottendorff. *Bevor Hitler kam* (Munich, 1934), 44.

70. "your blood pure": Wilhelm, 44.

71. "Hold Fast": Richard Hanser, *Putsch: How Hitler Made Revolution* (New York, 1970), 107–8.

71. "may as well be tried": Robert B. Asprey, *The German High Command at War* (New York, 1991), 460.

72. "to be done": ibid., 461.

72. "lost their heads"; "years of lies": ibid., 453, 467–73.

73. "deceived and duped": Mitchell, 76. See also Müller, 250–62.

73. "half sick": Thomas Mann, *Diaries 1918–1939* (London, 1984), 11.

74. "wish for this"; "from the other": ibid., 12.

74. "Stadelheim released me": Oskar Maria Graf, *Wir sind Gefangene* (Berlin, 1948), 336.

74. "will come first": Hanser, 119.

75. "the coming days": Graf, 344.

75. "prophet mane"; "sure of that": Müller-Meiningen, 29–31.

75. "going to happen": Mitchell, 91; Beckenbauer, 257.

CHAPTER 3: RED MUNICH

77. "Bolshevism its chance": Gerald D. Feldman, *The Great Disorder: Politics, Economics and Society in the German Inflation 1914–1924* (New York, 1993), 125.

77. "Follow us": Eberhard Buchner, *Revolutionsdokumente: Im Zeichen der roten Fahne* (Berlin, 1921), I:364.

78. "to be marching": Graf, 344.

78. "Long Live Freedom": Mitchell, 99.

79. "provisional prime minister": ibid., 100.

79. "I'm afraid of nothing": Beckenbauer, 263.

80. "dynasty is deposed": Mitchell, 101.

80. "all labor activity": Fishman, 53–54.

81. "That is the revolution": Thomas Mann, *Diaries,* 19–20.

82. "great German republic": Gordon Craig, *Germany 1866–1945* (New York, 1978), 402.

82. "with her baby": Alfred Döblin, *A People Betrayed* (New York, 1983), 55.

83. "go into politics": Hitler, 203–6.

83. "future will bring": Herbert Köpfler and Carl-Ludwig Reichert, *Umsturz in München* (Munich, 1988), 52.

83. "Boom! Boom! Boom": Sackett, 99.

83. "all be over": Hanser, 143.

84. "composing string quartets": ibid., 144.

84. for Munich's children: Fishman, 60; Mitchell, 113.

84. gripped the land: *MNN,* 18 Nov. 1918.

85. "shameful peace settlement": Josef Hofmiller, *Revolutionstagebuch 1918/19* (Leipzig, 1938), 59.

85. "maintenance of order": Mitchell, 114.

85. "of the land": Kurt Eisner, *Die neue Zeit* (Munich, 1919), 24–25.

85. "University of Munich": George D. Herron Papers, Box 1, HI.

86. "simpleminded"; *MNN,* 24 Nov. 1918.

86. "political and social life": Rudolf Herz and Dirk Halfbrodt, *Fotografie und Revolution: München 1918/19* (Munich, 1988), 28.

86. "an ignorant people": Toller, 145.

87. "good thing to do": Hanser, 145.

87. "want anarchy": *MNN,* 20 Dec. 1918.

88. "We want a Bavarian": Fishman, 101–2.

88. "of a littérateur": Hofmiller, 58.

89. "out a flue": ibid., 135.

89. "on election day": Herz and Halfbrodt, 104.

89. "a crushing defeat": Mitchell, 222.

90. "or a criminal": Müller, 312.

90. "cursed man in Germany": Fishman, 109.

90. "week is over": Herbert Haviland Field Papers. Private Diary, HI.

90. "me dead once": Richard Grunberger, *Red Rising in Bavaria* (London, 1973), 78.

91. "not a German": ibid., 84.

91. around his body: Friedrich Hitzer, *Anton Graf Arco* (Munich, 1988), 32.

91. with alacrity: Graf, 389.

91. "Down with Auer": Field Papers, Private Diary, HI.

91. "unsullied idealism": Hanser, 162.

92. in the head: Müller, 311.

92. "bullet for Eisner": Ricarda Huch, "Kurt Eisners Todestag," *Gesammelte Schriften: Essays, Reden, Autobiographische Aufzeichnungen* (Freiburg, 1964), 134.

92. "unifier of the proletariat": Müller, 312.

92. "the news came": Thomas Mann, *Diaries,* 34.

92. not to Arco-Valley: Hofmiller, 153.

92. "an evil spirit": Fishman, 112.

92. "meant to understand": Ricarda Huch, 131–32.

103. "never a Bavarian": Oswald Garrison Villard, *Fighting Years: Memoirs of a Liberal Editor* (New York, 1939), 418.

103. sacred spot: Sebottendorff, 83–84.

104. "he loved humanity": Fishman, 115.

104. "that went before": Heinrich Mann, "Kurt Eisner." *Macht und Menschen* (Frankfurt, 1989), 169–70.

104. "the near future": Field to American Commission to Negotiate Peace, 26 Feb. 1919, Field Papers, HI.

104. as a prostitute: Field Report, 15 March 1919, ibid.

105. "forth a mouse"; "to the left"; "is now accomplished": Mitchell, 289, 290.

105. "mentally unbalanced": Field Report, 26 Feb. 1919, HI.

106. such antics: *MNN,* 19 Feb. 1919.

106. "thing of impossibility": Mitchell, 296.

106. "Jew from Berlin": Diethard Hennig, *Johannes Hoffmann: Sozialdemokrat und bayerischer Ministerpräsident* (Munich, 1990), 250.

106. "like a bomb": Erich Mühsam, *Von Eisner bis Leviné* (Berlin, 1929), 39.

108. "Jewish goblin": Grunberger, 94; Mitchell, 304–8.

108. "against the Entente": Thomas Mann, *Diaries,* 43.

108. "ex-queen's bedroom": Toller, 158.

109. "creative revolutionary act": Ernst Niekisch, *Gewagtes Leben: Begegnungen und Begebnisse* (Cologne/Berlin, 1958), 67.

109. "a responsible office"; "bygone age"; "and noble humanity": ibid., 67–70.

110. "more appropriate date": Hofmiller, 177.

110. "reaction sets in": Thomas Mann, *Diaries,* 44.

111. "but a dream": Fishman, 166.

111. "would it end"; "be at hand": Toller, 159, 160–61.

112. "eggs, butter, and bacon": Franz Schoenberner, *Reflections of a European Intellectual* (New York, 1946), 114.

112. than a *y:* Hofmiller, 178.

112. toilet key crisis; "firmly taken away": Toller, 162, 163.

114. rear by rail: Max Siegert, *Aus Münchens schwerster Zeit: Erinnerungen aus dem Münchener Hauptbahnhof während der Revolutions- und Rätezeit* (Munich, 1928), 52–53.

114. "its Russian brothers": Mitchell, 319.

114. "the revolutionary sky": Wollenberg ms., Erich Wollenberg Papers, Box 1, HI.

115. "furnishings and books": Hayman, 310–11.

115. punishable by death: Mitchell, 323.

115. "of the proletariat": Grunberger, 125.

116. "of all Bavarians": Wolfgang Zorn, *Geschichte Bayerns im 20. Jahrhundert* (Munich, 1986), 194.

117. would send soldiers: Bürgerrat der Stadt München to Hoffmann, 10 Apr. 1919, MA 99902, BHSA.

117. and ill led: Toller, 181–86; Wollenberg, 171–78.

117. "purpose at all": Toller, 192.

118. *are not Russians*: Mitchell, 326–27.

118. "non-Jewish colleagues": Hofmiller, 206, 209.

118. "exemplary judgment": Thomas Mann, *Diaries,* 155.

118. "Schwabing intellectuals": Manfred von Killinger, *Ernstes und Heiteres aus dem Putschleben* (Munich, 1939), 11.

119. and shot: Josef Karl, *Die Schreckenherrschaft in München und Spartakus im bayerischen Oberland* (Munich, 1919), 77–96.

119. "frenzy of revenge": Toller, 199–200.

119. "morale collapsed entirely": Wollenberg, 202.

120. "well disciplined": Thomas Mann, *Diaries,* 54.

120. throne of the Wittelsbachs: Killinger, 23.

120. "into a washhouse": Toller, 248–49.

120. "pressure was abominable": Thomas Mann, *Diaries,* 55.

121. "to the soldiers": Graf, 436–37.

121. of his comrades: Joachimsthaler, 204–23.

121. blamed on "the Prussians": Grunberger, 145.

122. flat as well: Zorn, 209.

122. had Jewish ancestry: Der Generalstabschef Toller vor dem Münchener Standgericht, 15 July 1919, MA 99926, BHSA.

122. "Without Eisner, no Hitler": Hanser, 124.

122. "violent than in Munich": Franz, "Birthplace of Nazism," 334.

CHAPTER 4: BIRTHPLACE OF NAZISM

123. "pulled toward Munich": Lion Feuchtwanger, *Erfolg: Drei Jahre Geschichte einer Provinz* (Frankfurt, 1975), I:32. On *Erfolg*'s historical validity, see Reinhart Hoffmeister, *Wahrheit und Wirklichkeit in Lion Feuchtwangers Erfolg* (Munich, 1981).

124. king of Munich: Janet Barnhart, "Art beyond Art's Sake: Modern Movements and Politics in Munich, 1890–1924" (Ph.D. Dissertation, Harvard University, 1981), 270.

125. state like Bavaria: Robert S. Garnett, *Lion, Eagle and Swastika: Bavarian Monarchism in Weimar Germany, 1918–1933* (New York, 1991), 40–41.

125. "triumph of *Kirgistentum*": Thomas Mann, *Briefe 1889–1936* (Frankfurt, 1979), 162.

125. centralists at heart: Garnett, 42.

126. by the Entente: Lage in München, 18 May 1919, 14 June 1919, Polizeidirektion München, MA 99902, BHSA.

126. "in their nightshirts": Ernst Röhm, *Geschichte eines Hochverräters* (Munich, 1931), 28.

126. avant-garde culture: On the Einwohnerwehr, see David Clay Large, *The Politics of Law and Order: A History of the Bavarian Einwohnerwehr 1918–1921* (Philadelphia, 1980).

126. based in Moscow: On Orgesch and Orka, see ibid., and Rudolf Kanzler, *Bayerns Kampf gegen den Bolshevismus: Geschichte der bayerischen Einwohnerwehren* (Munich, 1931).

127. "for an Aryan": Karl Mayr, "I was Hitler's Boss," *Current History* (November 1941), 145.

127. "of the moment": Hitler, 208.

127. "a new party"; "of the students": ibid., 210, 215.

128. "glittered fanatically": Müller, 339.

128. "harmless prelude": ibid.

128. "I could 'speak' ": Hitler, 215–16.

129. "think his way": Joachim Remak, *Nazi Years* (Englewood Cliffs, 1969), 25.

129. "feelings of responsibility": Hitler to Gemlich, 19 Sept. 1919, in *Hitler: Sämtliche Aufzeichnungen, 1905–1924,* ed. Eberhard Jäckel and Axel Kuhn (Stuttgart, 1980), 88–90.

129. Schutz- und Trutzbund: On this, see Deutschvölkischer Schutz- und Trutzbund, Polizeidirektion München 6697, NSDAP, SA. A good secondary study is Uwe Lohalm, *Völkischer Radikalismus: Die Geschichte des Deutschvölkischen Schutz- und Trutzbundes 1919–1923* (Hamburg, 1970).

130. "could use him": Charles Bracelen Flood, *Hitler: The Path to Power* (New York, 1989), 67.

130. "so many others": Hitler, 218.

130. at the party; "resolve of my life": ibid., 220–24.

131. "everlasting glory": Mayr, 195.

132. "street peddlers": Lage in München, 28 June 1919, Polizeidirektion München MA 99902, BHSA.

132. another fourteen days: Rudloff, "Notjahre," 350.

132. "crisis in town": Thomas Mann, *Diaries,* 84.

132. "profiteering and smuggling": Lage in München, 22 Nov. 1919, Polizeidirektion München 6679, SA.

132. "weak-willed government": Lage Bericht, 23 Dec. 1919, ibid.

132. "by the Left": Staatsmin. des Innern to Polizeidirektion München, 3 May 1921, MA 100403, BHSA.

133. of their terms: Zorn, 221.

133. "academic trash": See Bavarian Interior Ministry discussion with Munich police, 26 June 1919 and 16 July 1919, in MA 99902, BHSA.

133. toward his victim: Hitzer, 284–313.

134. German iron: Hitler, 357–58.

134. Harrer out: Flood, 80.

134. "big capitalism": Bericht, 9 Jan. 1920, Polizeidirektion München, 6697, SA.

134. little producers: Jeremy Noakes and Geoffrey Pridham, eds., *Documents on Nazism, 1919–1945* (New York, 1975), 38.

135. "of the people": *VB,* 22 Feb. 1922.

136. "son of a bitch": Hanser, 224–25.

136. "has vanished": Flood, 111.

136. "bank robber": Hanser, 226.

137. "dress rehearsal": ibid., 228.

137. Kapp Putsch in Munich: Zorn, 227–29.

138. man-about-Munich: On Eckart, see Margareta Plewina, *Auf den Weg zu Hitler: Der völkische Publizist Dietrich Eckart* (Bremen, 1970).

138. "get the women": ibid., 62.

139. Kahr's personality: Zorn, 233.

141. "has judged you": Hanser, 260.

141. "enough of them": Wilhelm, 131.

141. "Socialist swine": Hanser, 261.

142. "high civilization": Wilhelm Hoegner, *Die verratene Republik: Geschichte der deutschen Gegenrevolution* (Munich, 1958), 107.

143. enemies from within: Bericht, 25 Nov. 1921. Polizeidirektion München 6803, SA.

143. "curse of God": Reinhard Bauer and Ernst Piper, *München: Die Geschichte einer Stadt* (Munich, 1993), 284.

144. "power I have behind me": Gordon Craig, "Under an Evil Star," *New York Review of Books* (5 Oct. 1995), 24.

144. "wind of Bavaria"; "insult to Bavaria"; "was visiting Munich": Seeds to Earl of Balfour, 13 June 1922, FO 371/7525, PRO.

145. "they might come": *MNN,* 26 June 1922; *BK,* 28 June 1922.

145. "with the Jew government": *MP,* 30 June 1922.

145. "the November treason": Hanser, 272.

146. "thousands as one": Kurt Ludecke, *I Knew Hitler* (London, 1938), 22–33.

146. "only 100": Nachlass Kapp, Box 92, BHSA.

147. origins of SA: Peter Longerich, *Die braunen Bataillone: Geschichte der SA* (Munich, 1989), 9–32.

147. "Throw him out"; "fresh fellows": Versammlung SA, 19 Oct. 1921, Polizeidirektion München, 6803, SA.

147. "hate the Jews too"; "We are anti-Semitic": 26 Oct. 1921, ibid.

148. "out of the hall": Hitler, 505.

148. "afraid of nothing"; "SA name": Versammlung SA, 9 Nov. 1921, 30 Nov. 1921, Polizeidirektion München, 6803, SA.

148. "from this standpoint": Röhm, 9.

149. fashionable men's club: Henry A. Turner, *German Big Business and the Rise of Hitler* (New York, 1985), 49.

150. "petite-bourgeois mentality": ibid., 50.

150. "remarkable fellow"; "look at him"; "Sieg Heil": Ernst Hanfstaengl, *Unheard Witness* (Philadelphia, 1957), 32–38.

151. valuable objets d'art: ibid., 65.

153. among the faithful: On Hitler and Hoffmann, see Heinrich Hoffmann,

Hitler Was My Friend (London, 1955); Rudolf Herz, *Hoffmann und Hitler: Fotografie als Medium des Hitler-Mythos* (Munich, 1994).

153. "of the church party": Hoffmann, 52.
153. "anti-Jewish demonstrations": Bauer and Piper, 304.
154. "devil with Beelzebub": Hellmuth Auerbach, "Hitlers politische Lehrjahre und die Münchener Gesellschaft 1919–1923," *VfZG* 25 (1977), 26.
154. "inspired prophet"; "provincial horizon"; "the Nazi cause": Ludecke, 92.
155. "its individual members": Flood, 207.
155. the Munich cadres: Ludecke, 98.
155. his long life: Joachim Fest, *The Face of the Third Reich* (New York, 1970), 187–97.
156. "Hitler's co-thinker": ibid., 163–74. See also profile of Rosenberg in Truman Smith Notebook, Truman Smith Papers, Yale University Archives.
156. "and Herr Hitler": John Toland, *Adolf Hitler* (New York, 1976), 110.
156. "inner unity": Hitler, 347.

CHAPTER 5: TO THE FELDHERRNHALLE

157. "of taking power": Anthony Nicholls, "Hitler and the Bavarian Background to National Socialism," in *German Democracy and the Triumph of Hitler,* ed. A. Nicholls and Erich Mathias (London, 1971), 116–17.
158. "Carnival gaieties": "Miscellaneous Material Concerning Life at Munich," 6 Feb. 1922, Munich Consular Reports, M336, Roll 79, NA.
158. "rolling in wealth": Hans Oertel to Gustav Gruner, 29 Sept. 1922, Gustav Gruner Papers, 257, Box 1, Yale Archives.
158. "had broken down": Hanser, 305–6.
159. "raise a trillion": Robert Murphy, *Diplomat among Warriors* (Garden City, 1964), 25.
159. "mistress-slave perversion": Hanser, 304–8.
159. "leaves of paper": Rudloff, 350.
159. golden denture: Schoenberner, 147–48.
160. "has to do": Gerald D. Feldman, "Bayern und Sachsen in der Hyperinflation 1922/23," *"Schriften des historischen Kollegs* 6 (1984), 28.
160. "old-time charm": Bissel to Gruner, 20 March 1922, Gustav Gruner Papers, 257, Box 1, Yale Archives.
160. "considered exorbitant": Gerald D. Feldman, "Welcome to Germany? The *Fremdenplage* in the Weimar Inflation," in *Geschichte als Aufgabe,* ed. Wilhelm Treue (Berlin, 1988), 642.
160. "the worst sort": Kurt Tucholsky, "Reisende, Meidet Bayern!" *Gesammelte Werke 1921–1924* (Hamburg, 1960), III:10.
161. "streaming to the Nazis": Edward Hamm to Theodor Wolff, 3 Jan. 1922, R431, 2621, BAK.
161. "new religious belief": Hanser, 310.
161. "avoid ruin": Seeds report, 5 Jan. 1923, FO 371/8753, PRO.

161. "name is Adolf Hitler": Hanser, 314.

161. "case in 1918": Department of State, Memo for Norweb, 13 Jan. 1923, M336, Roll 79, NA.

162. "future will bring": Thomas Mann, *Briefe 1889–1936,* I:204.

162. "November criminals": *Hitler: Sämtliche Aufzeichnungen 1905–1924,* ed. Eberhard Jäckel and Axel Kuhn (Stuttgart, 1980), 783–85.

162. "considered a Bavarian": Seeds reports, 17 Jan. 1923 and 25 Jan. 1923, FO 371/8753, PRO.

162. "Munich our own": Hitlerrede am 15 Jan. 1923, Polizeidirektion München, 6697, SA.

163. "hard to resist": Seeds report, 25 Jan. 1923.

163. "National Socialist outbreak": ibid.

163. "would be finished": Flood, 346.

164. "written in the *Münchener Post*": Karl Alexander von Müller, *Im Wandel einer Welt: Erinnerungen 1919–1932* (Munich, 1966), 145.

164. "will be held tomorrow": Harold J. Gordon, *Hitler and the Beer Hall Putsch* (Princeton, 1972), 191.

165. "fused together permanently": Müller, *Wandel,* 144–45.

165. "inner strength"; "come crumbling down": ibid., 145, 146.

165. "new German Reich": Flood, 352–53.

166. "Left and the Right": Wolfgang Benz, ed., *Politik in Bayern 1919–1933: Berichte des württembergischen Gesandten Carl Moser von Filseck* (Stuttgart, 1991), 120–21.

166. "stroke of fate": Flood, 328.

168. "overemphatic": Müller, *Wandel,* 30–31.

168. "That's my meat": Toland, 123.

168. "big man in it": Hanser, 298.

168. "cost me a cent": Ludecke, 131.

168. "collapsing fatherland": Lothar Gruchmann, "Hitlers Denkschrift an die bayerische Justiz vom 16. Mai 1923," *VfZG* 39 (1991), 306.

169. "his great triumph": Flood, 374.

169. "pitched battle": Röhm, 194–206.

170. confiscated and burned: Verlauf des 1. Mai bei den Nationalsozialisten, Polizeidirektion München, 6803, SA.

170. "will come soon": Hanser, 320.

170. "of the community": Murphy cable, 5 May 1923, M336, NA.

170. "Jewish materialism": Toland, 143.

170. "witches' cauldron": Hanser, 321.

171. "executive power": Gordon, 216.

171. "every right to sit": Hanser, 323.

171. "at all fairly": *Times* of London, 28 Sept. 1923.

171. "high collar politicians": Gordon, 220–21.

172. "since the war": Expulsion of Jews from Munich and Other Bavarian cities, 18 Jan. 1924, M336, NA.

172. popular anti-Semitism: For a scholarly account of the expulsions, see Reiner Pommerin, "Die Ausweisung von 'Ostjuden' aus Bayern," *VfZG* 34 (1986), 311–40."

173. "for the whole world": Hanser, 321–22.

173. "things to accomplish": ibid., 326.

173. "will sneak away": Gordon, 243–44.

174. "Kiss my ass": Hanfstaengl, 92.

174. radical nationalists: Gordon, 254–64.

174. "*hineinkompromittieren*"; "time to strike": Hanfstaengl, 91–92.

176. among the crowd: Müller, *Wandel,* 160.

176. "victory or jail": Johann Aigner, "Als Ordonanz bei Hochverräter: Ein Beitrag zur Geschichte der nationalen Erhebung," unplublished ms., Rehse Collection, Box 270, Reel 166, LC, 9.

176. "sinister motives"; "an uproar": Hanfstaengl, 101.

176. "and other weapons": Aigner, 10

177. "hall is surrounded"; "South America": Müller, *Wandel,* 161–62.

177. "headwaiter": Otto Gritschneder, *Bewährungsfrist für den Terroristen Adolf H. Der Hitler-Putsch und die bayerische Justiz* (Munich, 1990), 14.

177. "be undone": Gordon, 286.

177. "worrying about": Hanser, 341.

177. "actor might envy"; "to be heard"; "Yes, yes": Müller, *Wandel,* 162–63.

180. "*Glücklich entbunden*": Hanser, 347.

180. military headquarters: On Himmler and the putsch, see Peter Padfield, *Himmler* (New York, 1990), 66–67.

182. Bürgerbräu bill: Gritschneder, 21.

182. "We'll march"; "was decided on": Hanser, 370–71.

185. "to the heavens": Hans Hinkel, *Einer unter Hunderttausend* (Munich, 1938), 107.

185. "hadn't fought anybody": Hanser, 373.

185. "superfluous consumers": *München—Hauptstadt der Bewegung: Ausstellung in Münchener Stadtmuseum* (Munich, 1993), 104.

186. "in favor of the putsch": Aigner, 15.

186. "all higgledy-piggledy": Müller, *Wandel,* 166.

188. "and night stick": Gordon, 360–61.

189. "for Germany's youth": Aigner, 57.

189. "1 will follow you": Hanser, 386.

189. "for his fatherland": Gritschneder, 29.

189. "eliminates Hitler": *NYT,* 10 Nov. 1923.

190. "so-called better classes": Gordon, 413.

190. "Up with Hitler": *New York American,* 11 Nov. 1923.

191. "Tannhäuser in the Venusberg": Hanfstaengl, 112.

191. "shoot myself first": ibid., 113.

192. "a man so German": Gritschneder, 54–57.

192. "we sit in the dock": Harold J. Gordon, ed., *The Hitler Trial before the*

People's Court in Munich (Arlington, 1976), I:69.

193. "extremely poor figure": Clive to Foreign Office, 25 March 1924. FO 371/9799, PRO.

193. Fiehler testimony: Stadtrat Protokol, Fiehler, 2 June 1924, B.u.R. 1445, SAM.

193. "criminals of 1918": Bauer and Piper, 324.

193. "disgrace and despair": ibid., 323.

193. "leading men of Bavaria": Gritschneder, 92.

194. "All Fools' Day": *Times* of London, 2 April 1924.

194. "quasi-martyrdom": Geoffrey Pridham, *Hitler's Rise to Power: The Nazi Movement in Bavaria 1923–1933* (London, 1973), 18.

194. "I had two million": Hanser, 396.

CHAPTER 6: "THE DUMBEST CITY IN GERMANY"

195. "world-German city": Thomas Mann, "München und das Weltdeutsche" *Gesammelte Werke in Zwölf Bänden* (Frankfurt, 1960), X:911–13.

196. "a half-sob": Hoffmann, 57.

197. "from the warden": Otto Strasser in *Der Aufstieg der NSDAP in Augenzeugenberichten,* ed. Ernst Deuerlein (Düsseldorf, 1968), 234.

197. "all the stuff": Hanfstaengl, 119.

197. "beaten in games": ibid., 119–20.

197. "Machiavellian" means: Deuerlein, 234.

198. "urge to shit": Ralf Georg Reuth, *Goebbels* (Munich, 1990), 54.

198. "Things can't go on": Elke Fröhlich, ed., *Die Tagebücher von Josef Goebbels: Sämtliche Fragmente* (Munich, 1987), I:30.

198. "meaningful tasks": Reuth, 77.

199. "to do something": Pridham, 26.

199. "has suffered most": ibid., 37.

199. "a real leader": *Hitler: Sämtliche Aufzeichnungen,* 1238–39.

200. "discipline and order": Deuerlein, 238.

200. want Hitler back: Adolf Hitler, MA 100424, BHSA. See also Clive memo, 19 Feb. 1924, FO 371/9799, PRO.

200. "best-hated man in Bavaria": Clive memo, 19 Feb. 1924.

201. "sense of relief": Rudloff, 358.

201. "the people of London": Bentinck to Foreign Office, 24 Oct. 1924, FO 371/9799, PRO.

201. "chief misery of our people": Rudloff, 358.

203. "loosen the chain": Flood, 600.

203. "especially the youth": *Hauptstadt der Bewegung,* 157.

203. "walk over ours": Institut für Zeitgeschichte, ed., *Hitler Reden, Schriften, Anordnungen. Februar 1925 bis Januar 1933* (Munich, 1992), I:14–16.

203. "Moscow of our movement"; "holy ground": ibid., 99, 116.

204. "opposed most fiercely": Pridham, 46.

204. "man is an Austrian": Erhardt quoted in "Ernst von Solomon," *Berliner Zeitung,* 17 April 1994.

205. "shall convince Hitler": Goebbels, *Tagebücher,* I:121.

205. "petit bourgeois Hitler," Deuerlein, 255.

205. "Mecca of German socialism": Goebbels, *Tagebücher,* I:160.

205. "foundation of our ideology": Dietrich Orlow, *The History of the Nazi Party 1919–1933* (Pittsburgh, 1969), 70.

205. "swine from down under": Deuerlein, 257.

206. "am really happy": Reuth, 100–101.

206. "a political genius": ibid., 101.

206. "I love you very much": Toland, 217.

206. "Jewish movie house": Sackett, 120.

207. "good German architects": Fiehler to *VB,* B.u.R. 1505, SAM.

207. persecution of Feuchtwanger: Sackett, 120.

207. "excrement of Adolf Hitler": ibid.

208. "in wide circles": ibid., 121. See also *Hauptstadt der Bewegung,* 161; and W. Nerdinger, "Die 'Kunststadt München,' " in *Die zwanziger Jahre in München, Ausstellungskatalog,* ed. C. Stolzl (Munich, 1971), 99.

208. "rooted inheritances": Nerdinger, 106.

208. "joy or nobility": *MNN,* 11 April 1931.

208. "a city that respects itself": Akten Kulturamt, Nr. 420, SAM. See also Jean-Claude Baker and Chris Chase, *Josephine: The Hungry Heart* (New York, 1993), 161.

208. "in this direction": Stadtrat to Scharnagl, 24 April 1930. B.u.R. 306/3a, SAM.

208. "their German face"; quick removal: Nerdinger, 98–99.

209. "and German history": Gabriele Whetten-Indra, "Literarisches Leben in München 1918–1933," in Stolzl, ed., *Die zwanziger Jahre in München,* 40.

209. "intellectual intolerance," Bauer and Piper, 304.

210. "intellectual core"; "revival of Ur-Bajuwarentum"; "spirit of *Münchnertum*": Nerdinger, 98.

210. "reasons of tourism": Barnhart, "Art beyond Art's Sake," 250.

210. "yesterday and the day before": "Berlin and Munich," *Manchester Guardian,* 7 Feb. 1929.

210. "500 liters of beer": *Das Tagebuch,* quoted in *MNN,* 21 Sept. 1924.

210. "cultural and intellectual life": Scharnagl Rede, B.u.R., 5 May 1925, 306/2b, SAM.

211. artistic development: Scharnagl Rede, 18 March 1928, ibid.

211. views of democracy: Bauer and Piper, 299.

211. "be too dry": Scharnagl to Thomas Mann, 8 June 1925, B.u.R. 1879, SAM.

211. "must become republicans": Thomas Mann, "Von deutscher Republik," quoted in Kolbe, 349–54.

212. "of the swastika"; "idea of the future": Kolbe, 348.

212. "over his thoughts": Thomas Mann, *The Magic Mountain* (New York, 1992), 496–97.

212. "atmosphere of repression": Kolbe, 385.

213. "being represented": Nerdinger, 103.

213. "freedom and joyousness": Thomas Mann speech in *Kampf um München als Kulturzentrum* (Munich, 1926), 7–12.

213. "spiritual and artistic matters": Hamilton, 232.

213. "once so hospitable city": *Kulturzentrum,* 18–19.

214. "prosperous environment"; "adolescent dramas": Kolbe, 392.

215. "strain of hardness": Deuerlein, 247.

215. "it had in 1923": *Hauptstadt der Bewegung,* 159.

215. "for the Bavarian population": Pridham, 77.

216. "high expectations"; "hot sticky air": Hitler's erstes Wiederauftreten, MA 100427, BHSA.

217. "need for money"; "statesman like Mussolini": Hitlerversammlung, 30 March 1927, ibid.

217. "is definitely missing": Hitlerversammlung, 2 April 1927, ibid.

218. "60 to 80 at the most": *Hauptstadt der Bewegung,* 160.

218. recent statistical analysis: ibid., 179–86.

219. "of our cultural foundations": On the Combat League for German Culture, see ibid., 163.

219. "Hope of Germany": ibid., 161.

222. "in the country": Pridham, 157.

222. "race- and folk- and fellowship-": Hayman, 384.

222. "no longer needed": Rudloff, 363.

223. "public assistance": ibid., 364.

223. weddings or birthday parties: Orchestergemeinschaft München Berufsmusiker, B.u.R. 1492, SAM.

223. "irreparable loss": Marionettenbühne, ibid.

224. practicing homosexual: "Warme Brudershaft im Braunen Haus," *MP,* 22 June 1931.

224. "know your name": Klaus Mann. *Turning Point,* 236.

225. "adolescent infatuation"; "anatomical detail": Hanfstaengl, 169.

225. "an excellent monarch": Nerin E. Gun, *Eva Braun: Hitler's Mistress* (London, 1968), 64–65.

225. "with this man": Klaus P. Fischer, *Nazi Germany: A New History* (New York, 1995), 233.

225. "stuff her brassiere": Gun, 62.

226. came to power: Joachim Fest, *Hitler* (New York, 1974), 323; Robert G. L. Waite, *The Psychopathic God: Adolf Hitler* (New York, 1977), 262–63.

226. "hair on their heads": *Hauptstadt der Bewegung,* 164.

227. "above all as opium": Peter Gay, *Weimar Culture* (New York, 1968), 88.

227. tourist revenues: Scharnagl to Mitglieder des Hauptausschusses, 10 Oct. 1931, B.u.R. 1492, SAM.

227. "cultural centers in Germany": Münchens Stellung um Goethe Jahr, ibid.

227. rejected his application: Ministerialsitzung, 21 Dec. 1929, MA 100427, BHSA.

228. Röhm scandal: Toland, 263–64.

229. wait a little longer: *Hauptstadt der Bewegung,* 165.

230. "brutality and force": ibid.

CHAPTER 7: CAPITAL OF THE MOVEMENT

232. "It's like a dream": Goebbels, *Tagebücher,* ed. Ralf Georg Reuth (Munich, 1992), II:757.

233. "Hitler framed in": Fest, *Hitler,* 502.

233. "begin his work": Kurt Preis, *München unterm Hakenkreuz* (Munich, 1989), 9.

233. "a transition phase"; "this great event"; "all be pleased": ibid., 10–11.

234. "breach of the peace": Quoted in Erika and Klaus Mann, *Escape to Life* (Boston, 1939), 15.

234. "to its senses": Pridham, 298.

234. "boundless love for Munich": Zorn, 353.

235. "would have Communism": Pridham, 304.

235. "against the Red flood": ibid. 305.

235. "loved the most": Zorn, 355.

235. "separatist federalism": Pridham, 305.

236. "extremely painful": Thomas Mann to Scharnagl, 6.3.33, B.u.R. 1879, SAM.

236. "unpleasant consequences": Scharnagl to Thomas Mann, 9.3.33, ibid.

236. "house at all": Peter de Mendelssohn, *Der Zauberer: Das Leben des deutschen Schriftstellers Thomas Mann, Jahre der Schwebe, 1919 und 1933* (Frankfurt, 1992), 122.

236. "restore order": On the Nazi takeover in Munich, see Preis, 16–17; Zorn, 357–64; Pridham, 307–10; Wolfram Selig, ed., *Aspekte der nationalsozialistischen Machtergreifung in München* (Munich, 1983); Helmut Hanko, "München 1933 bis 1935," in *Die Städte Mitteleuropas im 20. Jahrhundert,* ed. Wilhelm Rausch (Linz, 1984), 287–92.

236. "our beloved city": Hans-Günther Richardi and Klaus Schumann, *Geheimakte Gerlich/Bell: Röhms Pläne für ein Reich ohne Hitler* (Munich, 1993), 150.

237. "triumphed after all": Zorn, 362.

237. "for our actions": Preis, 32.

238. "purely personal vendettas": *Hauptstadt der Bewegung,* 242.

238. "we have acted": *MNN,* 21 March 1933.

238. "to hold geese": Marita Krauss and Bernhard Grau, *Die Zeichen der Zeit: Alltag in München 1933–1945* (Berlin, 1991), 15.

239. "Prisoner Number One": Hans-Günther Richardi, "Mit der Anknuft der SS beginnt der Terror," *SZ,* 20–21 March 1993; see also Richardi, *Schule der Gewalt: Die Anfänge des Konzentrationslagers Dachau 1933–34* (Munich, 1983).

239. "off limits": Richardi, "Mit der Ankunft der SS."

239. "camp from inside": Barbara Diestel and Ruth Jakusch, eds., *Concentration Camp Dachau: Catalogue* (Munich, 1978), 46.

240. "You beat me": Richardi and Schumann, 124.

240. "camp at Dachau": Kolbe, 411.

241. "deepest German sensibilities": Kolbe, 402–5; Hans Rudolf Vaget, "Musik in München." *Thomas Mann Jahrbuch* 7 (1994), 41–69.

241. "against my Wagner essay": Hans Rudolf Vaget, "The Rivalry for Wagner's Mantle: Strauss, Pfitzner, Mann," in *Re-Reading Wagner*, ed. Reinhold Grimm and Jost Hermand (Madison, 1993), 144.

242. "Gypsy plague": Ludwig Eiber, *"Ich wüsste, es wird schlimm:" Die Verfolgung der Sinti und Roma in München 1933–1945* (Munich, 1993), 46–47.

242. Nazi persecution of Communists: see Heike Bretschneider, *Der Widerstand gegen den Nationalsozialismus in München 1933–1945* (Munich, 1968), 22, 54.

242. "slap the Nazis down": Wilhelm Hoegner, *Der schwierige Aussenseiter: Erinnerungen eines Abgeordneten, Emigranten und Ministerpräsidenten* (Munich, 1959), 84.

243. end of BVP: *Hauptstadt der Bewegung*, 240.

243. "officials of the old school": Ortwin Domröse quoted in Preis, 34.

243. "economic lifeblood of the city": Organisation und Aufbau der Wirtschaftspolizei, B.u.R. 452/20, SAM.

244. "entirely reliable persons": Baugenossenschaft Münchens, ibid.

244. "one after another": Schoenberner, 5–6.

244. "the new Germany": Ernst Piper, "Nationalsozialistische Kulturpolitik und ihre Profiteure," in *"Niemand war dabei und keiner hat's gewusst": Die deutsche Öffentlichkeit und die Judenvervolgung*, ed. Jörg Wollenberg (Munich, 1989), 152.

245. "Christian faith can come together": Bjorn Mensing, "Hitler hat eine göttliche Sendung," in *Irrlicht im leuchtenden München? Der Nationalsozialismus in der "Hauptstadt der Bewegung,"* ed. Bjorn Mensing and Friedrich Prinz (Regensburg, 1991), 111.

245. "unimpeded victory": ibid., 112.

246. "the national awakening": ibid., 116.

246. "the new government": Georg Denzler, "Ein Gebetssturm für den Führer"; in ibid., 127.

246. "is over anway": ibid.

247. state security: *Hauptstadt der Bewegung*, 398–99.

247. Jewish corpses: "Kündigung jüdischer Ärtze," 6.4.33, B.u.R. 305/8b, SAM.

247. authorities for reburial: *Hauptstadt der Bewegung*, 399.

248. "solving the Jewish Question": Ian Kershaw, *Popular Opinion and Political Dissent in the Third Reich: Bavaria 1933–1945* (Oxford, 1984), 245.

248. "exclusion of all non-German businesses": Kampfbund to Fiehler, 28.3.33, B.u.R. 453, SAM.

248. world capital of *Gemütlichkeit:* See, for example, "Wo unsere Stadt die Spitze hält," *VB,* 11 Sept. 1938; "München das Reiseziel der ganzen Welt," *Neues Münchener Tageblatt,* 12 Aug. 1936.

248. "Jewish cardinal": Kershaw, 247, 189.

248. "national blood": ibid., 248.

248. "disintegration of the [April] boycott": Denzler, 127.

249. preference for Old Fighters: Fiehler to Lenk, 5 June 1934, B.u.R. 452/19, SAM.

249. "nothing but rogues": Kershaw, 122–23.

249. great Bavarian pedigrees: Strassenbenennung, 30 May 1933, B.u.R. 305/6b, SAM.

249. figures in Bavarian history: Fellheimer to Fiehler, 28 May 1933, B.u.R., ibid.

249. Platz der deutschen Freiheit: Fiehler to Seyfferth, 29 May 1933, ibid.

250. city of destiny: On Night of the Long Knives, see David Clay Large, *Between Two Fires: Europe's Path in the 1930s* (New York, 1990), 101–37. Unless otherwise indicated, quotations are from Large.

255. "Prussians in Berlin": Zorn, 392.

256. in this enterprise: *Hauptstadt der Bewegung,* 331–57.

256. bizarre rite: SS-Eigene Veranstaltungen . . . in der Zeit von 7–9.33, B.u.R. 452/19, SAM.

257. "soul-stirring event": Robert Wistrich, *Weekend in Munich: Art: Propaganda and Terror in the Third Reich* (London, 1995), 44.

258. "wasteful pomposity": SOPADE Bericht, 1935, Wiener Library, London.

258. "stare and swear": SOPADE Bericht, 1938, ibid.

258. "an electric beam": Patrick Leigh Fermor, *A Time of Gifts* (Harmondsworth, 1979), 103.

259. spirit was Munich: "Ende der Rivalität," *MNN,* 23 April, 1936.

259. "most German of all German cities": Karl Arnold, "Das Haus der deutschen Kunst—ein Symbol der neuen Machtverhältnisse," in *Nationalsozialismus und Entartete Kunst,* ed. Peter-Klaus Schuster (Munich, 1987), 80 (note 8).

259. "favorite wish": ibid., 63.

260. "capital of German art": ibid., 62.

260. "strikes mightily": Toland, 414.

260. "destined to die": Albert Speer, *Inside the Third Reich* (New York, 1979), 49.

260. "in the German land": "München, die Stadt der Kunst und der Künstler," *Das Bayernland* (1934), 585–88.

261. "glare of shooting rockets": *Programmheft: Zweitausend Jahre deutscher Kultur* (Munich, 1937); also "Zweitausend Jahre deutscher Kultur im Festzug," *Das Bayernland* (Munich, 1937), 554–59.

262. "ecstatic meditation": Wistrich, 69.

262. gray limestone: "Das Haus der deutschen Kunst," *Das Bayernland* (1937), 523–28.

262. "national rejuvenation": Lynn H. Nicholas, *The Rape of Europa* (New York, 1994), 10.

263. "destruction of our people": *VB,* 19 July 1937.

263. "Accepted . . . Rejected": Nicholas, 16.

263. "old traditions": Wistrich, 76.

263. "renewal of the arts": *VB,* 20 July 1937; *MNN,* 20 July 1937.

263. element missing: Preis, 87.

263. "beer calendar": *Time* (24 July 1939).

264. On the Ausstellung Entartete Kunst, see Schuster, and Stephanie Baron et al., *Degenerate Art: The Fate of the Avant-Garde in Nazi Germany* (Los Angeles, 1994).

264. Barlach/Nolde protest: Reuth, *Goebbels,* 368.

265. "see for yourselves": Mario-Andreas von Lüttichau, "Deutsche Kunst und 'Entartete Kunst': Die Münchener Ausstellung 1937," in Schuster, 97.

265. recorded reactions: Toland, 416; Preis, 84.

265. "huge success": Willibald Sauerländer, "Un-German Activities," *New York Review of Books* (7 April 1994), 9.

265. "money from this garbage": Nicholas, 23.

266. "Bolshevism" show: *Hauptstadt der Bewegung,* 387–88.

266. "Der Ewige Jude" show: ibid., 409; "Der Ewige Jude," B.u.R. 305/9b.

CHAPTER 8: BABYLON ON THE ISAR

270. "the blitz technique": Ernest Pope, *Munich Playground* (New York, 1941), 8–12.

270. Hitler love affairs: Waite, 267–69.

270. successfully rebuffed: Leni Riefenstahl, *A Memoir* (New York, 1992), 107–8.

270. sleep with him: Hanfstaengl, 143.

271. "ideal of German womanhood": ibid., 225.

271. "most beautiful Nordic woman": Göring quoted in Pope, 131.

271. "did not shoot": Friedrich Percyval Reck-Malleczewen, *Diary of a Man in Despair* (New York, 1970), 28.

271. for this purpose: Jonathan Guinness, *The House of Mitford* (London, 1984), 363.

271. "that was her coup": David Pryce-Jones, *Unity Mitford: A Quest* (London, 1976), 126.

272. "deserve such an honor": Guinness, 369.

272. "shoot Jews": Pryce-Jones, 127.

272. "relief when we left": Guinness, 386.

272. "most dangerous woman in Munich": Pope, 133.

272. denounced anyone at all: Pryce-Jones, 95.

273. "unseemly familiarity": Speer, 45.

273. a respectful distance: Fiehler to Schaub, 27 Aug. 1937, B.u.R. 452/1, SAM.

274. Falstaff for Hitler's Munich: On Weber, see Pope, 30–42; *Hauptstadt der Bewegung,* 231–32.

274. "history of Munich carnivals": Pope, 37.

275. "profanation of the movement": Reinhard Bauer, Günther Gerstenberg, and Wolfgang Peschel, eds., *Im Dunst aus Bier, Rauch und Volk: Arbeit und Leben in München von 1840 bis 1945* (Munich, 1989), 260.

275. Oktoberfest exploitation: *Das Oktoberfest: Einhundertfünfundsiebzig Jahre Bayerische National-Rausch* (Munich, 1985), 86–87.

276. "green Freemasonry": David Irving, *Göring: A Biography* (New York, 1990), 180.

277. "Can-Can for Twelve": Richard D. Mandell, *The Nazi Olympics* (New York, 1971), 103–4.

277. "again a world city": "München das Reiseziel der ganzen Welt," *Neues Münchener Tageblatt,* 12 Aug. 1936.

277. "of the German people": "München—eine Antwort," *VB,* 5 Aug. 1937.

277. "people at home believe": Gordon Craig diaries, entry for 13 July 1935, unpublished ms., Stanford University Archives.

277. "fear in the air": entry for 25 July 1935, ibid.

278. "word in stone": *VB,* 24 Jan. 1938; "Hauptstadt der Bewegung." B.u.R. 305/6b, SAM.

278. "Forum of the Party": On Nazis' reconstruction of the Königsplatz, see Hans-Peter Rasp, *Eine Stadt für Tausend Jahre: München—Bauten und Projekte für die Hauptstadt der Bewegung* (Munich, 1981), 23–26.

279. "*Plattensee*": Preis, 66.

279. "its great culture": Krauss and Grau, 12.

280. "out of storage": Bauer, Gerstenberg, Peschel, 258.

281. to his specifications: Auszug aus einer Besprechung von 1.6.37, B.u.R. 305/4b, SAM.

281. "prepared to abandon": Preis, 118.

282. "works of architecture": Hermann Giesler, *Ein anderer Hitler: Bericht seiner Architekten Hermann Giesler* (Leoni am Starnberger See, 1978). 114.

282. Hitler's mausoleum: Rasp, 19.

282. "our entire existence": Elisabeth Angermair and Ulrike Haerendel, *Inszenierter Alltag. Volksgemeinschaft im nationalsozialistischen München 1933–1945* (Munich, 1993), 22.

282. "him in return": Preis, 63.

283. "Heil, heil, the king": ibid., 63–64.

283. nominal independence: Kershaw, 159–72.

284. "substitution of political motives": ibid., 181.

284. other minorities: Bjorn Mensing, "Hitler hat eine göttliche Sendung," in *Irrlicht im leuchtenden München?,* 119–20.

295. religious holidays: On Nazi harassment of the Bavarian Catholic Church, see Kershaw, 185–223; Denzler, "Ein Gebetssturm für den Führer." 124–53.

295. "Sun Tree": On Nazi paganism, see H. J. Gamm, *Der braune Kult: Das Dritte Reich und seine Ersatzreligion* (Hamburg, 1962).

295. "White Thor": Padfield, 175.

296. "ideological scuffle": Kershaw, 201.

296. "entered a new phase": *Hauptstadt der Bewegung,* 422.

296. "Red-Black conspiracy": ibid., 423.

297. "and her freedom"; "time to be silent": Kershaw, 219, 202.

297. On the Bayernwacht, see Zorn, 434–35.

297. an opponent of Jewry: Kershaw, 250.

298. uniforms to tin soldiers: *Hauptstadt der Bewegung,* 258–73.

299. *Zwangswirtschaft:* SOPADE Bericht, Sept.–Oct. 1934.

299. the other 2 percent: Kershaw, 149.

300. "all food products": Bauer, Gerstenberg, Peschel, 261.

300. not talk about their products: ibid., 235.

300. "Michl, look to the skies": Richard Bauer, *Fliegeralarm: Luftangriffe auf München 1940–1945* (Munich, 1987), 9.

300. loss of life: ibid., 10.

301. one quarter of the planned structures: ibid., 13–14.

301. "bring devastation to Germany": Kershaw, 151–52.

301. Czech crisis and Munich Conference: See Large, *Between Two Fires,* 317–63.

301. Chamberlain's reception: Paul Schmidt, *Staatist auf diplomatischer Bühne 1943–45* (Bonn, 1949), 417.

302. "demonstration against war": William Shirer, *Berlin Diary* (New York, 1941), 142–43.

303. "hugger-mugger affair"; "were a drill": Francis L. Loewenheim, *Peace or Appeasement?: Hitler, Chamberlain, and the Munich Crisis* (Boston, 1965), 138–39.

304. rumor of war: Kershaw, 107.

304. "without warlike entanglements": Marlis Steinert, *Hitlers Krieg und die Deutschen* (Düsseldorf, 1970), 39.

304. "undertone of criticism": Schmidt, 418.

305. "murder as a political weapon": *MNN* quoted in Peter Hanke, *Zur Geschichte der Juden in München zwischen 1933 und 1945* (Munich, 1967), 211.

305. "people's wrath": Goebbels, *Tagebücher,* III:1281.

306. neighboring buildings: On Night of the Broken Glass in Munich, see Hanke, 211–21.

306. "perfect discipline": ibid., 213.

307. "this disaster": Kershaw, 267.

307. *Schadenfreude:* Else Behrend-Rosenfeld, *Ich stand nicht allein: Erlebnisse einer Jüdin in Deutschland 1933–1944* (Munich, 1988), 61–63.

307. "much criticism": Hanke, 218.

308. "airhead Goebbels": Richard Breitman, *The Architect of Genocide: Himmler and the Final Solution* (New York, 1991), 53–54.

308. handsome profits: Hanke, 222–45; *Hauptstadt der Bewegung,* 411.

308. postage stamp collections: "Öffentliche Ankaufstelle, 30 March 1939, B.u.R. 305/7b, SAM.

308. Jewish property: Fiehler to Koglmeister, 5 Jan. 1939, B.u.R. 305/8b, SAM.

309. "with the mass of the people": *Time* (24 July 1939).

309. personal collection: ibid.

309. their VIP seats: On this film, see Wistrich, 101–43.

310. Interviews with festival participants: ibid.

310. "surprising": *Time* (24 July 1939).

CHAPTER 9. GÖTTERDÄMMERUNG

312. "Hurrah Patriotism of 1914": Ulrike Haerendel, "Das Rathaus unterm Hakenkreuz: Aufstieg und Ende der 'Hauptstadt der Bewegung' 1933 bis 1945," in *Geschichte der Stadt München,* ed. Richard Bauer (Munich, 1992), 391.

312. *The Curtain Falls:* Preis, 132.

313. "equality of distribution": ibid., 130.

313. "rich harvest": Zorn, 445–46.

313. would never surrender: Toland, 587.

314. *Ochsensepp:* On Müller's initiative, see his memoir, *Bis zur letzten Konsequenz* (Munich, 1975); also Klemens von Klemperer, *German Resistance against Hitler: The Search for Allies Abroad* (Oxford, 1992), 171–80.

314. just before sunrise: On the Elser plot, see Anton Hoch, "Das Attentat auf Hitler im Münchner Bürgerbräukeller 1939," *VfZG* 17 (1969), 383–413; Lothar Gruchmann, ed., *Autobiographie eines Attentäters Johann Georg Elser* (Stuttgart, 1989).

314. "direction of Christian Weber": Hoch, 408.

315. "called away": Toland, 591.

316. "reach my goal": ibid., 593.

316. "mission completed": Goebbels, *Tagebücher,* III:637.

316. Bavarian legitimists: ibid., 1347.

317. assassination attempt: S. Payne-Best, *The Venlo Incident* (London, 1950).

317. "another Reichstag Fire": Shirer, 247.

317. "hate the British": Pope, 20.

317. "halo of a martyr": Reck-Malleczewen, 94.

317. "*Verkohlte*": Vox Populi, *Geflüstertes: Die Hitlerei im Volksmund* (Heidelberg, 1948), 24.

317. "national tragedy": Preis, 137.

317. "Führer's fortunate escape": Toland, 594.

318. "attempt has failed": Reck-Malleczewen, 94.

318. "all kinds of shops": Haerendel, 488.

318. admitted by guards: Peter Hoffmann, *Hitler's Personal Security* (London, 1979), 169.

318. blow up the Führer: Klemperer, 160.

318. show trial: Anton Gill, *An Honourable Defeat: A History of the German Resistance to Hitler* (New York, 1994), 131.

318. cheat death: Preis, 140.

319. airport at Reim: Hans-Günther Richardi, *Bomber über München: Der Luftkrieg 1939 bis 1945* (Munich, 1992), 48–49.

320. "lyre and sword": Frederick Spotts, *Bayreuth* (New Haven, 1994), 190.

320. "weapon of the intellectal struggle": Frederike Euler, "Theater zwischen Anpassung und Widerstand," in *Bayern in der NS-Zeit,* ed. Martin Broszat (Munich, 1972), II:159.

320. "heart of the Reich": "München—des Reiches Herzstück," *VB,* 1 Sept. 1940.

321. "what they're getting": Richardi, *Bomber,* 57.

321. coal allotments: Kershaw, 301.

321. women's employment: Andreas Heusler, *Zwangsarbeit in der Münchener Kriegswirtschaft 1939–1945* (Munich, 1991), 30.

321. foreign workers: ibid., 31.

321. "meaning for the present era": Bormann-Fiehler correspondence, B.u.R. 452/4, SAM.

322. "suited to the present time": Kershaw, 341.

322. "unrest in the entire province": ibid., 353.

322. anything so "stupid": Edward N. Peterson, *The Limits of Hitler's Power* (Princeton, 1969), 219.

322. God's assistance: Preis, 151.

322. "cold chills": ibid., 154.

323. Munich producers: Verwaltung der städtischen Barakenanlagen, 9 May 1941, B.u.R. 305/4b. SAM.

323. church bell confiscation: Steinert, 160.

323. "most necessary of services": Preis, 159.

324. "last four years": Reck-Malleczewen, 137.

324. "drunkards and felons": ibid., 137–38.

324. "want to live there": *Hauptstadt der Bewegung,* 454.

324. north were showing: Steinert, 157.

325. "heavier raids in the future": Eva Berthold and Norbert Matern, *München im Bombenkrieg* (Düsseldorf, 1983), 32.

325. "hell for an entire hour": Ludwig Rosenberger, *Münchner Kriegstagebuch* (Munich, n.d.), 7.

325. "sea of destruction": Richardi, *Bomber,* 102.

325. "indistinct pearl gray sky": Wilhelm Hausenstein, *Licht unter dem Horizont: Tagebücher 1942–1945* (Munich, 1967), 38.

325. "historically deserved it"; "citadel of stupidity": Hayman, 479.

326. "joined the front": Richardi, *Bomber,* 116.

326. "pack of hangmen": ibid., 120.

326. "over the ice": Reck-Malleczewen, 167.

326. "The White Rose": On this, see David Clay Large, "White Rose in a Brown City," *Soundings* (Santa Barbara, 1994), 15–24; Inge Scholl, *The White Rose* (Middletown, 1983).

328. "decisive steps": "Vom Schmerz der Eltern tief bewegt," *SZ,* 12 Oct. 1993.

331. "cowardly to admit it": Michael Balfour, *Withstanding Hitler* (London, 1988), 237.

332. "go down in history"; "meet in eternity": Scholl, 61–62.

332. "Long live freedom": ibid., 62.

332. "dishonorable death": Preis, 173.

332. "God's will and mercy": "Vom Schmerz der Eltern . . ."

333. RAF leaflet drops; Thomas Mann broadcasts: Harold Marcuse, "Remembering the White Rose: (West) German Assessments, 1943–1993," *Soundings,* 28.

333. "commonwealth of nations": "On Not Signing an Appeal," *New York Review of Books* (12 Jan. 1995), 48.

333. streetcars: Hanke, 272–74.

334. "views of the Bavarian Alps": Behrend-Rosenfeld, 106.

334. latest inhumanity: Landeshauptstadt München, ed. *Verdünkeltes München* (Munich, 1987), 44.

334. "a dark time": ibid., 52.

334. arms factories: Hanke, 286–87.

335. "on to Poland"; "my best customers": Behrend-Rosenfeld, 166–67.

335. not paid much attention: Kershaw, 262–63.

335. "would not have happened"; "come to this pitch": ibid., 368.

335. in the East: ibid., 364. See also Wollenberg.

336. "exterminated them with gas": Kershaw, 367.

336. "storm break loose": Reuth, *Goebbels,* 515–20.

337. greater reliance on foreign labor: Heusler, 29–30.

338. "necessities of life": Donald Sheldon Papers, HI.

338. "Jewish brains": Richardi, *Bomber,* 223.

338. "European with disgust": Preis, 191.

338. cursed in the streets: ibid., 186.

338. "helper in hour of need": *Hauptstadt der Bewegung,* 456.

339. Troost award proposal: B.u.R. 305/1b.

339. Strauss appeal: Fiehler to Strauss, 14 June 1943, 306/6.

340. "five minutes after midnight"; "pumped up": Preis, 185–86.

340. "dirty wedge of July sun": Rosenberger, 25.

341. "Secret Germany": On the Stauffenberg-George connection, see Peter Hoffmann, *Stauffenberg. A Family History, 1905–1944* (Cambridge, 1995).

341. "Führer has been spared": Preis, 193.

341. stab in the back: Steinert, 265–68.

341. priests in the Wehrmacht: Zorn, 481.

342. "Germany's future leaders": Reck-Mallaczewen, 196.

342. "amid the ruins": Hausenstein, 265.

343. "hour will toll": *MNN* quoted in Preis, 190.

343. "difficulties of the moment": "Das Leben in München," *Aichbacher Zeitung,* 28 Nov. 1944.

343. "victory of the German Reich": Preis, 200.

343. "features and idiosyncrasies": Fiehler to Kuhlein, 9 Feb. 1945, B.u.R. 306/6, SAM.

343. "without fancy dress": Preis, 198.

344. last stand at Feldherrnhalle: Dieter Wagner, *München '45: Zwischen Ende und Anfang* (Munich, 1970), 12–13.

344. *Freiheitsaktion Bayern*: Zorn, 522; Wagner, 28–112.

344. "action against Himmler": Jürgen Heideking and Christof Mauch, eds., *American Intelligence and the German Resistance to Hitler* (Boulder, 1996), 390.

345. "inside the stack": Robert Abzug, *Inside the Vicious Heart: Americans and the Liberation of Nazi Concentration Camps* (New York, 1985), 92.

345. "even the liberators": ibid., 93.

346. soldiers as "Prussians": Zorn, 530.

346. "return sometime soon": Sheldon Papers, HI.

346. "for one G.I. to carry": ibid.

346. "born in this house": Klaus Mann, *Turning Point,* 368–69.

EPILOGUE

347. "great nonetheless": "O'zapft is," *Der Spiegel,* 23 Sept. 1964, 42.

348. "secret capital": see Karl Bosl, "München—Deutschlands heimliche Hauptstadt," *Zeitschrift für bayerische Landesgeschichte* 30 (1967), 288–313.

348. postwar appointments: Wolfram Selig, ed., *Chronik der Stadt München 1945–1948,* (Munich, 1980), 47–65.

349. denazification: See Nina Krieg, "Solang" der Alte Peter: Die vermeintliche Wiedergeburt Alt-Münchens nach 1945," in Richard Bauer, ed., *Geschichte der Stadt München* (Munich, 1992), 398–404; and Lutz Niethammer, *Die Mitläuferfabrik: Die Entnazifierung am Beispiel Bayerns* (Frankfurt, 1972).

350. "useful citizens": Krieg, 399.

350. "Mongolian savages": Carlo D'Este, *Patton: A Genius for War* (New York, 1995), 755.

350. "election fight": ibid., 766.

351. "with our population": Marita Krauss, "Die fremden Deutschen," *SZ,* 14–15 Aug. 1993, 117; Bauer and Piper, 364.

351. "are rid of all [the Jews]": Krauss, 117.

351. cursed three times: ibid.

352. blissfully ignorant: Nerdinger quoted in Wistrich, 91.

352. "cost too much": "Ratlos vor dem steinernen Grössenwahn," *SZ,* 2 May 1994; also "Kein Rauch ohne Feuer, kein Gedenken ohne Reue," *SZ,* 9

Nov. 1995.

352. "proud to be a German": *Chronik,* 54. See also Hannelore Kunz-Ott and Andre Kluge, *150 Jahre Feldherrnhalle: Ausstellung Katalog* (Munich, 1994), 70–74; "Welche Tradition heiligt was? Die Münchner Feldherrnhalle als Wille und Vorstellung," *SZ,* 29–30 Apr.–1 May 1995.

353. "enemy is listening in": Krieg, 400.

353. hiding in the city: Selig, 68, 210.

354. "to an equal degree": Krauss, 117.

354. slave laborers: "Zwangsarbeit—ein Stück verdrängte Geschichte," *SZ,* 28 Dec. 1994.

354. inconvenient memories: Harold Marcuse, "Nazi Crimes and Identity: Collective Memories of the Dachau Concentration Camp, 1945–1990" (Ph.D. Dissertation, University of Michigan, 1992); also Timothy Ryback, "Report from Dachau," *The New Yorker* (3 Aug. 1992), 43–61.

355. "opposed the government of the day": Ryback, 56.

356. White Rose monumentalization: Wilfried Breyvogel, "Die Gruppe 'Weisse Rose': Anmerkungen zur Rezeptionsgeschichte und kritischen Rekonstruktion," in Wilfried Breyvogel, *Piraten, Swings und Junge Garde. Jugendwiderstand im Nationalsozialismus* (Bonn, 1991), 159–221.

356. "of international tourism": "Auf geht's: Rama dama" *SZ,* 7 Jan. 1991.

357. "its old coziness": Bauer and Piper, 372–73.

357. "and the plastic arts": Friedrich Prinz, ed. *Trümmerzeit in München. Kultur und Gesellichkeit einer deutschen Großstadt im Aufbruch 1945–1949* (Munich, 1984), 9.

357. "among the Germans": Krauss, 117.

357. "looking the other way": Hayman, 564.

358. "nothing about the past": Bauer and Piper, 378–79.

359. "world its credentials": *800 Jahre München. Festwochen 14.6–31.8.1958* (Munich, 1958), 11.

359. "always remain the same": Bauer and Piper, 380–81.

359. icon of gay liberation: "Ewige Lust an Ludwig," *Der Spiegel,* 34/1995, 100–115.

360. "democracy, human rights, and federalism": "Historikerstreit auf bay-erisch," *SZ,* 6 Nov. 1993.

360. started years before: "Am Geburtsort der Nazis," *Die Zeit,* 10 Dec. 1993; "Exhibition Lets Munich Confront Its Nazi Past," *NYT,* 4 Jan. 1994.

360. Germany's neo-Nazi scene: Michael Schmidt, *The New Reich* (New York, 1993), 13.

INDEX

Page numbers in *italics* refer to illustrations.

Operation Barbarossa and, 322
Palm Sunday Putsch and, 113–14
in revolutionary period, 103–5, 107
compensation law, 354
concentration camps, 238, 306, 334–36
see also Dachau
Concordat, 284, 296
Confessing Church, 283
Congress of Bavarian Councils, 104
Conrad, Michael Georg, 6, 8–10
coordination campaign, 242–46, 248
Corinth, Lovis, 36
Cosmic Circle, 25–34, *99*
Cossmann, Paul Nikolaus, 240
Council of Love, The (Panizza), 10
Council of Workers, Soldiers, and Peasants, 78,
    80, 81, 86, 114, 117
Coventry, bombing of, 320
Craig, Gordon, 277
Crailsheim, Krafft von, 19
cultural politics, 206–14, 219, 232, 244
    and financial crisis (1929–1932), 223
    Great German Art Exhibit (1939),
        309–10
    Nazi aesthetics and, 258–67
    in World War II, 320, 339
culture, civilization vs., 53, 55, 57
currency restrictions, 299
Czechoslovakia, 301–4

Dachau, 118, 119, 238–42, 247, 296, 306, 337
    air raid damage to, 340
    Elser's internment at, 318
    inmate rebellion at, 345
    labor force in, 298
    liberation of, 344–45
    memorial service for victims of, 353
    postwar metamorphoses of, 354–55
Daladier, Édouard, 303, 304
Danaë (Slevogt), 37
DAP, *see* German Workers' Party
Dawes Plan, 201
Dawson, William, 158
Days of German Art, 261
Death's-Head SS unit, 345
Decline of the West, The (Spengler), 56–57, 61
Decree for the Protection of the Republic, 146
Degenerate Art Exhibition, 264–66
Dehmel, Richard, 49
Delvard, Marya, 18
demilitarization, 142, 143
democratization, xxi
denazification, 349–51
Depression, Great, 202, 220, 222, *294*
Derleth, Ludwig, 32
Deutsche Volksunion, 360
Deutsch-Sozialer Verein (DSV), xxiii–xxiv
Dietrich, Sepp, 253   .

displaced persons and refugees, after World
    War II, 351, 354
Dix, Otto, 264
Döblin, Alfred, 82
Doktor Faustus (Mann), 44
Drexler, Anton, 70, 88, 129–31, 134
Duensing, Frieda, 83
Durieux, Tilla, 207

East Prussia, 124
Ebert, Friedrich, 82, 136, 144–45
Eckart, Dietrich, 70, 137–39, 147, 150, 151, 155,
    165
Economic Police Force, 243, 244
economy:
    anti-Jewish boycott and, 247–48
    in Bavarian soviet period, 115
    Great Depression and, 202, 220, 222
    inflation, 87, 132, 158–60, 170
    Nazi policies and, 243–44, 298
    in postrevolutionary period, 132
    in revolutionary period, 105, 111–12
    stabilization of, after World War I, 201
    in World War I, 59–60
education, 64–65, 284
    see also Munich, University of
Edward VII, King of England, 15
Egelhofer, Rudolf, 114, 117, 119, 120
Ehrhardt, Captain, 139–40, 204
Ehrhardt Brigade, 119, 136, 137, 140, 141,
    147
Eicke, Theodor, 239, 254
Einstein, Albert, 153
Einwohnerwehren (Civil Guards), 126, 132,
    134, 138, 140–43
Eisenhower, Dwight D., 350, 354
Eisenstein, Alfred, 208
Eisner, Kurt, 67, 68, 74, 75, 77–81, 83–87,
    89–92, *100,* 103, 104, 166
    commemoration of, 360
    reburial of, 247
elections:
    of 1928, 218
    of 1929, 219–20
    of 1930, 221–22
    of 1932, 227–30
    of 1933, 234–35
Eleven Executioners, 17–20
Elser, Johann Georg, *293,* 314–18, 332
Epp, Franz Ritter von, 116, 144, 147,
    163, 218, 236, 237, 255, 322, 326,
    344, 349
Ernst, Max, 264
Erzberger, Matthias, 141–42
Escherich, Georg, 126, 138, 142, 143
Escherich, Karl, 153
Esser, Hermann, 154–55, 161, 183, 199, 200,
    205, 233, 349

München-Hauptstadt der Bewegung (exhibition), 360
Munich:
    Berlin vs., 142–46, 172–74, 210, 212–13, 232, 233
    golden age of, xviii
    Hitler in, xi–xii, xxv, 38–42, *102,* 340
    as Nazi playground, 268–78
    Nazi takeover of, 236–37
    recovery and growth of, after World War II, 347–48
    revolution in, *see* revolution of 1918–19
    titles bestowed on, 231, 232
    World War II casualties of, 325, 337, 338, 346
    see also specific individuals and movements
Munich, University of (Ludwig-Maximilians Universität), xxii, 127–28, 153–54, 190–91, 209, 212
    Nazi control of, 244–45
    White Rose group at, 327–32
    after World War II, 356, 359
Munich Conference (1938), *292,* 302–5
Munich Line, 361
Munich Poets' Circle, 5, 6
Munich Social Democratic Worker's Association, xxi
Murphy, Robert, 159, 161, 170
museums, 259, 339, 358
music, musicians, xv–xvi, xvii, 51, 55
    Nazi control of, 244
    unemployed, 223
    after World War II, 358
    in World War II, 320, 339, 343
Mussolini, Benito, 161, 171, 217, 266, *291,* 302, 303, 319
Muth, Karl, 327

Nationalist Association, 135–36
National Socialist Freedom Movement, 194
National Socialist German Workers' Party (NSDAP), 88, 134
    see also Nazi movement
Nazi movement, xvii, 124, 134–35, 194
    American Military Government and, 350
    anti-Munich campaign of, 203–5
    banning of, 215
    Bavarian symbols and, 249–50
    Beer Hall Putsch and, 175–94
    Christian churches and, 246, 248, 283–84, 295–97, 321–22
    civil defense and, 300–301
    colors and symbols of, 147–48
    coordination campaign of, 242–46, 248
    culture and, 206–8, 232, 258–67, 278–83
    demographic base of, 218–19
    early anti-Semitic measures of, 246–48
    economic and trade policies of, 298–99

elections and, *see* elections
elite supporters of, 149–56
financial difficulties of, 215, 217–18
growth of, 146, 157, 161–63, 224
Kahr's handling of, 172, 174
May Day fiasco and, 170
monument to victims of, 353
Munich as playground of, 269–78
Munich takeover by, 236–37
national headquarters of, 224, 232
Night of the Broken Glass and, 305–9
Night of the Long Knives and, 250–55
North-South division of, 199, 228, 229
outlawing of, 189
Party Day rally of, 163–66
persecutions and political terrorism of, 226, 238–42
political theater and, 256–58
Rathenau murder and, 145
relegalization of, 202, 203
resistance to, 356
stagnation of, 214–19
Storm Troopers and, 147
Thomas Mann's attack on, 214
Thule Society members in, 70–71
White Rose group and, 326–33
Neithardt, Georg, 192
neo-Nazis, 352, 360, 361
Nerdinger, Winfried, 352
Neue Pinakothek, 45
newspapers, 51, 111, 244, 343
    see also specific newspapers
Nicholas II, Czar of Russia, 15–16
Niekisch, Ernst, 104, 108–11
Niemöller, Martin, 283
Nietzsche, Friedrich, 21, 22, 29
Night of the Amazons (pageant), 274
Night of the Broken Glass, *293,* 305–9
Night of the Long Knives, 250–55
Nolde, Emil, 264
nonaggression pact (Germany-USSR), 310
Nordic·Winter Solstice festival, 295
North Africa, 326, 329
Nortz, Eduard, 163
Noske, Gustav, 112, 117, 136
NSDAP (National Socialist German Workers' Party), 88, 134
    see also Nazi movement
Nueva Germania, 27
Nuremberg, 110, 258, 307
Nuremberg Race Laws, 266
Nuremberg trials, 349

Obersalzberg, 273, 301
Obrist, Hermann, 36
OC, *see* Organisation Consul
Office for Festivals and Leisure Time, 275
Oktoberfest, xii, 58, 249, 275, 348, 361